CAPITAL MARKETS AND PRICES
Valuing Uncertain Income Streams

ADVANCED TEXTBOOKS IN ECONOMICS

VOLUME 25

NORTH-HOLLAND–AMSTERDAM·NEW YORK·OXFORD·TOKYO

CAPITAL MARKETS AND PRICES
Valuing Uncertain Income Streams

Clement G. KROUSE

University of California, USA

1986

NORTH-HOLLAND–AMSTERDAM·NEW YORK·OXFORD·TOKYO

ISBN 0 444 87931 5

Publishers
ELSEVIER SCIENCE PUBLISHERS B.V.
P.O. BOX 1991
1000 BZ AMSTERDAM
THE NETHERLANDS

Sole distributors for the U.S.A. and Canada
ELSEVIER SCIENCE PUBLISHING COMPANY, INC.
52 VANDERBILT AVENUE
NEW YORK, N.Y. 10017

Library of Congress Cataloging-in-Publication Data

Krouse, Clement G.
Capital markets and prices.

(Advanced textbooks in economics ; v. 25)
mR
Includes index.
1. Capital market. 2. Prices. 3. Commodity exchanges.
4. Stock-exchange. I. Title. II. Series.
HG4523.K76 1986 332.64 85-31224
ISBN 0-444-87931-5

PRINTED IN THE NETHERLANDS

INTRODUCTION TO THE SERIES

The aim of the series is to cover topics in economics, mathematical economics and econometrics, at a level suitable for graduate students or final year undergraduates specializing in economics. There is at any time much material that has become well established in journal papers and discussion series which still awaits a clear, self-contained treatment that can easily be mastered by students without considerable preparation or extra reading. Leading specialists will be invited to contribute volumes to fill such gaps. Primary emphasis will be placed on clarity, comprehensive coverage of sensibly defined areas, and insight into fundamentals, but original ideas will not be excluded. Certain volumes will therefore add to existing knowledge, while others will serve as a means of communicating both known and new ideas in a way that will inspire and attract students not already familiar with the subject matter concerned.

The Editors

To my father and mother,
for teaching me their way of valuing things

TABLE OF CONTENTS

PREFACE

This is a text in economic analysis. Its purpose is to set out, in a systematic way, the theoretical foundations underlying the valuation of uncertain income streams in a finite economy. As is the custom with a text, I shall not list my indebtedness to others for their ideas. I would, however, like to express my gratitude to many colleagues who have helped with earlier drafts of the manuscript: H. DeAngelo, K. Chung, J. Hirshleifer, S. LeRoy, D. Mayers, and C. Raymond deserve special mention in this regard. A more general debt I have is to J. Fred Weston, who has been mentor, colleague and friend since I began my study of economics. And, for typing and patience of the highest order, my thanks to Bee Hanson. That leaves me only to tell Elke and Bryan that I am no longer working on 'the book' and to thank them for their understanding and support during the seemingly endless time when I was.

INTRODUCTORY NOTE

As the literature on uncertain income stream valuation is relatively new its students face two difficulties. First, much of what is worthwhile reading is spread over many journals, written in a variety of formats, and set down in different notation and terminology. The second difficulty is more substantive: these journal writings often make only passing reference to each other and use conflicting assumptions about the economy under analysis. By both of these difficulties the student is left the onerous task of synthesizing what theory exists. This book is an attempt to set aside these problems. The material which results is intended as a graduate course in the theory of capital, or financial economics, requiring only that students have a good foundation in microeconomic theory and some basic mathematical skills.

The Table of Contents provides a clear view of the topics to be covered and their sequence. Here I only note that the fundamental method of analysis is the state preference framework suggested two generations ago by Irving Fisher. A characterization of commodities in this way, by dates and states of nature, permits the principles of neoclassical price theory to be applied. This should not come as a surprise, for capital theory too is a theory of price: it seeks to develop valuation formulae for uncertain income received (or paid) over time consistent with rational risk averse behavior and market equilibrium. The problems of capital theory under uncertainty are also the problems of price theory: a concern for the allocational efficiency of various market equilibria, the simplicity of valuation formulae, their statement in empirically observable parameters, and the extent to which they reflect all relevant costs. It is a mistake that students come much too late to understand these things.

As this book is meant mainly for students who will become researchers, equal weight is placed on the logical structure of the theory and its results. Because these are sufficient tasks in themselves, there are few comments concerning actual tests of the empirical regularities that are deduced. While the material is theoretical in this sense, it is not designed to require the powers of extensive abstraction. To accomplish this and to limit the required mathematics to the most basic calculus, linear algebra, and set operations, many ideas are not presented in their most rigorous, most condensed, or most general form. In addition, attention is restricted to finite economies. Those who wish to follow the developments with greater complexity are referred to original works throughout the text.

To help the student new to these topics, the book gives attention to the nuts-and-bolts of the model economies in varying degrees from the first to last chapter. At the onset, for example, each new concept is carefully defined and individuals, markets, and firms are specified prominently and in great detail. As the book proceeds and the maturity of the reader in these ideas develops, the same things are treated less explicitly, less formally, and more concisely. In addition to the definitions (D) and specifications (S), there is extensive use of propositions (P) and extensions/examples (E). For easy reference all of these things are indexed. For example P5.2 indicates Proposition 2 of Chapter 5, S9.7 indicates Specification 7 in Chapter 9, etc. As a further aid propositions, definitions, and specifications (but not examples) are given descriptive titles.

Some ten years ago Jack Hirshleifer in the introduction to his excellent book *Investments, Interest, and Capital* noted that his analyses would be limited generally to conditions of perfect markets and perfect competition. That was the state of theory then and, as he recognized, the theory which resulted was surprisingly robust in empirical tests. In the intervening decade not much has changed in this regard. Still, the major portion of theoretical work in capital asset valuation makes the same assumptions about markets, although there is somewhat more care given to the list of costs to be included in the models. And, the theories continue to be empirically robust. I have therefore generally continued the perfect market and perfect competition assumptions in this text. For this, no apologies are offered.

Before beginning, a word about notation is important. It is difficult to construct a system of symbolic representation for economic equilibrium analyses that is at the same time comprehensive, precise, concise, and easily readable. Many compromises are necessary and these have been made throughout the book. Some conventions were followed, however, which the reader will find useful. First of all, several specialized index sets are employed in a uniform way:

$t = 0, 1, \ldots, T,$ indexes dates, or periods,
$i = 1, 2, \ldots, I,$ indexes individuals,
$j = 1, 2, \ldots, J,$ indexes firms,
$s = 1, 2, \ldots, S,$ indexes states of nature, and,
$m = 1, 2, \ldots, M,$ indexes commodities.

Note that the first period is indicated by $t=0$ and not $t=1$. Also, in the frequent case that only one commodity is considered, that indexing is simply suppressed. It is further assumed that I, J, S, M, and T are finite unless noted otherwise

The above indexes are employed selectively both as subscripts and superscripts. Superscripts generally indicate individuals and firms as, for example, x^i will indicate the consumption plan of individual i and v^j will indicate the value of firm j. Subscripts generally indicate variables of a particular date, state, or commodity – for example, x_s^i will represent the consumption of individual i in state s and v_t^j will represent the value of firm j at period t.

Frequently, but not always, capital Greek or Latin letters are matrices whose respective elements are denoted by the corresponding lower case letter: $Z=[z_s^j]$ represents an $S \times J$ matrix with elements z_s^j. Vectors are generally written by lower case letters: for example, z^j might represent the S-vector with elements z_s^j, $z^j=[z_1^j \, z_2^j \ldots z_S^j]$.

The following representations are also used for vectors. First, for N-vectors x and y, $x \geq y$ means $x_n \geq y_n \, \forall n$, and similarly for the strict equality. The distinction between row and column vectors and the row-column order of matrices is not generally made. For example, for the N-vector y and the $N \times S$ matrix B we might write either yB or By without indicating transposition – the reader understands that both products are to be conformable. In the first case, we mean the $1 \times N$ row vector times the $N \times S$ matrix yielding the $1 \times S$ row vector and in the second case we mean the $S \times N$ matrix times the $N \times 1$ column vector yielding the $S \times 1$ column vector.

An appendix provided after the last chapter briefly reviews the mathematical notation and concepts employed throughout the book.

Clement G. Krouse

LIST OF PROPOSITIONS

Chapter 11

Chapter 1

THEORY OF CHOICE UNDER RISK

The purpose of an economic theory of choice in a market economy is to explain individual exchanges and, finally, individual consumption. The neoclassical microeconomic theory of demand in the certainty case is quite robust in this regard. Using a limited set of primitives, that theory provides answers to important questions: (1) given parameters of the market such as prices, endowments, and exchange arrangements, it is specific about the commodities consumers purchase; and, related to that solution, (2) it is specific about the way these choices are affected by changes in the original market parameters. Moreover, the derived information about the individual's choice of consumption is usefully summarized by the demand function, which gives prices and commodity amounts for each set of market parameters.

The tractability and robustness of the demand theory in the certainty case provides a strong rationale for constructing a theory of choice and demand under uncertainty with a parallel logical structure. That is the intent of this chapter. Because of this attempt at similarity, the study begins with the basic elements of demand under certainty.

1.A. Preferences, Scarcity and Demand

The world to which the economic theory of demand in a market economy is addressed has a specific structure. First of all, the economy consists of a collection of agents each of whom is a potential producer, consumer, and trader of two or more exchangeable objects called commodities. The commodities are defined to include all objects over which the agents may choose to produce or consume.

These ideas are formalized in a general way by considering an economy with $i=1,2,\ldots,I$ individuals (consumers) and $m=1,2,\ldots,M$ commodities, where both I and M are finite.[1] Each commodity is taken to be measurable

[1]The reader is reminded of the Mathematical Appendix, which briefly reviews the mathematical concepts, definitions and notations used throughout.

in specific units, to be continuously divisible, and to exist in a non-negative, finite quantity. A collection or bundle of the M commodities is termed a *consumption plan.* For the (typical) ith individual this plan is represented as the vector $x^i = [x_1^i\ x_2^i \ldots x_M^i]$, where x_m^i is the quantity of specific commodity m chosen.

Neglecting budget feasibility, the collection of all plans which are attainable using the exchange possibilities of the particular market is termed the *consumption set* and denoted X^i. For example, if by a government rationing system it were required that commodities 1 and 2 could be consumed by individual i only in a given ratio $k>0$, then the consumption set would, neglecting other possible restrictions, be defined as $X^i = \{x^i | x^i > 0$ and $kx_1^i = x_2^i\}$.[2] For the present such market limitations are not imposed and the simplest consumption set is chosen: consumption is unconstrained except that it be non-negative, i.e., $X^i = R_+^M$ for all i.

1.A.1. Some fundamentals of choice

In part on the basis of preferences, each individual chooses specific quantities of the various commodities thus forming a consumption plan. The concept of preference is that of a *binary relation* $(\geq)^i$ ordering the plans in the consumption set. For two consumption plans x^i, $\hat{x}^i \in X^i$, $x^i(\geq)^i\hat{x}^i$ means that x^i is at least as preferred by individual i as is the plan $\hat{x}^i$. If $x^i(\geq)^i\hat{x}^i$ and $\hat{x}^i(\geq)^i x^i$ jointly hold, then i is indifferent to the two plans, which is written compactly as $x^i(=)^i\hat{x}^i$. And, if $x^i(\geq)^i\hat{x}^i$ holds but $\hat{x}^i(\geq)^i x^i$ does not, then we write $x^i(>)^i\hat{x}^i$, which means that plan x^i is strictly preferred to plan $\hat{x}^i$ in the pairwise comparison.

Each commodity is assumed to be a good in the sense that more is preferred to less. Thus, for two plans x^i, $\hat{x}^i \in X^i$ such that $x^i \geq \hat{x}^i$ (x^i contains at least as much of every commodity as $\hat{x}^i$) then $x^i(\geq)\hat{x}^i$. Moreover, it is also assumed that individuals are *non-satiable*, so that if two consumption plans x^i and $\hat{x}^i$ have equal quantities for all goods except m and $x_m^i > \hat{x}_m^i$, then $x^i(>)\hat{x}^i$.

Consumption plans, consumption sets, and preferences are all individual specific. We understand this and hereafter omit the superscript i when no lack of precision results.

It is usual to define three sets of consumption plans based upon the binary relation and a reference plan $\hat{x} \in X$: the *preferred set* $\{x | x(\geq)\hat{x}$ for all $\hat{x} \in X\}$, the *inferior set* $\{x | x(\leq)\hat{x}$ for all $\hat{x} \in X\}$, and the *indifference set*

[2] Be careful not to confuse the consumption set with the budget set, which is introduced below.

$\{x|x(=)\hat{x}$ for all $\hat{x}\in X\}$. The indifference set is the intersection of the inferior and preferred sets, as the relation $(=)$ is equivalent to $(\geq)$ and $(\leq)$ jointly.

The greater the restrictions placed on the individual's preference ordering, the more specific will be the implications regarding individual choice behavior. With each restriction and each increase in predictive power of the associated theory there is, however, an accompanying loss in generality. Some balance is necessary. With this in mind, the usual formulation of economic choice theory employs five preference restrictions. For each individual *i*, the first four of these are:

(1) *Completeness.* For *all* x, $\hat{x}\in X$, either $x(\geq)\hat{x}$ or $\hat{x}(\geq)x$ or both.
(2) *Transitivity.* If x, $\hat{x}$, $\hat{\hat{x}}\in X$, then $x(\geq)\hat{x}$ and $\hat{x}(\geq)\hat{\hat{x}}$ imply $x(\geq)\hat{\hat{x}}$.
(3) *Reflexivity.* If $x\in X$ then $x(=)x$.
(4) *Regularity.* Let $\hat{x}\in X$. Every *preferred set* of consumption plans $\{x|x(\geq)\hat{x}$ with $x\in X\}$ contains every $x\geq\hat{x}$ and is closed. Further, the *inferior set* $\{x|x(\leq)\hat{x}$ with $x\in X\}$ is closed.

The completeness property presumes that each individual can order all possible plans in his consumption set according to preference. Transitivity provides consistency in the sense that pairwise comparisons can be used to unambiguously order the complete set of consumption plans from most to least preferred. Finally, reflexivity is an aspect of rationality assuring that the individual does not order identical consumption plans differently. When the binary relation $(\geq)$ is complete, transitive, and reflexive, it is said to *order by preference* all plans in the consumption set.

With regard to regularity, consider first the requirement that the preferred and inferior sets be closed. Such closedness implies continuity of the preference ordering. We say that the preference ordering is continuous if, with respect to any given consumption plan, (i) there is a sequence of plans each of which is at least as preferred as (or alternatively, not preferred to) the given plan, and (ii) the 'limit' plan to which the sequence converges is at least as preferred as (or not preferred to) the given plan. These ideas are illustrated in Figure 1.1A using an indifference contour relative to a given plan $\hat{x}$. The arrow in the figure represents a sequence of plans in the preferred set which converges to the limit plan x. When the plan x is at least as preferred as $\hat{x}$, then x is an element of the indifference set, as well as of the preferred and inferior sets, and the individual's preference ordering is continuous. On the other hand, when x is strictly less preferred than $\hat{x}$ then the individual's preference ordering is said to be discontinuous. The discontinuity occurs in this latter case because there is a jump at x in the

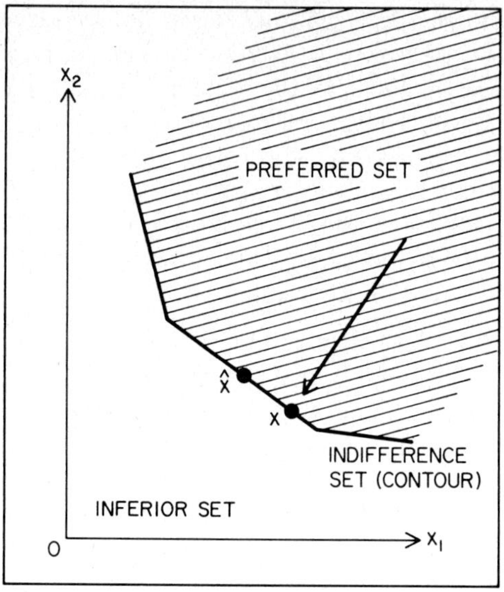

Fig. 1.1A. Convex indifference contour

preference ordering; as a result the preferred set is not closed and an indifference set for x is not defined.[3]

In addition to the indicated ordering properties, it is common to assume that the preference relation satisfies a final condition assuring that there exists a unique, preferred consumption plan when that choice is further subjected to a budget constraint (to be introduced below).

(5) *Convex preferences.* The preferred set is strictly convex.

The preferred set will be strictly convex when preferences themselves are strictly convex. *Preferences are strictly convex* if for every possible pair of consumption plans x, $\hat{x} \in X$ where $x(=)\hat{x}$ and $x \neq \hat{x}$, it is true that $[\lambda x + (1-\lambda)\hat{x}]\ (>)\hat{x}$ for any real constant λ, $0 < \lambda < 1$. That is, any convex combination of two non-equal plans to which the individual is indifferent is strictly preferred to each one of the plans. Graphically, strict convexity is present when the open line segment connecting x and $\hat{x}$ lies strictly in the

[3]An interesting case of this discontinuity in preference is found in the 'lexicographic' ordering, where a consumption plant containing more of some 'precedent' good is preferred to *all* other plans having less of that good.

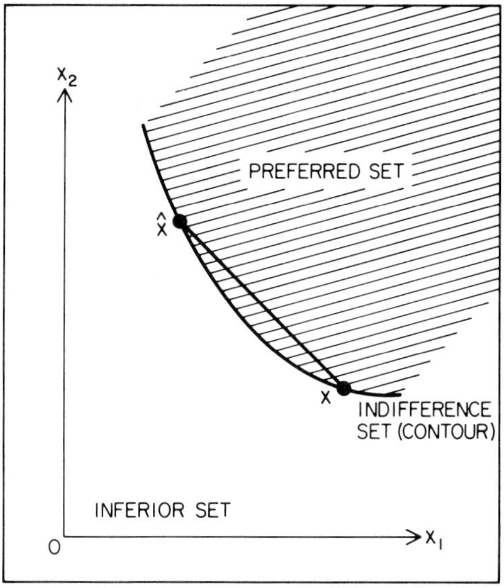

Fig. 1.1B. Strictly convex indifference contour

preferred set and not in the interior set, see Figure 1.1B. Somewhat differently, in Figure 1.1A the open line segment belongs to both the preferred and the inferior sets so that the preference ordering represented in the figure is not strictly convex, although it is convex.

Strict convexity of preferences has two important implications. First, it means that commodities (and consumption plans) are perfectly divisible. Second, it requires that the individual possess strictly decreasing rates of substitution between any pair of commodities and thus always prefers mixtures to extremes. This is, perhaps, an unnecessarily strong requirement. Simple convexity, permitting 'perfect substitutes' and constant substitution rates, would be somewhat more general, but the value of this additional realism is questionable and gained only with some technical complication.

1.A.2. Representation of preferences by utility functions

The above Assumptions (1) through (5) define an ordering of consumption plans in a way consistent with reasonable, and minimally restricted, individual preferences. A useful device for cataloging this ordering is to attach a real number to each *plan* in the consumption set in a way such that for any pairwise comparison the preferred plan is given a larger number and when there is indifference the plans are given the same number.

The existence of such a numbering scheme implies the existence of a rule of correspondence, a functional relationship, whose domain is the set of feasible plans and whose range is the set of real numbers. When such a function exists it is said that preferences are *representable*; the function itself is termed a *utility function.*

D1.1. Utility function. A real-valued function, u, defined on the consumption set X is a utility function and represents an individual's preferences provided that $u(x) \geq u(\hat{x})$ if and only if $x(\geq)\hat{x}$ for all x, $\hat{x} \in X$.

The existence of a continuous utility function is assured by the completeness, transitivity, continuity and regularity restrictions.[4]

Since the utility function represents all the properties of the individual's preference system, it is redundant to simultaneously specify both the details of an individual's preference structure and the utility function. At the same time it is not proper to take just any function and call it a utility function, for the definition clearly requires the admissible utility function be order-preserving relative to the preferences of the individual. Does this then mean that corresponding to each individual's preference structure there is a single utility function?

From the definition of the utility function it is apparent that every increasing function of a utility function is also a utility function, for the numbers assigned by this new function too preserves the ordering of the consumption plans. That is, if $u = u(x)$, then $F(u)$ is equivalent to u as a utility function if F is increasing in u. Thus, when we are interested only in the ordering of bundles as described by $(\geq)$, utility functions are uniquely defined only 'up to' an increasing functional transformation. To recall this essential indeterminacy such utility functions are referred to as *ordinal.*

Finally it is noteworthy that the existence proof of the utility function requires only the first four preference assumptions and not the final convexity Assumption (5). But, if the preference ordering follows that additional restriction and is thus (strictly) convex, indifference curves are (strictly) convex to the origin and, being level contours, the utility function is by definition (strictly) quasi-concave.

Given that preferences satisfy all of the above properties, the rational consumer, when presented with choices from among the consumption plans in his consumption set which are also feasible (in terms of his budget to be introduced shortly), chooses the plan which is most preferred or, equivalently, that plan which has the largest real number assigned it by an

[4]Arrow and Hahn (1971, pp. 82–87) provide the existence proof.

appropriate utility function. Without resource constraints, it is apparent that the individual with non-satiable preferences would choose infinite amounts of all commodities. As the next section notes, however, such a fortuitous plan is not generally selected because of budget limitations.

1.A.3. Utility functions and demand

Consider a pure exchange economy with fixed, strictly positive amounts of each commodity available in the aggregate. Individuals in this market economy possess preferences over consumption plans which are bundles of the M different commodities. Associated with each commodity is an exchange rate, or price. We represent the *price system* for the $(M-1)$ markets in the economy by the M-vector $p=[p_1\, p_2 \dots p_M]$, with $p_m=1$ when the mth commodity is designated as numeraire. Prices are relative in the sense that each indicates an amount of the numeraire commodity paid in exchange for each unit of the considered commodity.

To account for the history of the economy it is usual to assume that individuals enter into market exchange with an *endowment* of the consumption goods. For individual i the endowment is indicated by $\bar{x}^i=[\bar{x}^i_1\,\bar{x}^i_2 \dots \bar{x}^i_M]$, where each $\bar{x}^i_m$ measures i's exogenously given, initial holding in units of commodity m. When valued at market prices the endowment determines *initial wealth*, which is denoted by $\bar{w}^i$ for each i:

$$\bar{w}^i=\sum_m p_m \bar{x}^i_m.$$

Generally, only strictly positive prices and non-negative initial wealths are considered relevant. In this case we designate the market parameters by the *data set* $\Delta^i=\{p, \bar{w}^i \mid p>0 \text{ and } \bar{w}^i \geq 0\}$.

When endowments are given exogenously and individuals are takers of market prices, no consumer has control over the elements of Δ^i. Once prices and wealth are set forth in this fashion (by either an auctioneer or the particular operation of a market) and each Δ^i is fixed, the set of consumption plans achievable in exchange by any individual i are specified by a *budget set*:

$$B^i(p, \bar{w}^i)=\left\{x \mid \sum_m p_m x^i_m \leq \bar{w}^i\right\}.$$

The *equation* $\bar{w}^i=\Sigma_m p_m x^i_m$ is specifically termed i's *budget constraint* and defines the collection of consumption plans which, given prices, have exactly the same value in exchange as i's initial wealth.

For convenience in notation the superscript i is generally omitted from the individual's endowment $\bar{x}$, initial wealth $\bar{w}$, data set Δ, and budget set B when dealing with a typical individual.

Given the assumptions made to this point, it is well-known that there is a unique solution to each individual's choice of consumption. The proof proceeds by contradiction. First note that, for $p>0$ and $\bar{w}\geq 0$, the set B is closed and bounded and there exists at least one consumption plan, call it $\mathring{x}$, maximizing $u(x)$. Suppose now that some second plan, $\hat{x}$, also maximizes $u(x)$, which means $u(\mathring{x})=u(\hat{x})$. Let x_α be a proper convex combination of $\mathring{x}$ and $\hat{x}$, so that it lies in the budget set if both $\mathring{x}$ and $\hat{x}$ do. If u is strictly quasi-concave (indifference curves are strictly convex to the origin), then x_α has a higher utility than either $\mathring{x}$ or $\hat{x}$, which means that neither $\mathring{x}$ nor $\hat{x}$ is a utility maximizing plan. This contradicts the initial hypothesis and implies that, given $u(x)$ is strictly quasi-concave, corresponding to every specific $(p, \bar{w})\in\Delta$ there is exactly one plan contained in $B(p, \bar{w})$ which maximizes $u(x)$. Consumption plans chosen in this manner can be represented functionally.

D1.2. Demand function. For each $(p, \bar{w})\in\Delta$, the individual chooses the one consumption plan $\mathring{x}\in B(p, \bar{w})$ which is preferred. This act of choice defines a function from Δ to X: $\mathring{x}=f(p, \bar{w})$ such that $u(\mathring{x})>u(x)$ for all $x\in B(p, \bar{w})$, and $x\neq\mathring{x}$. f is called the demand function.

Given prices and initial wealth parameters, the range of the demand function is that single consumption plan which is optimal for the individual from among those which are budget feasible. Geometrically, the demand function for any commodity is derived from the familiar points of tangency of an indifference hypersurface with the budget constraint hyperplane as the price of the commodity is changed, other parameters of the data sets $\Delta^i \forall i$ being held constant.

1.A.4. Indirect utility functions

An important property of the demand function from an analytical viewpoint is its continuity in both prices and wealth. Specifically, if the utility function $u(x)$ is continuous in x and strictly quasi-concave, then for every $(p, \bar{w})\in\Delta$ the demand function $f(p, \bar{w})$ is continuous and differentiable both in p and $\bar{w}$.[5] It is of particular importance in equilibrium analyses to notice that $w=\Sigma_m p_m \bar{x}_m$, so that wealth too is a function of the price system

[5]See Barten and Boehn (1982, Ch. 9) for a formal proof.

with given endowments. This fact is generally noted by the functional notation $\bar{w}(p)$ and, in this case, the demand function may be written $f(p, \bar{w}(p)) = g(p)$, where we understand the relationship between f and g.

D1.3. Indirect utility function. Let f indicate a demand function on X and denote the function U on Δ given by

$$U(p, \bar{w}) = u(f(p, \bar{w})) = \max_{x} u(x) \quad \text{s.t.} \quad x \in B \wedge X,$$

as the indirect utility function (of price and wealth).

By the continuity of u on X and the fact that f is continuously differentiable in both p and $\bar{w}$ for $(p, \bar{w}) \in \Delta$, the indirect utility function is also continuous and differentiable in p and $\bar{w}$.[6]

E1.1. Consider the utility function defined on two goods x_1 and x_2 given by

$$u(x_1, x_2) = x_1^{\alpha} x_2^{(1-\alpha)}.$$

As any increasing transformation of a utility function represents identical preferences we can equivalently write

$$u(x_1, x_2) = \alpha \ln x_1 + (1 - \alpha) \ln x_2.$$

There is also the usual budget restriction

$$p_1 x_1 + p_2 x_2 = \bar{w},$$

where prices and wealth are strictly positive and constant. The stationarity conditions for an interior optimum are

$$\frac{\alpha}{p_1 x_1} = \frac{(1-\alpha)}{p_2 x_2}.$$

Using the budget constraint to remove x_2 yields the (Marshallian) demand for x_1:

$$x_1^*(p_1, p_2, \bar{w}) = \alpha \bar{w} / p^1,$$

which, incidentally, is independent of p_2. A similar method yields the

[6]Again, see Barten and Boehn (1982, Ch. 9).

demand for x_2:

$$x_2^*(p_1, p_2, \bar{w}) = (1-\alpha)\bar{w}/p_2.$$

Substituting these expressions into the utility function gives

$$U(p, \bar{w}) = u(x_1^*, x_2^*) = \ln \bar{w} - \alpha \ln p_1 - (1-\alpha) \ln p_2,$$

which is the indirect utility function. ■

E1.2. The Marshallian (uncompensated) demand for commodities is often derived using *Roy's Identity*, which can be stated as follows: let $U(p, \bar{w})$ be the indirect utility function, then assuming suitable differentiability and strictly positive prices and wealth

$$x_m(p, \bar{w}) = \frac{-\partial U(p, \bar{w})/\partial p_m}{\partial U(p, \bar{w})/\partial \bar{w}},$$

for all commodities $m = 1, 2, \ldots, M$. For example, with the conditions in E1.1. we have

$$-\partial U/\partial p_1 = \alpha/p_1, \qquad \partial U/\partial \bar{w} = 1/\bar{w}.$$

Roy's identity then gives

$$x_1(p, \bar{w}) = \frac{\alpha/p_1}{1/\bar{w}} = \alpha\bar{w}/p_1,$$

which is the form shown in E1.1.

Proof of the identity is straightforward. Suppose that $x^* = [x_1^* \, x_2^* \ldots x_M^*]$ maximizes utility at some specific prices p and wealth $\bar{w}$. Then $u(x^*) \equiv U(p, \bar{w})$ and we can differentiate partially with respect to any p_m to derive

$$0 = \frac{\partial U}{\partial p_m} + \frac{\partial U}{\partial \bar{w}} \frac{\partial \bar{w}}{\partial p_m}.$$

Solving for $\partial \bar{w}/\partial p_m = x_m$ and recognizing that the result holds for all p and $\bar{w}$ proves the identity. ■

Notice that the use of an indirect utility function assumes only optimal consumption plans are chosen for any price system and initial wealth, and thus shifts attention from consumption commodities to initial wealth and price as potential choice criteria.[7] An extremely important property of the indirect utility function is based on this notion and on the fact that, prices fixed, any (other) consumption plan which is at least as preferred as a chosen plan must cost more than the chosen consumption plan. This is stated somewhat conversely in the following sufficient-conditions proposition:

P1.1. More wealth is better. With $u(x)$ a continuous utility function on the non-empty, compact set $B(p, \bar{w})$, the indirect utility function defined by

$$U(p, \bar{w}) = \max_x u(x) \quad \text{s.t.} \quad \langle p, x \rangle \leq \bar{w},$$

is continuous in its arguments. Moreover, when $B(p, \bar{w})$ is convex and u is strictly quasi-concave and increasing in x, then U is strictly quasi-concave and, holding prices constant, increasing in wealth $\bar{w}$.

Katzner (1970, Section 3.5) and Cox (1973) provide alternative proofs of this proposition. (E1.4 and E1.5, to follow, sketch the logic of the proof.)

Two aspects of the proposition are important. First is the positive result: if prices are fixed, then, as the indirect utility function is increasing in wealth, *optimal* consumption plans for the individual are ordered by their exchangeability with wealth. This means, for example, that an increase in wealth allows the individual to choose a commodity bundle which is unambiguously preferred to an original bundle, providing the price system is fixed. More wealth is better. The second important implication is one *not* set forth in the proposition: if a wealth effect, say a wealth increase, comes through changes in the prices of goods, then one cannot in general say whether the post-change optimal consumption plan is preferred to or inferior to the original, pre-change plan.

E1.3. For the utility function $u(x_1, x_2) = x_1 x_2$, maximization of utility subject to the budget constraint $p_1 x_1 + p_2 x_2 \leq \bar{w}$ yields the demand functions $x_1 = \bar{w}/2p_1$ and $x_2 = \bar{w}/2p_2$. Substitute these into the utility function to obtain the indirect utility function $U(p, \bar{w}) = \bar{w}^2/4p_1 p_2$. It is clear that $U(p, \bar{w})$

[7]The Slutsky, and typical, development of consumer demand is concerned with maximizing $u(x)$ subject to the linear constraint $\langle p, x \rangle = \bar{w}$, where p and $\bar{w}$ are fixed parameters. A dual problem is to minimize 'expenditures' $\Sigma_m p_m x_m$ subject to some value of the indirect utility function $U(p, \bar{w})$, but where x is the 'parameter' and prices are chosen. It is well-known, see Samuelson (1965), that the solutions to these problems are related: if $\mathring{x}$ solves the primal problem given specific prices and wealth $(\mathring{p}, \bar{w}) \in \Delta$, then $(\mathring{p}, \bar{w})$ solves the dual problem given $\mathring{x}$.

is increasing in $\bar{w}$ when p is fixed and that accompanying variations in p can alter this result.

The 'more wealth is better' P1.1 is a key proposition in the analysis of capital markets and prices. To understand its implications in an immediately useful context, it is useful to introduce uncertainty to consumption choices.

1.B. Uncertainty and State Contingent Consumption

It is analytically convenient to regard the M consumption commodities as differentiated both in time and 'space' even when otherwise identical. In situations subject to uncertainty an especially useful form of commodity differentiation is by *states of nature*. Each such *state* is defined to be a description so complete that when known to be true it determines completely and precisely the size and distribution of supply for every relevant commodity. In an uncertain world the state to obtain at each future period is generally unknown in the present. In turn, each commodity is differentiated by the state and time period in which it is to be contingently available.

Suppose there to be only two time periods (now and then, or the present and the future) and a single, 'composite' good. The supply of the composite good is certain in the present, but differentiated by $s=1,2,\dots,S$ (finite) states of nature at the future period. In this case think of each individual as choosing a consumption plan given by the $(S+1)$-vector $\chi=[x_0\, x_1 \dots x_S]$ with x_0 consumption in the present period, $t=0$, and each x_s consumption in state s at the future period, $t=1$. In an analogous way the individual's endowment $\bar{\chi}=[\bar{x}_0\, \bar{x}_1 \dots \bar{x}_S]$ is also uncertain, or state contingent, at period one.

Consider now a market economy where trading occurs only at the present period. Taking the current consumption commodity as the basis of exchange, or numeraire, S markets result with associated prices $\phi=[p_0\, p_1 \dots p_S]$, where $p_0 \equiv 1$. Each price p_s is required to be paid irrevocably at $t=0$, before it is known what state will realize at $t=1$, for a unit of the commodity delivered if and only if state s obtains. For emphasis: exchange takes place now, at $t=0$, deliveries on current consumption also take place now, but deliveries arising from state contingent claims take place in the next period, at $t=1$, after it is unambiguously known to all individuals which state has occurred.

In the contingent claims market the preferences of individuals are expressed with respect to plans of current and next period (state contingent) consumption and represented by the increasing, strictly quasi-concave utility function $u(\chi)$. There is also an associated indirect utility function $U(\phi, \bar{w})$ and the budget constraint $\Sigma_s p_s x_s + p_0 x_0 = \bar{w}$ limiting feasible consumption plans. Given that $u(\chi)$ is increasing in x, $U(\phi, \bar{w})$ is increasing in $\bar{w}$ when the prices ϕ are held fixed, and it follows from P1.1 that initial wealth orders optimal consumption plans for the individual. For example, each individual having an extended set of choices (say, with respect to some specific aspect of the market organization or with respect to the production or 'financial structure' decisions of firms) will simply take those which act to maximize his wealth, *providing* market prices are not also altered. When such decisions lead to changes in both ϕ and w, then without further restrictions either on the changes or on utility functions the decision is more complex.

E1.4. When there are simultaneous changes in price and wealth such that the individual's old budget set is a proper subset of the new one, then too the individual will reach a preferred consumption plan. More exactly, let $(\phi, \bar{w})$ indicate original prices and wealth levels and let $(\phi^*, \bar{w}^*)$ indicate new values. Define $\hat{x}_\theta(\phi, \bar{w})$ as the maximum level of good $\theta = 0, 1, \ldots, S$ that can be purchased with ϕ and $\bar{w}$; $\hat{x}_\theta(\phi^*, \bar{w}^*)$ similarly corresponds to the new price and wealth situation. If $\hat{x}_\theta(\phi, \bar{w}) \leq \hat{x}_\theta(\phi^*, \bar{w}^*)$ for all θ, with strict inequality for some θ, then the new budget set dominates the old and (neglecting corner solutions) the individual is better-off with the change. ■

E1.5. Let there be just two states of nature and imagine an individual with the utility function $u(x_1, x_2) = x_1 x_2$. Given the initial endowments $(\bar{x}_1, \bar{x}_2) = (5, 1)$ and prices $(p_1, p_2) = (1, 1)$, initial wealth is $\bar{w} = p_1 x_1 + p_2 x_2 = 6$. To maximize utility in this case the individual chooses the bundle $(x_1, x_2) = (3, 3)$ with $u(3, 3) = 9$ 'utils'. Now let the individual's endowment change to $(\bar{x}_1, \bar{x}_2) = (6, 1)$ holding prices constant. This change increases initial wealth to $\bar{w} = 7$; in turn, the optimal consumption choice becomes $(x_1, x_2) = (3\frac{1}{2}, 3\frac{1}{2})$ and there is an increase in utility to $u(3\frac{1}{2}, 3\frac{1}{2}) = 12\frac{1}{4}$. In this case more wealth is better.

Next assume that both endowments *and* prices are changed to $(\bar{x}_1, \bar{x}_2) = (6, 1)$ and $(p_1, p_2) = (1, 3)$, respectively. (Note that x_1 has been taken to be the numeraire, $p_1 = 1$.) The individual's initial wealth is now $\bar{w} = 9$, which is greater than in the previous case. At the new price ratio the optimal consumption choice is $(x_1, x_2) = (4\frac{1}{2}, 1\frac{1}{2})$, which yields $u(4\frac{1}{2}, 1\frac{1}{2}) = 6\frac{3}{4}$ 'utils'. The individual is worse off relative to the former situation despite the fact that his endowed wealth both in terms of physical units and of the numeraire (x_1 here) has been increased. (It is to be observed that his level of wealth is actually lower in the new situation if it is measured alternatively in terms of x_2 as the numeraire.) Thus, in the absence of knowledge of specific utility functions, wealth unambiguously orders optimal consumption plans only when the price ratio does not change.

A geometric illustration of this choice is provided in Figure 1.2. Let $\bar{x}_A$ be the initial state 1 and state 2 endowment of the individual. As a first case, assume that prices obtain such that $\bar{w}_A$ is the individual's initial wealth, with $\bar{w}_A$ being used in the figure to mark the associated budget constraint. With preferences given by the indifference curves, the plan x_A is selected in this case. With state contingent price remaining unchanged, now alter the individual's endowment by increasing consumption claims in state 1 while holding those in state 2 constant: in the figure this new endowment is represented by $\bar{x}_B$. The change leads to an increase in wealth denoted by $\bar{w}_B > \bar{w}_A$ and a corresponding shift out in the budget constraint from $\bar{w}_A$ to $\bar{w}_B$. The increase in initial wealth leads to optimal bundle x_B which is strictly preferred to the original x_A. Holding prices fixed, the result is that greater wealth leads to a more preferred consumption plan.

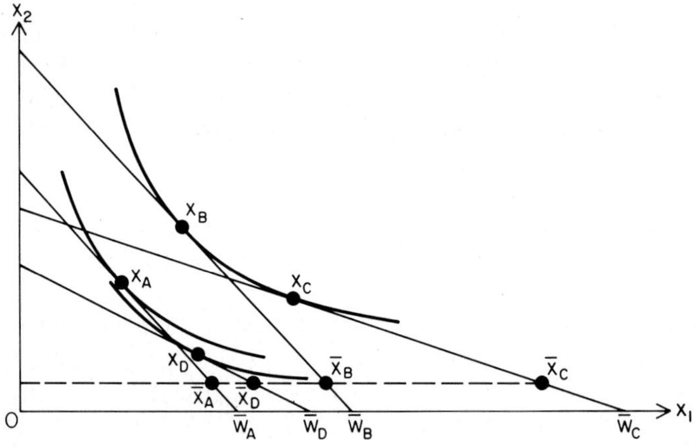

Fig. 1.2. Optimal consumption plans

Now consider simultaneous changes in both prices and endowments. Specifically, let the endowment position move from $\bar{x}_A$ to $\bar{x}_C$, which represents an increase in state 1 claims while holding state 2 claims fixed. Without a change in prices this would unambiguously lead to an increase in wealth and to a preferred optimal consumption plan. In this case, however, prices do change as the budget constraint $\bar{w}_C$ shifts in a non-parallel manner now passing through $\bar{x}_C$. The optimal bundle is now x_C, which is preferred to the original optimum x_A. The converse might also have occurred as represented by case D. In this alternative there is an increase in the endowment of state 2 claims, with prices changing simultaneously to yield budget constraint $\bar{w}_D > \bar{w}_A$. Notwithstanding the increase in wealth, the optimal consumption plan x_D is *less* preferred relative to the original optimal plan x_A. Note that $\bar{w}_D > \bar{w}_A$ in terms of x_1, but this inequality is reversed if wealth is measured in x_2 units (which explains how it is possible for the individual to be worse off with $\bar{x}_D$ than with $\bar{x}_A$). ■

1.B.1. Expected utility

In the remaining parts of this chapter we focus on the uncertain part of choice. This is done simply by assuming each individual i's consumption at period zero to be fixed at some specific level $\mathring{x}_0^i$. Each relevant utility maximization problem is then only concerned with the choice of future consumption $x^i = [x_1^i \, x_2^i \ldots x_s^i]$ conditional on the 'parameter' $\mathring{x}_0^i$. In this case we write $u^i(x^i)$ rather than $u^i(\chi^i)$, where the difference in the utility functions is not explicit, but nonetheless understood. To be sure, the choice of x_0^i and x^i must be made at once, and we will later approach the problem in this more general way, but it is easier for the moment (and correct for present purposes, see Section 5.A) to proceed without the bookkeeping involved in an initial period consumption choice.

It is intuitive to think of the individual's preference ordering over consumption plans at period one to contain elements of judgments about the likelihood with which different states will occur as well as the evaluation of tastes. Can these notions be made part of $u^i(x^i)$? Such a decomposition of the ordinal utility function into distinct elements of belief about the likelihood of certain states and pure taste has been frequently considered. The treatises of von Neumann and Morgenstern (1947) and Savage (1954) provide plausible and reasonably weak sets of axioms under which such a decomposition can be made. The result of their alternative sets of assumptions are that consumer preference can be summarized by an *expected utility function* of the form $\Sigma_s h_s^i u_s^i(x_s^i)$.[8] In the Savage development the

[8]Two assumptions are crucial to the expected utility representation of preferences in both the Savage and the von Neumann and Morgenstern developments. (These are in addition to the completeness, transivity and reflexivity assumptions which provide the underlying preference ordering.) First, there is a continuity assumption requiring that if (possibly uncertain) distinct plans x, $\hat{x}$, and $\hat{x}$ are formed in a way that x is preferred to $\hat{x}$ and in turn $\hat{x}$ is preferred to $\hat{x}$ then there exists a number λ, $0 < \lambda < 1$, such that the individual becomes indifferent to the

weights h_s^i are subjective (or personal) probabilities and satisfy the conditions: $h_s^i \geq 0\ \forall i, s$ and $\Sigma_s h_s^i = 1\ \forall i$. (We note also that the number of states is required to be finite in this case.) The von Neumann and Morgenstern development alternatively takes probabilities to be objective, so that in each state $h_s^i = h_s\ \forall i$, where h_s is the 'objectively' measured probability of the state s occurrence.

In the expression for expected utility the *elementary utilities* $u_s^i(x_s^i)$ are functions which represent the ordering of consumption amounts in each state.[9] It is important to note that it is an assumption in both the Savage and von Neumann and Morgenstern developments that preferences, and therefore the elementary utility functions, are additive across states. In spite of some criticisms concerning its plausibility [see Samuelson (1961)], this assumed additive property gives great usefulness both in theory and in empirical work to the expected utility representation of individual choice under uncertainty.

In the following, as is usual in the literature, we make a final assumption: that preferences, and thus elementary utility functions, are independent of the state to occur. That is, we require $u_s^i(x_s) = u^i(x_s)\ \forall s$. Hirshleifer (1969) and others call this the *uniqueness* assumption. Lastly, we define the *expected utility function* $\mathrm{E}u^i(x^i) = \Sigma_s h_s^i u^i(x_s)$, which is a convex combination of the elementary utility functions.[10]

1.B.2. Cardinality and ordinality

Given the axioms which imply the expected utility criterion, any elementary utility function that provides the same ordering of consumption as $u(x_s)$

'simple' plan $\hat{x}$ and the 'compound' plan $[\lambda x + (1-\lambda)\hat{\hat{x}}]$. The second crucial aspect of the expected utility development is what is referred to as the independence assumption. That is, it is assumed that for two uncertain plans x and $\hat{x}$ such that $x(\geq)\,\hat{x}$, and third plan $\hat{\hat{x}}$, it is true that for all λ, $0<\lambda<1$, $[\lambda x + (1-\lambda)\hat{\hat{x}}]$ is preferred to $[\lambda\hat{x} + (1-\lambda)\hat{\hat{x}}]$. The reason that the above is termed an independence assumption is that it rules out any interrelationships, such as substitutability or complementarity, between plans. More particularly, if $x\ (\geq)\hat{x}$, then it is required that this preference not be changed just because both x and $\hat{x}$ are offered in conjunction with some other plan $\hat{\hat{x}}$. This independence assumption leads directly to the fact that the elementary utilities are additive (with probability weights) across states.

[9]Elementary utility functions such as $u(x_s) = \ln(x_s)$ which are unbounded in x_s do not order all prospects by expected utility and thus violate the first of the von Neumann/Morgenstern and Savage axioms concerning completeness. The St. Petersburg Paradox describes such a prospect, see Ellsberg (1961). In the sequel we do not generally impose a boundedness condition on elementary utility functions, but we do consider only a bounded opportunity set for consumption claims. With suitable regularity of the utility function, then the ordering of all prospects in the opportunity set will be complete in this case. See also Kennan (1981).

[10]Note that Eu is 'double lettering' of the (single) function. Eu, which is defined on the vector of variables $x_1, x_2, \ldots, x_S$, is distinct from the elementary utility u, which is defined on the scalar x_s.

and orders plans in the same way as $\Sigma_s h_s u(x_s)$, i.e., according to the expected utility criterion, is said to be equivalent to $u(x_s)$. Any positive linear transformation of $u(\cdot)$ is, in such a way, equivalent to $u(\cdot)$. Proof of this equivalence goes as follows: Let $v(\cdot)=\alpha+\beta u(\cdot)$ where $\beta>0$ is a constant, and consider two arbitrary consumption plans x and $\mathring{x}$. With given probabilities h, $u(\cdot)$ orders these plans by the values of the expected utilities $\Sigma_s h_s u(x_s)$ and $\Sigma_s h_s u(\mathring{x}_s)$. The elementary utility function $v(\cdot)$ in turn orders x and $\mathring{x}$ by the expected utilities as

$$\sum_s h_s v(x_s)=\alpha+\beta\sum_s h_s u(x_s), \quad \text{and}$$

$$\sum_s h_s v(\mathring{x}_s)=\alpha+\beta\sum_s h_s u(\mathring{x}_s).$$

From these equations we see that, with $\beta>0$, the ordering by expected utility of the two plans x and $\mathring{x}$ using $u(\cdot)$ is the same as that using its positive linear transformation $v(\cdot)$.

To prove that only linear transformations preserve the preference ordering, consider an increasing transformation of $u(\cdot)$:

$$v=g[u(\cdot)],$$

where $g'>0$. It will ease the notation to use subscripts to denote the level of the consumption at which utility is evaluated. That is, for x_1 the original utility will be indicated by u_1 and the corresponding transforms of that by v_1. Now, let $x_1>x_2>x_3$. There then must exist some probability h such that

$$u_2=hu_1+(1-h)u_3.$$

Moreover, if v is to be a valid utility it must also be that

$$v_2=hv_1+(1-h)v_3.$$

Substituting in this last equation from the former gives

$$g(u_2)=hg(u_1)+(1-h)g(u_3),$$

and substituting in turn for u_2 we have

$$g(hu_1+(1-h)u_3)=hg(u_1)+(1-h)g(u_3).$$

For arbitrary probabilities and consumptions this last equation can be satisfied only if $g(\cdot)$ is a linear function.

It is usual to refer to a utility function which is equivalent only 'up to' a positive linear transformation as a *cardinal* utility function. By this terminology a cardinal utility index does not possess all the typical properties of 'cardinality'. Specifically, it does not have a unique origin (like distance and volume) and thus the cardinal utility index numbers are not so meaningful as to indicate the absolute amount of utility. On the other hand, the cardinal utility function does provide an interval scale, as shown in the following example:

E1.6. Consider three consumption plans x_a, x_b and x_c such that the following preference by expected utility (given probabilities) occurs:

$$\mathrm{E}u(x_a) > \mathrm{E}u(x_b) > \mathrm{E}u(x_c).$$

Moreover assume that, as measured by expected utility, the preference for x_a relative to x_b is greater than that of x_b relative to x_c:

$$\mathrm{E}u(x_a) - \mathrm{E}u(x_b) > \mathrm{E}u(x_b) - \mathrm{E}u(x_c). \tag{1.B.1}$$

We want to show that this inequality is preserved if the utility function u is replaced by the linear transformation $v(u) = \alpha + \beta u$, $\beta > 0$. Using v, the expected utility of plan x_a is $\mathrm{E}v(x_a) = \alpha + \beta \mathrm{E}u(x_a)$ as shown above. Some reorganization yields

$$\mathrm{E}u(x_a) = \frac{\mathrm{E}v(x_a) - \alpha}{\beta}.$$

Similar linear transformations for x_b and x_c can also be made. Substituting these in (1.B.1) gives us

$$\left[\frac{\mathrm{E}v(x_a) - \alpha}{\beta}\right] - \left[\frac{\mathrm{E}v(x_b) - \alpha}{\beta}\right] > \left[\frac{\mathrm{E}v(x_b) - \alpha}{\beta}\right] - \left[\frac{\mathrm{E}v(x_c) - \alpha}{\beta}\right],$$

from which it follows that

$$\mathrm{E}v(x_a) - \mathrm{E}v(x_b) > \mathrm{E}v(x_b) - \mathrm{E}v(x_c). \tag{1.B.2}$$

The conclusion: the ranking of differences in expected utility is not changed by the linear transformation. ■

The invariance of utility differences under linear transformations is a key distinction between the usual axioms of choice under certainty and the von Neumann–Morgenstern (or Savage) axioms of choice under uncertainty.

The properties of the marginal utility function which are commonly specified under certainty provide no information about preferences, because that marginal utility is not generally invariant to arbitrary monotonic transformations. When marginal utility is decreasing in some interval in the certainty case it is in general possible to find a monotonic transformation of the utility function such that the 'new' marginal utility is constant, or increasing, in that same interval. In contrast, marginal utility is an invariant property of the utility function when individuals maximize expected utility, which means that marginal utility in this second case contains information about individual preferences. What is that information?

1.B.3. Risk aversion

Consider an individual endowed with some consumption plan $\bar{x}=[\bar{x}_1\, \bar{x}_2 \ldots \bar{x}_S]$ and let the associated state probabilities be given by $h=[h_1\, h_2 \ldots h_S]$. It is said that trade at *actuarially fair* rates of exchange occurs if the individual is able at most to trade his endowment for any consumption plan x which has the same expected value, $\Sigma_s h_s x_s = \Sigma_s h_s \bar{x}_s$. That is, plans of the same expected values bear the same market price, and greater expected values command greater prices. With trade actuarially fair, the consumer's optimization problem is

$$\max_x \; \mathrm{E}u(x) \quad \text{s.t.} \quad \sum_s h_s(x_s-\bar{x}_s)=0. \tag{1.B.3a}$$

There is the corresponding Lagrange function

$$L(x,\lambda)=\mathrm{E}u(x)-\lambda\left[\sum_s h_s(x_s-\bar{x}_s)\right], \tag{1.B.3b}$$

where λ is the usual multiplier. In part, the stationarity conditions for an interior optimum are, for all s,

$$\partial L/\partial x_s = h_s(\partial u/\partial x_s) - \lambda h_s = 0. \tag{1.B.4}$$

The obvious solution is $\mathring{x}_\theta = \Sigma_s h_s \bar{x}_s$ for all $\theta = 1, 2, \ldots, S$.[11] That is, the

[11] If each $u(\cdot)$ is strictly concave, then as $\mathrm{E}u(x)$ is the sum of the functions it too must be strictly concave and hence the preferred set $\{x \mid \mathrm{E}u(x) \geq \mathrm{E}u(\mathring{x})\}$ is convex. As a result, if $\mathring{x}$ is a maximum to this problem it is also the unique maximum.

optimum plan $\mathring{x}$ is riskless with each element equal to the expected value of the individual's endowment. If allowed to exchange contingent claims at actuarially fair exchange rates, an individual with a strictly concave utility function will choose to avoid all uncertainty and consume an amount equal to the expected value of his endowment. This observation leads in a natural way to the definition of risk aversion and its association with the concavity of elementary utilities.

D1.4. Risk aversion. Let $x>0$ be a risky consumption plan, one such that at least two of its elements are unequal. An individual is said to be *risk averse* if he strictly prefers receiving the expected consequence of that consumption plan to receiving the plan itself. The individual is said to be *risk neutral* if he is indifferent to these two alternatives. Conversely, if the individual prefers the plan to its expected value he is said to have a *risk affinity*.

Written somewhat differently, an individual is *risk averse* if

$$u[\mathrm{E}(x)]>\mathrm{E}u(x), \tag{1.B.5a}$$

risk neutral if

$$u[\mathrm{E}(x)]=\mathrm{E}u(x), \tag{1.B.5b}$$

and *risk affinitive* if

$$u[\mathrm{E}(x)]<\mathrm{E}u(x), \tag{1.B.5c}$$

where all expectations are with respect to the state probabilities h: $\mathrm{E}x=\Sigma_s h_s x_s$ and $\mathrm{E}u(x)=\Sigma_s h_s u(x_s)$. It is important to notice that the definition of risk aversion is limited to properties of the individual's utility function (his preferences) and therefore is a concept placed logically prior to the consideration of prices, endowments, budget limitations, and conditions of market exchange generally. When all such effects are considered, we will find that in spite of 'pure' preferences risk averse individuals do not generally choose riskless plans. But, first some intermediate results.

P1.2. Risk aversion and concavity of u. A consumer is risk averse if and only if his elementary utility function u is strictly concave. He is risk neutral if and only if u is linear and has a risk affinity if and only if u is strictly convex.

Proof. Consider an uncertain, non-zero plan yielding x_1 with probability h_1 and x_2 with probability $h_2=(1-h_1)$, $0<h_1<1$. The expected outcome is $\mathrm{E}x=h_1x_1+(1-h_1)x_2$. For risk aversion it is required that

$$u[h_1x_1+(1-h_1)x_2]>h_1u(x_1)+(1-h_1)u(x_2),$$

which is the definition of strict concavity for the function u. To prove the converse (with finite S), consider a non-zero plan x yielding x_s with probability $h_s \forall s$. Since u is strictly concave, we have

$$u\left[\sum_s h_s x_s\right]>\sum_s h_s u(x_s), \tag{1.B.6}$$

which defines risk aversion. The demonstration of risk neutrality if and only if u is linear is obvious, as is the fact that strict convexity implies and is implied by a risk affinity. □

D1.4 and P1.2 jointly imply the following proposition:

P1.3. Jensen's inequality. Let $x>0$ be a risky plan. Then a (strictly) concave expected utility function evaluated at the expected value of some uncertain consumption plan is (strictly) greater than the expected utility of the consumption plan.

E1.7. Jensen's equality can be similarly stated for (strictly) convex functions, with the (strict) inequality being reversed. For example, consider the uncertain plan x and the strictly convex function $f(x)=1/x$. Then,

$$\mathrm{E}(1/x)>1/\mathrm{E}(x),$$

that is, the expected value of the strictly convex function $f(x)$ is strictly greater than the value of the function evaluated at the expectation of x. (Note that the equality holds for non-random x.) ■

1.B.4. Measuring risk averseness

P1.2 suggests that some index of concavity would be appropriate as a measure of risk averseness. Restricting attention to only increasing utility functions, two properties of the measure, however specified, are desirable: (1) it should indicate whether a utility function exhibits risk aversion (which might be done with the second derivative of u in that, as we have noted, strict concavity implies risk aversion); and, (2) it should be identical for equivalent utility functions. It is easy to construct one measure with these properties. Consider two elementary utility functions u and v which are equivalent, so that $v=a+bu$ with $b>0$. Letting primes indicate derivatives, it follows immediately that $v'=bu'$ and $v''=bu''$and therefore $v''/v'=u''/u'$, which is a non-positive ratio for increasing concave utilities. Thus, one candidate for the measure of aversion to risk is simply the ratio of u'' to u'. Hold this possibility aside for the moment and consider the following two definitions:

D1.5. Certainty equivalent. For every consumption plan, x and set of state probabilities h, define the certainty equivalent as that amount of the consumption good, x^* (a scalar), such that the individual is indifferent between receiving x^* for certain and taking the uncertain consumption plan. That is, x^* is such that $\mathrm{E}u(x)=u(x^*)$.

D1.6. Risk premium. The risk premium, r^*, related to a set of state probabilities and a consumption plan is the difference between the expected (actuarial) value of the plan, Ex, and its certainty equivalent x^*, i.e.,

$$r^*=\mathrm{E}x-x^*.$$

The risk premium is measured in units of the consumption good. It is the amount by which the mean value of the consumption plan must be changed such that an individual is indifferent between receiving $(\mathrm{E}x-r^*)$ for certain and taking the plan. That is, $u(\mathrm{E}x-r^*)=\mathrm{E}u(x)$. The risk premium exists if Ex, u and Eu exist; moreover, it depends on the functional form of u, the probability distribution, and the consumption plan under consideration.

E1.8. Suppose there is an individual with elementary utility function $u(x_s)=(x_s)^{0.5}$. Let there be just two states with probabilities $h_1=0.6$ and $h_2=(1-h_1)=0.4$ and consider the consumption plan $x=[4\ 9]$. The indivudual's expected utility of this plan is

$$\mathrm{E}u(x)=0.6(4)^{0.5}+0.4(9)^{0.5}=1.2+1.2=2.4,$$

and the certainty equivalent is

$$(x^*)^{0.5}=2.4, \qquad x^*=5.76.$$

In turn, the risk premium can be calculated as

$$\begin{aligned} r^* &= \mathrm{E}x-x^* \\ &= [0.6(4)+0.4(9)]-5.76=0.24. \end{aligned}$$

■

Our intuition relative to the definition of risk aversion, certainty equivalence, and risk premium is helped by reference to Figure 1.3. A simplified plan x having only two outcomes x_1 and x_2 with probabilities h_1 and $(1-h_1)$, respectively, is indicated in the figure. These outcomes are represented on the horizontal axis along with the expected (or actuarial) value of the plan, $\mathrm{E}x = h_1 x_1 + (1-h_1)x_2$. With the increasing, strictly concave utility function u, the utility of the expected wealth is given on the vertical axis by $u(\mathrm{E}x)$. In distinction, there is the expected utility of the consumption plan: $u(x_1)$ is the elementary utility in case of outcome x_1, $u(x_2)$ and x_2 are similarly related, and $\mathrm{E}u(x) = h_1 u(x_1) + (1-h_1)u(x_2)$ is the expected utility. With risk aversion and thereby the strict concavity of u, then $u(\mathrm{E}x) > u(x^*)$. From the figure it is also seen how both the certainty equivalent x^* and the risk premium r^* are defined relative to the plan x. Note that both are measured in the units of the consumption good rather than in 'units of utility'.

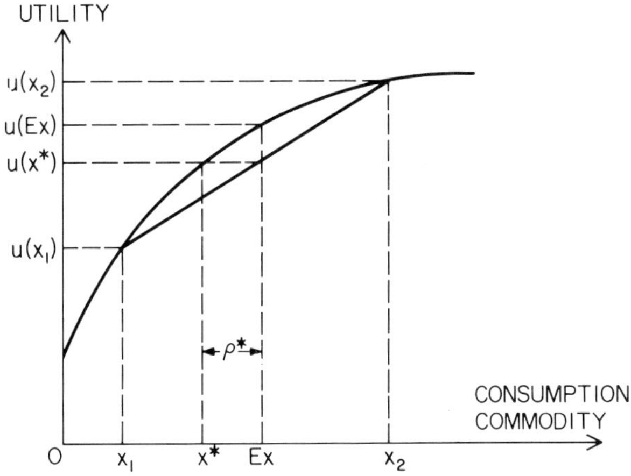

Fig. 1.3. Utility analysis of choice under risk

For completeness we state formally the now obvious relationship between risk aversion and the risk premium.

P1.4. Risk aversion and the risk premium. For utility functions increasing in consumption, an individual is risk averse if and only if his risk premium is positive, he is risk neutral if and only if his risk premium is zero, and he is risk affinitive if and only if his risk premium is negative.

Proof. Follows immediately from Definitions D1.4 and D1.6. □

Pratt (1964) develops a useful approximation to the risk premium by expanding $u(\mathrm{E}x - r^*)$ and $\mathrm{E}u(x)$ in Taylor series for a consumption plan with small variance and then letting the variance approach zero. His development is instructive and easily replicated. Assume, as Pratt, that $u(\cdot)$ is suitably continuous with finite derivatives and consider some specific consumption plan x. Separate the plan into two parts: a sure amount to be received in each state, which is referred to as (final) wealth and denoted by w, and the remaining portion, which is referred to as being *at risk* and represented by the S-vector $\xi = [\xi_1\, \xi_2 \ldots \xi_S]$. That is, we write $x_s = w + \xi_s\ \forall s$. For convenience take the part of x at riak as actuarially neutral, i.e., choose ξ such that $\mathrm{E}\xi = 0$, which implies $w = \mathrm{E}x$.

By the definition of the certainty equivalent and risk premium we have

$$u(x^*) = u(w - r^*) = \mathrm{E}u(w1_S + \xi), \tag{1.B.7}$$

where 1_S is the S-vector of 1's. It is assumed that $\mathrm{E}u(w1_S + \xi)$ exists and is finite. Expand the utility functions around w for both sides of the rightmost equality. For the LHS obtain

$$u(w - r^*) = u(w) - r^* u'(w) + \frac{(r^*)^2}{2} u''(w) + \ldots,$$

and for the RHS obtain

$$\begin{aligned} \mathrm{E}u(w1_S + \xi) &= u(w) + \mathrm{E}\xi u'(w) + \tfrac{1}{2}\mathrm{E}\xi^2 u''(w) + \ldots \\ &= u(w) + \tfrac{1}{2}\mathrm{E}(\xi^2) u''(w) + \ldots . \end{aligned}$$

Next, equate these expansions and retain terms of comparable order to give

$$-r^* u'(w) = \tfrac{1}{2}\mathrm{E}(\xi^2) u''(w).$$

Recognizing $\mathrm{E}(\xi^2) = \sigma_\xi^2$ as the variance of the at-risk portion of the plan (since $\mathrm{E}\xi = 0$), we solve for the risk premium as follows

$$r^* = -\frac{1}{2}\sigma_\xi^2 \frac{u''(w)}{u'(w)}. \tag{1.B.8}$$

The individual's risk premium for a small variance, actuarially neutral risk is approximately $-u''(w)/u'(w)$ times one half the variance of the prospect.

This measure of the premium is local in the sense that there are limitations on the accuracy of the expansion about the specific wealth level w.

Notice that the term $-u''/u'$ appears in the expression and contains all of the utility function 'information' (σ_ξ^2 is specific to the risk). This finding accords well with the earlier, intuitively proposed measure of risk aversion and leads to the following definition:

D1.7. Absolute risk measure. The absolute risk aversion function, written $r(w)$, is defined as (assuming the differentiability of u)

$$r(w) = -\frac{u''(w)}{u'(w)} = -\frac{\mathrm{d}\log u'(w)}{\mathrm{d}w}. \tag{1.B.9}$$

As risk aversion occurs when u is concave then $u''<0$ and, with $u'>0$ by non-satiation, $r(w)>0$; i.e., the risk-aversion measure is strictly positive for strictly risk-averse individuals. Considering the sign of u'', note also that $r(w)<0$ indicates an affinity to risk, and $r(w)=0$ when the individual is risk neutral.

E1.9. Consider the elementary utility function given by the natural logarithm $u(\cdot)=\ln(\cdot)$. For this case note that $u'(w)=1/w$ and $u''(w)=-1/w^2$, which for strictly positive wealth yields non-satiation and strict concavity as usually required. The absolute risk aversion measure takes the form

$$r(w) = -\frac{u''(w)}{u'(w)} = +(1/w)>0,$$

which is decreasing in wealth. Also, $r(\mathrm{w})$ is strictly positive indicating a risk averse individual. ■

1.B.5. Absolute risk aversion

What happens to r^* and $r(w)$ as wealth changes? It seems intuitive that as wealth increases individuals would be willing to take a smaller risk premium in place of a given random prospect. The reasoning would seen to be that as individuals become richer they can better sustain the adverse consequences of a particular prospect and therefore would forego less to avoid it. Whether the risk premium increases, remains constant, or decreases with w is, of course, finally a question of fact. We consider these three possibilities in turn after first noting the technical relationships between changes in r^* *and* $r(w)$ as w changes.

P1.5. The risk premium and risk aversion function. The risk premium r^* is decreasing (increasing, constant) in wealth if and only if the risk-aversion function $r(w)$ is decreasing (increasing, constant) in wealth.

Proof. Trivial from (1.B.8). See also Fishburn (1968) or Kuenne and Raiffa (1976). □

P1.5 establishes an important relationship between the effect of the individual's wealth on his risk-premium and degree of risk-aversion. This, in turn, leads to the following cases:

D1.8. Constant (decreasing, increasing) absolute risk aversion. An individual is said to exhibit constant (decreasing, increasing) absolute risk aversion if and only if $r(w)$ is a constant (decreasing, increasing) function.

By direct integration of $r(w)=c$ it is possible to catalogue all utility functions yielding *constant absolute risk aversion* (CARA). These are:

$$u(w)\sim -\mathrm{e}^{-cw} \quad \text{iff} \quad r(w)=c>0 \quad \text{(risk aversion)},$$

$$u(w)\sim w \quad \text{iff} \quad r(w)=0 \quad \text{(risk neutrality), and}$$

$$u(w)\sim \mathrm{e}^{-cw} \quad \text{iff} \quad r(w)=c<0 \quad \text{(risk affinity)}.$$

The 'negative exponential' case indicating risk aversion is, of course, the one of principal interest.

Unlike the situation with CARA, it is not possible to catalogue all of the utility functions yielding decreasing or increasing risk aversion. The best that can be done in these instances is to study the several utilities which are commonly considered. Take first the power function

$$u(w)=-(b-w)^c,$$

with $w<b, c>1$, and b and c are constants. First and second derivatives are

$$u'(w)=c(b-w)^{c-1}, \quad \text{and}$$

$$u''(w)=-c(c-1)(b-w)^{c-2}.$$

Thus, the risk-aversion function is, after simplification and noting again that $w<b$ and $c>1$,

$$r(w)=\frac{c-1}{(b-w)}>0.$$

Because $r(w)>0$, the individual is risk averse and

$$\frac{\mathrm{d}r(w)}{\mathrm{d}w}=\frac{c-1}{(b-w)^2}>0,$$

which implies increasing absolute risk aversion for all w.

As one specific example of the above case, choose $c=2$ to give the quadratic utility function $u(w)=\alpha+\beta w-w^2$. When w is constrained to amounts less than $\beta/2$ then the individual has utility increasing in wealth. In this region there is risk aversion, but the individual is increasingly risk averse. Quadratic utility is therefore inappropriate when decreasing risk aversion is a desideratum.

As a second example, consider the logarithmic utility function $u(w)=\ln(w+b)$ with the constant $b\geq 0$. Again, taking derivatives yields

$$u'(w)=\frac{1}{(w+b)} \quad \text{and} \quad u''(w)=\frac{-1}{(w+b)^2}.$$

These then give (for $w>0$)

$$r(w)=\frac{1}{w+b}>0 \quad \text{and} \quad \frac{\mathrm{d}r(w)}{\mathrm{d}w}=-\frac{1}{(w+b)^2}<0.$$

The logarithmic utility function has intuitive appeal in that, for positive wealth levels, the individual is risk averse and decreasingly so.

Pratt (1964) has further shown, and it should now be obvious, that two utility functions are equivalent if and only if they have the same risk aversion function. This means that the function $r(w)$ preserves all essential information concerning the elementary utility function while eliminating everything that is arbitrary.[12]

[12]That $r(w)$ determines all equivalent $u(w)$ – unique, up to a linear transformation – is seen by the following integrations:

(1) $-r(w)=u''(w)/u'(w)=\mathrm{d}\ln u'(w)/\mathrm{d}w$,

(2) $\int -r(w)\mathrm{d}w=\int \mathrm{d}\ln u'(w)=\ln u'(w)+\text{const.}$,

(3) $e^{\int -r(w)\mathrm{d}w}=e^{\text{const.}}u'(w)$,

(4) $\int e^{\int -r(w)\mathrm{d}w}=e^{\text{const.}}u(w)+\text{const.}$

1.B.6. Proportional risk aversion

To this point the concern has been with risks which were not altered as the individual's wealth varied. One might alternatively think of 'proportional risks' in the sense that the individual's choice is with respect to the *fraction* (as opposed to the dollar amount) of his wealth to allocate to a risky plan. Then, as the individual becomes wealthier, holding constant the proportion of his wealth allocated in this way increases the dollar amount to be put at risk. For prospects of this kind it is useful to have a measure of *relative risk aversion* and again to investigate cases under which that measure is constant, decreasing, or increasing in initial wealth.

D1.9. Relative risk measure. Define

$$wr(w) = -w\frac{u''(w)}{u'(w)} \tag{1.B.10}$$

as the relative (or proportional) local risk-aversion function.

The relative risk measure can be interpreted in a manner analogous to the absolute measure. To see this, let r^{**} be the *relative risk premium*, meaning that the individual is indifferent to the consumption plan wz with probabilities h and the sure amount $\mathrm{E}(wz) - wr^{**}$. The term r^{**} must equal the (absolute) risk premium r^{*} with $x = wz$, and one can proceed to derive a relative risk measure in exactly the same manner as the absolute risk-aversion measure was earlier derived.

D1.10. Constant (decreasing, increasing) relative risk aversion. An individual is said to exhibit constant (decreasing, increasing) relative risk aversion if $wr(w)$ is a constant (decreasing, increasing) function.

The case of constant relative risk aversion (CRRA) is especially important, as the following illustrations suggest. Consider an individual with initial wealth $\bar{w}$ which is to be allocated to one alternative from among an exhaustive and mutually exclusive set of *investment portfolios* $\{z_1, z_2, \ldots, z_K\}$. Each such portfolio provides (per dollar of invested wealth) a specified *rate of return* in each state of nature, that is, each $z_k (k = 1, 2, \ldots, K)$ is an S-vector of dollars paid off per dollar invested. If, for example, the individual chooses specific portfolio z_k, then his consumption plan will be the product $x = \bar{w}z_k$; in this sense risks are proportional to wealth, for the choice of a given portfolio fixes the proportion in which wealth is divided into state claims.

Since the specific choice of a portfolio determines the consumption plan, it should maximize $\mathrm{E}u(\bar{w}z_k)$. The simplest case to consider in this regard is that of a linear utility function, $u(w) \sim w$. In this instance the optimal portfolio choice z_k is such that

$$\max_k \mathrm{E}u(\bar{w}z_k) = \max_k \mathrm{E}(\bar{w}z_k) = \bar{w}\left(\max_k \mathrm{E}z_k\right).$$

When $u(w) \sim w$, the result is simple: the choice of the optimal portfolio does not depend on the wealth position $\bar{w}$ of the individual. Is this a general result? Before answering this question, consider the power utility function $u(w) = w^{1-c}$ for $0 < c < 1$, which provides the consumption problem

$$\max_{z_k} \mathrm{E}u(\bar{w}z_k) = \max_{z_k} \mathrm{E}(\bar{w}z_k)^{1-c} = (\bar{w})^{1-c} \max_{z_k} \mathrm{E}z_k^{1-c}.$$

Again, the optimal portfolio is independent of initial wealth.

These examples provide a basis for the more general conclusions given in the following two propositions:

P1.6. Choice of consumption plan independent of wealth. Let individuals be risk-averse expected utility maximizers with suitably continuous elementary utility functions. If the optimal choice of portfolio does not depend on initial wealth, then $wr(w)$ is constant. The converse also holds: a utility function for which the measure $wr(w)$ is constant as w varies yields a choice of portfolio which is independent of wealth.

The proof of this proposition is somewhat long and complex and is delayed until (the next) Section 1.C. For a concise, but less instructive, proof the interested reader is referred to Kuenne and Raiffa (1976).

P1.7. Constant relative risk aversion. The following three statements are equivalent, each implying the other two:

(a) $wr(w) = c$, where c is a constant,

(b) $u(w) \sim \ln(w)$ for $c = 1$,

$u(w) \sim w^{1-c}$ for $0 < c < 1$,

$u(w) \sim w^{-(c-1)}$ for $c > 1$, and

$u(w) \sim w$ for $c = 0$,

(c) the choice of optimal portfolio is independent of initial wealth.

Proposition 1.6 establishes the equivalence of parts (a) and (c), and remaining part of the proof is by straightforward integration of $wr(w)=c$ and left to the reader.

E1.10. Consider an individual with logarithmic (CARA) elementary utility function: $u(x_s)=\ln(x_s)$. The choice problem is

$$\max \mathrm{E}\ln(x_s) \quad \text{s.t.} \quad \sum_s p_s x_s = \bar{w}.$$

Stationarity conditions for an optimum are

$$(h_s/x_s) - \lambda p_s = 0 \quad \forall s,$$

where λ is the multiplier associated with the budget constraint. This implies optimal portfolio fractions, for all states s and e,

$$\frac{x_s}{x_e} = \frac{h_s/p_s}{h_e/p_e} = \frac{h_s}{h_e}\left(\frac{p_e}{p_s}\right)$$

independent of wealth. ■

In the above example the optimal consumption amount in any state is strictly proportional to the consumption amount of any other state with the proportionality constant determined by prices and probabilities, but not wealth. Does this property hold for other utility functions? That is our next subject.

1.C. Linear Risk Tolerance and Proportional Risk Claims

Again setting aside consumption in the initial period, we assume that each individual maximizes expected utility by solving

$$\max_x \sum_s h_s u(x_s), \tag{1.C.1a}$$

subject to

$$\sum_s p_s x_s = \bar{w}, \tag{1.C.1b}$$

where $\bar{w}$ is endowed wealth. The solution to this problem depends, of course, on the 'parameter' $\bar{w}$, which leads to the following definition:

D1.11. Wealth consumption curve (WCC). The WCC is the locus of points in the S-dimensional space of consumption plans which solve problem (1.C.1) as the individual's initial wealth is varied holding constant all probabilities and prices.

An equivalent characterization of the WCC is possible using the stationarity conditions of (1.C.1): the WCC is the collection of points in the consumption state space at which the marginal rate of substitution between consumption in any two states just equals the ratio of the state claim prices.

D1.12. Linear wealth consumption curve. When, for all levels of initial wealth, optimal consumption in every pair of states s and e is related by the equation

$$x_s = a_{se} + b_{se} x_e, \tag{1.C.2}$$

where a_{se} and b_{se} are constants, then the wealth consumption curve is said to be linear. When $a_{se} = 0 \, \forall s, e$ then the wealth consumption curve is more exactly said to be proportional.

The reason for our interest in the linearity of the WCC will become clear as we proceed to the next few propositions. A first concern is with the class of utility functions implying linear WCC. As a preliminary in this regard, first note that an indifference contour for an expected utility function is that set of x's satisfying $\Sigma_s h_s u(x_s) = \text{constant}$. Using the implicit function theorem, the *marginal rate of substitution* of x_2 for x_1 along such a contour is given by

$$MRS_{12} = -\frac{dx_1}{dx_2} = \frac{h_2 u'(x_2)}{h_1 u'(x_1)}, \tag{1.C.3}$$

where primes indicate partial derivatives. Moreover, along the WCC the MRS is constant, which in turn implies[13]

$$\frac{dx_1}{dx_2} = \frac{T(x_1)}{T(x_2)}, \tag{1.C.4}$$

[13]For emphasis: dx_1/dx_2 in the above equations (1.C.3) and (1.C.4) do not mean the same thing. In (1.C.3) dx_1/dx_2 is the rate of substitution of x_1 and x_2 for a constant level of expected utility. In (1.C.4) the MRS is held constant and dx_1/dx_2 is the slope of the WCC projected onto the x_1, x_2 plane.

where $T(\cdot)=-u'(\cdot)/u''(\cdot)=1/r(\cdot)$. $T(x_s)$ is termed the *risk tolerance* of the utility function $u(x_s)$ and is the inverse of the absolute risk aversion measure. The slope of the WCC (projected from the S-dimensional claims space onto the two-dimensional x_1 and x_2 plane) is the ratio of the state 1 and 2 risk tolerance functions.

For the WCC to be linear, the rate of change of x_1 for x_2 is everywhere constant. When this rate is constant, then from (1.C.4) the risk tolerance in these states is proportional. Moreover, such a proportionality must occur between all pairs of states. Hold these facts aside for the moment and consider two final definitions.

D1.13. Linear risk tolerance. We say the elementary utility function u exhibits linear risk tolerance if its associated risk tolerance function is such that, for all s,

$$T(x_s)=\alpha+\beta x_s, \tag{1.C.5}$$

where parameters α and β are independent of both w and x_s. In addition, u is said to exhibit proportional risk tolerance if (1.C.5) holds with

$$\alpha\equiv 0.$$

Note that the definition of linear risk tolerance means the risk aversion measure is of the form $r(x_s)=1/(\alpha+\beta x_s)$, which explains the alternative *hyperbolic absolute risk aversion* (or HARA) label given this case.

P1.8. Utility functions with linear risk tolerance. The class of elementary utility functions exhibiting linear risk tolerance solve the differential equation

$$T(x_s)=-\frac{u'(x_s)}{u''(x_s)}=\alpha+\beta x_s.$$

There are three solution forms (exponential, logarithmic, and power functions) depending on the parameter β:

$$u(x_s)\sim-\alpha\exp(-x_s/\alpha) \qquad \text{for } \beta=0, \tag{1.C.6a}$$

$$u(x_s)\sim\ln(\alpha+x_s) \qquad \text{for } \beta=1, \tag{1.C.6b}$$

$$u(x_s)\sim[(\beta-1)/\beta](\alpha+\beta x_s)^{(\beta-1)/\beta} \qquad \text{for } \beta\neq 0,1. \tag{1.C.6c}$$

Proof. The derivation is by straightforward integration and left to the reader. □

The utility functions listed as solutions are those exhibiting risk aversion, which generally requires $\alpha \geq 0$ and, more specifically, for (1.C.6a) requires $\alpha > 0$ and for (1.C.6c) requires $\beta > 0$ and $\alpha = 0$. Note that the class of utility functions with linear risk tolerance is somewhat general. For example, $\beta = 0$ gives the constant absolute risk aversion function, $\alpha = 0$ gives the constant relative risk aversion function results, and when $\beta = -1$ we have the familiar quadratic utility function.

D1.14. Demand linear in wealth. Let $\{f_1(p, \bar{w}), f_2(p, \bar{w}) \ldots f_S(p, \bar{w})\}$ denote the collection of demand functions determining optimal consumption in the S states. When these functions have the form

$$x_s = f_s(p, \bar{w}) = \gamma_s(p) + \delta_s(p)\bar{w} \quad \forall s \tag{1.C.7a}$$

demand is said to be linear *in wealth* (not prices). When $\gamma_s(p) \equiv 0 \, \forall s$, then

$$x_s = \delta_s(p)\bar{w} \quad \forall s \tag{1.C.7b}$$

and demand is said to be proportional to wealth.

We now show the relationship between linearity of WCC and the linearity of demand in wealth.

P1.9. Linear WCC and demand linear in wealth. Demand is linear (proportional) in wealth iff wealth consumption curves are linear (proportional).

Proof. First necessity is shown, that demand linear in wealth implies a linear WCC. Let $x_1 = \gamma_1(p) + \delta_1(p)\bar{w}$ and $x_2 = \gamma_2(p) + \delta_2(p)\bar{w}$. Thus,

$$\bar{w} = \frac{x_1 - \gamma_1(p)}{\delta_1(p)} = \frac{x_2 - \gamma_2(p)}{\delta_2(p)}.$$

Solving the rightmost equation for x_1 in terms of x_2 yields

$$\begin{aligned} x_1 &= [\gamma_2(p) - \gamma_1(p)]\frac{\delta_1(p)}{\delta_2(p)} + \frac{\delta_1(p)}{\delta_2(p)} x_2 \\ &= a + bx_2, \end{aligned}$$

where a and b are constants since p is fixed. Similar linear equations can be obtained relating x_1 to all other state claims.

Next is sufficiency, that linear WCC implies demand linear in wealth. By hypothesis $x_1 = a + bx_2$ so that $dx_1/dx_2 = b$. From the demand functions we have $dx_1 = f'_1(p, \bar{w})d\bar{w}$ and $dx_2 = f'_2(p, \bar{w})d\bar{w}$, where the prime indicates partial differentiation by $\bar{w}$. Therefore, $dx_1/dx_2 = f'_1/f'_2$ and, in turn, linear WCC implies $dx_1/dx_2 = f'_1/f'_2 = b$. That is, the ratio of the *marginal* demands is independent of wealth and constant. The only functions f consistent with both of these conditions are those which are linear in wealth. This result can be similarly shown to hold for all pairs of x's.

The final requirement is to prove that linear WCC pass through the origin iff demand is proportional to wealth. This is straightforward. Follow the above proof, but let $\gamma_1 = \gamma_2 = 0$ when showing necessity and set $a = 0$ when showing sufficiency. □

Not only is linear WCC 'equivalent to' demand linear in wealth, it is 'equivalent to' linear risk tolerance.

P1.10. Linear WCC and linear risk tolerance. A necessary and sufficient condition for the wealth consumption curve to be linear (proportional) is for the utility function to exhibit linear (proportional) risk tolerance.

Proof. First necessity is shown. Along the WCC the rate of substitution is constant so that $dx_1/dx_2 = T(x_1)/T(x_2)$, see (1.C.4). The linearity of the WCC implies $x_1 = a + bx_2$ so that $dx_1/dx_2 = b$. Thus $T(x_1) = bT(x_2)$ and therefore $T'(x_1)dx_1/dx_2 = bT'(x_2)$. Since $dx_1/dx_2 = b$ we have $T'(x_1) = T'(x_2)$ or $T'(a + bx_2) = T'(x_2)$, which implies that $T(x_2)$ is linear in x_2 or, more generally, that $T(x_s) = \alpha + \beta x_s \forall s$. The proof of sufficiency is straightforward. Start with $dx_1/dx_2 = T(x_1)/T(x_2)$, use the substitution $T(x_s) = \alpha + \beta x_s$, and then solve.[14] □

Finally, there is now the obvious link between risk tolerance and demand.

P1.11. Linear risk tolerance and demand linear in wealth. A necessary and sufficient condition for linear (proportional) risk tolerance is that the utility function be such that demand is linear (proportional) in wealth.

Proof. This proposition follows immediately by reference to P1.9 and

[14]Note that a and b in this proof are specific to the states 1 and 2, and we might more exactly use a_{12} and b_{12}.

P1.10 which provide that a linear (proportional) WCC is both necessary and sufficient for linear (proportional) risk tolerance *and* for demand linear (proportional) in wealth. □

The importance of the propositions P1.9–P1.11 lies in their implications for the range of optimal consumption plans chosen by individuals. For example, if we restrict individuals to have the same proportional risk tolerance function, so that they differ only in initial wealth, then all optimal consumption plans (for all individuals) must lie along the same linear WCC. This means that all optimal plans are specified by a ray, 1-dimensional subspace, in the S-dimensional consumption set. And, every optimal plan is simply a scale multiple of every other. While the results of this specific situation are convenient, the requirement that individuals differ only in initial wealth is, to be sure, overly restrictive. There is, however, a much less pathological case.

Consider, alternatively, that all optimal consumption plans lie in a 2-dimensional subspace of R^S_+, a plane, which means that each optimal plan can be written as a linear combination of two 'basic' consumption plans. Assuming one of these basic plans to be riskless then i's optimal consumption in any given state s can be written in terms of optimal consumption in any other state e as follows.[15]

$$[x^i_s - g^i(\bar{w}^i)]/[x^i_e - g^i(\bar{w}^i)] = k_{se}, \tag{1.C.8}$$

where k_{se} is the same constant for all i, and $g^i(\bar{w}^i) \geqq 0$ is a function representating the optimal amount of consumption held risklessly. For concreteness we can limit our discussion to the three states $s = 1, 2, 3$. Using one equation to eliminate $g^i(\bar{w}^i)$ yields a pair of equations, and adding these two equations in turn gives

$$kx^i_1 + (1-k)x^i_2 = x^i_3, \tag{1.C.9}$$

where $k = (1 - k_{13} - k_{23})/(1 - k_{12})(k_{13} - k_{23})$, which is independent of i.

Equation (1.C.9) is the equation of a plane and thus is nothing more than the original requirement that all optimal consumption plans lie in a 2-dimensional 'solution' subspace. (Note further that $x^i_1 = x^i_2 = x^i_3$ satisfies the equation so that the riskless plan, as required, is one of these used to

[15]The riskless plan $[x_1, x_2 \ldots x_s]$ is such that $x_s = x_e$ for all states s and e. We have assumed that one of the basic plans from which all optimal consumption plans can be created is the riskless plan. That this is in fact a proper choice is shown below.

generate the optimal solution plane.) But that is not all to be seen in equation (1.C.9): the equation also implies that each individual's WCC is linear with one constant common to all individuals. To see this fix x_3^i at some level a^i and look at the (x_1^i, x_2^i) projection of the optimal solution plane. This gives

$$kx_1^i + (1-k)x_2^i = a^i \quad \text{or} \quad x_1^i = a^i + bx_2^i, \tag{1.C.10}$$

where $b = (1-k)/k$.

In summary, when every individual's optimal consumption plan can be written as a linear combination of (the same) two basic plans, and one of these basic plans is riskless, then the elementary utility functions of all individuals must be such that they lead to linear WCC and linear risk tolerance, with common slope parameters as given above. Proof of sufficiency proceeds in the obvious way and is left to the reader. As shall be seen in later chapters, the case where two basic consumption plans 'span' the optimal solution subspace of all individuals is rich in both theoretical and empirical implications.

The 1-dimensional optimal solution subspace noted earlier is a specialization of the 2-dimensional case. To see this, let $g^i(\bar{w}^i) = 0$ in the above equation (1.C.8). This gives $x_s^i = k_{se} x_e^i$ along a WCC with the same proportionality constant for all individuals. By (1.C.6c) this requires all individuals to have elementary utility functions of the form $u^i(x_s^i) = (\beta - 1)(x_s^i)^{(\beta-1)/\beta}$. Finally, we note that this is the constant relative risk aversion utility function, which provides the promised proof of P1.6 and P1.7.

E1.11. Consider an economy with two individuals $\mathrm{i} = 1, 2$ and three states of nature with probabilities $h_1 = 0.2$, $h_2 = 0.3$, and $h_3 = 0.5$. Suppose the individuals have logarithmic elementary utilities

$$u^1(x_s^1) = \ln(1 + x_s^1) \quad \text{and} \quad u^2(x_s^2) = \ln(2 + x_s^2)$$

and maximize expected utility. Let $\bar{x}^1 = [1 \;\; 2 \;\; 3]$ and $\bar{x}^2 = [2 \;\; 2 \;\; 4]$ be the state contingent endowments. For this case we show that (1) the individuals have linear risk tolerance, (2) linear wealth consumption curves, and (3) have demand linear in wealth. We also derive (4) the exchange equilibrium price system.

(1) *Linear risk tolerance.* $\partial u^1/\partial x_s^1 = h_s/(1 + x_s^1)$ and $\partial^2 u^1/\partial(x_2^1)^2 = -h_s(1 + x_s^1)^2$ and therefore $T^1(x_s^1) = 1 + x_s^1$. Similarly, $T^2(x_s^2) = 2 + x_s^2$.

(2) *Linear WCC.* Stationarity conditions for an optimum of expected utility include $p_e h_s \partial u^1/\partial x_s^1 = p_s h_e \partial u^i/\partial x_e^i$, for pairs of states s and e. With individual 1 this becomes $p_e h_s(1+x_e^1)=p_s h_e(1+x_s^1)$, which gives

$$x_e^1 = a_{se}^1 + b_{se}^1 x_s^1,$$

where $b_{se}^1=(p_s h_e/p_e h_s)$ and $a_{se}^1=b_{se}^1-1$. Following similar steps, for individual 2 we get

$$x_e^2 = a_{se}^2 + b_{se}^2 x_s^2,$$

where $b_{se}^2=b_{se}^1$ and $a_{1e}^2=2(a_{se}^1)$. Note that the a's and b's are market constants and that WCC are thus linear.

(3) *Demand linear in wealth.* Stationarity conditions for individual 1 are

$$h_1/p_1(1+x_1^1)=h_2/p_2(1+x_2^1)=h_3/p_3(1+x_3^1).$$

[Fact: When $a/b=c/d=e/f$ then $a/b=(a+c+e)/(b+d+f)$.] From this we have

$$\begin{aligned} p_1(1+x_1^1)/h_1 &= p_1+p_2+p_3+(p_1x_1^1+p_3x_2^1+p_3x_3^1) \\ &= \sum_s p_s + w^1 \end{aligned}$$

or, solving for x_1^1,

$$x_1^1 = \left(\frac{h_1}{p_1}\sum_s p_s - 1\right) + \frac{h_1}{p_1} w^1.$$

More generally,

$$x_s^1 = \left(\frac{h_s}{p_s}\sum_s p_s - 1\right) + \frac{h_s}{p_s} w^1.$$

Similar results obtain for individual 2 where

$$x_s^2 = 2\left(\frac{h_s}{p_s}\sum_s p_s - 1\right) + \frac{h_s}{p_s} w^2.$$

(4) *Exchange equilibrium prices.* Define $k_{es}=p_s h_e/p_e h_s$ and choose $p_1=1$ so that $k_{12}=0.6p_2$, $k_{13}=0.4p_3$, and $k_{23}=0.6(p_2/p_2)$. As shown above, demand

functions are of the form

$$x_e^1 = (k_{es} - 1) + k_{es} x_s^1,$$

$$x_e^2 = 2(k_{es} - 1) + k_{es} x_s^2.$$

Substitute the values of k_{es} in terms of prices in these equations and then use the identities $\bar{x}_1^1 + \bar{x}_1^2 = 3$ and $\bar{x}_2^1 + \bar{x}_2^2 = 4$ to solve for prices $p_3 = \frac{9}{7}$ and $p_3 = \frac{3}{2}$. Thus, $[1\ \frac{9}{7}\ \frac{3}{2}]$ are the exchange equilibrium prices. ■

1.D. A Typology of Consumer Preferences

In the previous sections a variety of specifications of consumer preferences have been set forth. Here we catalog three frequently used specifications. In each, attention is restricted to a two-period, S state of nature characterization of uncertainty with $\chi = [x_0\, x_1 \ldots x_S]$ the plan of current and next period consumption.

D1.15 I1 individuals. We say individuals are type I1 if they rank consumption plans by preferences represented by a utility function $u(\chi)$ having the following properties:

(i) $u(\mathring{\chi}) \geq u(\chi)$ iff $\mathring{\chi}(\geq)\chi$,
(ii) $u(\chi)$ is continuous and at least twice continuously differentiable in each argument, and
(iii) $u(\chi)$ is monotone increasing, strictly quasi-concave.

D1.16. I2 individuals. We say individuals are type I2 if they rank consumption plans by an expected utility function E$u(\chi)$ having the following properties:

(i) elementary utility functions at period one are state independent so that E$u(\chi)$ is of the form

$$\mathrm{E}u(\chi) = u_0(x_0) + \sum_s h_s u(x_s),$$

where $h_s \geq 0$ are probability weights, $\Sigma_s h_s = 1$,
(ii) $u_0(x_0)$ and $u(x_s)\ \forall s$ are continuous and at least twice continuously differentiable, and
(iii) $u_0(x_0)$ and $u(x_s)\ \forall s$ are monotone increasing, strictly concave and thus E$u(\chi)$ is strictly quasi-concave.

It is to be emphasized that the I2 specification presumes $h_s^i = h_s \ \forall i$ in each state s, that is, there are either homogeneous subjective probability estimates or all probabilities are objective. This is commonly termed the identical 'expectations' or homogeneous belief assumption. The reason that identical expectations is specified here, and has been extensively employed in the literature, is partly that it is analytically difficult to introduce non-homogeneous expectations into models and still obtain simple results, partly that differing expectations are 'non-observable' and can explain too much too early, and partly that many real world facts can be explained in other terms. For example, differences in consumption plans can be explained in terms of individual differences in wealth and risk aversion as well as probability beliefs. The reason we focus on the former effects and not on heterogeneous expectations when specifying I2 individuals is not that that is not the true explanation of the phenomena under investigation. Rather, it is merely that the several effects can best be studied in isolation and, unfortunately, economists have relatively less skill in analyzing models when individuals differ in expectations.

A final word about the notation is helpful here. For I1 individuals the ordinal utility function is written as $u^i(\chi^i)$, while for I2 individuals the elementary utility function is written as $u^i(x_s^i)$. Some care must be taken that these two cases are not confused; while the distinction is usually obvious from the context of the analysis, the reader is advised to always carefully note the proper argument for each 'utility function'.

It is quite clear that the set of I2 individuals are a proper subset of those who are I1. At times, however, neither the I1 nor I2 specifications are suitably restrictive, and we consider a particularly useful subset of I2 individuals.

D1.17. I3 individuals. We say individuals are type I3 if they satisfy all the conditions of I2 individuals and furthermore have elementary utility functions which are linear in risk tolerance.

Chapter 2

EQUILIBRIUM IN A CONTINGENT COMMODITY MARKET ECONOMY

The theory of exchange, production, and finance in a multiperiod, uncertain economy has its foundation in the sequence of studies by Fisher (1930), Debreu (1959), Arrow (1964), and Hirshleifer (1965, 1966). While these analyses are elegant and powerful, they rest upon a simple proposition: a timeless, certain economy can be generalized to include multiple periods and risk by defining commodities, and commodity claims, not only by their physical properties, but also by time periods and states of nature in which the commodities are contingently available.

With contingent claim contracts the basis of exchange, the economy deals with time and uncertainty in a standard way. First of all, there are the typical agents: firms as producers and individuals as consumers. As usual, each firm is characterized by a technology set listing feasible production plans. Because of the uncertainty, however, each plan determines inputs and outputs of the commodities not simply at each time period, but also in each possible state of nature at each period. The firm acquires its inputs and sells claims to its future outputs only in the present, meaning that markets, and thus prices, exist in the present for delivery of every commodity in all later periods contingent on every state of nature to then occur. Because there exist these forward markets to claims in every date and state, the value of any (even uncertain) production plan is exactly known in the present by all individuals – it is simply the appropriate price-weighted sum of inputs and outputs.

In the time and uncertainty extended economy individuals are also characterized in the usual way by consumption sets, preferences, and endowments. For each individual the consumption set is the collection of technically feasible plans for current and future consumption extended to every period and state of the world. Endowments are similarly associated with time periods and states, with each individual's wealth determined as the value of endowed consumption plus ownership fractions in the firms' profits.

Because the above construction is the one usual in price theory, a production and exchange equilibrium in the contingent commodity economy has the usual meaning: a set of prices together with plans by individuals and firms such that each consumer maximizes his utility subject to his budget constraint, each firm maximizes its value within its production set, and total demand equals total supply at each period and in each state. Moreover, since the contingent commodity economy has the same logical structure as the timeless, certainty economy, it is possible to demonstrate in conventional ways (i.e., under convexity and continuity of production and consumption sets and preferences) that a competitive production and exchange equilibrium exists, that the resulting allocation under uncertainty is efficient in the Pareto sense, and that every efficient allocation corresponds to a competitive equilibrium relative to some distribution of individual endowments and set of prices.

A systematic analysis of these results is our concern in this chapter, with particular attention being given to the 'allocation of risk' in the economy.

2.A. Contingent Commodity Markets

Individuals do not have perfect foreknowledge; they do not know exactly all the conditions to occur in the future. The notion underlying the formulation of a contingent commodity economy is that each individual, while unsure about future events, can nonetheless make exhaustive lists of conceivable future *states of nature.* In this manner identical commodities available in different states become distinct goods, have different prices, and enter uniquely into individual preferences and firm production processes. While the essential structure of the economy under certainty remains unchanged by this extension of the commodity concept, there are nonetheless important economic implications that go beyond the equivalency of logical structure.

2.A.1. Markets in contingent commodity claims

Many of the interesting questions concerning the equilibrium of the contingent commodity market economy can be posed and answered in a two-period world with just one physical commodity. In view of our present, limited objectives, the principal effect of considering more periods or physically different goods would be only to introduce notational complexity.[1]

[1]Allowing more than two periods would require a reinterpretation of the S claims to future consumption. That is, we might think of partitions of the future states such that those indexed

In the initial (current, $t=0$) period of this economy a particular state prevails and is known to all individuals. With respect to the next (future, $t=1$) period, however, there is uncertainty about two things: individual endowments and firm outputs. This uncertainty is made specific by having the endowment and production amounts depend on the state of nature to occur in the future.[2] For concreteness let there be S (finite) possible states at the next period. In turn, there are $S+1$ distinct consumption goods: the commodity for consumption at the initial period and the commodity differentiated by the S states of nature in the future period. Using the consumption commodity at the initial period as numeraire, there are then S markets on which exchanges take place.

Trading on the S markets to current consumption and state contingent consumption claims occurs in the current period. Thus, the S markets are *forward markets* in the sense that the contingent claims contracts are made in the current period with deliveries to occur in the future. Specifically, each *state contingent claim* is a promise providing for the delivery of one unit of the physical commodity at the next period if and only if a specified state of nature in fact occurs at that period. The current consumption numeraire is, however, paid irrevocably on the S current markets for claims before it is known what state will hold in the future.

As usual, in the market economy only individuals, not firms, have endowments. These endowed amounts may be received both in the first period (with certainty) and in the future period contingent upon the state to then occur. According to personal preferences and market rates of exchange, individuals trade portions of their current period endowment to firms as inputs (to production processes). In addition, individuals trade their current endowment and claims to future period endowments with other individuals, and they purchase claims to the firms' state contingent outputs for delivery at the future period. As all such exchanges occur simultaneously in the initial period, each firm achieves its net income at that time and immediately distributes this to the owners according to exogenously given sharing fractions. Because of the presumed simultaneity of events, the net

---

$s=1,2,\ldots,S^1$ pertain to period $t=1$, those indexed $s=S^1+1, S^1+2,\ldots, S^2$ pertain to period 2, and so on. Of course, if markets opened conditional on dates and states so that all trading does *not* occur in the present, then a two-period model would not have this generality. Chapter 3 considers these complications and deals explicitly with more than one physical commodity.

[2]The states are mutually exclusive, and their list is exhaustive and identical for all individuals. To avoid unmanageable circularities, each state is defined as a description of the economy complete in all aspects that are beyond the control of any individual or firm. That is, the full list of states is precisely described (or given) exogenously to the workings of the model economy. The alternative definition of 'result states', whose occurrence can be affected by the actions of agents, gives rise to the well-known problem of moral hazard. See, for example, Marshall (1974).

income disbursed by firms is available to individuals as initial period consumption. Finally, by the operation of the forward markets the production plans (and therefore the demand for inputs and the supply of outputs) and the trading plans of individuals (and therefore the supply of inputs and demand for outputs) are determined through a price system established in trading at the initial period.

What has been implied by the above discussion, largely by the omission of any explicit consideration, is that the markets of concern operate without many usual complications. Most real markets have associated commodity assurance problems, holding costs, price and quality information asymmetries among traders, transaction costs, taxes, etc. Furthermore, real markets are generally required to reflect the complications of bargaining time and *ex post* uncertainty about which state has in fact realized, and some system is required to exclude non-buyers from the use of the commodity exchanged. In contrast, such complications are here assumed to be absent.

S2.1. Perfect markets. All markets are perfect in the sense that:

(1) all potential and actual traders costlessly observe all rates of exchange and other relevant properties of both the commodity and the claims contract governing the assignment of property rights to a commodity,
(2) there are no brokerage fees, taxes, or any other transfer costs associated when either commodity or claims contract is exchanged, and
(3) there are no costs to determining *ex post* the state of nature obtaining in any period, and there is no haggling and thus no contract enforcement cost.

There are several notable implications of a perfect market. First, even though there is uncertainty it is only with respect to the knowledge individuals have concerning the state to occur in the next period. In distinction, once some state realizes, each individual costlessly knows that state (that is, each has a full description of the economy in all relevant aspects). Second, in a perfect market there is no role for middlemen (and thus no middleman fees) as there is no need for concern over the efficiency of exchange in the absence of transaction and information costs. Third, there is an instantaneous equilibrium in the perfect market as costless information and transactions mean that a stable set of supply and demand contracts, and associated market clearing prices, are immediately found. Speculation by specialists to minimize trading at non-equilibrium prices is therefore unnecessary. Finally, a perfect market implies a 'one price law',

Only one price can obtain for any commodity claim (or any bundle of them), for no seller would choose to sell at less than the maximum price and no buyer would choose to buy at more than the minimum. It is only when the maximum and minimum price exactly coincides that buyer–seller transactions take place, with every buyer and seller choosing to exchange at that price doing so.

2.A.2. Competition

As suggested by the discussion of market perfection, the definition of market equilibrium to be employed is static in the sense that it does not set forth any *process* of economic activity. In particular, the fact that markets are perfect implies nothing about the manner in which market equilibrium will be reached. All that market perfection requires is that, no matter how the price system is determined, every market exchange takes place at those prices. There is thus a second, distinct concept. If, in the process of arriving at some transaction price, the market contains no individual who can exert an influence on the determination of that price by controlling his own supplies and/or demands for the commodity, the market is further said to be 'competitive'. The significance of this situation is that price becomes a datum, a parameter, for every individual over the range of his consumption and supply choices.

The above specification of competition is not generally useful, for when there are only a finite number of individuals in a given market and some do not behave idiosyncratically to exactly offset the decisions of others, every individual will in fact influence price by his own decisions, notwithstanding the smallness of his effect. Thus, it is more appropriate to think of competitive exchange as occurring when each individual *perceives* the price as fixed and *acts* as a price-taker regardless of his ability to minimally influence the formation of the market price.

S2.2. Competition in exchange. Individuals are small relative to each market in the sense that each perceives his exchange decisions not to affect aggregate quantities demanded (or supplied) in any market and thereby claim prices – even though there may be a minimal effect. In this case markets are said to be competitive. Equivalently, individuals are said to be competitive traders or price-takers in exchange.

Competition in exchange arises from restrictive conditions on markets and specific trader reactions to prevailing market prices with given aggregate supplies of commodities. Firms, being the agents of production, make decisions which affect aggregate commodity supplies and, as in the case of exchange, there is the symmetrical question concerning what firms assume about market prices. Again, the usual assumption removes the difficulties of circularity.

S2.3. Competition in supply. Each individual as a shareholder directs each firm in which it has a share to act *as if* changes in supply decisions do not affect (i) the aggregate supply of the relevant commodity in any state and, in turn (ii) the claims prices. In this case it is said that there is competition in supply. Equivalently, each firm is said to be a competitive producer, or price-taker, in supply.

As with price-taking in exchange, the rationale for price-taking in supply is one involving an approximation argument. Firms are assumed small relative to total market supplies so that none can significantly alter aggregate output and thus significantly affect either consumption plans or equilibrium prices.

Finally, it is of note that the above definition does not require that the owners of firms be unanimous with respect to production decisions. Rather, all that is assumed is that each owner of each firm, when assessing the production decision from the viewpoint of his own interest, acts *as if* the supply decision of that single firm will not alter prevailing prices.[3]

With these general descriptions and market conditions as a foundation, we move next to the detailed specification of firms, individuals, and then the organization of markets. Throughout, the following indices are employed.

S2.4. Index sets. Elements of the contingent claims market economy are indexed in the manner:

$t=0, 1$ the two discrete time periods,
$i=1, 2, \ldots, I$ individuals,
$j=1, 2, \ldots, J$ firms, and
$s=1, 2, \ldots, S$ states of nature at $t=1$.

It is further assumed that I, J, and S are finite.

2.A.3. *Individuals, consumption, and preferences*

In an uncertain economy the fundamental objects of each individual's

[3]Whether, at these fixed prices, some individual owners favor a specific production change while others do not is a separate question. See Rubinstein (1978) and Chapter 8 to follow.

choice are contingent commodity claims. In turn, the claims are fashioned into consumption plans, to form the fundamental elements of preference. The following three specifications formalized these ideas and lay the basis for individual behavior.

S2.5. Consumption plan. Associated with each individual i there is an $(S+1)$-vector $\chi^i=[x_0^i\ x^i]$ termed a consumption plan. Each such plan represents a consumption amount in the current period, x_0^i, and in all states of the future period, $x^i=[x_1^i\ x_2^i \ldots . x_S^i]$.

S2.6. Consumption set. The set of all consumption plans which are technically feasible for some individual i is termed his consumption set and denoted X^i. With S distinct markets in claims to next period consumption (exchanges are with respect to the initial period consumption good), this feasible set of consumption plans is the non-negative $(S+1)$-dimensional orthant.

S2.7. Individual preferences. Individuals express preferences for consumption plans. The preferences are represented, for each individual i, by an ordinal utility function, $u^i(\chi^i)$, which is monotone increasing, strictly quasi-concave and differentiable on the interior of its domain.

2.A.4. Firms and production

Individuals represent the demand side of the contingent commodity claim market and the supply side of the factor market, the market for resources employed in production. Firms are the specialized agencies employed by individuals in the time and state production process. In this regard firms do not consume, they have null resource endowments, and they are the sole agents of production in the economy. Firms represent the supply side for contingent commodities and the demand side for resources.

At the onset it is necessary to deal with the supply of commodities only at an aggregate level and each firm can be treated as a simple input–output process. The description of production is thus straightforward: each firm selects an input level at period 0, its investment, and an output level technically consistent with that input occurs at the next period. A complication arises in that the output level is subject to uncertainty. The complication is minimal, however, when we think of the output in each state as a distinct good, so that there are simply S different contingent commodities 'produced'. Although only one 'kind' of good is delivered *ex post*, the firm chooses *ex ante* a bundle across all states from those technically feasible.

S2.8. Production plan. Let $y_0^j \leq 0$ denoted the number of units of the composite commodity employed as firm *j*'s input at period 0 and $y^j = [y_1^j \; y_2^j \ldots y_S^j]$ denote the composite commodity outputs at period 1 in each of the S possible states. The production plan of firm j is the $(S+1)$-vector $\psi^j = [y_0^j \; y^j]$ specifying input and state contingent outputs.

As with consumption plans, the production plan can be thought of not only as an input–output collection or as a point in a production set, but in geometric terms as a vector in an $(S+1)$ space.

Some production plans represent technically feasible transformations of the input to state contingent outputs while others do not. For the moment this specification is best done in a way that is least restrictive while still satisfying our intuition about reasonableness and insuring that a production and exchange equilibrium (to be defined later) exists for the contingent claims economy.

S2.9. Production set. The set of all technically feasible production plans for each firm j $(j = 1, 2, \ldots, J)$ is termed its production set and denoted by Ψ^j. Each production set possesses the following properties:

(1) the origin is in Ψ^j,
(2) no point in the positive orthant belongs to Ψ^j (except the origin),
(3) Ψ^j is closed, and,
(4) Ψ^j is convex.

Although each firm's production set is presumed to satisfy these conditions, this does not mean that all firms, or even a subset of them, has the same production set.

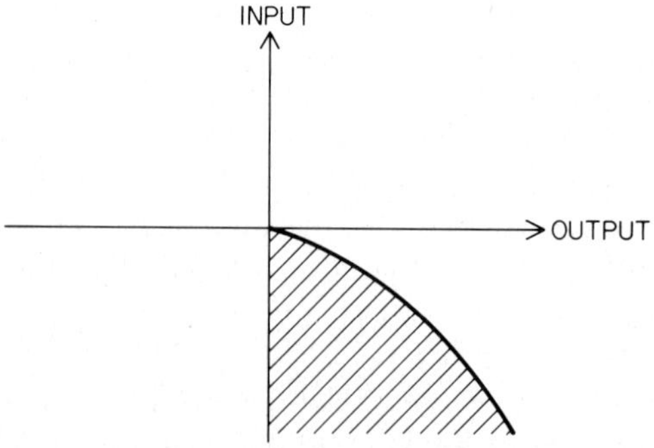

Fig. 2.1. Production set

The purpose of properties (1) and (2) of S2.9 are quite obvious. Property (3) is concerned with continuity: specifically, if each element of a sequence of production plans is feasible then so must its limit. Finally, the convexity property (4) requires that convex combinations of any two (distinct) feasible production plans be feasible. That is, for two feasible, but non-equal plans, $\psi^j, \hat{\psi}^j \in \Psi^j$ and $\psi^j \neq \hat{\psi}^j$, the plan $[\lambda\psi^j + (1-\lambda)\hat{\psi}^j]$ is also an element of Ψ^j providing $0 \leq \lambda \leq 1$. The convexity of Ψ^j provides two important implications: it means that increasing returns to scale do not exist (thus ruling out fixed, or overhead costs) and it assures there is perfect divisibility of every production plan (as the zero plan belongs to ψ^j). The production set is illustrated intuitively by the shaded area in Figure 2.1.

2.A.5. *Endowments*

In addition to preferences, consumption sets, and production sets, a private ownership economy is described by a specification of the initial resources possessed by each individual. These are termed endowments to stress the fact that they are given *exogenously*, i.e., prior to and outside the workings of the model economy.

S2.10. Endowment position. Each individual i is endowed with non-negative amounts of the consumption commodity in both the current period, $\bar{x}_0^i$, and in every state of the future period, $\bar{x}_s^i$ $\forall s$. These define i's *endowed resources* $\bar{\chi}^i = [\bar{x}_0^i\ \bar{x}^i]$, an $(S+1)$-vector. In addition, each individual is endowed with non-negative fractional ownership shares in each firm. Let $[\bar{\alpha}_1^i\ \bar{\alpha}_2^i \ldots \bar{\alpha}_J^i]$ be the vector of i's *endowed ownership shares* in the J firms. The collection $\{\bar{\chi}^i, \bar{\alpha}^i\}$ forms i's total endowment.

It is important to note that the endowments at the future period are uncertain prospects, for they depend on the state of nature to occur. Again, these endowments and the outputs of the firms' production processes are the (only) two sources of uncertainty in the contingent claims economy.

2.A.6. *Prices and the budget set*

In a market economy exchanges conform in part to the prices given to the different goods.

S2.11. Contingent claim prices. A contingent claims price system is defined by the $(S+1)$-vector $\phi = [p_0\ p]$. Taking the price per unit of period zero consumption as numeraire $(p_0 \equiv 1)$, the S-vector $p = [p_1\ p_2 \ldots p_s]$ represents prices (normalized to the current consumption good) whose sth element is the price established at period 0 for the delivery of one unit of the composite commodity if and only if state s occurs.

Given a price system ϕ, the *value* of any consumption plan $\chi=[x_0\, x_1 \ldots x_S]$ is given by its price-weighted sum

$$x_0+\sum_{s=1}^{S} p_s x_s=\langle\phi,\chi\rangle.$$

Two plans of consumption, χ' and χ, are said to be *exactly exchangeable* in the S markets when they have the same value under the prevailing price system, that is, $\langle\phi,\chi\rangle=\langle\phi,\chi'\rangle$. If $\langle\phi,\chi\rangle\leq\langle\phi,\chi'\rangle$ then plan χ', having a greater value, is then said to be *at least* exchangeable with plan χ.

Given a claims price system ϕ, the *endowed wealth*, $\bar{w}^i$, of any individual i is determined as the sum of the value of endowed resources and endowed ownership shares in firms. The first of these, the value of the endowment in the consumption good, is determined quite simply as $\langle\phi,\bar{\chi}^i\rangle$. The value of the endowed ownership shares is more complicated since it in turn requires knowledge of the value of each firm. This complication is only slight, however, as the *market value* of firm j, v_0^j, is given by the difference between its revenues from the sale of claims and the cost of its factor input (note $y_0^j\leq 0$),

$$v_0^j=\langle\phi,\psi^j\rangle=y_0^j+\sum_s p_s y_s^j. \tag{2.A.1}$$

With the value of all firms determined similarly, define $v_0=[v_0^1\, v_0^2 \ldots v_0^J]$ as the derivative *security price system.* Using the two price systems and the two forms of endowment, individual i's total endowed (or initial) wealth can be written as

$$\bar{w}^i=\langle\phi,\bar{\chi}^i\rangle+\langle v_0,\bar{\alpha}^i\rangle. \tag{2.A.2}$$

In a market economy individuals engage in exchange to acquire consumption plans more preferred than their endowment. Only trades which are at least exchangeable with the endowment are market feasible for each individual and this leads to a budget, or wealth, restriction.

S2.12. Budget set. Given a claims price system, ϕ, the set of consumption plans economically feasible for each individual i is that collection which is at least exchangeable with endowed wealth:

$$B^i(\phi,\bar{w}^i)=\{\chi^i\,|\,\langle\phi,\chi^i\rangle\leq\bar{w}^i\}.$$

The set $B^i(\phi,\bar{w}^i)$ is termed i's budget set.

It follows immediately that: (1) with competition in exchange, individuals are price-takers and the budget set B^i is an uncontrollable datum for each individual; (2) B^i depends explicitly upon the price system and endowed wealth and, in turn, on endowed resources and ownership shares; and (3) B^i is closed, bounded, and convex.

Consider finally the set of consumption plans which are at the same time physically *and* economically feasible. This is termed the individual's opportunity set and denoted O^i.

S2.13. Opportunity set. The opportunity set for individual i, O^i, is the intersection of consumption and budget sets: $O^i(\phi, \bar{w}^i) = X^i \wedge B^i(\phi, \bar{w}^i)$.

The opportunity set is compact and convex, which follows directly from the properties of its constituent sets X^i and B^i. Note especially that O^i is not empty since it at least contains the zero vector (which belongs to X^i by assumption and to B^i when endowed wealth is non-negative).

In the contingent commodity claims market organization the consumption set is the entire $(S+1)$-dimensional, non-negative orthant: claims to current consumption and consumption in each of the S states at the second period are independently available on the forward markets. In this case the opportunity set is identical to the budget set. This is, however, a special case, for the consumption set need not always have such an extent. For example, substantial fixed costs in the operation of a market, high costs of unambiguously identifying the particular state that has occurred, or 'point rationing' schemes might lead to the availability of only very specific combinations of state claims (or bundles of state claims). In such circumstances only a subset of consumption plans in the non-negative orthant would be feasible. These restrictions would affect the consumption set and, in turn, limit the individual's opportunity set. In all cases, however, these considerations are prior to (and thus separate from) the effects of market prices and endowments and therefore the budget feasible set.

2.B. Contingent Claims Exchange

While prices are considered to be exogenous data when consumer's decisions are taken in isolation, they are endogenous in the determination of an exchange equilibrium and therefore lead to a theory of price or a 'theory of value'. In this section the concern is specifically with exchange equilibria and particularly with providing an answer to the question, 'What are the factors determining the price system in competitive contingent commodity claims markets?'

2.B.1. Exchange equilibrium conditions

Given a (not necessarily equilibrium) claims price system ϕ along with endowments, production plans of firms, and ownership shares, individual wealth $\bar{w}^i$ is determined by equation (2.A.2). In such a situation the individual's choice of consumption plan can be written as the solution to the problem

$$\max_{\chi^i} u^i(\chi^i) \quad \text{s.t.} \quad \langle \phi, \chi^i \rangle = \bar{w}^i \quad \text{and} \quad \chi^i \in X^i. \tag{2.B.1}$$

The strict concavity of u^i and the convexity of the opportunity set provide necessary and sufficient conditions for a unique solution to (2.B.1). Restricting attention to positive, interior solutions, there exists a Lagrange multiplier $\lambda^i \geq 0$ such that, at the optimum,

$$u_0^i - \lambda^i = 0, \tag{2.B.2}$$

$$u_s^i - \lambda^i p_s = 0 \; \forall s, \tag{2.B.3}$$

and the budget constraint holds. In these equations the subscripts to u^i represent partial derivatives: e.g., $u_s^i \equiv \partial u^i / \partial x_s^i$ is the marginal utility of period 1, state s consumption.

Using (2.B.2) and (2.B.3), eliminate λ^i and in turn introduce the notation $(u_s^i / u_0^i) \stackrel{\Delta}{=} \pi_s^i \; \forall s$ to yield

$$p_s = \pi_s^i \; \forall s. \tag{2.B.4}$$

Each π_s^i is i's rate of substitution of period 1, state s consumption for period 0 consumption at the optimum. These S equations therefore have the same sense as those appearing in classical demand theory: they require that the marginal rate of substitution between any two claims (commodities) be equal to the ratio of appropriate market prices. We refer to the $\pi_s^i \; \forall s$ as individual i's *implicit demand prices* for consumption claims.

A market equilibrium in the exchange of contingent claims is also determined in the usual way.

D2.1. Contingent claims exchange equilibrium. An exchange equilibrium in competitive contingent claims markets consists of a collection of individual consumption plans $\mathring{\chi} = [\mathring{\chi}^1 \, \mathring{\chi}^2 \ldots \mathring{\chi}^I]$ along with a price system $\mathring{\phi}$, such that

$$\mathring{\chi}^i \text{ maximizes } u^i(\chi^i) \text{ with } \mathring{\chi}^i \in O^i(\mathring{\phi}, \bar{w}^i) \; \forall i, \quad \text{and} \tag{2.B.5}$$

$$\sum_i (\mathring{\chi}^i - \bar{\chi}^i) = \sum_j y^j. \tag{2.B.6}$$

The conditions of the equilibrium are straightforward: (2.B.5) provides that each individual choose the preferred consumption plan subject to the restrictions of his opportunity set; (2.B.6) provides that the price system is such that the total quantity demanded of each commodity (differentiated by time and state) at these individual optima exactly equals the sum of the amounts endowed to individuals and the (fixed) amounts produced by firms. [Recall that the vectors in (2.B.6) contain current consumption as the first element.] It is of note, and the basis of some later analyses, that the claims price system, and thus the consumption plans, of the exchange equilibrium depend on the specific set of production plans adopted by the firms. If, for example, some firm were to alter its production, individual budget sets would in general change and the position of the exchange equilibrium, both in claims prices and consumption plans, would generally be affected.

Finally, note that at the exchange equilibrium each individual's rate of claim substitutions across any two states equals that of all other individuals: $\pi_s^i\ \forall i$ is equal to the (common) state s, equilibrium price $\mathring{p}_s$ and this holds for all s. The implications of this fact for the efficiency of exchange should be apparent and will be emphasized shortly.

E2.1. Consider an exchange economy with two individuals and two future states of nature. Suppose that the utilities for the individuals are identicai and given by

$$u(x_0, x_1, x_2) = x_0^{0.4} x_1^{0.2} x_2^{0.2}$$
$$\sim 2 \ln x_0 + \ln x_1 + \ln x_2.$$

In addition, let $[1\ p_1\ p_2]$ indicate market prices, with $\bar{w}^i$ the endowed wealth of individual i at these prices. The conditions of consumption optimality, (2.B.2) and (2.B.3), then imply the following demand functions for each individual

$$x_0^i = \bar{w}^i/2, \qquad x_1^i = \bar{x}^i/4p_1, \qquad x_2^i = \bar{w}^i/4p_2.$$

With individual endowments given by $\bar{\chi}^1 = [4\ \ 4\ \ 6]$ and $\bar{\chi}^2 = [2\ \ 4\ \ 4]$, then $(4 + 4p_1 + 6p_2) = \bar{w}^1$ and $(2 + 4p_1 + 4p_2) = \bar{w}^2$. In turn, equality of aggregate demand and supply of $x_0 (\bar{x}_0^1 + \bar{x}_0^2 = x_0^1 + x_0^2)$ implies

$$6 = \frac{4 + 4p_1 + 6p_2}{2} + \frac{2 + 4p_1 + 4p_2}{2}.$$

Similarly, for x_1 we have

$$8=\frac{4+4p_1+6p_2}{4p_1}+\frac{2+4p_1+4p_2}{4p_1}.$$

Solving these last two equations simultaneously for market clearing prices yields $p_1=\frac{3}{8}$ and $p_2=\frac{3}{10}$ at the exchange equilibrium. Using the demand functions the following equilibrium allocation then results:

individual 1	*individual 2*
$x_0^1=3.65,$	$x_0^2=2.35,$
$x_1^1=4.87,$	$x_1^2=3.13,$
$x_2^1=6.08,$	$x_2^2=3.92.$

■

For a claim paying one unit if and only if state s occurs, the equilibrium price implies a corresponding (one plus) *conditional rate of return* given by

$$r_s=(1/p_s). \tag{2.B.7}$$

There is also a corresponding rate of return S-vector with r_s in state s and zeros elsewhere. Note that p_s, or r_s, is determined as a function of individual preferences and endowments since these are the factors affecting the underlying demand for and supply of contingent claims.

Since the states are mutually exclusive and the list of them is exhaustive, it is apparent that an unconditional (riskless) claim to one unit of commodity is equivalent to S contingent claims, one for each state of nature. And, because markets are perfect, the price of this unconditional claim must equal the sum of the claims prices $\Sigma_s p_s$. This in turn determines the (one plus) *riskless (interest) rate*,

$$\rho=\left(1\bigg/\sum_s p_s\right), \tag{2.B.8}$$

and there is a corresponding interest rate S-vector with ρ as each entry. As the riskless claim gives title unconditionally to one unit of the commodity at $t=1$, the price $\Sigma_s p_s$ is the marginal rate of substitution of one unit of consumption for sure at $t=1$ in terms of one unit of consumption foregone at $t=0$. The rate ρ is the inverse of this price, that is, it is the marginal rate of substitution of $t=0$ consumption in terms of a certain unit of consumption at $t=1$. As this substitution rate is the same for all individuals at equilibrium we say that personal 'impatience' for time is equalized at the margin. And, since each p_s is determined by individual preferences and endowments, ρ is determined by the same factors.

Finally, from optimality conditions (2.B.2) and (2.B.3) it is noticed that non-satiation is sufficient to insure that all marginal rates of state claim substitution are strictly positive, i.e., $\pi_s^i > 0 \; \forall i, s$. This means that all contingent claims prices are positive and therefore that each conditional rate r_s and the riskless rate ρ must be strictly greater than zero in this two-period, pure exchange model.

E2.2. What is the rate of return on a risky consumption plan? There are two usual answers to this question. The first is to describe the (one plus) rate of return as a vector (random variable), one generally different conditional rate of return for each possible state. The second is based on an *ex ante* expected rate of return.

A numerical illustration will clarify these concepts. We use an economy with three future states to occur with probabilities $h_1 = 0.1$, $h_2 = 0.4$, and $h_3 = 0.5$. Let the prices for contingent claims be $p_1 = 0.3$, $p_2 = 0.4$, and $p_3 = 0.2$ and consider a specific consumption prospect $x = [1 \; 5 \; 2]$. The present market value (price) of that prospect is

$$v_0^x = (0.3)1 + (0.4)5 + (0.2)2 = 2.7.$$

The *ex ante*, stochastic rate of return to holding the prospect as part of a consumption plan is 1/2.7 if state 1 occurs, 5/2.7 if state 2, and 2/2.7 if state 3. We write these as the vector

$$r^x = [0.37 \quad 1.85 \quad 0.74],$$

where each entry r_s^x is the state conditional rate of return.

Alternatively, the rate of return can be expressed as a single number

$$\bar{r}^x = \mathrm{E}x / v_0^x,$$

called the *ex ante* expected rate. In the present case this is

$$r^x = [0.1]1 + (0.4)5 + (0.5)2]/2.7 = 3.1/2.7 = 1.148,$$

with $\bar{r}^x$ being a 14.8% 'return'. In passing note that

$$\sum_s p_s = 0.9,$$

which implies a riskless 'rate of return' of 11.1%. ■

2.C. Comparative Statics of Risk Aversion

Recall from equations (2.B.2) and (2.B.3) that the plan satisfying conditions for a consumptive optimum depends on several parameters: those of the price system, the endowment positions, and the preferences for consumption in the various states and periods. As the contingent commodity claims formulation of the individual's choice problem is an immedate extension of the classical problem with multiple commodities under certainty, the standard Slutsky equations hold along with the usual price and wealth effect interpretations. The particular aspect of comparative statics at the consumptive optimum which is unique to the analysis of demand under uncertainty, and therefore the aspect we considered in some detail here, is the effects of the individual's risk averseness. To proceed at all with such an analysis means, however, that some measure of risk aversion is necessary.

One of the principal rationales for expected utility as a choice criterion is that it yields a natural, quantitative measure of risk aversion. (This is in distinction to the more general representation of preferences by ordinal utility functions, which leaves the specification of risk attitudes abstract.) Because of this we now restrict attention to I2 individuals. And, to allow some insights provided by graphical analysis we further limit our focus to period one consumption with only two states. In this case each individual's preference is represented by the expected utility function (suppressing superscript i)

$$\mathrm{E}u(x)=hu(x_1)+(1-h)u(x_2), \tag{2.C.1}$$

where h is the probability of state 1 occurring and the elementary utility function $u(\cdot)$ is monotone increasing and strictly concave. Finally, let $\bar{x}=[\bar{x}_1\,\bar{x}_2]$ denote the individual's endowment position so that with price system $p=[p_1\,p_2]$ initial wealth is $\bar{w}=p_1\bar{x}_1+p_2\bar{x}_2$.

With these notations and restrictions the optimality condition corresponding to (2.B.3) becomes

$$p_1/p_2=h_1u_1/(1-h_1)u_2, \tag{2.C.2}$$

where subscripts to the utility function indicate appropriate partial derivatives. Given the endowment $\bar{x}$, the conditions of this solution are satisfied at the point $\mathring{x}$ shown in Figure 2.2. The steps to the solution are as usual: the slope of the budget line AB is p_1/p_2, the slope of each indifference curve is everywhere $h_1u_1/(1-h_1)u_2$, and the optimal consumption plan $\mathring{x}$ is obtained at the point of tangency.

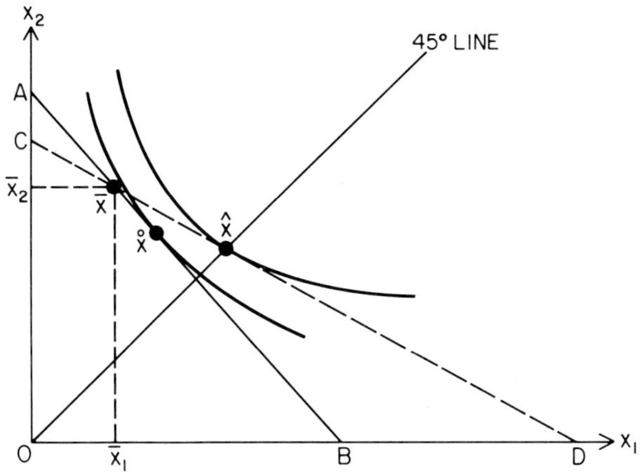

Fig. 2.2. Insurance

Suppose now that the price ratio p_1/p_2 is equal to the ratio of probabilities $h_1/(1-h_1)$, which is the 'odds' that state 1 occurs. In this case the optimality condition simplifies to

$$1 = u_1/u_2.$$

Since u is a monotone increasing function (by non-satiation), this implies $x_1 = x_2$ at the new optimum $\hat{x}$. In the figure, this requires that the absolute slope of the budget line represented by CD be equal to the $h_1/(1-h_1)$ ratio of state probabilities. That is, the movement of the optimal consumption plan in reaction to this specific change in prices decreases the chosen difference beween the two contingent claims and thus amounts to an act of insurance. In this way we can think of the market rate of exchange from state to state as the price of insurance: one unit of x_1 is purchased for p_1/p_2 units of x_2. If the price of insurance so defined is actuarially fair, meaning that it equals the probability ratio as above, then a maximizer of expected utility with strictly concave elementary utility functions always chooses the position of certainty, $x_1 = x_2$ (see Section 1.B.2). The converse also holds: the individual will choose to gamble, or disinsure, by moving further away from the 45° line at a sufficiently high price of insurance (in spite of the fact that he is risk-averse).

2.C.1. Relative risk aversion

For reasons which will be clear in a moment, consider the manner in which the slopes of indifference curves change along a given ray from the origin. Each indifference curve everywhere has its (absolute) slope equal to $h_1u_1/(1-h_1)u_2$. By taking the derivative of this slope function subject to $\alpha x_1 = x_2$, where α determines the slope of the ray from the origin, derive the expression

$$\frac{\mathrm{d}}{\mathrm{d}x_1}\left[\frac{h_1u_1}{(1-h_1)u_2}\right]=\frac{h_1(u_{11}u_2-u_1u_{22}\alpha)}{(1-h_1)u_2^2}. \tag{2.C.3}$$

Thus, for outward movements along the ray the change in indifference curve slope at the points of intersection is negative if $u_{11}u_2 < u_1u_{22}\alpha$, or equivalently if

$$-x_1(u_{11}/u_1) > -x_2(u_{22}/u_2), \tag{2.C.4}$$

(which is obtained by multiplying both sides of the former inequality by $-x_1(u_1u_2)$ since $u_1u_2 > 0$). But (2.C.4) simply indicates decreasing proportional risk aversion when $x_1 < x_2$. That is, if the slopes of indifference curves decrease along a ray from the origin, then the individual's preference is characterized by decreasing relative risk aversion. Note that the decrease in the slope of indifference curves along a given ray necessarily implies a

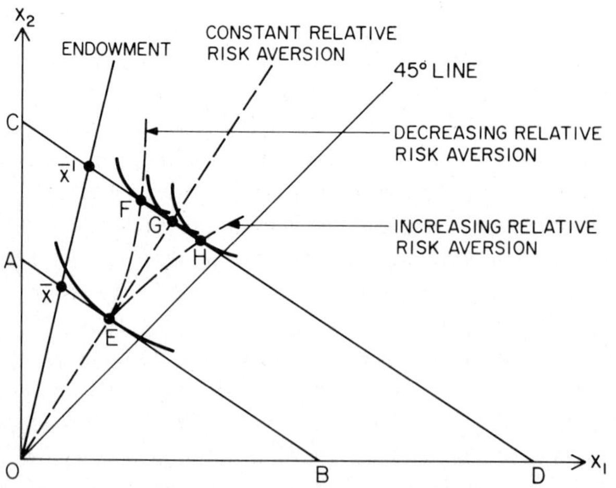

Fig. 2.3. Relative risk aversion

wealth consumption curve that is bowed away from the 45° line, which is shown as *EF* in Figure 2.3.

This result has a useful interpretation. Consider a proportional increase in endowed contingent claims in the two states, for instance from $\bar{x}$ to $\bar{x}'$ in Figure 2.3. For the wealth consumption curve *EF*, it is clearly seen that the individual's demand for insurance (the horizontal distance between the endowment and optimum points along the budget lines) has increased in a smaller proportion than the wealth increase.[4]

If the slope of the indifference curves remain constant along a given ray, then the inequality in (2.C.4) becomes an equality, which is, of course, the case of constant relative risk aversion. When this occurs, the wealth expansion path becomes a ray from the origin, such as the line *EG* in Figure 2.3, and the individual's demand for insurance increases in the same proportion as the increase in wealth. The final, increasing relative risk aversion case is obtained when the expression (2.C.3) is positive and $x_2 > x_1$, so that the expansion path bows toward the 45° line. These results are stated more generally in the following proposition.

P2.1. Equalization of state claims and relative aversion to risk. For an I2 individual possessing decreasing (constant, increasing) relative risk aversion, the demand for claims to equalize state claim holdings relative to an endowment increases in a smaller (equal, greater) proportion than increases in wealth.

Proof. Follows by induction from the case with two claims. □

2.C.2. Absolute risk aversion

The demand to equalize state claims, to 'insure' relative to an endowment, is also related to the individual's absolute risk aversion measure. This relationship can be developed in a way similar to the above case. First take the derivative of the indifference curve slope along a line parallel to the 45° line, that is, subject to a constraint of the form $x_2 - x_1 = \text{constant}$. Doing so yields

$$\frac{\mathrm{d}}{\mathrm{d}x_1}\left[\frac{h_1 u_1}{(1-h_1)u_2}\right] = \frac{h_1(u_{11}u_2 - u_1 u_{22})}{(1-h_1)u_2^2}, \tag{2.C.5}$$

[4]Ehrlich and Becker (1972) provide examples of market and self-insurance in this context.

which is negative if $u_{11}u_2 < u_1 u_{22}$ or if

$$-(u_{11}/u_1) > -(u_{22}/u_2). \tag{2.C.6}$$

The inequality (2.C.6) defines decreasing absolute risk aversion in the region where $x_2 > x_1$. Thus, when the slopes of indifference curves decrease along a line parallel to and above the 45° line there is decreasing absolute risk aversion and the associated wealth expansion path gains increasing distance from the 45° line. The wealth expansion path *EF* in Figure 2.4 corresponds to this case: note that the distance between the optimum and the riskless bundle of claims achievable with the same budget increases with wealth.

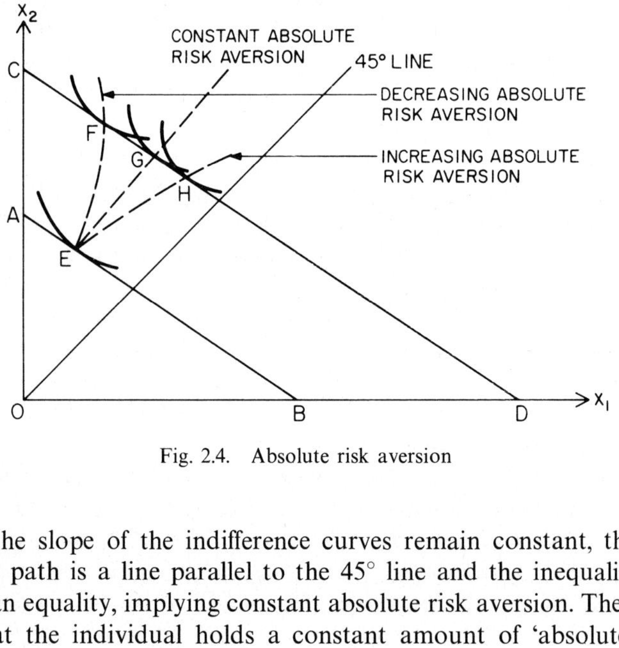

Fig. 2.4. Absolute risk aversion

When the slope of the indifference curves remain constant, the wealth expansion path is a line parallel to the 45° line and the inequality (2.C.6) becomes an equality, implying constant absolute risk aversion. The path *EG* shows that the individual holds a constant amount of 'absolute risk' at different levels of wealth. The obvious results for increasing absolute risk follow, and are also graphed in the figure.

P2.2. Equalization of state claims and absolute aversion to risk. For an I2 individual possessing decreasing (constant, increasing) absolute risk aversion, the demand for claims to equalize state claim holdings relative to an endowment absolutely decreases (remains constant, increases) with increases in wealth.

Proof. This follows by induction from the above case with two claims. □

In conclusion, note again that contingent state claims are equalized whenever an individual is faced with an actuarially fair price of insurance. In this very special case the measures of both absolute and relative risk aversion stay constant along the 45° line irrespective of the shape of individual preference (as long as elementary utilities are strictly concave).

2.D. Production and Exchange Equilibrium

With production decisions given, individual choices of state claims and market clearing conditions determine equilibrium prices for all date and state contingent claims. Strict convexity of indifference sets and the convexity of opportunity sets provide that the equilibrium price system is unique. These prices equalize rates of substitution appropriately between all claims and individuals. When production is taken explicitly into account prices must also satisfy other properties. The nature of these other conditions, again with perfect markets and price-taking behavior assumed, is now of concern.

2.D.1. Separation

With production, the first question concerns the objectives of the producing firms. Ignoring costs of information and transaction, we shall assume each firm is operated directly in the interest of its shareholders. This, however, does not solve the problem of a relevant objective. For example, one immediate issue is how the firm can make decisions when its production process is subject to an essential uncertainty and the individual firm owners have diverse risk preferences. Under such circumstances isn't it likely that shareholders, looking only to their own interests, will disagree on what constitutes an optimal output plan? Under certain conditions the answer is no, for there is an 'invisible hand' in terms of market prices for contingent claims which acts to ensure consistency.

P2.3. Functional separation. When contingent claims markets are perfect, there is competition in supply and exchange, and individuals are I1, then the production decision which maximizes the net market value of the firm is in the best interest of every shareholder of that firm.

With respect to any individual and firm, the importance of the proposition lies in the fact that production decisions can be 'separated from' consumption decisions in the sense that the individual shareholder does not need to know the technical aspects of the firm's production processes, nor need he take part in the firm's internal decisions. Rather, the individual simply supports a straightforward rule for managerial behavior: maximize the firm's market value at given claims prices. Ignoring problems of agency, the consumer is indifferent as to whether he himself or someone else manages the firm: all that is required is for market value to be at its maximum.

Proof. The key elements of the proof are (1) that markets are perfect and (2) that indirect utility is increasing in wealth. Let consumer i with ownership fraction $\bar{\alpha}_k^i > 0$ (i is a shareholder in firm k) have a vote in altering the production plan of firm k. Suppose further the kth firm is small relative to the market, so that i perceives all market prices to be unaffected both by any decision to alter k's output and his subsequent choice of consumption plan. That is, i considers the decision problem, see (2.A.1) and (2.A.2),

$$\max_{\chi^i, \psi^k} U(\chi^i), \quad \text{subject to} \tag{2.D.1}$$

$$\langle \phi, \chi^i \rangle = \langle \phi, \bar{\chi}^i \rangle + \langle v_0, \bar{\alpha}^i \rangle$$

$$= \langle \phi, \bar{\chi}^i \rangle + \left[\sum_{j \neq k} \bar{\alpha}_j^i v_0^j \right] + \bar{\alpha}_k^i \left(y_0^k + \sum_s p_s y_s^k \right)$$

and $\chi^0 \in X^i$, $\psi^k \in \Psi^k$. $\phi > 0$ is the price system for current consumption and contingent claims. Since $v_0^k = y_0^k + \Sigma_s p_s y_s^k$ and the contingent claims prices are by assumption fixed, firm k's choice of production plan affects i's opportunity set only through changes it can bring about in his wealth (*not* by any alteration in either his consumption set or the claims price system). Firms which maximize market value under these conditions then maximize shareholder wealth. With the consumption set fixed, claims prices fixed, and individuals I1, Proposition 1.1 holds and 'more wealth is better' for every individual. □

It is to be emphasized that Proposition 2.3 has only been shown in 'partial equilibrium' in the sense that it holds for individuals one at a time. The subsequent definition of a simultaneous production and exchange equilibrium for the contingent claims market economy will, however, make clear that in such a (perfect market, competitive) equilibrium, functional separation occurs for every consumer and every firm.

Observe finally that in maximizing market value the firm's production decisions entail no risk. Each firm simply arranges for inputs and for state contingent delivery of its output at known prices in the initial period markets; it thus immediately (at $t=0$) realizes the sure value of any production plan adopted. As a consequence, all the firm need do is compare the value of each available production plan, selecting the one with the greatest market value. The physical consequences of production are nonetheless uncertain and, as individuals hold contingent claims to output, they bear all the risk as consumers. That is, while each has sure knowledge of every firm's production technology and thus every feasible consumption plan, the state to occur at $t=1$ is not certain and aversion to risk is a part of the individual's demand analysis.

2.D.2. General Equilibrium

Taking claims prices as fixed, suppose that firms maximize market value. Individuals as price-takers in exchange and supply determine their preferred production plans for firms and demands for claims to maximize their utility. The supply and demand of the commodity which follows from these 'individual' cases are summed appropriately over firms and individuals in the economy to yield aggregate supplies and demands. The individual plans are achievable as a collection if and only if there is also an equality of aggregate supplies of and demands for claims in each state and period. These conditions describe a simultaneous production and exchange equilibrium.

D2.2. Competitive contingent claims equilibrium. Given perfect markets and competition in both exchange and supply, a price system $\mathring{\phi}$, a collection of production plans $\mathring{\psi}^j \in \Psi^j\ \forall j$, and a collection of consumption plans $\mathring{\chi}^i \in X^i\ \forall i$ constitute a competitive contingent claims equilibrium if[5]

$$\mathring{\phi} > 0, \qquad (2.D.2)$$

[5]That there exist a unique price system satisfying the conditions of the competitive contingent claims equilibrium is guaranteed by the earlier specification of consumption, budget, and production sets. Negishi (1960) provides an existence and uniqueness proof by first showing that such a competitive equilibrium is a maximum of a social welfare function which is a linear combination of utility functions of individual consumer (with the weights in the combination in inverse proportion to the marginal utilities of wealth). The proof of existence of an equilibrium is then equivalent to a proof that there exists a maximum of this special welfare function which, in a straight-forward way, only involves proper convexity–concavity conditions. An alternative proof of existence not requiring divisibility, continuity, and the representation of preferences or production transformations by functions, and therefore not involving the use of the differential calculus, is provided by Arrow and Hahn (1971, Chapter 5).

$$\sum_i \mathring{\chi}^i \leq \sum_j \mathring{\psi}^j + \sum_i \bar{\chi}^i, \tag{2.D.3}$$

$$\mathring{\psi}^j \quad \text{maximizes} \quad \langle \mathring{\phi}, \psi^j \rangle \quad \text{s.t.} \quad \psi^j \in \Psi^j \, \forall j, \quad \text{and} \tag{2.D.4}$$

$$\mathring{\chi}^i \quad \text{maximizes} \quad U^i(\chi^i) \quad \text{s.t.} \quad \chi^i \in 0^i(\mathring{\phi}^i, \bar{w}^i) \, \forall i. \tag{2.D.5}$$

The definition of production and exchange equilibrium is relative to the given production sets $\psi^j \, \forall j$, the given consumption sets $X^i \, \forall i$, and the given endowment positions in resources $\bar{\chi}^i$ and ownership shares $\bar{\alpha}^i \, \forall i$. It is intuitive that changes in production or consumption sets and/or endowment positions will generally alter the specific equilibrium prices and allocation.

Because the same consumption conditions appear in the functional separation theorem and in the definition of production and exchange equilibrium, the proof of separation can easily be shown with the market clearing price system $\mathring{\phi}$. The separation property thus insures that value maximization is in the unanimous and best interest of every shareholder.

E2.3. Consider the case in which there are only two states $s=1,2$ and, for simplicity, let some particular firm j be owned by a single individual i who is an expected utility maximizer. Assume that the period zero commodity is fixed. Holding constant the factor inputs, write the firm's production transformation possibilities as $Q(y_1, y_2)=0$, which is strictly concave to the origin in the contingent claims space (implying increasing opportunity costs for the specialization of production in any state).[6] Because of functional separation, the optimization problem of the individual can be expressed in two separate parts:

$$\max_y \langle p, y \rangle \quad \text{s.t.} \quad Q(y)=0 \quad \text{and} \quad y \in Y, \tag{P1}$$

$$\max_x \{hu(x_1)+(1-h)u(x_2)\} \quad \text{s.t.} \quad \langle p, x \rangle = \langle p, \mathring{y} \rangle. \tag{P2}$$

In the above $\mathring{y}$ is the solution of the first problem (P1) and the firm and individual superscripts have been suppressed.

Look first at problem (P1), which concerns the individual's choice of production holding aside the subsequent opportunities for exchange. In this

[6]In the sequel some analyses are more clearly seen with the use of the calculus. In these cases we will make the further assumption that the production set can be represented by a (suitably differentiable) production function. A production function f defined on R^{S+1} is such that $f(y_0, y_1, \ldots, y_s)=0$ if and only if ψ is a technically efficient plan and $f(y_0, y_1, \ldots, y_s) \leq 0$ if and only if ψ is a plan in the production set Y.

case the optimum consumption bundle is depicted by point G in Figure 2.5 where, starting from the $\bar{x}$ endowment, the individual chooses to produce at the tangency of the production transformation locus with his highest achievable indifference curve, Eu^*. With no possibilities for exchange the claims bundle G represents a combined production–consumption optimum; the marginal rate of claims substitution (in consumption) equals his marginal rate of claims transformation (in production). Along with the appropriate continuity, the concavity of the production possibility locus and the convexity of the indifference schedules assure that a unique tangency bundle of claims exists.

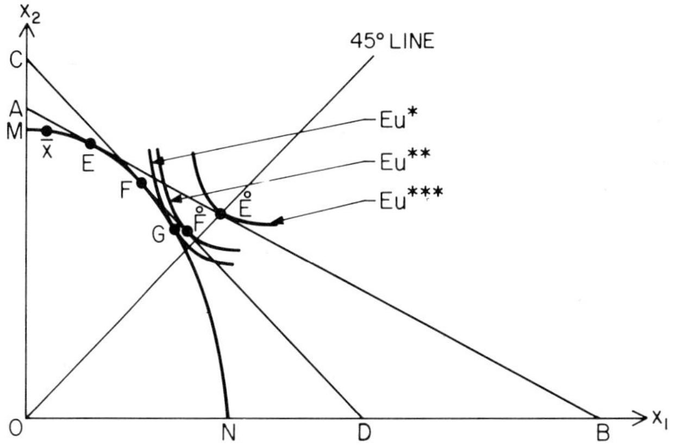

Fig. 2.5. Individual production and exchange optimum

Now drop the restriction of no trade and consider problems (P1) and (P2) in sequence. With the individual a price-taker, let the price system be such that line CD represents his market opportunities for exchange (the absolute slope of CD is the market price ratio p_1/p_2). The existence of the exchange market permits the separation of production and consumption. Specifically, the individual can now achieve a consumptive optimum at $\mathring{F}$ on indifference curve Eu^{**} by a two-step process. First, he moves along MN from his endowment $\bar{x}$ to his production optimum F, the tangencies of the production transformation possibility locus with the market line CD. Note that at the prevailing prices this maximizes the market value of the production plan, so that this step corresponds exactly to problem (P1). From F, by exchanging x_2 for x_1, the individual then moves along the market line CD to his final consumptive optimum $\mathring{F}$. A comparison of the production-only solution at G with the combined production-exchange solution at $\mathring{F}$ makes clear the advantages in the separation of productive and consumptive optimum positions made possible by trade.

Using the calculus we can directly write the first-order conditions for the production and exchange problems,

$$\frac{Q_1(y)}{Q_2(y)}=\frac{p_1}{p_2}, \tag{C1}$$

$$\frac{h_1 u_1(x)}{(1-h_1)u_2(x)}=\frac{p_1}{p_2} \tag{C2}$$

Conditions (C1) and (C2), respectively, define the productive and subsequent consumption optima as the tangencies between the production transformation and the indifference curves and the market exchange line. Since the firm is owned by the single individual in the present case, we may appropriately view the transformation possibility as a locus of self-insurance (or gambling) opportunities. At the actuarially fair price of market insurance, represented by the slope of the line AB, the individual chooses the production plan E, which maximizes the market value of the firm. The individual insures further by trading x_1 for x_2 to arrive at the point $\mathring{E}$ where his consumption claims for both states are equal.

At the higher price of insurance given by the slope of line CD, *self*-insurance is increased by moving from the endowment point $\bar{x}$ to F rather than E, while market insurance is reduced in that the horizontal distance F–$\mathring{F}$ is smaller than the distance and E–$\mathring{E}$. Thus, self-insurance and market-insurance are substitutes. Comparison of the points G and F also reveals this substitution effect: provided with market opportunities, the individual decreases self-insurance from G to F, using instead the market insurance, distance $F-\mathring{F}$.

It is important to see that the combined effect of the two sources of insurance is a function of market prices of insurance. The conclusions: any judgment on risks and insurance taken must be in part dependent on available opportunities in the marketplace. ■

2.E. Optimality of the Competitive Contingent Claims Equilibrium

The statement of the contingent claims equilibrium with price-taking makes clear that, relative to a set of claims prices, no individual can make himself better off without spending more (than his budget constraint permits). While this is surely an important aspect of an equilibrium allocation of claims, it does not tell us whether or not there might be gains to additional transfers among individuals. Judgments concerning the worth of such inter-agent transfers in general involve some value weighting of individual welfares (e.g., more weight to me and my friends, less to others). To avoid such value judgments, it is usual to employ the concept of *Pareto optimality* as a criterion to (partially) order alternative allocations of consumption claims among individuals. The Pareto criterion is applied with respect to a given allocation to determine whether or not there exists a reallocation capable of making some individual(s) better off while not making any other worse off.

2.E.1. Pareto optimality and competitive exchange

The meaning of, and conditions for, Pareto optimality can be stated as follows. For each consumption amount x^i_θ–$\theta=0,1,\dots,S$ indexes both the current state and all future states–consider some small change. This leads to changes in utility given by

$$\mathrm{d}u^i=\sum_\theta u^i_\theta \mathrm{d}x^i_\theta \quad \forall i, \tag{2.E.1}$$

where u^i_θ is the marginal utility of x^i_θ. Any change in i's consumption must be offset by changes in the consumption of other individuals to assure that aggregate consumption exactly equals the fixed supply, i.e.,

$$\sum_i \mathrm{d}x^i_\theta=0 \quad \forall^\theta. \tag{2.E.2}$$

An allocation of consumption amounts to individuals is said to be Pareto optimal if there is no feasible reallocation making at least one individual better off while not making any other worse off. For example, an original allocation $\{\chi^i\,\forall i\}$ is Pareto optimal if and only if any reallocation results in differential utilities which are not all non-negative (or all zero). What are the conditions for this to hold?

P2.4. Pareto optimality. Let individuals be I1. An equilibrium allocation $\{\chi^i\,\forall i\}$ is unconstrained Pareto optimal if and only if

$$\lambda^i u^i_\theta=u^1_\theta \quad \forall i,\theta, \tag{2.E.3}$$

where $\lambda^i>0$ are arbitrary constants.[7]

[7] This theorem and proof follows Borch (1967, 1968).

Proof. First we show sufficiency. To this end, consider a reallocation of $x_\theta^i \; \forall i, \theta$. If (2.E.3) holds then the reallocation must satisfy

$$\lambda^i \mathrm{d}u^i = \sum_\theta u_\theta^1 \mathrm{d}x_\theta^i.$$

Summing this over all i and using (2.E.2) in turn yields,

$$\sum_i \lambda^i \mathrm{d}u^i = \sum_i \sum_\theta u_\theta^1 \mathrm{d}x_\theta^i = \sum_\theta u_\theta^1 \sum_i \mathrm{d}x_\theta^i = 0.$$

As each $\lambda^i \geq 0$ the individual $\mathrm{d}u^i$ cannot be of the same sign (otherwise they are all zero), which proves sufficiency.

The proof of necessity is only somewhat more complicated. Let the reallocation be only with respect to (typical) state 1 and 2 claims and only for any two individuals i and k. In this case the reallocation is feasible only when

$$\mathrm{d}x_1^i = -\mathrm{d}x_1^k \quad \text{and} \quad \mathrm{d}x_2^i = -\mathrm{d}x_2^k.$$

As a result the corresponding changes in utility become

$$\mathrm{d}u^i = u_1^i \mathrm{d}x_1^i + u_2^i \mathrm{d}x_2^i,$$

$$\mathrm{d}u^k = -(u_1^k \mathrm{d}x_1^i + u_2^k \mathrm{d}x_2^i).$$

For a Pareto optimal allocation the product $(\mathrm{d}u^i)(\mathrm{d}u^k)$ must be nonpositive, which requires

$$(u_1^i \mathrm{d}x_1^i + u_2^i \mathrm{d}x_2^i)(u_1^k \mathrm{d}x_1^i + u_2^k \mathrm{d}x_2^i) \geq 0.$$

This inequality is preserved for all values of $\mathrm{d}x^i$ and $\mathrm{d}x^k$ only if

$$(u_2^i u_1^k + u_1^i u_2^k)^2 \leq 0.$$

Obviously, this last inequality only holds when the LHS is zero, or when

$$u_1^i / u_2^i = u_1^k / u_2^k, \tag{2.E.4a}$$

which is the usual interior optimality condition: the rate of state claim substitution must be equal across individuals. This implies

$$u_1^i = \lambda^i u_1^k, \tag{2.E.4b}$$

$$u_2^i = \lambda^i u_2^k, \tag{2.E.4c}$$

which is exactly the condition set forth in P2.1. □

P2.4 provides an immediate basis for the following well-known result.

P2.5. Pareto optimality of competitive claims exchange. The exchange equilibrium of a competitive contingent commodity claims market is Pareto optimal.

Proof. The result follows immediately from the comparison of equations (2.B.2) and (2.B.3) with Pareto optimality conditions (2.E.3). □

E2.4. Let individuals be I1 and consider the following problem

$$\max \sum_i k^i u^i(\chi^i),$$

subject to $\Sigma_i x^i_\theta = \bar{z}_\theta \geq 0$ for all $\theta = 0, 1, \ldots, S$ and where the $k^i > 0\ \forall i$ are constants. Stationarity conditions for an interior maximum are

$$k^i u^i_\theta(\chi^i) = \lambda_\theta \quad \forall i, \theta,$$

with the λ_θ being Lagrange multipliers associated with the $S+1$ feasibility constraints. For individual 1 this condition becomes

$$k^1 u^1_\theta(\chi^1) = \lambda_\theta \quad \forall \theta.$$

And, using these last two equations to eliminate λ_θ yields

$$\lambda^i u^i_\theta(\chi^i) = u^1_\theta(\chi^1) \quad \forall i, \theta,$$

where $\lambda^i \equiv k^i/k^1$. As utility functions are equivalent when scaled by a positive constant, it is possible to choose λ^i in this last equation to be identical to λ^i in (2.E.3). Thus, a sufficient condition for an allocation to be Pareto optimal is that it be the maximum of a positively weighted sum of individual utilities.

E2.5. What is the specific form of the Pareto optimality conditions when individuals maximize expected utility

$$\mathrm{E}u^i(\chi^i) = \sum_\theta h^i_\theta u^i(x^i_\theta) \quad \forall i, \tag{2.E.5}$$

where $\theta = 0, 1, 2, \ldots, S$; h_0 is i's intertemporal preference parameter; h^i_1, $h^i_2, \ldots, h^i_S$ are state probabilities; and, $u^i(x^i_\theta)$ is the elementary utility function. In this case the marginal utility of each state s consumption is $h^i_\theta u^i_\theta(x^i_\theta)$ with $u^i_\theta(x^i_\theta) = \partial u^i(x^i_\theta)/\partial x^i_\theta$. In turn, the Pareto optimality conditions

(2.E.3) become

$$\lambda^i h^i_0 u^i_0 = h^1_0 u^1_0, \qquad \text{(2.E.6a)}$$

for all i and θ, which can be rewritten as

$$h^i_\theta u^i_\theta / h^i_e u^i_e = h^k_\theta u^k_\theta / h^k_e u^k_e, \qquad \text{(2.E.6b)}$$

for any two states, θ and e, and any two individuals, i and k. ■

2.E.2. Optimality of the general equilibrium

An *allocation* under uncertainty is a specification of consumption plans for all individuals and production plans for all firms such that aggregate demand does not exceed aggregate supply (including endowments):

$$\sum_i \chi^i \leq \sum_j \psi^j + \sum_i \bar{\chi}^i. \qquad \text{(2.E.7)}$$

Section 2.D has set forth the detailed properties of the allocation resulting from production and exchange in competitive contingent claims markets. At that equilibrium no consumer could make himself better off without spending more (than his budget constraint permitted) and no firm could further increase its market value. Does that then imply that the competitive production and exchange equilibrium is also Pareto optimal?

Analogous to the pure exchange case, a set of production plans $\{\mathring{\psi}^j \, \forall j\}$ and consumption plans $\{\mathring{\chi}^i \, \forall i\}$ are said to be a Pareto optimum if (a) the material balance requirement of an allocation is satisfied, and (b) there exists no other feasible set of production plans and therefrom consumption plans $\{\chi^i \, \forall i\}$ such that $U^i(\chi^i) \geq U^i(\mathring{\chi}^i) \, \forall i$ with strict inequality for at least one consumer.

P2.6. Pareto optimality of a general equilibrium. If $\{\mathring{\chi}^i, \forall i; \mathring{\psi}^j, \forall j; \mathring{\phi}\}$ is a competitive equilibrium, the corresponding allocation is a Pareto optimum.

Proof. We proceed by contradiction. Suppose that there exists a candidate set of production plans $\{\psi^j \, \forall j\}$ and similarly a candidate set of consumption plans $\{\chi^i \, \forall i\}$ such that $U^i(\chi^i) \geq U^i(\mathring{\chi}^i) \, \forall i$ with strict inequality holding for at least one i. With $\mathring{\chi}^i$ the most preferred plan in the opportunity set, then $\forall i$

$$\langle \mathring{\phi}, \chi^i \rangle \geq \langle \mathring{\phi}, \bar{\chi}^i \rangle + \sum_j \bar{\alpha}^i_j \langle \mathring{\phi}, \mathring{\psi}^j \rangle, \qquad \text{(2.E.8)}$$

which must be an inequality for at least one individual if the consumption plans χ^i are to Pareto dominate the competitive equilibrium plans. Next, sum (2.E.8) over all i to yield

$$\left\langle \mathring{\phi}, \sum_i \chi^i \right\rangle > \left\langle \mathring{\phi}, \sum_i \bar{\chi}^i \right\rangle + \left\langle \mathring{\phi}, \sum_j \psi^j \right\rangle. \tag{2.E.9}$$

The strict inequality holds since $\langle \mathring{\phi}, \Sigma_j \mathring{\psi}^j \rangle \geq \langle \mathring{\phi}, \Sigma_j \psi^j \rangle$ is required by value maximization and (2.E.8) is to be an inequality for at least one individual.

For the candidate set of consumption and production plans to be feasible they must satisfy the conservation equation (2.E.7). Premultiplying that equation by the equilibrium price vector $\mathring{\phi}$ yields

$$\left\langle \mathring{\phi}, \sum_i \chi^i \right\rangle \leq \left\langle \mathring{\phi}, \sum_i \bar{\chi}^i \right\rangle + \left\langle \mathring{\phi}, \sum_j \psi^j \right\rangle. \tag{2.E.10}$$

The inequalities (2.E.9) and (2.E.10) are a contradiction; as a result there exists no alternative to the competitive equilibrium allocation which makes one individual better off while not making another worse off. □

2.F. The Firm

To this point the market value of the firm was considered without making explicit any distinction between the value of its distributive shares to several potential classes of claimants. We cannot, however, ignore the fact that the capitalistic firm is a special legal entity in which owners generally have access to only a specified portion of the returns from production with the other portion being claimed by various debt holders. If this is the case, how does the debt-equity capital structure of the firm affect the market value of equity? And, what constitutes an optimal policy for financing the production activity of the firm? It is to these, and closely related questions concerning mergers and partitions of firms, that the analysis of this section is addressed.

2.F.1. Capital structure

The interaction of firms and individuals in the context of frictionless claims markets forms a system of transfers and transformations that is, by the perfection of the markets, free from external drains. There are, in particular, no losses from the system arising from transaction or underwriting costs, personal and/or corporate taxes, transfer taxes, etc. and therefore, with production plans fixed and endowments in both periods given exogenously, the aggregate total of consumptive claims in the economy is a constant. When such conditions prevail our concern need only be with how the 'packaging' of the firm's claims into debt and equity parts affects the market value of the firm.

In the above model economy firms do not consume and they possess no endowments. Having a null endowment, it is therefore required that each firm j obtain funds from 'outside' sources to finance its factor input level y_0^j. To this point it has been assumed that the firm borrowed amount $p_0 y_0^j$ in the markets at period zero, repaying that sum also at period zero with the proceeds from its sale of state contingent claims. The firm's earnings in excess of this payment were proportionately distributed to individuals according to their ownership shares as endowed. All of this is implicit in equation (2.A.1), which is repeated here:

$$\sum_s p_s y_s^j = v_0^i - p_0 y_0^j, \tag{2.F.1}$$

where the market value of the firm's uncertain output is given as the value of it equity, v_0^j, plus its debt, $p_0 y_0^j$ (recall that $y_0^j \leq 0$ by convention).

The firm finances its input factor usage by the borrowed amount $p_0 y_0^j$. Alternatively, what if it were not all-debt financed, but used some fraction of equity?

P2.7. Capital structure irrelevance. In perfect contingent claims markets the equilibrium market value of each firm is independent of the proportion of debt to equity in its capital structure.

Proof. Consider only two kinds of claims on the firm: simple debt and simple equity. With the contingent claims market organization these are indistinguishable, as unit claims to each are perfect substitutes for the other. Under the single-price law of perfect markets, unit claims which are identical must sell for the same price. Without some special form of differentiation (for example, as might occur if debt and equity had different tax status), the single price p_0 must therefore apply to both unit debt and equity claims. This means the market value of the firm's output can be written as

$$\sum_s p_s y_s^j = p_0(\bar{e}_0^j - y_0^j), \tag{2.F.2}$$

where $\bar{e}_0^j$ is the sum (across individuals) of endowed unit equity claims.

Partition y_0^j as follows:

$$-y_0^j = d_0^j + e_0^j,$$

where d_0^j is debt and e_0^j is equity, both of which are externally acquired to finance production. Finally, rewrite (2.F.2) as

$$\sum_s p_s y_s = p_0(\bar{e}_0^j + e_0^j + d_0^j), \tag{2.F.3}$$

by which it is immediately seen that the market value of the firm's output is the same regardless of the e_0^j and d_0^j combination (as long as total investment y_0^j is fixed). □

The proof has a minimum of complication (and content) in the contingent commodity claims economy, for debt and equity are simply perfect substitutes. It is on this basis that the usual microeconomic theory of the firm ignores all mention of the firm's choice of capital structure.

2.F.2. Mergers and partitions

The above capital structure proposition is concerned with the formation of alternative debt and equity assets by a single firm. Is that same theory applicable to combinations of assets across firms? Yes, absent any technological gains or losses from joint production and scale, neither conglomeration nor divestiture has an economic advantage. The whole, again, is quite simply the sum of parts.

P2.8. Conservation of value. Let there be no gains or losses to joint production or scale. Then, in a competitive contingent claims equilibrium the merger of existing firms yields a value of the combined firm exactly equal to the sum of the values of the constituents. Conversely, the partition of an existing firm results in constituent firm values whose sum equals the value of the original, whole firm.

Proof. Consider a firm formed by merger of the M firms $j = 1, 2, \ldots, M$, where $M \leq J$. At equilibrium, the value of this 'merged' firm is

$$\max_{\psi^m \in \Psi^m} \langle \phi, \psi^m \rangle = \langle \phi, \mathring{\psi}^m \rangle, \tag{2.F.4}$$

where ψ^m is the production plan of the merged firm (indicated by subscript m) chosen from production set Ψ^m. When there are no gains or losses to joint production or scale, i.e., the production decision of each original firm does not affect the plans of others, the production set of the firm formed by the merger is simply the sum of production sets of the merged firms: $\Psi^m = \Psi^1 + \Psi^2 + \ldots + \Psi^M$. Given the pre-merger equilibrium prices are unchanged with the merger, then the (maximum) value of the new firm is determined by

$$\max_{\psi^m \in \Psi^m} \langle \phi, \psi^m \rangle = \sum_{j \in M} \left[\max_{\psi^j \in \Psi^j} \langle \phi, \psi^j \rangle \right]$$
$$= \sum_{j \in M} \langle \phi, \mathring{\psi}^j \rangle$$
$$= \left\langle \phi, \sum_{j \in M} \mathring{\psi}^j \right\rangle. \tag{2.F.5}$$

At the old price system the new firm's optimal production plan would simply equal the sum of the optimal production plans of the original firm; this fact in turn guarantees that the equilibrium prices will not change following the merger. In consequence,

$$v_0^m = \langle \phi, \mathring{\psi}^m \rangle = \sum_{j \in M} \langle \phi, \mathring{\psi}^j \rangle = \sum_{j \in M} v_0^j.$$

The (post-merger) equilibrium market value of the merged firm, v_0^m, equals the simple sum of the (pre-merger) equilibrium market values of its constituents. The proof of conservation of value by partitioning is analogous and not repeated here. □

2.G. The Contingent Claims Economy: Some Reservations

The correspondence between an economy under certainty and one under uncertainty with contingent claims markets (CCM) is achieved at considerable expense. To begin with, the CCM requires that individuals possess extraordinary information gathering, processing and calculation skills, surely at levels much beyond what is reasonable to suppose. The model, similarly, requires a system of markets which are numerous, complex, and refined. In part due to these presumptions, the model fails to consider many key institutional features of modern capitalist economies; e.g., the pervasiveness of money, the existence of a stock market, and the presence of operating markets at each date.

These several criticisms have a common basis, which suggests the manner in which the CCM might be further developed. If, as in the CCM, each production plan has a certain, observable present value at the beginning of time, then individuals have no motive to trade in ownership shares, so that there is no role to be played by a stock market. Moreover, if all accounts are settled at the beginning date, there is then no need for money during the evolution of the economy. In contrast, once we recognize the limited rationality and information processing capabilities of individuals and, for this reason, fashion a model economy with a sequence of markets, one for each date, and no one of them providing claims against all future contingencies, then more realistic phenomena and institutions, not part of the CCM, take a role. It is to these issues that the next several chapters turn.

Chapter 3

CONTINGENT CLAIM AND SECURITY MARKET ECONOMIES

In a contingent commodity claims market economy exchanges for future consumption take place on forward markets opening and closing at the initial period. A key feature of such markets is that all claims prices, both by date and state, are observable at once. As a consequence there is no price uncertainty and the risks that arise are only those fundamentally associated with quantities.

The absence of price uncertainty brings about many simplifications. For example, with all prices sure it is a relatively simple matter for the firm to maximize the (market) value of its production plan. Since the value of each firm's production is certain, value maximizing behavior does not in itself imply any attitude toward risk. Moreover, this sure value is distributed to individuals in proportion to their ownership claim, which means that the initial wealth of the individual, when it comes only from these claims and from the sure value of an initial endowment, is also riskless. This, unfortunately, ends the sequence of certain events for, with initial wealth given in this way, each individual must choose a state contingent (quantity risky) consumption plan to maximize utility. Thus, although each individual has a sure wealth in the initial period, the choice of consumption plan depends in part on personal attitudes toward risk.

A second feature of exchange by contingent commodity claims is that it yields a Pareto optimal alocation of risk-bearing when markets are perfect and competitive. This optimality was seen in Chapter 2 to be achieved at some expense, however, for the number of different commodity claims must equal the number of states times the number of physically distinct commodities. Optimality thus seems to require a large number of markets.

Because we see only a small number of actual markets in which contingent claims are actively traded, does this then mean that allocations are inefficient? Perhaps not, for Arrow (1964) has shown that, without impairing the optimality of allocation, it is possible to replace the full set of markets for contingent commodity claims with forward markets for contingent claims to only one commodity of account and then future spot markets in all other commodities. The interesting aspect of this arrangement is its similarity to a security market economy, particularly when one thinks of the securities as contingent claims in a 'money' commodity of account.

What are the conditions under which it is possible to make an exact substitution of security markets followed by spot markets in commodities for the alternative contingent commodity claims markets? That is our principal concern in this chapter. Part of this concern, as we shall see, is that future markets introduce the complexities of price uncertainty.

3.A. *The Organization of Exchange*

In the model economy to be considered the list of agents and elements are, with one exception, the same as in Chapter 2. For completeness we recall these by indices.

S3.1. Index sets. The elements of the economy are:

$t = 0, 1$ (two, discrete) time periods,
$i = 1, 2, \ldots, I$ individuals,
$j = 1, 2, \ldots, J$ firms,
$s = 1, 2, \ldots, S$ states, and
$m = 1, 2, \ldots, M$ consumption commodities.

The exception? We now deal explicitly with M different consumption commodities rather than the single, composite commodity.

As remarked above, various combinations of forward and spot markets in both consumption commodities and securities will be considered. In each, markets are taken to be perfect and competition is assumed to prevail throughout.

S3.2. Perfect markets. The markets for consumption claims are assumed to be such that

(i) (frictionless exchange) there are no transaction costs or taxes, and all traded claims are divisible,
(ii) (one price law) there are no arbitrage opportunities, so that like claims or bundles of claims which yield the same set of consumptions trade at the same price, and
(iii) (full price information) except as noted, each individual possesses full information of equilibrium prices on all markets (present and future).

Full price information, item (iii), requires further comment, but this is delayed until Section 3.D. That leaves the final specification.

S3.3. Competition in exchange. Every individual acts as if his choice to trade any claim does not affect the market price of that claim or any other claim.

3.A.1. *Firms*

It is usual to think of each firm's factor usage at an initial period as an investment which yields amounts of the M commodities at the subsequent period 1. That characterization is useful here, providing the M commodities produced are also differentiated by the S future states. While there are in this fashion MS potential outputs for each firm, only one amount of each of the M goods is produced *ex post* depending on the state to actually occur. Subject to the technical limitations of its production set, each firm nonetheless chooses *ex ante* a plan describing the production of each of the M goods in each of the S states.

S3.4. Production plan. Let the combination of inputs and associated outputs of each firm j, the production plan, be given by $\psi^j = [y_0^j \, y^j]$. The vector y_0^j represents firm j's input of the M commodities in period 0 ($y_0^j \leq 0$ is again used as a convention for inputs) and $y^j = [y_1^j \, y_2^j \ldots y_S^j]$ is the corresponding, non-negative MS output matrix of each commodity in each period 1 state.

S3.5. Production set. The production set for each firm j, denoted Ψ^j, is the collection of technically feasible production plans. The set $\Psi^j \subset R^{M(S+1)}$ is assumed to be closed, convex, and contain the null vector $\psi^j = 0$.

Since the concern of the next several sections is with exchange equilibria, the production plans of firms are assumed to be given exogeneously. Other than the technical feasibility of these plans, it is only required that aggregate production be strictly positive in each state: $\Sigma_j y_{sm}^j > 0$ for each s and m. (In section 3.E. consideration is given to investment and output decisions and to production-exchange equilibria.)

3.A.2. *Individuals*

As with production and firms, the characterization of consumers and their decisions closely parallels that of Chapter 2.

S3.6. Consumption plans. Each individual i's consumption plan is represented by the non-negative $M(S+1)$-vector $\chi^i=[x_0^i\, x^i]$, where x_0^i is the M-vector of consumptions at period 0 and $x^i=[x_2^i\, x_2^i \ldots x_s^i]$, each x_s^i being the M-vector of consumptions in period 1, state s (x_{sm}^i indicating the specific consumption of commodity m at that state and date).

None of the market arrangements to be considered in this chapter will limit any individual's consumption set. Until this is apparent, however, we simply assert that the consumption set is given by the non-negative orthant, $R_+^{M(S+1)}$, for each individual. Again, the consumption set should not be confused with the budget set (to be specified later) which does depend on the specific market arrangements to be employed.

S3.7. Endowment position. Each individual i is endowed with exogenously specified, non-negative amounts of the M commodities both at period 0 and 1. Designate these by the M-vector $\bar{x}_0^i$ and the SM-vector $\bar{x}^i=[\bar{x}_1\, \bar{x}_2 \ldots \bar{x}_S^i]$, respectively. Let $\bar{\chi}^i=[\bar{x}_0^i\, \bar{x}^i]$.

The possible sources of individual endowments include non-capital income, claims on capital assets which are non-marketable, and claims on marketable capital assets.[1] The issues of interest here are dealt with most directly by limiting endowments to only the last kind. Thus, $\bar{x}_0^i$ indicates each individual i's previously purchased claims delivered at period 0 by firms after their (exogenously) fixed, $t=0$ investments have been made. The next period endowment, $\bar{x}_s^i$, for each individual similarly arises from ownership claims to period 1 firm outputs (purchased prior to period zero), but now we let these $\bar{x}_s^i$ occur *before* the future investment decision is made by the firms. With given, positive aggregate production amounts the aggregate amount available for consumption of each commodity m is simply the sum of individual endowments:

$$\sum_i x_{0m}^i=\sum_i \bar{x}_{0m}^i \quad \text{at period 0, and} \tag{3.A.1a}$$

$$\sum_i x_{sm}^i=\sum_i \bar{x}_{sm}^i=\sum_j y_{sm}^j>0 \quad \text{in each state } s \text{ at period 1.} \tag{3.A.2b}$$

The final specification of individuals is usual.

[1]Under specific 'mean-variance' assumptions, Mayers (1971) has developed a theory of asset pricing where non-marketable assets are present. Fama and Schwert (1977) provide empirical tests of that theory.

S3.8. Consumer preferences. Each individual i's preferences are given by specification I2 and indicated here by the two-period, expected utility function

$$\mathrm{E}u^i(\chi^i)=u_0^i(x_0^i)+\sum_s h_s u^i(x_s^i), \tag{3.A.2}$$

where $\Sigma_s h_s=1$ and $h_s \geq 0$ is the probability of the occurrence of the sth state of nature. See D1.16.

3.A.3. Markets

The simplest case for analysis is the absence of exchange. In that instance, each individual's consumption exactly equals his endowment: $x_{0m}^i=\bar{x}_{0m}^i$ and $x_{sm}^i=\bar{x}_{sm}^i$ for all i, s, and m. With exchange and heterogeneous individuals, however, there is the potential that consumption plans more preferred than those given by endowments can be obtained. But, how to organize the exchange to achieve the greatest benefits? When there is uncertainty, Chapter 2 provides arguments for organizing forward markets in contingent claims to consumption at each date and state. Such an arrangement gives considerable freedom in trading and, given markets are perfect and there is price-taking, the resulting allocation is Pareto optimal. When, however, there are costs in organizing such an extensive set of markets and/or there are economies of scale in market transactions, it becomes important to balance the gains to such extensive trading possibilities with the associated costs. While the economics of this balance are straightforward in principle once some criterion is selected, there is a *fortuitous* case where no such balancing is necessary. That is, under certain conditions it is possible to devise an organization of exchange which decreases the number of markets without any diminution in relevant exchange possibilities.

3.B. Contingent Commodity Claim Markets

As a reference case, suppose first that exchange is organized as in Chapter 2, by contingent commodity claims markets. To call full attention to the fact that all exchanges occur at period 0 with this market organization, we refer to the markets as being *pre-state*. Specifically, the model economy includes pre-state markets in claims to each of M commodities in each period and state: $[M(S+1)-1]$ markets in the M current and MS state-contingent commodities. Corresponding to these markets define the (pre-state) price system $\phi=[p_0\ p]$ made up of period 0 consumption and period 1 claims prices as follows:

$$p_0 = [p_{01}\, p_{02} \cdots p_{0M}], \quad \text{and} \tag{3.B.1a}$$

$$p = [p_1\, p_2 \cdots p_S], \tag{3.B.1b}$$

with, for each s,

$$p_s = [p_{s1}\, p_{s2} \cdots p_{sM}].$$

Relative to a numeraire commodity claim, p_{0m} is the price paid at period 0 for one unit of commodity m delivered in that period and p_{sm} is, similarly, the price paid at period 0 (and thus *before* it is known what state will obtain in period 1) for a claim to one unit of commodity m to be delivered in period 1 if and only if state s occurs. Again, it is emphasized that all exchanges and payments take place on forward markets (pre-state, at $t=0$) with deliveries either in the next period (post-state, at $t=1$) contingent on the state to occur. In the case of the period 0 consumption claims, deliveries occur at the instant trading is closed. (For convenience of expression, it is sometimes useful to refer to period 0 claims as 'contingent' on the occurrence of a state which happens to be known and numbered 0.)

3.B.1. Market organization 1

When markets are open to trades among all combinations of the $M(S+1)$ contingent claims, each individual faces a single, comprehensive budget restriction.

S3.9. Budget set with contingent commodity claims. The budget (wealth restricted) set of consumption plans available to individual i with trading in contingent commodity claims is

$$B^i(\phi, \bar{W}^i) = \left\{ \chi^i \geq 0 \,\middle|\, \sum_m p_{0m} x^i_{0m} + \sum_s \sum_m p_{sm} x^i_{sm} \leq \bar{W}^i \right\}, \tag{3.B.2}$$

where

$$\bar{W}^i = \sum_m p_{0m} \bar{x}^i_{0m} + \sum_s \sum_m p_{sm} \bar{x}^i_{sm}, \tag{3.B.3}$$

is the market value (in exchange at $t=0$) of i's endowment.

The budget restriction makes clear that markets organized in contingent commodity claims permits trading across all combinations of time periods, states, and commodities. For example, an individual relatively well endowed in some specific commodity in the initial period might exchange that commodity for claims to any commodity in any state at period 1 in which he has a relatively poor endowment.

Over the range of consumption opportunities provided by his budget set, each individual maximizes expected utility. Formally, each individual's choice is given as the solution to the following problem:

$$\max_{\chi}\left[u_0(x_0)+\sum_s h_s u(x_s)\right], \quad \text{subject to} \tag{3.B.4a}$$

$$\sum_m p_{0m}x_{0m}+\sum_s\sum_m p_{sm}x_{sm}=\bar{W}. \tag{3.B.4b}$$

Introducing the multiplier λ, the associated Lagrange problem is:

$$\max_{\chi}\left[u_0(x_0)+\sum_s \mathrm{h}_s u(x_s)-\lambda\left(\sum_m p_{0m}x_{0m}+\sum_s\sum_m p_{sm}x_{sm}-\bar{W}\right)\right]. \tag{3.B.5}$$

Stationarity conditions for an optimum closely follow those with a single, composite commodity – see Section 2.B.1.

E3.1. Consider an individual with logarithmic elementary utility in an economy with contingent commodity claims markets. Let there be two equiprobable states and two commodities, so that the choice problem is:

$$\max[(\ln x_{01}+\ln x_{02})+0.5(\ln x_{11}+\ln x_{12}+\ln x_{21}+\ln x_{22})],$$

subject to

$$\sum_\theta\sum_m p_{\theta m}x_{\theta m}=\bar{W},$$

where $\theta=0, 1, 2$ and $\mathrm{m}=1, 2$. Conditions for an interior optimum include

$$(x_{\theta m})^{-1}=\lambda\left(\frac{p_{\theta m}}{h_\theta}\right),$$

for each θ and m, with $h_0=1$ and $h_1=h_2=0.5$. The original budget restriction is also part of the stationarity conditions. Suppose the following prices and endowment: $p_{01}=1$, $p_{02}=2$, $p_{11}=0.25$, $p_{12}=0.5$, $p_{21}=0.5$,

$p_{22}=0.2$, and $\bar{W}=4$. Using these conditions it is immediately shown that the individual's optimal consumption plan is $x_{01}=1$, $x_{02}=0.5$, $x_{11}=2$, $x_{12}=1$, $x_{21}=1$, and $x_{22}=2.5$. ■

To close this first case, we note that an *exchange equilibrium* with contingent commodity claims is a set of claims prices $\mathring{\phi}$ and an allocation $\mathring{\chi}^i\,\forall i$ such that $\mathring{\chi}^i$ maximizes $\mathrm{E}u^i$ for each i and there is equality in the aggregate number of claims bought and sold for each state and each commodity, i.e.,

$$\sum_i \bar{x}^i_{0m}=\sum_i \mathring{x}^i_{0m} \quad \forall m, \quad \text{and} \tag{3.B.6}$$

$$\sum_i \bar{x}^i_{sm}=\sum_i \mathring{x}^i_{sm} \quad \forall m, s. \tag{3.B.7}$$

To avoid confusion with other forms of market organization to be introduced shortly, we label this usual, pre-state form of the contingent commodity claims exchange *Market Organization 1* (MO1).

3.B.2. Sequential markets: Market organization 2

With MO1, consumption at period 1 is achieved using only forward contracts with no trading at the future period after the realization of the state. At this point it is natural to ask whether the lack of post-state markets constrains consumption opportunities. Under certain (ideal) conditions the answer is no and those conditions, being commonly assumed, are our present focus. To begin, we suppose that, in addition to the forward markets usual in the MO1 organization of exchange, markets in the M consumption commodities open after the state occurs at the future period. This sequence of $(MS+M-1)$ pre-state and $(M-1)$ post-state markets is labeled *Market Organization 2* (MO2). Our intention is to show the conditions under which the post-state markets of the MO2 offer no new trading opportunities.

Suppose that some specific state s has occurred at $t=1$ and that on the then occurring commodity markets an auctioneer calls out prices $p^*_s=[p^*_{s1}\,p^*_{s2}\cdots p^*_{sM}]$. Choose commodity $m=1$ numeraire so that $p^*_{s1}=1$. The sequence of markets gives each individual the opportunity to trade at period one on post-state markets with these p^*_s prices as well as in the pre-state markets for contingent claims at prices p_s. Further, suppose that the post-state prices p^*_s are known (exactly anticipated) at date zero. Arbitrage opportunities will then be absent only if, for each state s and commodity m at date 1,

$$p^*_{sm} = p_{sm}/p_{s1}. \tag{3.B.8}$$

How do individuals faced with the possibility of both pre- and post-state trading reach an optimal plan? Whatever their specific calculus, each can be thought to be involved in a stage-wise analysis: one problem at $t=0$, where an optimal plan of consumption at that period and contingent claims to consumption at the next period are determined, and a subsequent (post-state) problem at $t=1$ in which the paying contingent claims are then traded on spot markets to acquire optimal consumption amounts. In such analyses it is convenient to consider the post-state, period 1 problem first, then working backwards in time to the period 0 problem.

To this end, assume state s has occurred at $t=1$. Each individual then chooses the consumption amounts x'_s to solve the spot market problem

$$\max u(x'_s), \quad \text{subject to} \tag{3.B.9a}$$

$$\sum_m p^*_{sm} x'_{sm} = \sum_m p^*_{sm} x_{sm}, \tag{3.B.9b}$$

where the x_{sm} $\forall m$ in this problem are the period one claims 'endowed', i.e., given from the period $t=0$ foreward market choices. Let the indirect utility function $U(w_s, p^*_s)$ correspond to this solution with

$$w_s = \sum_m p^*_{sm} x_{sm}, \tag{3.B.10}$$

defining the state s, *conditional wealth* arising from the 'endowment' valued at spot market prices p^*_s.[2]

E3.2. Recall the situation of E3.1. Using the data given there and (3.B.8) we derive the spot market prices:

$$p^*_{11} = 1, \qquad p^*_{21} = 1,$$

$$p^*_{12} = 0.5/0.25 = 2, \qquad p^*_{22} = 0.2/0.5 = 0.4.$$

Suppose now that state $s=1$ realizes, then the spot market problem

[2]Because of the two period structure, this indirect utility is frequently referred to as a 'derived' utility. See Chapter 9 for details.

corresponding to (3.B.9) and (3.B.10) becomes

$$\max[\ln x'_{11}+\ln x'_{12}],$$

subject to $x'_{11}+2x'_{12}=w_1$. Stationarity conditions of this optimization are

$$1/x'_{11}=\lambda_1, \qquad 1/x'_{12}=2\lambda_1,$$

and the budget constraint (λ_1 being the multiplier). The commodity demands are

$$x'_{11}=0.5w_1, \qquad x'_{12}=0.25w_1,$$

where w_1 is the state 1 conditional wealth. More generally, the solution is

$$x'_{s1}=0.5w_s, \qquad x'_{s2}=0.5w_s/p^*_{s2},$$

where w_s is given by (3.B.10). Finally, the indirect utility function associated with the solution for each s is

$$U(w_s, p^*_s)=\ln(0.25w_s)-\ln(p^*_{s2}),$$

which is also of the logarithmic form and, for this special case, separable in prices and wealth. ■

The choice of period one consumption claims on the period zero markets determines the conditional wealth levels which are critical to the individual's utility on the period 1 spot market. This wealth 'link' between period 0 and 1 consumptions is clarified in the following period 0 problem.

$$\max_{\chi}\left[u_0(x_0)+\sum_s h_s U\left(\sum_m p^*_{sm}x_{sm}, p^*_s\right)\right], \quad \text{subject to} \tag{3.B.11a}$$

$$\sum_m p_{0m}x_{0m}+\sum_s\sum_m p_{sm}x_{sm}=\bar{W}. \tag{3.B.11b}$$

where, for each state s, equation (3.B.8) defines the spot prices p^*_s based on the pre-state market prices p_s and $w_s=\Sigma_m p^*_{sm}x_{sm}$.

Algebraic manipulations of the solution conditions for the MO2 problem (3.B.9)–(3.B.11) and the earlier MO1 problem provide the following result.

P3.1. Spot market redundancy. Let $\mathring{\chi}$ indicate some (typical) individual's optimal consumption plan in MO1 at prices $[p_0\, p]$ and let $\hat{\chi}$ indicate that person's optimal plan in MO2 at the same forward market prices and subsequently spot market prices p_s^*. Then one choice of $\hat{\chi}$ is $\mathring{\chi}$, and with this choice the individual will *not* revise his consumption plan using the post-state markets.

Proof. The definition of state conditional wealth

$$w_s = \sum_m p_{sm}^* x_{sm} \tag{3.B.12a}$$

implies

$$p_{s1} w_s = \sum_m p_{sm} x_{sm} \tag{3.B.12b}$$

for all states s. Substituting these appropriately in the period zero, MO2 problem (3.B.11) gives

$$\max_{x_0, w} \left[u_0(x_0) + \sum_s h_s U(p_{s1} w_s, p_s^*) + \lambda \left(\sum_m p_{0m} x_{0m} + \sum_s p_{s1} w_s - W \right) \right], \tag{3.B.13}$$

where $w = [w_1, w_2, \ldots, w_S]$ is the S-vector of conditional wealths and λ is a Lagrange multiplier. The corresponding MO1 problem (3.B.4) is

$$\max_{\chi, w} \left\{ u_0(x_0) + \sum_s h_s \left[u(x_s) + \zeta_s \left(\sum_m p_{sm} x_{sm} - p_{s1} w_s \right) \right] + \lambda \left(\sum_m p_{0m} x_{0m} + \sum_s p_{s1} w_s - W \right) \right\}, \tag{3.B.14}$$

where the ζ_s are Lagrange multipliers.

Since expected utility is simply additive across states, the maximization with respect to each x_s can be simply applied to the separate terms in this last problem. Doing so makes (3.B.14) identical to (3.B.13). (The equality of prices in the two problems is crucial to this conclusion, as we shall stress in a moment.) □

The structure of the MO2, two stage problem provides a final important fact: when trading is allowed on post-state markets in addition to the full contingent claims markets at $t=0$, then the optimal choice of consumption claims at $t=0$, $\mathring{\chi}$, at contingent claim prices $[p_0\ p]$ is not unique. That is, if $\mathring{\chi}$ is an optimal choice of claims on the forward markets at $t=0$, then so are all plans $\hat{\chi}$ such that they yield the same consumption at period 0 and (only) the same conditional wealth in each state of period 1. The conditions which are required in this case are $\mathring{x}_0=\hat{x}_0$ and $\Sigma_m p^*_{sm}\mathring{x}_{sm}=\Sigma_m p^*_{sm}\hat{x}_{sm}\ \forall s$, which are $(S+M)$ equations in $M(S+1)$ unknowns. With the opportunity for post-state market exchange at prices $p^*_s\ \forall s$, then in the $t=0$ forward markets each individual need only concern himself with the conditional wealth distribution across states at period 1 (and his initial period consumption). In short, so long as the period one wealth distribution across states is optimal, the individual is fully able to trade on appropriate post-state markets to obtain the preferred, future consumption of specific commodities.

E3.3. Consider again the situation of E3.1. The solution of the MO1 problem given there was, in part, $x_{11}=2$ and $x_{12}=1$. Now, allow the MO1 solution to be selected in the $t=0$ forward markets with MO2. Suppose next that $s=1$ realizes. The spot prices p^*_1 (derived in E3.2) then imply a conditional wealth in that state 1 of

$$p^*_{11}x_{11}+p^*_{12}x_{12}=1(2)+2(1)=4=w_1.$$

Also from E3.2 note that the solution to the state 1 spot market problem with $w_1=4$ is $x'_{11}=0.5w_1=2$ and $x'_{12}=0.25w_1=1$, which is exactly the period 1, state 1 consumption claims purchased on the (MO1 and MO2) pre-state markets. Similar results occur for state 2 as the reader can verify. ■

E3.4. Recall, one last time, the situation of E3.1, assuming now that both forward and spot markets occur (MO2). In E3.1 it was shown that the optimal MO1 consumption plan was also optimal with MO2. Suppose now that the purchase of period 1 claims is changed from $x_{11}=2$ and $x_{12}=1$ to $x_{11}=4$ and $x_{12}=0$, holding all other consumption choices the same. Note that the new plan satisfies the budget restriction. These changes imply a state 1 conditional wealth of

$$x_{11}p^*_{11}+x_{12}p^*_{12}=4(1)+0(2)=4=w_1,$$

which is exactly the same as with the original choices. If such choices were made at $t=0$, the individual would then, with exchange on the post-state spot market, optimally choose $x'_{11}=2$ and $x'_{12}=1$ (see E3.2) and replicate the original solution. With MO2 it is the distribution of state conditional wealths created using the forward market trading that is important, for they represent consumptions claims that can be traded to form a variety of commodity bundles on the post-state markets. ■

The solution indeterminacy when trading occurs in the sequence of markets with MO2 contingent commodity claims combined with spot markets is not to be overlooked, for it means that additional constraints can be placed on exchange without affecting the ability of individuals to achieve optimal consumption plans. For example, the MO1 restriction, that there be no post-state trading, is sufficient to provide a unique Pareto optimal equilibrium solution. Is it possible to achieve the same optimum of consumption by, say, eliminating some of the pre-state claims markets and in turn substituting post-state markets?

Suppose momentarily that trading at $t=0$ in $t=1$ consumption claims is prohibited and that in substitution there are only post-state, or spot, markets. The result of this particular market arrangement is that individuals cannot exchange their contingent claims endowments of a particular state with those of any other. Obviously, this is too great a restriction. If, however, we add to this arrangement S forward (pre-state) markets which allow individuals to trade contingent claims to a 'base' commodity across states at $t=1$, then the inter-state wealth transfer difficulty is solved. That in fact is what we plan: a restriction of the forward markets at $t=0$ to trading in contingent claims to a single (base) commodity and then the addition of post-state markets in all M commodities. This means that the SM claims markets at $t=0$ are replaced by S claims markets and then spot commodity markets. Can this be done without any diminution in the individual's optimal plan and loss of allocative efficiency?

3.C. *A Security Market Economy*

Recall the (3.B.8) spot prices taking commodity one as numeraire, which are rewritten here in vector notation as

$$p_0 = p_0^* p_{01} \quad \text{at period 0, and} \tag{3.C.1a}$$

$$p_s = p_s^* p_{s1} \quad \forall s \quad \text{at period 1.} \tag{3.C.1b}$$

In anticipation of what is to follow, note that the price of a period one, commodity one claim (p_{s1}) may be thought of as the price of a claim yielding one unit of 'wealth', or unit of account, if and only if state s occurs. As each claim represents a sure promise to pay, this unit of account can in turn be used in the $t=1$ contingent exchange markets of the M commodities at prices p_s^*. In this way transactions in S contingent claims to this base commodity and contingent exchange in the remaining M-1 commodities can, under certain conditions, substitute for a full set of markets in contingent claims. What are the conditions?

3.C.1. Conditional wealth and pure securities

With MO2, the value of claims in amount x_s if state s realizes is

$$w_s = \sum_m p_{sm}^* x_{sm}, \qquad (3.C.2)$$

or, on multiplying this identity by p_{s1},

$$p_{s1} w_s = \sum_m p_{sm} x_{sm}. \qquad (3.C.3)$$

An important interpretation arises from this last equation. When the consumer holds w_s claims of commodity 1 valued at p_{s1} per unit, then at spot prices p_s the period 1 consumption plan x_s can be acquired in exchange. That is, w_s is the number of units of account (commodity one) against which the individual's total period 1 consumption could be exchanged conditional on state s. In this way we can think of w_s as the quantity of a security held by the individual, where each such security yields one unit of account if and only if state s occurs.

D3.1. Pure security.[3] A claim which provides one unit of account if state s obtains and zero units of account otherwise is termed a state s pure security.

D3.2. Pure Security Market (*PSM*). Let there be S states of nature and S different pure securities, one pure security corresponding to each state. The markets on which these state contingent claims trade are referred to as pure security markets.

With a little additional notation it is straightforward to formulate the individual's choice problem in pure securities. To this end, define

$$w_0 = \sum_m p_{0m}^* x_{0m}, \qquad (3.C.4)$$

[3]Such securities are often called Arrow–Debreu securities, as Arrow (1964) and Debreu (1959) provided their original specification.

which is the value of the individual's period 0 consumption in terms of period 0, commodity 1 units. And, as a notational convenience introduce the $(S+1)$ vector $\omega=[w_0\, w]$, where $w=[w_1\, w_2 \ldots w_S]$ represents the individual's holdings of the pure securities. The final step is to add the (3.C.2) and (3.C.4) definitions to problem (3.B.4), rewriting it as

$$\max_{\chi,\omega}\left\{u_0(x_0)-\zeta_0\left(\sum_m p^*_{0m}x_{0m}-w_0\right)\right.$$
$$+\sum_s h_s\left[u(x_s)-\zeta_s\left(\sum_m p^*_{sm}x_{sm}-w_s\right)\right]$$
$$\left.-\lambda\left(p_{01}w_0+\sum_s p_{s1}w_s-\bar{W}\right)\right\}, \tag{3.C.5}$$

where the multipliers ζ_0 and $\zeta_s\,\forall s$ accommodate the (3.C.4) and (3.C.2) identities. The contingent claims problem is stated now in terms not only of the choice of specific contingent commodities, but also the state-by-state and period-by-period planned consumption of units of account, that is, the pure securities. As the terms of (3.C.5) are additively separable, the maximization operation with respect to x_0 and each x_s can be appropriately distributed across terms to yield

$$\max_{\omega}\left[U_0(w_0,p^*_0)+\sum_s h_s U(w_s,p^*_s)\right.$$
$$\left.-\lambda\left(p_{01}w_0+\sum_s p_{s1}w_s-\bar{W}\right)\right], \tag{3.C.6}$$

with as usual (capital) U representing indirect utilities.

When the p^* prices are given, (3.C.6) can be thought of as a pure securities problem where the individual is concerned with the choice of current and future state-conditional wealths w_0 and w_s, respectively.[4] In this case, the individual chooses amounts of the pure securities to maximize expected (indirect) utility – the functions U imply that the subsequent allocation of conditional wealth to commodities on the spot markets is optimal in each state s at the then prevailing spot prices p^*_s. The trading in the S pure

[4]With strict convexity of preferences the indirect utility functions U^i_0 and $U^i(w_s,p^*_s)$ are continuous, increasing and quasi-concave in initial and state contingent wealth, respectively. The 'securities problem' is thus well formed.

securities is, of course, also subject to a budget constraint which provides that the sum of prices paid for any choice of securities cannot exceed endowed wealth $\bar{W}$.

In summary note that, relative to the contingent commodity claims market organization, the pure securities play a dummy role which allows the decomposition of each individual's utility maximization problem into two linked steps. The first determines initial consumption and the allocation of wealth to various states represented by the choices of the pure security amounts w. The second determines the allocation of that state conditional wealth among commodities, as indicated by the indirect utility functions.

3.C.2. Pure security and contingent claims market economies

Problem (3.C.6) and the above arguments cannot yet be taken to mean that there is an equivalence in allocation between (1) the sequence of S pure security and $(M-1)$ other commodity markets at $t=0$ and the $(M-1)$ spot markets in commodities at $t=1$, and (2) the $[M(S+1)-1]$ contingent claims markets at $t=0$. Rather, (3.C.6) establishes an equivalence only when all transactions are effectively concluded at period 0. That is, the *sequential* structure of pre-state security markets and the post-state commodity markets can precisely replicate the contingent claims market allocation only if each individual knows exactly that the $p_s^* \forall_s$ prices will hold on the period 1 spot markets. But how are these post-state market prices to be known if no exchange in period 1 consumption commodities takes place until after the period 1 state realizes? The required knowledge of prices can result from a simultaneous determination, by actual exchange of contracts at period 0 or a simulation of those exchanges in the minds of every individual, of all the equilibrium prices on all claims markets (including the period 0 spot commodity markets).[5] Thus, if we mean by a security market economy the *sequence* of security markets and then post-state (spot) markets, the equivalence to a contingent claim market economy is not yet established. One more assumption is necessary.

D3.3. Full Information Price Expectations. Consider a market organized with trading at two dates, with security markets occurring at $t=0$ and commodity spot markets occurring at $t=1$. If at the first trading period each individual, with perfect foresight, anticipates the future prices $p_s^* \forall s$ that would be implicit in trading on a full set of forward markets to future

[5]See Hayek (1945) for a detailed discussion of such simulations.

consumption claims, then full information price expectations are said to obtain.

Full information price expectations is an equilibrium concept. From the discussion of MO2 equilibrium it is known that, given each individual expects the prices $p_s^* \forall s$ to occur and makes choices of conditional wealths $\mathring{w}_s \forall s$ on that basis, then these expected prices will actually result in the spot market tradings. From this it is easy to understand why it is often said that expectations are 'rational' in this case.[6]

When price expectations are presumed to be formed as in D3.3 the 'problem' of price indeterminancy (uncertainty) in the sequence of markets is solved and we have our long-sought result.

P3.2. Consumptive optimum equivalence. Let individuals be I2 with full information price expectations and let all trading occur on perfect and competitive markets. Then each individual's exchange optimum arrived at on markets for contingent claims to all commodities can be replicated in markets for contingent claims to a single base commodity (pure securities) at $t=0$ and on contingent (post-state spot) markets for commodities at $t=1$.

Proof. The steps to the proof are those used in deriving equation (3.C.6); perfect markets and competitive exchange, I2 individuals, and the requirement of full information price expectations are the bases for the proof. □

Notice that Proposition 3.2 is concerned only with the individual consumptive optimum at fixed prices. It specifically does not establish that the derived pure securities market and spot commodity markets clear as a result of the clearance of the contingent commodity claim markets. This final result is, however, not difficult to show.

3.C.3. Market clearing

When the contingent claims market clears at $t=0$, inputs and consumption amounts must balance with endowments; this requires

[6]Since Muth (1961) it has been recognized that full information price expectations is a strong assumption. It implies that, at date zero, all plans of the individuals are *consistent*; that is, for each commodity, each date, and each state, the planned excess supply is zero. This is as Radner (1972) first noted, 'An equilibrium of plans, prices, and price expectations for the future is a set of prices on the first market, a set of common price expectations for the future, and a consistent set of individual plans, one for each trader, such that, given the current prices and price expectations, each individual trader's plan is optimal for him, subject to an appropriate sequence of budgetary constraints'.

$\Sigma_i x_0^i = \Sigma_i \bar{x}_0^i$. Premultiplying by the period 0 conditional market price vector yields the corresponding value balance

$$\left\langle p_0^*, \sum_i x_0^i \right\rangle = \left\langle p_0^*, \sum_i \bar{x}_0^i \right\rangle,$$

which can be written as

$$\sum_i w_0^i = \sum_i \bar{w}_0^i. \tag{3.C.7}$$

Similarly, for each s,

$$\sum_i x_s^i = \sum_i \bar{x}_s^i,$$

when market clearing conditions hold in the period $t=1$ contingent claims. Again, premultiply by the appropriate conditional price vector to yield the value balance for each s

$$\left\langle p_s^*, \sum_i x_s^i \right\rangle = \left\langle p_s^*, \sum_i \bar{x}_s^i \right\rangle, \quad \text{or}$$

$$\sum_i w_s^i = \sum_i \bar{w}_s^i. \tag{3.C.8}$$

Thus, the pure security market clears at base commodity prices $[p_{01}\, p_{11} \cdots p_{S1}]$ if the contingent claims market does with the price system $\phi = [p_0\, p]$.[7] This proves the following proposition:

P3.3. Equilibrium Equivalence. Let the conditions of Proposition 3.2 be satisfied. Then, the allocation $[\mathring{\chi}^1\, \mathring{\chi}^2 \ldots \mathring{\chi}^I]$ of a competitive exchange equilibrium in a contingent claims market economy with price system $\mathring{\phi} = [\mathring{p}_0\, \mathring{p}]$ is also the allocation of a competitive exchange equilibrium in a (sequential) pure security market economy with security price system $[p_{01}\, p_{11} \cdots p_{S1}]$ defined by equation (3.C.1).

[7]Hahn (1971) proves the existence of equilibrium in a sequence of contingent claims markets with transaction costs are proportional to the size of the transaction. (The proportionality constant may be zero as above.) The effect of such costs, when positive, is to encourage traders to move commitments closer to the date of claims delivery, thus giving value to the sequence of markets. See also Foley (1974) and Kurz (1974).

3.D. Partial Equilibrium Analysis

The following chapters focus on the workings of security markets and not conditional exchange markets in real commodities. These analyses assume that the demand and supply of securities is determined only by *security* prices; the spot market *commodity* prices are not given attention. Such an equilibrium analysis is to be regarded as a special case of general equilibrium where the relative prices of the real commodities are assumed to be fixed.

D.3.4. Composite commodity of account (money). Suppose that the *relative* prices of the set of M commodities on contingent markets remain constant. We then define a single composite commodity with price proportional to the price of every member of the set and quantity units measured so that expenditure on the composite commodity is equal to the total expenditure on the several commodities in the set. We call the composite commodity *money* and denominate it in *dollar* units.[8]

The assumption of fixed relative prices for the real commodities cannot be strictly true in all cases, but as an approximation it will have practical importance. On this basis it is usual to adopt a security market, partial equilibrium approach and refer to money as the numeraire for security market prices. It should be emphasized that by this convention money is a commodity yielding direct utility.

3.D.1. Security markets

Using money, full information price expectations, and the sequence of markets, equation (3.C.6) is now our basic utility maximization problem. We repeat that problem here:

$$\max_{\omega}\left[U_0(w_0, p_0^*)+\sum_s h_s U(w_s, p_s^*)\right], \quad \text{subject to}$$

$$\left(p_{01} w_0+\sum_s p_{s1} w_s=\bar{W}\right). \tag{3.D.1}$$

[8]This definition is based on the composite commodity theorem first developed by Hicks (1939, p. 312) and Mosak(1944, p. 29).

The assumption of full information for future spot market commodity prices, while helpful, is not enough to make this problem all we would like it to be. Unfortunately, the p_s^*, while known for each s, still will generally differ across the states; that is, the spot prices p_s^*, viewed from date 0, are state dependent (stochastic). In turn, this means that the indirect utilities are state dependent and, when suppressing the spot commodity prices, we then write $U_s(\cdot)$. Even though we began with the assumption of state independent, elementary utility functions (defined on contingent commodity claims) the corresponding security market formulation with two trading periods has state contingent utilities (defined on next-period wealth). This state dependence can be resolved by the assumption of particular classes of utilities and probability distributions for the states. We shall delay consideration of these special cases until Chapter 9 and, in the interim, simply 'assume away' this problem. That leads to the following definition.

D3.5. Two period security market economy. By a two-period security market economy we mean:

(1) state contingent claim markets in money,
(2) post-state (spot) markets in real commodities,
(3) full information price expectations of all spot market commodity prices, and
(4) state independent indirect utilities (defined on next-period wealth).

3.E. Theory of the Firm with Pure Securities

In this section, and in the remaining chapters generally, it is presumed that security markets arise to economize on the number of forward markets. As this requires the sequential arrangement of security and post-state spot commodity markets, it is also generally assumed that the basic elements of a security market as given in D3.5 obtain. And, specifications S3.2 (perfect markets in commodities) and S3.3 (price-taking in exchange) are too assumed.

3.E.1. Value maximizing firm decisions

Proposition 2.7 established that, in a perfect and competitive contingent-commodity claims market, each firm operates in the (unanimous) best interest of its shareholders by maximizing market value. For firm j this value, $\mathring{v}_0^j$, is given as

$$\mathring{v}_0^j = \max_{\psi^j \in \Psi^j} \langle \phi, \psi^j \rangle = \langle \phi, \mathring{\psi}^j \rangle, \tag{3.E.1}$$

which we note is defined with respect to the optimum production plan. Using the normalization by commodity 1 given in (3.C.3), the maximum of market value can be rewritten as follows:

$$\mathring{v}_0^j = \sum_s \langle p_s^*, \mathring{y}_s^j \rangle p_{s1} + \langle p_0^*, \mathring{y}_0^j \rangle p_{01}. \tag{3.E.2}$$

A useful simplification of this expression occurs if we use $\mathring{w}_s^j = \langle p_s^*, \mathring{y}_s^j \rangle \; \forall s$ to designate the revenues associated with optimal outputs of firm j in state s and, similarly, let $-\mathring{w}_0^j = \langle p_0^*, \mathring{y}_0^j \rangle$ designate the costs (negative revenues) of the optimal input combination. These substitutions yield

$$\mathring{v}_0^j = \sum_s p_{s1} \mathring{w}_s^j - p_{01} \mathring{w}_0^j. \tag{3.E.3}$$

Using the structure of this last equation, we can think of the firm as supplying a set of pure securities which yield $\mathring{w}_s^j$ units of account in period 1 in each state s, and $-\mathring{w}_0^j$ units of account at period 0. In turn, the value of the corporation can be measured as the market value of those outputs at the p_{s1} pure security prices less the market value of input factors at price p_{01}. Moreover, in this equation the prices $p_{s1} \; \forall s$ and p_{01} are market-observable, so that subjective (personal) evaluations are not required to value any production plan.

Because the ownership shares held in firms are risky they, in general, need not be perfect substitutes for shares of debt in the same firm. As this substitutability was the basis for the Chapter 2 proof of the irrelevancy of capital structure in a contingent commodity claims market, the reformulation of the economy to a sequential security market arrangement potentially destroys that earlier result. The potential is not borne out, however.

P3.4. Capital structure irrelevance. Let the basic elements of a security market obtain. Given a fixed production plan, perfect markets, and price-taking in exchange, the value of the firm is independent of the proportion of debt to equity in its capital structure.

Proof. Consider firm j and fix its level of investment at y_0^j, which represents the amount of composite commodity used as input. Partition y_0^j into debt $y_d^j \leq 0$ and equity $y_e^j \leq 0$ components such that the following input balance holds,

$$y_0^j = y_d^j + y_e^j \leq 0. \tag{3.E.4}$$

If $y_d^j = 0$, then the firm is all equity financed, which implies the debt/equity ratio is zero. With p_0 the price of the composite commodity, then (3.E.4) is also the market value of firm j's input. This value has the two obvious parts, that of the shareholders and bondholders, respectively.

Let each unit of composite commodity purchase one corporate bond, and designate by b^j the promised payment to each bond issued by firm j. Bonds are potentially subject to default risk, meaning that for some states it is possible that the firm's receipts from the sale of its output will be insufficient to pay $b^j y_d^j$ at $t=1$. In such a case bondholders simply receive whatever is available while shareholders receive nothing. These ideas can be made more specific by considering the following two sets of states

$$D = \{s \mid p_s y_s^j < b^j y_d^j\}, \quad \text{and} \tag{3.E.5a}$$

$$N = \{s \mid p_s y_s^j \geq b^j y_d^j\}, \tag{3.E.5b}$$

where p_s represents the $t=0$ market price of one dollar and y_s^j represents the firm j output dollars at $t=1$ in state s. It is clear that D denotes the set of bond *default states* and N denotes the *non-default states.* With these definitions write the $t=0$ value of the firm's bonds as

$$v_d^j = \left[\sum_{s \in D} p_s y_s^j + \sum_{s \in N} p_s b^j y_d^j \right] + y_d^j, \tag{3.E.6}$$

and the $t=0$ value of its equity shares as

$$v_e^j = 0 + \left[\sum_{s \in N} p_s y_s^j - \sum_{s \in N} p_s b^j y_d^j \right] + y_e^j. \tag{3.E.7}$$

The present value of debt is equal to its yield in default states plus its value in nondefault less the debt investment. Similarly, the present value of equity is equal to zero in default plus the excess of its gross receipts over the promised debt payment in non-default less the equity investment. The overall value of the corporation, v_0^j, simply equals the sum of debt and equity market values. That is,

$$v_0^j = v_d^j + v_e^j = \left[\sum_{s\in D} p_s y_s^j + \sum_{s\in N} p_s b^j y_d^j\right] + y_d^j$$

$$+ \left[\sum_{s\in N} p_s y_s^j - \sum_{s\in N} p_s b^j y_d^j\right] + y_e^j$$

$$= \left[\sum_{s} p_s y_s^j\right] + y_d^j + y_e^j = \langle \phi, \psi^j \rangle. \tag{3.E.8}$$

This proves capital structure irrelevancy: $v_0^j = \langle \phi, \psi^j \rangle$ irrespective of the relative sizes of v_d^j and v_e^j. □

Because of some confusion in the literature, it bears some emphasis that the above proposition on capital structure irrelevancy clearly allows for risky debt. There is no requirement that bonds be default-free for y_d^i, and thus the value $b^j y_d^j$, might be small (or large) enough so that that value does not (or does) exceed $p_s y_s^j$ for any s.

Chapter 4

COMPLETE AND INCOMPLETE SECURITY MARKETS

An example best indicates the issues to be considered in this chapter. The model economy of the example is quite simple: two periods, two firms, and three states of nature at the future date. Each firm uses an amount of a composite commodity of account at the current period to produce state contingent amounts of that same commodity in the future period, each financing its input by selling claims against its uncertain output. Label the firms A and B and let their output plans be as given in Table 4.1. Across the three states firm A produces the quantities [2 1 1] while B produces [3 1 2]. With only these two producing firms and no exogeneous endowments, aggregate supplies are [5 2 3].

Table 4.1
Output plans

	State		
Firm	1	2	3
A	2	1	1
B	3	1	2
Aggregate	5	2	3

Suppose first that the firms issue pure securities; that is, each sells separate claims to its state 1, state 2, and state 3 output. In selecting an optimal plan of claims for the future period, individuals choose specific amounts of these three state-differentiated securities. Each person is, of course, indifferent to whether firm A or firm B pure securities are held for any given state. And, in the absence of arbitrage opportunities every state s claim must have the same market price at $t=0$.

Ignoring budget limitations, the feasibility of aggregate supplies, and assuming securities to be fully divisible, individuals can choose claims to period one consumption which are a linear combination of the 3 pure security vectors [1 0 0], [0 1 0], and [0 0 1] as shown in Figure 4.1. These securities, being linearly independent vectors, span the R^3_+ state space

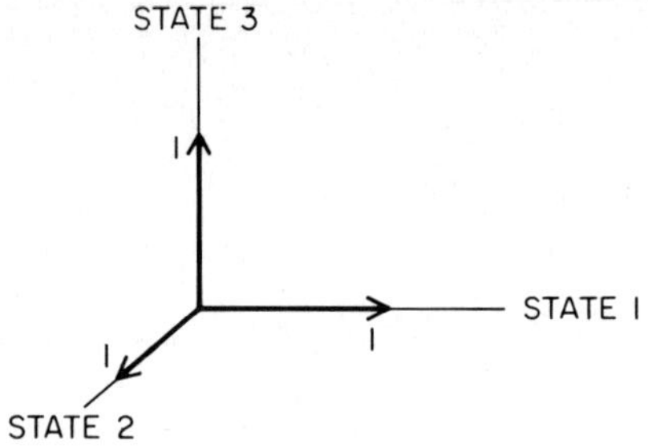

Fig. 4.1. Consumption set with pure securities

and define the consumption claims set of the example. In short, pure securities provide claims against every state contingency.

To be precise about what is meant by 'provide claims against every contingency', suppose now that it is prohibitively costly to distinguish among states so that only securities which do not require such a differentiation are traded. Specifically consider the exchange of *shares*, which are promises by a firm to pay a constant fraction of its output at the future period regardless of the state to occur. In this case it is not necessary for either buyers or sellers (of shares) to incur any costs to distinguish among the states.[1]

The resulting restriction to trade in shares, or 'bundles' of pure securities, means that the possible consumption claims at the future period are those formed as linear combinations of the firm A and B payout vectors [2 1 1] and [3 1 2].[2] Unlike the pure securities, linear combinations of these 'composite security' vectors only generate a 2-dimensional subspace, or plane, in the 3-dimensional consumption state space, see Figure 4.2.

The point of the example is that restrictions on the available securities can place limits on individual consumption sets. How do the altered consumption sets in turn affect exchange equilibrium prices, security holdings, and optimal consumption plans? And, are there resultant effects on the efficiency of the allocation with competitive exchange? These are the essential questions to which this and the next several chapters are addressed.

[1]It is further assumed that financial intermediaries and individuals, like the producing firms, find it prohibitively costly to 'unbundle' the underlying contingent claims and in turn sell them as pure securities on secondary markets.

[2]We here allow positive and negative amounts (respectively, long and short positions) to be taken in all securities without transaction costs. See S4.2 below.

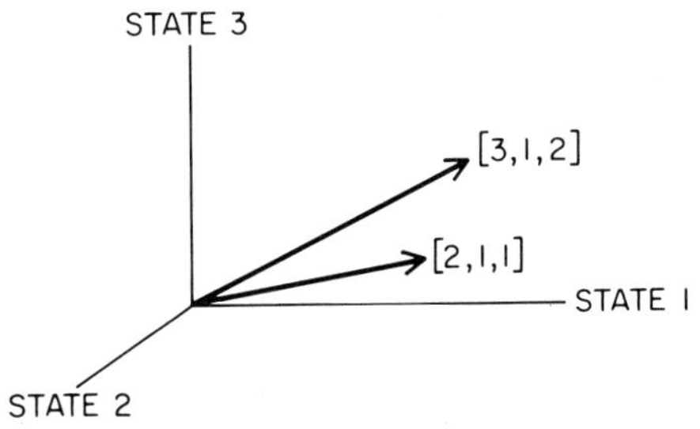

Fig. 4.2. Consumption set with shares

4.A. The Model Economy

We consider a discrete time, two period security market economy with the usual list of agents, events, and commodities, which are made explicit by their indices.

S4.1. Index sets. Elements of the economy are indexed in the following manner:

$t=0, 1$ discrete time periods,
$i=1, 2, \ldots, I$ individuals,
$j=1, 2, \ldots, J$ firms, and
$s=1, 2, \ldots, S$ states of nature at $t=1$.

In the several security market arrangements to be considered all claims are bought and sold at $t=0$ on markets which are perfect and conditions for such trading too are noted for emphasis.

S4.2. Perfect markets. The markets for security exchange are assumed to be such that:

(i) (no price uncertainty) the elements of a security market are present, see D3.5,
(ii) (frictionless exchange) there are no transaction costs or taxes, and all securities are infinitely divisible,
(iii) (one price law) there are no arbitrage opportunities, meaning that all securities or combinations of securities which yield the same output pattern across states sell at the same price, and,

(iv) (interior solutions) the short sale of every security is permitted without either margin or escrow requirement.[3]

Finally, all security markets are assumed competitive.

S4.3. Competition in security exchange. Each individual acts as if his choice to trade any security does not affect the market price of that or any other security.

Again, when there is competition in security exchange individuals are said to be competitive traders or price-takers in exchange.

4.A.1. Individuals

As usual, the key aspects in the description of individuals are those relating to consumption plans, preferences, consumption sets, and budgets sets.

S4.4. Consumption plans. Each individual i's consumption plan is represented by the vector $\omega^i=[w_0^i\, w^i]$, where w_0^i is period 0 consumption and $w^i=[w_1^i\, w_2^i \ldots w_S^i]$, with w_s^i representing consumption claims in dollars at period 1, state s.

S4.5. Consumption set. Let $*$ indicate some security market exchange arrangement. The consumption set Ω_{0*} for each individual i is given by the Cartesian product

$$\Omega_{0*}=\Omega_0 \times \Omega_*,$$

where

$$\Omega_0=\{w_0^i | w_0^i \geq 0\}, \quad \text{and}$$

$$\Omega_*=\{w^i | w^i \geq 0 \quad \text{plus restrictions of market arrangement } *\}.$$

The specification involves three consumption sets. Ω_0, the *period zero consumption set*, contains all non-negative consumption amounts at the current period. Next is Ω_*, the set of achievable $t=1$ consumption claim S-

[3]While in actual markets there are restrictions on short sales, these limitations may not be analytically important in that 'derivative' securities (e.g., put and call options) can provide essentially the same type of output across states as the short sale of any original security. See Chapters 8 and 10 for details.

vectors using the * security market arrangements. With no exogenous endowment at future periods, this set is restricted to non-negative values to avoid problems of personal bankruptcy. And, depending on the detailed description of the security market and the specific instruments available, other restrictions too may be imposed. Ω_* is called the *period one claims set* or, more simply, the *claims set*. Notice that neither Ω_0 nor Ω_* carry superscripts to indicate individual dependences: the operation of all markets is assumed to apply identically to every individual. Finally, the *consumption set* Ω_{0*} is the product of Ω_0 and Ω_*. It is the collection of all achievable period zero consumptions and period one claims: the set of all plans $\omega = [w_0\ w_1]$ feasible on current consumption good and security markets.

Each individual chooses his preferred (and budget feasible) consumption plan from the consumption set according to preferences as follows.

S4.6. Individual preferences. Except as noted, all individuals are I1 (see D1.15) and have utility functions represented by $U^i(w_0^i, w^i)$.

4.A.2. Firms

As we focus on security exchange, details of the production process of firms are secondary. All that matters are the basic constraints which technology imposes on production.

S4.7. Production plans. The combination of firm j's period 0 inputs and period 1 outputs (across states) is given by the vector $\xi^j = [z_0^j\ z^j]$, with $z_0^j \leq 0$ the dollar input level and $z^j = [z_1^j\ z_2^j \ldots z_S^j]$ the dollar outputs across states at period 1. The S-vector z^j is termed firm j's *output plan.*

The set of technically feasible production plans for firm j, its production set, is assumed to be closed, convex and to contain the origin. Further, if ξ^j is feasible and is such that $z_0^j = 0$, then $z^j = 0$.

S4.8. Output program. Let z^j be a (feasible) output plan for some firm j. By an output program we mean a J-fold collection of such output plans, one for each firm in the economy: $Z = [z^1\ z^2 \ldots z^J]$. As each z^j is an S-vector, an output program Z is represented by an $S \times J$ (or, when appropriate, $J \times S$) matrix.

Throughout this chapter the production plans of firms, and in consequence the output program for the economy as a whole, are considered to be known and fixed.

For each individual i define a *distribution* of the firms' outputs by the numbers $a^i_{js} \geq 0 \; \forall s, j$. Each a^i_{js} indicates the quantity of firm j's production delivered to individual i contingent upon the occurrence of state s at period one. In the aggregate a distribution of each firm j's output is feasible only if it satisfies a conservation constraint, $\Sigma_i a^i_{js} = z^j_s \; \forall s$. And, for such a constraint to hold for all firms and all individuals it is additionally required that $\Sigma_j a^i_{js} = w^i_s \; \forall i, s$. That is, in the absence of exogenous (period one) endowments, equilibrium individual consumptions in each state s must sum to the aggregate supplies available from firms.

4.A.3. Markets in pure securities

If markets are perfect in the sense that no information or transaction costs are present, then a distribution $\{a^i_{js}\}$ can be specified in a very general way. What then results is trading on *Pure Security Markets* (PSM).[4]

S4.9P. Pure security ownership plan. Each individual i's security ownership plan in a pure security market is represented by the $J \times S$ matrix $A^i = [a^i_{js}]$ where each element a^i_{js} represents the dollars of state s claims which i holds in firm j.

S4.10P. Consumption set with pure securities. The set of consumption plans attainable in PSM exchange is given by

$$\Omega_{0P} = \Omega_0 \times \Omega_P,$$

where Ω_0 is defined in S4.5 and the consumption claims set is given by

$$\Omega_P = \left\{ w^i \geq 0 \,\middle|\, w^i_s = \sum_j a^i_{js} \quad \forall s \right\}.$$

The period one consumption claims set is seen to depend only on the PSM exchange organization and not at all on individual characteristics, which explains the P subscript and the absence of any individual superscript. (Again, all individuals are considered to have identical access to markets.) We note also that the definition of the consumption set excludes

[4]A dollar is a dollar, and the state s primary securities of all firms are, of course, perfect substitutes so that one might be inclined to drop the j subscript and all references to firms in the following specifications. The similarity between pure and 'conventional' securities (to be introduced in a moment) can be made quite conveniently, however, if the distinction is retained.

any consideration either of budget feasibility or the attainability of any plan in the aggregate. If the aggregate output of the firms is strictly positive in each state ($\Sigma_j z_s^j > 0\ \forall s$), then $\Omega_P \equiv R_+^S$. Unless stated otherwise this condition is always assumed and Ω_P and R_+^S are used interchangeably.

An equilibrium ownership plan requires that aggregate material balances be satisfied. That leads to the following specification.

S4.11P. Pure security ownership program. A collection of pure security ownership plans $A = [A^1\ A^2 \ldots A^I]$ is termed a PSM ownership program iff $\Sigma_i a_{js}^i = z_s^j\ \forall j, s$.

Ignoring non-capital income and claims on non-marketable capital assets, an ownership program implies

$$\sum_i w_s^i = \sum_i \sum_j a_{js}^i = \sum_j z_s^j \quad \forall s,$$

so that aggregate production equals aggregate consumption in each state. Finally, at the onset of trading in PSM the claims to the output of the firms are specified as follows.

S4.12P. Endowments in pure security markets. Let $\bar{A}^i = [\bar{a}_{js}^i]$ indicate individual i's endowment, which is made up only of the pure securities issued by firms. In turn, let $\bar{A} = [\bar{A}^1 \bar{A}^2 \ldots \bar{A}^I]$ indicate the endowed ownership program, which necessarily requires $\Sigma_i \bar{a}_{js}^i = z_s^j\ \forall j, s$.

4.A.4. *Markets in conventional securities*

As a result of the costs of unambiguously differentiating among states at any date, firms generally do not issue pure securities. Rather, they generally issue securities whose payoff does not depend on knowledge of the state to occur. While the full detail and variety of such *conventional securities* need not concern us at this moment, it is useful in developing intuition to mention the two most common forms: debt (or bonds) and equity (or stocks).

D4.1. Debt (bonds) and equity (stocks). Let z^j be the output plan of firm j. Suppose there are no corporate or personal taxes, security brokerage or transaction fees, or bankruptcy costs. Define the debt (d) and equity (e)

securities (payout vectors) of firm j as, $\forall s$,

$$z_s^{jd} = \min[b^j, z_s^j],$$

$$z_s^{je} = \max[z_s^j - b^j, 0],$$

where b^j is the promised payment to debt. Notice that $z_s^j = z_s^{jd} + z_s^{je}\ \forall s$, so that the payout is feasible and exact. Given b^j, investors need only observe the output level of the firm, z_s^j when state s obtains, to determine the payoff to debt and equity. In a sense, debt is the senior claim, receiving its promised payment b^j if the firm's output is not less than the payment: otherwise, the firm defaults, bankruptcy occurs, and the debt security holders claim the total output (without transfer fees). If the firm does not default, then the equity security holding receives the excess over the promised (and actual) payment to debt. Finally, when the promised payment to debt is less than the firm's output in every state then debt is riskless. It is the possibility of bankruptcy, where the promised payment is not made in full, that causes risky debt.

We might use both debt and equity when dealing with conventional securities. Preferred stock, warrants, and convertible bonds too could be considered explicitly. This generality would be notationally cumbersome, however, and add little to the basic issues to be considered. As a result, it is convenient to assume that firms issue only one kind of security. These securities are fractional shares in the firms' output plans and, as above, termed stocks or equities. When we speak, then, of conventional securities here (and through Chapter 7) we will exactly mean these equities, but the adjustments necessary to deal with other forms of securities will be slight as finally shown in Chapter 8.

The nature of exchange in conventional securities is the same as that in pure securities; in fact, the formal model of conventional security exchange can be most simply derived by adding constraints to the distributions possible with the PSM. More exactly, if for each individual i and firm j it is required that $a_{js}^i = \alpha_j^i z_s^j\ \forall s$, where α_j^i is a proportionality constant, then the specification of markets in conventional securities derives directly from the pure security market specification.

S4.9C. Conventional security ownership plan. Each individual i's conventional security ownership plan is given by the vector $\alpha^i = [\alpha_1^i\ \alpha_2^i \ldots \alpha_J^i]$, where α_j^i is the *fractional* holding by i of firm j's conventional security.

It is understood that ownership has been defined differently in the two market arrangements: the a^i_{js} are dollar amounts of output claims while the α^i_j are fractions of total output (and thus dimension-free numbers). This points to the two crucial features of conventional securities. First, such securities are a composite of claims across states. Secondly, these composites can only be held by individuals in linear combinations given by the $[\alpha^i_j]$ weights. That is, the operation of the conventional security market is to allocate firm outputs, composite claim vectors, by *linear sharing rules.* What are the limits of such trade?

S4.10C. Consumption set with conventional securities. Let $Z=[z^1 z^2 \ldots z^J]$ be the output program for the economy. Then, the set of attainable consumption plans with trading on conventional security markets (CSM) is the same for all individuals and given by:[5]

$$\Omega_{0C}=\Omega_0 \times \Omega_C(Z),$$

where Ω_0 is defined in S4.5 and

$$\Omega_C(Z)=\{w^i \geq 0 \mid w^i=Z\alpha^i \; \forall \alpha^i\}.$$

Because conventional securities are traded by rules of linear combination, it is at times useful to think of the $\Omega_C(Z)$ geometrically, as a vector space. When doing so, the restriction that each individual i's period one claims be a linear combination of the output plans of firms is equivalent to the requirement that each feasible consumption vector w^i lies in that space. Since $\Omega_C(Z)$ is generated by linear combinations of the output plans, its dimension is equal to the maximum number of linearly independent output vectors and, therefore, the dimension of $\Omega_C(Z)$ equals the column rank of the output program $Z=[z^1 z^2 \ldots z^J]$.[6]

E4.1. Consider some firm j's output plan, z^j. $\Omega_C(Z)$ is easily shown to be unaltered if

(i) z^j is replaced by a scale replica, γz^j where $\gamma>0$ is a constant; or,
(ii) z^j is replaced by $(z^j+\delta z^k)>0$, where δ is a constant and z^k is the output plan of a second firm k with $z^j \neq z^k$.

[5]Again, it is assumed that individuals receive no non-capital (or non-marketable capital) income at period one. Otherwise, the consumption set would additionally have to reflect these future consumption claims. Also, note 1 above still obtains.

[6]Recall that equities are the only conventional securities being considered here. If, for example, bonds were also issued by some firms then an augmented securities payout matrix would replace Z.

From these results, certain aspects of firm decisions can be seen. For example, by (i) it is immediately seen that the individual is not concerned with production scale expansion choices, except as they might affect his wealth and budget constraint. By (ii), the individual is similarly indifferent to the merger of firm j with (some portion or all of) firm k, providing there is no change in production opportunity sets. ■

While the above example gives two cases to the contrary, $\Omega_C(Z)$ generally changes with the firm's production decision and, as we will see later, the kinds of securities they issue. Some firm might, for example, alter its production in such a way as to make its output plan not a linear combination of other firms' plans where it previously was. In this case the rank of Z, and dim $\Omega_C(Z)$, will increase and there will be new trading opportunities. Alternatively, the firm might partition its output, say, by issuing both debt and equity. Such a purely financial arrangement, with the firm's output plan itself unchanged, may increase (decrease) the number of linearly independent output patterns available. If it does, it will also increase (decrease) the rank of the output program and thereby increase (decrease) trading possibilities.

In summary, the extent of the consumption claims set is generally determined by two factors: the organization of exchange and the output program Z. With markets in pure securities the consumption claims set extends over R^S_+ for every specification of Z (providing only that aggregate output in each state is strictly positive). When, alternatively, trading is limited to conventional securities, then the properties of the output program also become an important second factor in determining the dimension of the consumption set, which explains the $\Omega_C(Z)$ notation. These considerations lead to the following two cases.

D4.2. Complete security market. Let there be S states of nature and let $\Omega_*(Z)$ be the period one consumption claims set determined by trading in the security market arrangement with output program Z. When $\Omega_*(Z) = R^S_+$ the $*$ security market is said to be complete.[7]

As noted above, $\Omega_P = R^S_+$ and thus the PSM is always complete. Because the

[7] Let there be three dates $t = 0, 1, 2$ with uncertainty characterized by states of nature at dates 1 and 2 (but not at $t = 0$). In this case a complete market in the sense of Debreu (1959, pp. 98–102) would require unit claims for all possible *evolutions* through date 2. That is, if s indicates the typical state at $t = 1$ and θ similarly indicates typical states at $t = 2$, a complete securities market would be required to pay not only in each s and θ independently (the 'subevents') but for all possible combinations of s and θ. See Chapter 9 for details.

consumption set is maximal in this case, the PSM is often used as a standard for comparison of trading and consumption opportunities. When $\text{rank}(Z)=S$, then it is also true that $\Omega_C(Z)=R^S_+$ and the corresponding CSM is complete. There is, however, what is often thought to be the more usual case of 'not complete' security markets.

D4.3. Incomplete security market. Let the number of linearly independent conventional securities (vectors) be K: $\text{rank}(Z)=\dim \Omega_C(Z)=K$. When $K<S$, the attainable set of consumption claims is a proper subset of the S-space of state claims, $\Omega_C(Z)<R^S_+$, and the security market is said to be incomplete.

E4.2. Consider a conventional security market economy with three firms and three states of nature at the future period. Let the output plans, and thus conventional securities, of the firms by given by $z^1=[1\ \ 2\ \ 3]$, $z^2=[0\ \ 1\ \ 2]$, and $z^3=[0\ \ 0\ \ 1]$. These are linearly independent vectors in R^S_+; thus $\text{rank}(Z)=3$ and the security market is complete. One implication of this completeness is that it is possible to form a consumption plan with equal output in every state as a linear combination of the three securities. In the specific case here,

$$w^f=z^1-z^2=[1\ \ 1\ \ 1].$$

The plan w^f is riskless for it yields the same amount in all states.

What happens if we change the output of firm 3 to $z^3=[1\ \ 1\ \ 1]$, leaving z^1 and z^2 as defined above? In this case $\text{rank}(Z)=2$, as $z^1-z^2=z^3$, the three securities are linearly dependent, and the conventional security market is incomplete. The riskless plan is still feasible, however – either as z^3 or as the linear combination z^1-z^2. The plane which defines the consumption claims set in this case contains the point $[1\ \ 1\ \ 1]$.

As a final case let $z^1=[1\ \ 2\ \ 3]$ as above, but now suppose $z^2=[1\ \ 2\ \ 2]$ and $z^3=[0\ \ 0\ \ 1]$. Again, $\text{rank}(Z)=2$ and the market is incomplete, but a riskless plan is no longer achievable, which is to say the plane in R^3_+ defining the consumption claims set no longer contains any point on the '45 degree ray' in that space. ■

The following two specifications parallel those in the pure security market and provide a convenient terminology when describing market equilibrium conditions.

S4.11C. CSM ownership program. The collection $[\alpha^1\ \alpha^2 \ldots \alpha^I]$ of individual security ownership plans is termed a CSM ownership program iff

$$\sum_i \alpha_j^i = 1 \quad \forall j.$$

And, of course, an equilibrium CSM ownership program requires that the supply and demand be equal for each security.

S4.12C. Endowments in conventional security markets. Let $\bar{\alpha}^i = [\bar{\alpha}_1^i \, \bar{\alpha}_2^i \ldots \bar{\alpha}_J^i]$ denote i's endowment of conventional securities. The collection of such endowments, $[\bar{\alpha}^1 \, \bar{\alpha}^2 \ldots \bar{\alpha}^I]$, is called the endowed ownership program for the economy, and necessarily satisfies the conservation condition

$$\sum_i \bar{\alpha}_j^i = 1 \quad \forall_j.$$

4.A.5. Budget sets in PSM and CSM

Each individual's consumption choice depends in part upon risk preferences and the production program (which generally determines the consumption set). In market economies it depends on more than these things: from among the consumption plans which are in the consumption set, each individual is further restricted in his choice to those plans which have value in exchange less than or equal to the value of his endowment. That is, there is the usual budget constraint. We specify the budget set first in PSM and then in CSM.

S4.13P. Pure securities price system. Corresponding to the markets in pure securities define the S-vector of relative prices $p = [p_1 \, p_2 \ldots p_S]$, taking current consumption as numeraire ($p_0 \equiv 1$). Each p_s represents the price paid at $t = 0$ for a claim delivering one dollar in (only) state s at $t = 1$.

S4.14P. Pure securities budget set. Let $\bar{a}^i = [\bar{a}_1^i \, \bar{a}_2^i \ldots \bar{a}_S^i]$ be individual i's endowed security portfolio (state claims to future consumption) and $\bar{w}^i$ be his endowment of period 0 consumption. The set of all period 1 consumption plans available to the individual, termed his budget set, is given by

$$B_P^i(p, \bar{a}^i, \bar{w}^i) = \{w^i \mid \langle p, (w^i - \bar{a}^i) \rangle \leq \bar{w}^i - w_0^i\},$$

where p is as in S4.13P.

The equation $\langle p, (w^i - \bar{a}^i) \rangle = \bar{w}^i - w_0^i$ is termed the PSM budget constraint. With U^i increasing in its arguments and prices positive, any plan optimally chosen solves this equation.

S4.13C. Conventional securities price system. Let the J-vector of relative prices $v_0 = [v_0^1\, v_0^2 \dots v_0^J]$ be the price system corresponding to the J markets in conventional securities (taking current consumption as numeraire), where v_0^j is the period $t=0$ value of firm j – i.e., the price of a full (100%) share of its output in period $t=1$.

S4.14C. Conventional securities budget set. The set of all security ownership plans available to the individual in exchange, termed the budget set, is given by

$$B_C^i(v_0, \bar{\alpha}^i, \bar{w}^i) = \{\alpha^i \mid \langle v_0, (\alpha^i - \bar{\alpha}^i)\rangle \leq \bar{w}^i - w_0^i\},$$

where v_0 is as in S4.13C.

Again, the equation $\langle v_0, (\alpha^i - \bar{\alpha}^i)\rangle = \bar{w}^i - w_0^i$ is called the budget constraint.

The collection of all period 1 consumption plans which are simultaneously attainable and budget feasible with the exchange of pure securities, termed the *opportunity set*, is given by

$$O_P^i(p, \bar{a}^i, \bar{w}^i, Z) = \Omega_P(Z) \wedge B_P^i(p, \bar{a}^i, \bar{w}^i).$$

As $\Omega_P(Z)$ is the positive orthant, the opportunity set and budget set are identical in PSM. The distinctive feature of CSM exchange is the reduction in trading opportunities and the potential difference between opportunity and budget sets. Specifically, the opportunity set in CSM exchange is given by

$$O_C^i(v_0, \bar{\alpha}^i, \bar{w}^i, Z) = \{w^i = \alpha^i Z \mid \alpha^i \in B_C^i\}.$$

4.B. Constrained Pure Security Markets

Let $K = \operatorname{rank}(Z)$ be the number of linearly independent conventional securities for some economy. When $K < S$, then necessarily $\Omega_C(Z) < \Omega_P$ and there cannot in general be equivalence between conventional security and pure security market arrangements in the economy. The conventional security market is incomplete in this case and some consumption plans attainable in the PSM are not attainable in the described CSM. There are, in turn, two subcases to consider: $K < J < S$ and $K = J < S$. When $K < J < S$ the conventional security market is such that, given no market imperfections and the absence of opportunities for arbitrage (the market values of all security ownership plans providing identical claims are equal), every feasible consumption plan can be arrived at from an infinite number of security ownership plans. That is, in this case the α-solutions of $w = Z\alpha$ are infinite in number for each $w \in \Omega_C$. This leads to the following definition.

D4.4. Redundant securities. When two (or more) different conventional security ownership plans provide the same plan of period one claims and arbitrage opportunities are absent then the output program Z is said to contain redundant securities.

In the second subcase, when $K = J < S$, then to each feasible claims plan at $t = 1$ there corresponds a unique conventional security ownership plan; that is, for a given $w \in \Omega_C(Z)$ there is exactly one α which solves $w = Z\alpha$. Although incomplete ($K < S$), the conventional security market does not possess redundant securities in this subcase.

While it is common to restrict attention to conventional securities and incomplete markets, it is at times helpful to fashion equilibrium analyses in terms of pure securities with trading *constrained* in a way which is fully 'equivalent' to some CSM. Equivalence, of course, requires that the opportunity set of *each* individual be the same in the constrained PSM as in the CSM, which in turn generally means the respective equivalence of both consumption and budget sets.

Designate a *constrained pure security market* equivalent to some CSM by the symbol ₱SM, with the ₱ subscript then indicating the consumption and budget sets for that market specification. The remainder of this section sets out conditions for constructing a ₱SM such that $\Omega_₱(Z) = \Omega_C(Z)$ and, for each individual i, $B^i_₱(\cdot) = B^i_C(\cdot)$. Section 4.C then shows that, when this equivalence in consumption and budget sets holds, there is an exchange equilibrium in an appropriately specified ₱SM which is equivalent to each exchange equilibrium in the corresponding CSM. A key byproduct of the ₱SM analysis is the development of an (implicit) state claims price system which will sustain, or support, the conventional security prices of the corresponding CSM.

4.B.1. Consumption sets

P4.1. The relationship between $\Omega_₱(Z)$ and $\Omega_C(Z)$. The output program Z for an economy defines the consumption set achievable in a CSM, $\Omega_C(Z)$, as a (perhaps proper) subset of Ω_P.

Proof. To avoid uninteresting complications assume there are no redundant securities, i.e., rank$(Z) = K = J$. In CSM exchange the feasible period one consumption claims satisfy $w=Z\alpha$ (i superscripts are omitted). Partition Z into a nonsingular $K\times K$ matrix Z_K and a residual $N\times K$ matrix Z_N where $N=S-K$. (Such a partition is always possible by a suitable labeling of rows.) In a like manner, partition the consumption plan w into the obvious w_K and w_N parts. With these definitions the equation of any plan $w=Z\alpha$ can be partitioned as

$$w_K=Z_K\alpha \quad \text{and} \quad w_N=Z_N\alpha.$$

As Z_K has an inverse, solve the first equation for $\alpha=Z_K^{-1}w_K$, substituting this in the second equation to give

$$w_N=Z_N Z_K^{-1} w_K.$$

With some algebraic manipulation this can be rewritten as

$$[-Z_N Z_K^{-1} \vdots I_N]w=\theta \tag{4.B.1a}$$

or, with the obvious definition of Γ, as

$$\Gamma w=\theta. \tag{4.B.1b}$$

As $-Z_N Z_K^{-1}$ is $N\times K$ and the identity matrix I_N is $N\times N$, the (augmented) constraint matrix Γ is $N\times S$. The null vector θ must, of course, be $N\times 1$. The N equations $\Gamma w=\theta$ are termed the *fundamental system* of the CSM.

The rank of Γ is $N=S-K$, which means that the fundamental system provides exactly N constraining equations. As a result, the set of all consumption claims which solve $\Gamma w=\theta$ define the claims set $\Omega_C(Z)$, a subspace of R^S_+ whose dimension is $K=S-N$,

$$\Omega_C(Z)=\{w\geq 0 \mid \Gamma w=\theta\}. \tag{4.B.2}$$

□

E4.3. With three states and two firms, let the output program be given by the dollar amounts

$$Z=\begin{bmatrix} 4 & 6 \\ 2 & 2 \\ 2 & 4 \end{bmatrix}.$$

What is the implied consumption set with a conventional security market?

Partition Z as

$$Z_K = \begin{bmatrix} 4 & 6 \\ 2 & 2 \end{bmatrix} \quad \text{and} \quad Z_N = [2 \quad 4].$$

Then

$$-Z_N Z_K^{-1} = -[2 \quad 4] \begin{bmatrix} -\frac{1}{2} & \frac{3}{2} \\ \frac{1}{2} & -1 \end{bmatrix} = [-1 \quad 1].$$

The single equation of the fundamental system is

$$\Gamma w = [-Z_N Z_K^{-1} : I_N] w = [-1 \quad 1 \quad 1] \begin{bmatrix} w_1 \\ w_2 \\ w_3 \end{bmatrix}$$

$$= -w_1 + w_2 + w_3 = 0,$$

which describes a plane in the three dimensional state space. That is, trading in the conventional securities limits every individual's consumption in states 2 and 3 to be equal in sum to consumption in state 1. All consumption claim vectors achievable by the conventional securities are bound by this restriction. Note, incidentally, that a riskless plan is not feasible in this specific case.

If the consumptive optimum for any individual is to be the same with trading either in conventional or constrained pure securities, then it is generally required that opportunity sets be identical under the two exchange arrangements. The conditions for equality of period 1 consumption sets are given above (in P4.1) and provide for a set of $N = S - K$ constraints to properly restrict pure security exchange. The final requirement is to equate the individual's budget sets in the two security market arrangements. Before doing this, it is first useful to point out several key properties of the individual's consumptive optimum. This is done in the next section, with the then following section returning to the problem of assuring appropriate equality in budget sets.

4.B.2. CSM consumption optimum

Price-taking in the exchange of conventional securities means that each individual acts as if the price system $v_0=[v_0^1 v_0^2 \ldots v_0^J]$ is unaltered in any component by his choice of security ownership plan. When such conditions hold, each individual solves

$$\max U^i(w_0^i, w^i), \qquad \text{subject to} \tag{4.B.3a}$$

$$w^i = Z\alpha^i, \tag{4.B.3b}$$

$$\bar{w}^i - w_0^i = \langle v_0, \alpha^i - \bar{\alpha}^i \rangle, \tag{4.B.3c}$$

where α^i and w_0^i are the decisions. Treat (4.B.3b) by direct substitution and, with λ^i the multiplier pertaining to the budget constraint, write the Lagrange function

$$U^i(w_0^i, Z\alpha^i) - \lambda^i[\langle v_0, \alpha^i - \bar{\alpha}^i \rangle - (\bar{w}^i - w_0^i)]. \tag{4.B.4}$$

With subscripts to U^i indicating the obvious partial derivatives, stationarity conditions for an interior optimum are[8]

$$U_0^i - \lambda^i = 0, \tag{4.B.5a}$$

$$\sum_s U_s^i z_s^j - \lambda^i v_0^j = 0 \quad \forall j, \tag{4.B.5b}$$

and the original constraints.

Define $\pi_s^i = U_s^i / U_0^i \ \forall s$, which is the marginal rate of substitution of period one, state s consumption and period zero consumption. In turn, for each firm j rewrite equation (4.B.5b) as

$$v_0^j = \sum_s \pi_s^i z_s^j. \tag{4.B.6}$$

At the consumptive optimum each π_s^i is i's *implicit demand price* for a consumption claim in that state s. The market value of each firm j is in turn equal to the sum of its state contingent output valued at these implicit state-claim prices.

For *each* individual i of the economy, necessary conditions for state contingent consumption to be optimal are that the associated implicit state claim prices $\pi^i = [\pi_1^i \ \pi_2^i \ldots \pi_S^i]$ satisfy the equations $v_0 = Z\pi^i$. Suppose now

[8] Recall that short sales are admissible without transaction cost.

that the security market is incomplete ($J=\text{rank}(Z)<S$); then corresponding to every composite security price system v_0 there are an infinite number of state claim price systems capable of satisfying this condition. In this case variations in preferences and wealth positions in the cross-section of individuals (even with v_0 and Z fixed) mean that the implicit state claim prices will generally differ across individuals.

D4.5. Sustaining state claim price system. Let $\pi=[\pi_1\,\pi_2\ldots\pi_s]$ denote an S-vector of non-negative state claim prices where each π_s is denominated in $t=0$ dollars per dollar paid in state s at $t=1$. We say that π is a sustaining state claim price system relative to some vector of CSM prices v_0 and output program Z if and only if $v_0^j=\Sigma_s\pi_s z_s^j\,\forall j$.

It is possible to show that for any conventional security market at equilibrium (and particularly when arbitrage opportunities are absent) that there exists a sustaining state claim price system, one which 'supports' the equilibrium security values. In general this set of claims prices will not be unique, but it will be when the security market is complete.

P4.2. Sustaining state claim prices. Let the output program Z and conventional security prices v_0 be given such that there are no arbitrage opportunities (in the sense described below). Then:

(i) there exists a (non-negative) sustaining state claim price system,
(ii) the implicit state claim prices of every individual, π^i, constitutes a sustaining price system,
(iii) every sustaining price system yields the same value for every consumption plan in the CSM consumption set $\Omega_C(Z)$, and
(iv) if the CSM is complete then there is a unique sustaining price system – otherwise, when the market is incomplete, there is an infinite number of such price systems.

Proof. Let $\alpha^*=[\alpha_1^*\,\alpha_2^*\ldots\alpha_J^*]\neq 0$ represent a combination of long and short security holdings using no wealth: $\Sigma_j\alpha_j^* v_0^j=0$. Then *arbitrage opportunities* are lacking only if a solution for α^* both to the equation $\Sigma_j\alpha_j^* v_0^j=0$ and the inequalities $\Sigma_j\alpha_j^* z_s^j>0\,\forall s$ does not exist. When there is no such α^*-solution, then by the Minkowski–Farkas Lemma there must exist a set of non-negative constants $\pi_s\,\forall s$ which solve $v_0^j=\Sigma_s\pi_s z_s^j\,\forall j$.[9] Proof of part (ii), that the implicit state claim prices of any individual are sustaining prices, follows

[9]See the Appendix to this Chapter for a detailed statement of this Lemma.

immediately from the optimality conditions (4.10). To prove part (iii), choose an arbitrary plan $w \in \Omega(Z)$ where $w = \Sigma_j \alpha_j z^j$. Next let π^1 and π^2 be two sustaining price vectors with the prices π_s^1 $\forall s$ such that

$$\sum_s \pi_s^1 w_s = \sum_s \pi_s^1 \sum_j \alpha_j z^j = \sum_j \alpha_j \sum_s \pi_s^1 z^j = \sum_j \alpha_j v_0^j,$$

and prices π_s^2 $\forall s$ such that

$$\sum_s \pi_s^2 w_s = \sum_s \pi_s^2 \sum_j \alpha_j z^j = \sum_j \alpha_j \sum_s \pi_s^1 z^j = \sum_j \alpha_j v_0^j.$$

As π^1 and π^2 are arbitrary sustaining price systems, then every such price system yields the same value for every feasible consumption plan.

It is only left to show part (iv) of the proposition. Again, let π^1 and π^2 be sustaining price systems. Then $v_0 = \pi^1 Z$ and $v_0 = \pi^2 Z$, which implies $(\pi^1 - \pi^2)Z = \theta$. When the CSM is complete Z has (full) rank S and the only solution to this last equation is $\pi^1 = \pi^2$, which implies uniqueness of the sustaining state claim prices. When, on the other hand, the CSM is incomplete and Z has rank $K < S$, then an infinite number of sustaining price systems exist. □

Consider an incomplete CSM where some particular pattern of claims is *not* feasible, say, the riskless plan for convenience. Question: Is every set sustaining state claims price such that the sum $\Sigma_s \pi_s$ takes on the same constant value, implying a given riskless rate of interest? More generally, is it possible to unambiguously impute prices to non-exchanged patterns using a sustaining set of claims prices? The answer is, of course, no. If the riskless plan is not feasible, and thus not traded (or created as a linear combination of traded plans), it cannot be unambiguously priced. That is true of any pattern of claims which is not traded; indeed, that is the essence of an incomplete market.

E4.4. A key feature of the Modigliani and Miller (1958) analysis of investment is the proportional valuation rule

(Rule 1) $z^j = \delta z^k$ implies $v_0^j = \delta v_0^k$,

for any two firms j and k, where δ is a positive constant. (Two firms are said to be in the same *risk class* when their output plans are scale replicas.) In perfect markets this proposition is easily proved:

$$v_0^j = \sum_s \pi_s z_s^j = \sum_s \pi_s(\delta z_s^k) = \delta \sum_s \pi_s z_s^k = \delta v_0^k.$$

It is common to extrapolate from this proposition to the conclusion that a firm adopting an investment which increases its output by a given fraction in all states of the world also increases its market value by that same fraction. That is, it is said that

(Rule 2) $z^{j'} = \delta z^j$ implies $v_0^{j'} = \delta v_0^j$,

where the prime indicates post-investment quantities and $\delta > 1$. This second proposition Rule 2 does not generally follow from Rule 1. Rather, such proportionality holds only as an approximation. Notice that the post-investment demand for j becomes:

$$\sum_s U_s^{i'} z_s^{j'} - \lambda^{i'} v_0^{j'} = 0 \quad \text{or} \quad \sum_s \frac{U_s^{i'}}{\lambda^{i'}} z_s^j = v_0^{j'}/\delta.$$

If the ratio of post-investment marginal utilities $U_s^{i'}$ and $\lambda^{i'}$ were equal to the pre-investment levels then the proportional valuation rule would obtain. However, these marginal utilities will generally be affected as the individual amounts consumed in each state generally depends on aggregate supplies (see P2.3) and aggregate supplies are altered by the adoption of the investment. For the proportion rule (Rule 2) to hold it is more generally required that

$$\frac{U_s^{i'}}{\lambda^{i'}} = \frac{U_s^i}{\lambda^i} = \pi_s \quad \forall s,$$

which is to say that the sustaining state claims prices are unaltered by the investment decision. This issue is given close attention in Chapter 8. ■

4.B.3. Budget sets in CSM and ⱣSM

Given the notion of a sustaining state claims price system corresponding to a conventional securities market it is a straightforward matter to derive the conditions for equality of budget sets in CSM and ⱣSM.

P4.3. Budget set equality in CSM and ⱣSM. Let π be a sustaining state claim price system associated with an output program Z and a conventional security price system v_0. Moreover, let $\bar{a}^i = Z\bar{\alpha}^i$ so that i's endowment is identical in both CSM and PSM arrangements. Then the budget set in CSM exchange

$$B_C^i(v_0, \bar{w}^i) = \{w^i | w^i = Z\alpha^i \text{ and } \alpha^i \text{ solves}$$
$$\langle v_0, \alpha^i - \bar{\alpha}^i \rangle \leq \bar{w}^i - w_0^i\},$$

and the budget set in the (constrained) exchange of primary securities

$$B_P^i(\pi, \bar{w}^i) = \{w^i | w^i \text{ solves } \langle \pi, w^i - \bar{a}^i \rangle \leq \bar{w}^i - w_0^i\},$$

are equal.

Proof. As current consumption is numeraire both for v_0 and π, all that is required to show is the condition under which identical amounts will be spent on period 1 consumption claims in the two security markets. Let π^* be a system of sustaining state claims prices in the CSM. It is required that $\langle \pi^*, w^i \rangle = \langle v_0, \alpha^i \rangle$ and $w^i = Z\alpha^i$ simultaneously hold in this cases. These conditions imply $v_0 = Z\pi^*$, which is true by the definition of π^* as a sustaining state claim price system. □

E4.5. Consider an individual with expected utility function defined only by period one consumption as

$$Eu(w) = \sum_s h_s u(w_s),$$

where the elementary utility function is quadratic with the specific form $u(w_s) = w_s - 0.0005w_s^2$. Suppose further that there are three states of nature occurring with probabilities $h_1 = 0.5$, $h_2 = 0.1$, and $h_3 = 0.4$, and let there be two firms such that

$$Z = \begin{bmatrix} 4 & 2 \\ 1 & 2 \\ 3 & 2 \end{bmatrix}.$$

Firm 1 produces a risky output, while firm 2's output is riskless. Assume the price of each asset in CSM exchange to be unity: $v_0^1 = 1$ and $v_0^2 = 1$. A sustaining set of state claim prices $\pi = [\pi_1\ \pi_2\ \pi_3]$ must satisfy $\langle \pi, z^1 \rangle = 1$ and $\langle \pi, z^2 \rangle = 1$ or

$$4\pi_1 + \pi_2 + 3\pi_3 = 1 \quad \text{and} \quad 2\pi_1 + 2\pi_2 + 2\pi_3 = 1.$$

These are two equations in three unknowns. The reader can easily verify that one sustaining price system is $\pi = [0.1\ 0.3\ 0.1]$.

From equation (4.B.1) the fundamental system of the CSM is constructed as

$$\Gamma w = -(\tfrac{2}{3})w_1 - (\tfrac{1}{3})w_2 + w_3 = 0.$$

All admissible consumption plans in CSM exchange lie on this plane in R^3_+.

Set aside initial consumption and, as an additional convenience, assume a null endowment of securities, $\bar{\alpha}_j = 0\ \forall j$ and $\bar{a}_s = 0\ \forall s$. Each individual thus solves the CSM problem

$$\max_{\alpha} \mathrm{E}U(Z\alpha) \quad \text{s.t.} \quad \langle v_0, \alpha \rangle = \bar{w},$$

where $\bar{w}$ is the total dollar investment in securities. The corresponding ₱SM problem becomes

$$\max_{w} \mathrm{E}u(w) \quad \text{s.t.} \quad \Gamma w = 0,\ \langle \pi, w \rangle = \bar{w}.$$

The solution to these problems, as we have shown, is equal and given by $\mathring{w} = Z\mathring{\alpha} = [998\ \ 962\ \ 986]$ when $\bar{w} = 487$. This solution derives from the demand functions resulting from the CSM problem

$$\mathring{\alpha}_1 = 520 - 1.1\bar{w},$$

$$\mathring{\alpha}_2 = -520 + 2.0\bar{w},$$

and the demand functions resulting from the ₱SM problem,

$$\mathring{w}_1 = 2.9\bar{w} - 451,$$

$$\mathring{w}_2 = 1.1\bar{w} + 451,$$

$$\mathring{w}_3 = 0.2\bar{w} + 903.$$

It is finally of interest to note that both conventional security and state claim demand functions are linear in wealth, as the quadratic utility function exhibits linear risk tolerance (see P1.11). ■

4.C. Exchange Equilibrium in Incomplete Security Markets

Each individual's consumptive optimum with trading in an incomplete securities market can be represented either in asset form with conventional security prices and share fractions or, alternatively, in state claim form with pure security prices, dollar holdings, and an appropriate constraint limiting the set of feasible consumption plans. These individual equivalences make it straightforward to show that every exchange equilibrium in conventional securities corresponds to an exchange equilibrium with constrained trading in pure securities (i.e., when each individual's PSM consumptions are constrained by the fundamental system defined by the CSM).

We begin with the definition of an exchange equilibrium in the conventional security market.

D4.6. Exchange equilibrium in CSM. Let Z represent a given output program. An equilibrium in CSM exchange is a conventional security ownership program $\mathring{\alpha}^i\ \forall i$, an allocation of period zero consumption $\mathring{w}_0=[\mathring{w}_0^1 \mathring{w}_0^2 \ldots \mathring{w}_0^I]$ and period one consumption claims $\mathring{w}=[\mathring{w}^1 \mathring{w}^2 \ldots \mathring{w}^I]$, and a conventional security price system $\mathring{v}$ such that for each individual:

(i) $\bar{w}^i - w_0^i = \langle \mathring{v}_0, \mathring{\alpha}^i \rangle$,

(ii) $\mathring{w}^i = Z\mathring{\alpha}^i$,

(iii) $[\mathring{w}_0^i\ \mathring{w}^i]$ maximizes $U^i(\mathring{w}_0^i, \mathring{w}^i)$ and is both budget and consumption set feasible, and, in the aggregate,

(iv) $\Sigma_i \mathring{w}^i = \Sigma_j z^j$ and $\Sigma_i(\bar{w}_0^i - \mathring{w}_0^i) = \Sigma_j z_0^j$.

Conditions (i), (ii), and (iii) simply provide that each individual chooses his most preferred consumption plan from among those satisfying both the restriction of the budget and consumption sets. Lastly, condition (iv) is the usual market clearing restriction, that aggregate supply and demand be equal at the equilibrium prices.[10]

There is a corresponding definition of an exchange equilibrium in a $\not{P}$SM.

D4.7. Exchange equilibrium in a constrained pure security market. Again, let Z represent a given output program. An equilibrium in a $\not{P}$SM exchange is a pure security ownership program $\mathring{a}^i = \mathring{w}^i\ \forall i$, an allocation of period zero

[10]For each state s, sum (ii) over all individuals to derive

$$\sum_i \mathring{w}_s^i = \sum_i \sum_j \mathring{\alpha}_j^i z_s^j = \sum_j z_s^j \sum_i \mathring{\alpha}_j^i.$$

If each firm's output is exactly distributed by its composite securities, then $\Sigma_i \mathring{\alpha}_j^i = 1\ \forall j$, and therefore $\Sigma_i \mathring{w}_s^i = \Sigma_j z_s^j\ \forall s$, which is condition (iv) of D4.5. That is to say, equilibrium market clearing conditions can be stated either in terms of aggregate output plans and consumption plans or in terms of the full subscription of ownership shares in the security market.

consumption $\mathring{w}_0=[\mathring{w}_0^1\,\mathring{w}_0^2\ldots\mathring{w}_0^I]$ and period one consumption $\mathring{w}=[\mathring{w}^1\,\mathring{w}^2\ldots\mathring{w}^I]$, and a state claims price system $\mathring{\pi}=[\mathring{\pi}_1\,\mathring{\pi}_2\ldots\mathring{\pi}_s]$ such that for each individual:

(i) $\langle\mathring{\pi},\mathring{w}^i\rangle=\bar{w}^i-\mathring{w}_0^i$,

(ii) $\Gamma\mathring{w}^i=0$,

(iii) $[\mathring{w}_0^i\;\mathring{w}^i]$ maximizes $U^i(w_0^i, w^i)$ and is both budget and consumption set feasible, and, in the aggregate,

(iv) $\Sigma_i\mathring{w}^i=\Sigma_j z^j$ and $\Sigma_i(\bar{w}_0^i-\mathring{w}_0^i)=\Sigma_j z_0^j$.

The explanation of the equilibrium conditions for ⱣSM exchange directly parallels those in CSM exchange.

P4.4. Equivalence of exchange equilibria. Let $\mathring{v}$ be an exchange equilibrium price system in a conventional security market with output program Z. Then any sustaining state claim price system solving $\mathring{v}=Z\mathring{\pi}$ is an equilibrium price system in the corresponding ⱣSM.

Proof. This is a straightforward application of P4.1 and P4.3 and left to the reader. □

The importance of P4.4 is clear: any analysis done in a conventional security market can be equivalently accomplished in a properly formed market with pure securities. Not only will the optimality conditions for each individual be equivalent, so will the conditions of exchange equilibrium. In later chapters there will be occasion to use the insights provided by this equivalence, particularly in the analysis of firm production and capital structure decisions.

4.D. Optimality of Risk-Bearing in Incomplete Security Markets

Let $[z_0^j\;z^j]\;\forall j$ be the fixed production plans of the J firms in the economy. An *allocation* is a collection of state contingent consumption plans, one for each individual in the economy, such that aggregate consumption at every date and state not exceed aggregate supplies. Finally, an allocation $\mathring{\omega}$ $[\mathring{w}_0\mathring{w}]$ is said to be Pareto optimal if there exists no other allocation $\omega=[w_0\;w]$ such that $U^i(w_0^i, w^i)\geq U^i(\mathring{w}_0^i, \mathring{w}^i)\;\forall i$ with strict inequality for at least one individual, where $\mathring{\omega}^i=[w_0^i\;w^i]$ is the ith element of $\mathring{\omega}$ and $\omega^i=[w_0^i\;w^i]$ is the ith element of ω.

4.D.1. Constrained Pareto optimality

Other than the requirement that aggregate consumption claims in any date and state not exceed aggregate production, notice that the test for optimality places no restrictions on the period one consumption claims w that are to be compared with the competitive equilibrium amounts $\mathring{w}$. When the output of the firms is allocated by pure securities, the extent of this comparison seems appropriate, for in the PSM all period one consumption claims in R^S_+ are feasible in exchange. When, alternatively, the output of the firms is allocated by conventional securities, it seems unreasonable to expect the allocation resulting from competitive exchange to be fully Pareto optimal, for in the CSM not all consumption plans and therefore allocations are generally available. The most that should be expected is that such an equilibrium allocation is Pareto optimal in a constrained sense, i.e., efficient *relative* to the set of period one consumption claims attainabe using linear combinations of the existing conventional securities.[11] This suggests the following definition and proposition.

D4.8. Constrained Pareto optimality. An allocation $\mathring{\omega}=[\mathring{w}_0\ \mathring{w}]$ where $\mathring{w}^i \in \Omega_C(Z)\ \forall i$ is said to be (linearly) constrained Pareto optimal, or Pareto optimal in CSM exchange, if there exists no other allocation $\omega=[w_0\ w]$ where $w^i \in \Omega_C(Z)\ \forall i$ such that $U^i(\omega^i) \geq U^i(\mathring{\omega}^i)\ \forall i$, with strict inequality holding for at least one individual.

P4.5. Optimality of CSM exchange. Let Z be the fixed output program of the economy. The allocation resulting from competitive exchange in conventional security markets is constrained Pareto optimal.

Proof.[12] Let $\mathring{\omega}=[\mathring{w}_0\ \mathring{w}]$ with $\mathring{w}^i \in \Omega_C\ \forall i$ be the exchange equilibrium allocation resulting from competitive trading in composite securities with a given production program. Let π represent a sustaining state claims price system corresponding to this equilibrium. Suppose there is a second, different allocation. $\omega=[w_0\ w]$, $\omega^i \in \Omega_C\ \forall i$, such that $U^i(w^i_0, w^i) \geq U^i(\mathring{w}^i_0, \mathring{w}^i)$ for every i, with the strict inequality holding for at least one individual. For this second collection of consumption plans to be an (equilibrium) allocation it is required that aggregate demand equal aggregate supply at every date and state: $\Sigma_i(w^i_0 - \bar{w}^i_0)=0$ and, for all s, $\Sigma_i w^i_s = \Sigma_j z^j_s$.

[11] Suppose there are no barriers to making markets other than resource costs. Thus, if some markets do not exist, it is presumably because their cost of opening and operation are greater than their benefits and a claim of inefficiency should not therefore be based upon incomplete markets.

[12] See Radner (1974).

Given $\mathring{w}^i$ is the competitive equilibrium plan for individual i, it is his optimal consumption plan in $\Omega_C(Z)$ at the prices π. This means that the alternative w^i, if it yields greater utility, must be more costly with π, i.e., it requires that

$$\langle \pi, w^i \rangle \geq (\bar{w}_0^i - w_0^i) + \sum_j \bar{\alpha}_j^i \langle \pi, z^j \rangle \quad \forall i, \tag{4.D.1}$$

with the inequality holding for at least one individual. Summing this restriction over all i yields

$$\sum_i \langle \pi, w^i \rangle > \sum_j \langle \pi, z^j \rangle. \tag{4.D.2}$$

This last inequality uses two facts: $\Sigma_i \bar{\alpha}_j^i = 1$, the firm's original ownership plan is feasible, and $\Sigma_i(\bar{w}_0^i - w_0^i) = 0$, borrowing and lending in the current consumption good must be equal in the aggregate.

A collection of consumption plans is an allocation only if it is feasible, i.e., only if $\Sigma_i w_s^i \leq \Sigma_j z_s^j$ for all s. As this feasibility condition is contradicted by the strict inequality of (4.D.2), there exists no alternative to the competitive CSM allocation which, constrained to the consumption and budget sets available to individuals in CSM exchange, makes one individual better off while not making another worse off. □

While constrained Pareto optimality seems the best that can be expected for incomplete markets, there is one set of circumstances in which the allocation, and thus prices, reached in an incomplete market is the same as would occur in a corresponding complete market, meaning that the allocation is (fully) Pareto optimal.

4.D.2. Universal portfolio separation

Consider a somewhat modified form of the CSM problem given by (4.B.3) above, now allowing individuals to be time additive, risk averse, expected utility maximizers in the manner

$$EU(w_0, w) = U(w_0) + \gamma \sum_s h_s U(w_s), \tag{4.D.3}$$

where $h_s \geq 0$ are state probabilities and $\gamma > 0$ is the individual's time impatience parameter. The i superscripts are also omitted as a convenience.

Suppose that a riskless security is feasible and consider the individual's choice of the portion of his optimal plan which results from holding the riskless security and that which derives from holding risky securities. That is, we think of the individual's consumption in each state s as

$$w_s = \alpha_1 z_s^1 + \sum_k \alpha_k z_s^k, \tag{4.D.4a}$$

where z^1 is chosen as the riskless security and $k=2,3,\ldots,J$. This we rewrite as

$$w_s = \alpha z_s^1 + (1-\alpha)\sum_k \delta_k z_s^k, \tag{4.D.4b}$$

where $(1-\alpha) \equiv \Sigma_k \alpha_k$, $\delta_k = \alpha k/(1-\alpha)$, and $\alpha_1 = [1-(1-\alpha)] = \alpha$. It is clear that $\Sigma_k \delta_k = 1$, which means that each δ_k denotes the proportion of the 'at risk' consumption in state s associated with risky security k.[13] We say that the $\delta_k (k=2,\ldots,J)$ form a portfolio of the risky securities. In turn, the choice parameter α can be thought of as the individual's leverage, the greater α is, the greater the riskless to risky investment proportion.

With these notations the individual's choice problem (4.B.3) can be rewritten as

$$\max \left[U(w_0) + \gamma \sum_s h_s U\left(\alpha z_s^1 + (1-\alpha)\sum_k \delta_k z_s^k \right) \right], \tag{4.D.5a}$$

subject to:

$$\bar{w} - w_0 = \alpha v_0^1 + (1-\alpha)\sum_k \delta_k v_0^k, \tag{4.D.5b}$$

$$\sum_k \delta^k = 1, \tag{4.D.5c}$$

where for simplicity it is further assumed that $\bar{w}$ includes any endowment in

[13] With $\bar{w} - w_0$ the investment amount and $\hat{\alpha}$ the proportion of that amount allocated to the riskless asset then we can write

$$w_s = (\bar{w} - w_0)\left[\hat{\alpha} z_s^1 + (1-\hat{\alpha})\sum_k \delta_k z_s^k \right].$$

In this way $(1-\hat{\alpha})\delta_k$ is the proportion of investment wealth allocated to risky security k.

securities. In this form the choice variables are current consumption w_0, leverage α, and the $\{\delta_k\}$ portfolio fractions. With the $U(\cdot)$ exhibiting strict risk aversion, stationarity conditions for an interior optimum are

$$U'(w_0)=(z^1/v_0^1)\left[\sum_s h_s U'(w_s)\right], \tag{4.D.6a}$$

$$\sum_s h_s U'(w_s)[(z_s^k/v_0^k)-(z_s^1/v_0^1)]=0, \tag{4.D.6b}$$

and the constraints of (4.D.5). At an exchange equilibrium these conditions plus the requirements that aggregate demand at each date and state equal aggregate supplies are satisfied by the equilibrium prices $v_0^1, v_0^2, \ldots, v_0^J$ (taking current consumption as numeraire).

P4.6. Universal Portfolio Separation (UPS).[14] Let individuals be I3 (see D1.17) so that

$$-\frac{U'(w_e)}{U''(w_e)}=A+Bw_e \quad \text{for all } e=0,1,\ldots,S.$$

Restrict parameter B to be common across individuals, but allow individual variations in A. Then the optimal equilibrium portfolio of risky securities $\{\delta_k\}$ is the same for all individuals. (Recall that I3 individuals have homogeneous probability beliefs, which is necessary for the following proof.)

Proof. As the algebra is somewhat tedious we only sketch the proof here. For $B\neq 0$, $U'(w_s)=(A+Bw_s)^{-1/B}$. Substitute this in (4.D.6). Now consider two individuals indexed i and n which are distinguished in A, w_0, α, and $\{\delta_k\}$. The optimality conditions of the two imply

$$(1-\alpha^i)\delta_k^i=\frac{A^i+Bz^1}{A^n+Bz^1}[(1-\alpha^n)\delta_k^n].$$

Summing this equation over all k and using the portfolio identities $\Sigma_k\delta_k^i=\Sigma_k\delta_k^n=1$ gives

$$(1-\alpha^i)=\frac{A^i+Bz^i}{A^n+Bz^1}(1-\alpha^n).$$

[14]This proposition was first shown by Pye (1967). See also Rubinstein (1974).

Dividing the last equation into the immediately preceding one leads to the sought-after result, $\delta_k^i = \delta_k^n$ for all k. Similar steps are used in the proof with $B=0$. □

Under the conditions of the proposition all individuals hold the same portfolio of *risky* securities even though they potentially differ in time patience (γ), initial wealth, current consumption, and the preference parameter A. It is important to recognize that the proposition applies with both complete and incomplete markets. This fact leads to the following result.

P4.7. Complete market equivalence with UPS. In an economy with perfect and competitive markets and universal portfolio separation, the allocation at an exchange equilibrium is the same as in a corresponding complete market economy.

Proof. A *corresponding* market economy is one where (1) individuals and (2) the social (aggregate) total of claims at $t=0$ and in each state at $t=1$ are identical to those in some original economy. When UPS occurs, then from P4.6 the equilibrium current consumption and consumption in each state at $t=1$ are the same for every individual, regardless of the choice of economies. Choosing one of the economies to have a complete market fulfills the proof. □

There are two immediate consequences of the above proposition. First, security prices in an economy with UPS but with incomplete markets will be determined *as if* there were a (corresponding) complete market. Secondly, since with UPS the allocation is equivalent to that of a (corresponding) complete market, then the allocation must be fully (not constrained) Pareto optimal. That is, with UPS any 'loss' of trading opportunities is inconsequential to allocative efficiency so long as the social total of claims at each date and state are unaffected (and the riskless asset persists). Stated alternatively, the 'completion' of a market provides 'no surplus' to individuals when there is UPS.

Chapter 4 Appendix

MINKOWSKI–FARKAS LEMMA

Let A be an $M \times N$ real matrix, let b and y be $N \times 1$ vectors, and let w be a $M \times 1$ vector.

Minkowski–Farkas lemma. A vector b will satisfy $b'y \geq 0$ for all y satisfying $Ay \geq 0$ if and only if there exists a non-negative vector $w \geq 0$ such that $A'w = b$.

Proof. To prove sufficiency, assure there exists a vector $w \geq 0$ such that $A'w = b$ or $w'A = b'$. Thus for any y, $w'Ay = b'y$. Then, if $Ay \geq 0$ it must be that $w'Ay \geq 0$ and $b'y \geq 0$ as we require. Proof of necessity makes use of the duality of linear programs. If $b'y \geq 0$ for every y in $Ay \geq 0$, then the program

$$Ay \geq 0; \min b'y$$

has the solution $y = 0$. As a result the dual program

$$A'w = b,\ w \geq 0; \max 0w,$$

also has an optimal solution, i.e., there exists at least one $w \geq 0$ solution to $A'w = b$. □

The Lemma can also be proved without using the duality of linear programs, see Nikado (1963, p. 38).

Chapter 5

RISK AND RETURN: THE EFFICIENT SET

While the theory of security price developed in Chapter 4 is both elegant and analytically tractable, it has limited practical use. The problem is the one typical in general equilibrium analyses: particularly, the demand functions for securities, security portfolios, and finally equilibrium prices and consumption plans remain dependent on unspecified aspects both of security returns and individual preferences. What is required, of course, are those clever (and restrictive) specifications of the theory which identify the characteristics of securities, security portfolios, and consumption plans relevant to individual choice in such a way that the parameters of the valuation equation can be observed. Holding the organization of exchange aside, limitations of two kinds can be considered. First, restrictions can be placed on the class of risk-averse individuals in the economy. In addition, or alternatively, restrictions can be placed on the properties of, and relationships among, security output vectors. How do these provide a theory of security price? That is the concern here and in the next several chapters.

5.A. Security Markets

Consider a two period $(t=0,1)$ security market economy with $s=1,2,\ldots,S$ states of nature at the future period, see D3.5. As usual, it is also assumed that security markets are perfect (S4.2) and there is competition in exchange (S4.3).

With two exceptions the CSM economy of Chapter 4 forms the model of exchange used here. First, rather than using a more general, ordinal specification of preferences, all individuals are now required to be expected utility maximizers. Not only is this necessary as a basis for the two period security market model, it also provides explicit measures of risk and risk premia. Secondly, all consumption and output plans are now expressed in a 'return' form and therefore denominated in dollars/dollar numbers rather than dollars. The ways in which these particular revisions enter into the analysis are seen in the description of the security market economy to follow.

5.A.1. Firms and securities

Recall the notation of Chapter 4:

$z^j=[z_1^j\, z_2^j \ldots z_S^j]$	the output plan of each firm $j=1,2,\ldots,J$,
$Z=[z^1\, z^2 \ldots z^J]$	the output program (collection of output plans of the J firms), and
$v_0=[v_0^1\, v_0^2 \ldots v_0^J]$	the security price system, with v_0^j being the market price of plan z^j for each j.

The price system v_0 uses the current consumption good as numeraire. As one unit of that consumption good, the composite commodity of account, is called one dollar, each v_0^j too is denominated in dollars.

D5.1. Securities and outputs. Let $\underline{z}_s^j=z_s^j/v_0^j$ define the state s (one plus) *rate of return*, or *return*, to holding one dollar of security j. In turn, $\underline{z}^j=z^j/v_0^j=[\underline{z}_1^j\underline{z}_2^j\ldots\underline{z}_S^j]$ denotes the state contingent return to each firm j's security and $\underline{Z}=[\underline{z}^1\,\underline{z}^2\ldots\underline{z}^J]$ denotes the *security program* of the economy.

In the above definition, and hereafter, bar underscores are used to represent the return form of variables. As in common, $\underline{z}^j$ is referred to as firm j's security, and similarly $\underline{Z}$ is called the security program. The reader should understand, however, that in these cases we now mean state-contingent vectors, or matrices, of returns.

It should be noted that changes either in the (dollar) output plans of firms or in the price system generally affects the security returns and therefore the return program. The 'normalization' of outputs by prices to define return variables thus leaves prices one step removed in analysis. The danger of this construction is that one can easily overlook the fact that a different price system generally implies a different return vector for each firm. Be advised and therefore careful in this regard.

While the security market here is restricted to one security for each firm, as we noted in Chapter 4 this is an assumption of convenience only. While such an extension has implications for firm valuation, the only effect of allowing the additional securities in the following discussion is an increase in dimensionality.[1] We thus restrict attention simply to the case of one conventional security per firm.

[1]Alternatively, we might allow that each firm j issues $k=1,2,\ldots,N^j$ securities with the payoff of each such security being z^{jk}. In this case the condition $z^j=\Sigma_{k=1}^{N}z^{jk}$ would be required for each firm j when there are no external drains or subsidies.

5.A.2. Individuals: The security market problem

Again, recall the notation from Chapter 4:

w_0 period zero consumption of the composite commodity of account (money) measured in dollar units,

$w=[w_1\, w_2 \ldots w_S]$ the S-vector of state contingent consumption claims for period $t=1$, and

$\bar{w}_0$ exogeneously given, period zero endowment.

The above consumption variables are defined for each of the $i=1,2,\ldots I$ individuals in the market economy. When dealing with a typical individual as above, the differentiating superscript is generally neglected.

While the individuals of the model may differ, each is nonetheless presumed to be I2; i.e., a risk averse expected utility maximizer with homogeneous probability beliefs (see D1.16). In this two period model $U_0(w_0)$ indicates the period zero utility function and, similarly, $U(w_s)$ indicates the elementary utility at period one, state s with $h_s \geq 0$ being the state probability ($\Sigma_s h_s = 1$). The individual's optimal choice of w_0 and w is given as the solution of

$$\max\left[U_0(w_0)+\sum_s h_s U(w_s)\right], \tag{5.A.1a}$$

subject to the budget restriction

$$\bar{w}_0 - w_0 = \sum_s \pi_s w_s, \tag{5.A.1b}$$

where $\pi=[\pi_1, \pi_2, \ldots, \pi_S]$ is a system of sustaining state claims prices and current consumption is numeraire. Non-negative consumptions are assumed and endowments at $t=1$ are ignored.

It is convenient in much of what follows to focus on the individual's choice of period 1 consumption claims by securities while setting aside current period consumption. This focus is based on the following decomposition. First, define $\bar{w}=\bar{w}_0 - w_0$ as *investment wealth*, or simply *investment*, which is that portion of the individual's endowment not consumed at $t=0$ and thus available for the purchase of securities paying claims at $t=1$. Using the investment variable, next consider the *security market problem*

$$G(\bar{w}, \pi) = \max_w \sum_s h_s U(w_s) \quad \text{s.t.} \quad \bar{w} = \sum_s \pi_s w_s. \tag{5.A.2}$$

The indirect utility $G(\bar{w}, \pi)$, the maximum of period 1 expected utility, generally depends on the investment amount $\bar{w}$ brought to the security market by the invidual. G is in fact monotone increasing, strictly concave in $\bar{w}$ providing the prices π are fixed and the utility function $U(\cdot)$ exhibits risk aversion, see P1.1. Finally, the optimal choices of (period one) consumption claims $w^*(\bar{w})$ arising from this problem are also dependent on the investment level.

But what about the current period consumption? That choice can be considered (indirectly) as the choice of investment to[2]

$$\max_{w} \, [U_0(\bar{w}_0 - \bar{w}) + G(\bar{w}, \pi)]. \tag{5.A.3}$$

The solution value of this problem, $\bar{w}^*$, not only yields current consumption, it determines the preferred choice of (period 1) claims using the *rule* developed from the solution of (5.A.2), i.e., $w^*(\bar{w}^*)$.

In summary, the determination of the period 1 consumption claims function (of investment) occurs in problem (5.A.2), the choice of investment (and, derivatively, period zero consumption) occurs in (5.A.3). Don't be mislead, the two problems are not (generally) independent, but are linked as explained. The interconnection indicates, however, that a security market problem, (5.A.2), can be meaningfully defined using investment $\bar{w}$ as a parameter, with this problem providing the optimal *rule* for the choice of period one claims. These things understood, the focus for much of the discussion in this and the following two chapters will be limited to the security market and problem (5.A.2).

E5.1. P1.7 and P1.11 show that the individual's choice of relative amounts consumed in any two states is independent of investment wealth iff elementary utility is constant relative risk averse. That is, at any given price system the optimal consumption *ratio* w_s/w_e of any pair of states s and e is independent of $\bar{w}$ iff U is CRRA. This specific degree of independence between problems (5.A.2) and (5.A.3) is commonly termed 'portfolio myopia'. ■

How is the choice of claims $w = [w_1 \; w_2 \ldots w_S]$ related to the selection of securities? Using conventional securities and the implied linear combination

[2]The two-stage decomposition relies on the time additive, state separable utility function. See Green (1964).

rule, the claims held in each state s are

$$w_s = \sum_j \alpha_j z_s^j, \tag{5.A.4}$$

where the choice variable α_j is the fraction of firm j's total security issue held by the individual.

D5.2. Portfolio Fractions and Budget Constraint. Let $\delta_j = \alpha_j v_0^j / \bar{w}$ be the fraction of the individual's investment wealth allocated to security j. The J-vector $\delta = [\delta_1\ \delta_2 \ldots \delta_J]$ represents (security) *portfolio fractions* when $\Sigma_j \delta_j = 1$.

A *long* ($\delta_j > 0$), *short* ($\delta_j < 0$), or *no* ($\delta_j = 0$) position may be taken in any security when forming portfolio fractions. All that is required is $\Sigma_j \delta_j = 1$, which translates to $\Sigma_j \alpha_j v_0^j = \bar{w}$ and assures that the associated portfolio is budget feasible. Also, when short positions are indicated these are assumed to be without margin and/or escrow requirements.

E5.2. Let $\pi = [\pi_1\ \pi_2 \ldots \pi_S]$ be a sustaining state claim price system for a given collection of securities. Then securities are valued by the equation

$$v_0^j = \sum_s \pi_s z_s^j \quad \forall j,$$

or, dividing by v_0^j to yield the return form,

$$1 = \sum_s \pi_s \underline{z}_s^j \quad \forall j.$$

The price weighting of each security's returns across states must exactly sum to one. ■

While the final object of individual choice in a security market is a plan of state-contingent claims, it is analytically convenient to scale this plan by the individual's investment wealth. The result is termed a *portfolio*.

D5.3. Consumption portfolio. A period one consumption portfolio, given by the S-vector $\underline{w} = [\underline{w}_1\, \underline{w}_2 \ldots \underline{w}_S]$ results from a choice of portfolio fractions δ in the fashion $\underline{w} = \delta \underline{Z}$.

For every state s there is the identity $\underline{w}_s = \Sigma_j \delta^j \underline{z}_s^j = \Sigma_j (\alpha_j v_0^j / \bar{w})(z_s^j / v_0^j) = w_s / \bar{w}$. That is, state-contingent portfolio returns are defined relative to investment wealth: $w_s = \bar{w}\underline{w}_s \; \forall s$.

D5.4. Portfolio opportunity set. For each security program $\underline{Z}$ the set of consumption portfolios feasible at period one is given by

$$\theta(\underline{Z}) = \{\underline{w} \in R_+^S \mid \underline{w} = \delta \underline{Z} \text{ for all portfolios } \delta\},$$

and called the portfolio opportunity set.

Viewing consumption in terms of protfolios is a key step, for it means the opportunity set is common to all individuals regardless of differences in investment wealth. This is in fact the principal reason for expressing variables in returns, as opposed to dollar amounts.[3] A complicating effect of this construction is that wealth must somehow be explicit in the specification of individual utility, for dollar consumption must still be the final choice object.

S5.1. Individual preferences. Let individuals be I2 with expected utility function given in the form

$$EU(\omega) = U_0(w_0) + \sum_s h_s U(w_s), \tag{5.A.5}$$

see D1.16. In turn, the expected utility function for the security market problem (5.A.2) written in return form becomes

$$EV(\underline{w}) = \sum_s h_s V(\underline{w}_s), \tag{5.A.6}$$

where $V(\underline{w}_s) = U(\bar{w}\underline{w}_s) = U(w_s)$ for each state s and, again, $\bar{w}$ is investment wealth. Finally, note that when U is monotone increasing, strictly concave in w_s and $\bar{w} > 0$ is a constant, then V is also monotone increasing, strictly concave in $\underline{w}_s$.

It is to be emphasized that each elementary utility function $V(\cdot)$ represents a different I2 individual with unique risk index and/or level of investment wealth. As the utility function depends on investment wealth in this way, it

[3]In contrast, the opportunity set differs across individuals when consumption is denominated in dollars. The reason is, of course, that investment wealth, and thus the budget constraint, differs from individual to individual.

also depends on the security price system which values that wealth. When individuals are price takers this functional dependency causes no problems, otherwise it introduces a complexity that must be explicitly treated. Note, finally, that with security prices fixed and investment wealth strictly positive, EV has the properties of an I2 utility function in terms of consumption portfolios provided that the expected utility function given in terms of (dollar) consumption plans also possesses those properties.

E5.3. Let $U(w_s)$ and $V(\underline{w}_s)$ be defined as in S5.1. Differentiating the identity gives

$$\frac{\partial V(\underline{w}_s)}{\partial \underline{w}_s}=\frac{\partial U(w_s)}{\partial w_s}\bar{w}, \quad \text{and}$$

$$\frac{\partial^2 V(\underline{w}_s)}{\partial \underline{w}_s^2}=\frac{\partial^2 U(w_s)}{\partial w_s^2}\bar{w}^2.$$

From these expressions it is seen that $V(\underline{w}_s)$ exhibits constant relative risk aversion (CRRA) with parameter c if $U(w_s)$ does:

$$w_s\frac{\partial U/\partial w_s}{\partial^2 U/\partial w_s^2}=\underline{w}_s\frac{\partial V/\partial \underline{w}_s}{\partial^2 V/\partial \underline{w}_s^2}=c.$$

More generally, when $U(w_s)$ is not CRRA, i.e.,

$$w_s\frac{\partial U/\partial w_s}{\partial^2 U/\partial w_s^2}=f(w_s),$$

with $f(\cdot)$ a non-constant function, then neither the non-constant relative or absolute risk aversion functions for U and V are the same. Thus, the elementary utility function $U(w_s)$ is equivalent in Pratt risk aversion measure to the function $V(\underline{w}_s)$ if and only if U, and thus V, is CRRA. ■

5.B. *Optimal Portfolios*

Using return notation each individual's choice of period one consumption is given by the solution of the security market problem (5.A.2)

$$\max_{\delta} \mathrm{E}V(\delta \underline{Z}) \quad \text{s.t.} \quad <\delta, 1_J> =1, \tag{5.B.1}$$

with, again, i superscripts omitted.

5.B.1. Gains to arbitrage

The solution to (5.B.1) is of interest only when the security program does not offer opportunities for riskless arbitrage. Such a *gain to arbitrage*, or an *arbitrage opportunity*, is said to occur when there are two portfolios $\underline{w}^{\alpha}=\delta^{\alpha}\underline{Z}$, $\underline{w}^{\beta}=\delta^{\beta}\underline{Z}$ such that:

$$\mathrm{E}\underline{w}^{\alpha} > \mathrm{E}\underline{w}^{\beta}, \quad \text{and} \tag{5.B.2a}$$

$$\underline{w}^{\alpha}=\mathrm{E}\underline{w}^{\alpha}1_S+\varepsilon, \tag{5.B.2b}$$

$$\underline{w}^{\beta}=\mathrm{E}\underline{w}^{\beta}1_S+\varepsilon, \tag{5.B.2c}$$

where 1_S is the S-vector of 1's and the S-vector ε is the (common) risky element of both portfolios. When these conditions occur the portfolio $\underline{w}=\underline{w}^{\alpha}-\underline{w}^{\beta}$ (and choice of securities requiring no wealth $\delta^{\alpha}-\delta^{\beta}=0$) provides a strictly positive dollar payoff risklessly. Then, simply by increasing the scale of $\delta^{\alpha}-\delta^{\beta}$, and thus the scale of $\underline{w}=\underline{w}^{\alpha}-\underline{w}^{\beta}$, each individual could create an infinite payoff. Stated conversely, arbitrage opportunities are absent only if $\mathrm{E}\underline{w}^{\alpha}=\mathrm{E}\underline{w}^{\beta}$ whenever (5.B.2b) and (5.B.2c) hold for any two unit plans $\underline{w}^{\alpha}$ and $\underline{w}^{\beta}$. In the following it is assumed that prevailing prices do not permit gains to arbitrage.

One particular implication of the no-arbitrage condition is that the riskless portfolio is unique. To show this let $\rho=\mathrm{E}\rho 1_S$ and $\hat{\rho}=\mathrm{E}\hat{\rho}1_S$ indicate two potentially riskless portfolios with different returns, say $\mathrm{E}\rho>\mathrm{E}\hat{\rho}$. In this case the arbitrage position $\underline{w}=(\delta\rho-\delta\hat{\rho})$ with $\delta>0$ provides a positive riskless return $\delta(\mathrm{E}\rho-\mathrm{E}\hat{\rho})1_S$ without using any investment. On 'scaling up' the investment amounts, an infinite period one wealth would result. The absence of profitable arbitrage thus requires $\mathrm{E}\rho=\mathrm{E}\hat{\rho}$ and, in turn, $\rho=\hat{\rho}$. Thus when such a portfolio exists it must be unique, there can be no other riskless asset of different mean. In what follows we shall use $\rho=\mathrm{E}\rho 1_S$ to indicate this *riskless portfolio*. (Incidentally, the portfolio may be constructed from a single security or by a combination of securities, or both.)

Are there arbitrage opportunities when security markets are in equilibrium? In Chapter 4 an equilibrium was defined in part by the existence of a non-negative sustaining state claims price system $\pi=[\pi_1\ \pi_2 \ldots \pi_S]$ such that

$$v_0^j=\sum_s \pi_s z_s^j \quad \forall j.$$

A zero-wealth arbitrage position $\alpha=[\alpha^1\ \alpha^2 \ldots \alpha^J]$ with $\Sigma_j\alpha^j=0$ can provide arbitrage gains only if $\underline{w}^{\alpha}=\alpha\underline{Z}\geq 0$, i.e., the position provides strictly positive returns in at least one state. If this were the case, $\lambda\alpha$ would yield arbitrarily large returns without risk in the indicated state(s) as the scale parameter λ increased. This observation leads to the following proposition.

P5.1. Arbitrage and sustaining prices. Arbitrage opportunities are absent in a security market if and only if securities are valued by a sustaining state claims price system.

Proof. Using the notation given above, P4.2 shows that the existence of a non-negative π is equivalent to the non-existence of a positive $\underline{w}^{\alpha}$. □

5.B.2. The solution conditions

Recall now the security market problem (5.B.1), assuming that $\underline{Z}$ does not provide arbitrage opportunities. Then, $\mathring{\delta}$ are optimal portfolio fractions when they satisfy the following stationarity conditions

$$\sum_s h_s(\partial V(\mathring{\underline{w}}_s)/\partial \underline{w}_s)\underline{z}_s^j = \lambda \quad \forall j, \tag{5.8.3a}$$

where $\mathring{\underline{w}} = \mathring{\delta}\underline{z} \geq 0$ and λ is the marginal utility of wealth $\bar{w}$ at the optimum. Short positions may be used at this optimum, and we assume as usual that $\mathring{\underline{w}} \geq 0$. Eliminating λ gives

$$\sum_s h_s(\partial V(\mathring{\underline{w}}_s)/\partial \underline{w}_s)(\underline{z}_s^j - \hat{\underline{w}}_s) = 0 \quad \forall j, \tag{5.B.3b}$$

with $\hat{\underline{w}} = [\hat{\underline{w}}_1\, \hat{\underline{w}}_2 \ldots \hat{\underline{w}}_S]$ being any feasible portfolio such that $\underline{z}_s^j \neq \hat{\underline{w}}_s$ for some s. This solution is written compactly as

$$\mathrm{E}[V'(\mathring{\underline{w}})(\underline{z}^j - \hat{\underline{w}})] = 0 \quad \forall j, \tag{5.B.3c}$$

using the prime to denote partial differentiation with respect to claims in the various states. When the riskless portfolio is feasible it is usual to choose $\hat{\underline{w}} = \rho$. While suppressed by the notation, notice for completeness that the $\mathring{\delta}$-solution to the above problem, and in turn $\mathring{w}$, is a function of investment $\bar{w}$. This occurs as changing levels of investment generally changes the specification of the utility function $V(\cdot)$, see S5.1.

Sufficient conditions for the portfolio $\mathring{\underline{w}}$ to be optimal are that it be a solution to (5.B.2) and that individuals not have a risk affinity. With risk aversion (strictly concave V) $\mathring{\underline{w}}$ is unique. Moreover, when the security program $\underline{Z}$ has rank J there is a unique set of security portfolio fractions corresponding to the optimal portfolio $\mathring{\underline{w}}$. Otherwise, when rank $(\underline{Z}) = K < J$ and there are redundant securities, only K of the J portfolio fractions can be uniquely specified and the remaining $(J–K)$ portfolio fractions are arbitrary – providing they, along with the first K fractions, sum to one.

5.C. The Efficient Set

The properties of optimal portfolios must, of course, be made up of the properties of their constituent securities. The manner in which the separate security properties 'add-up' in the portfolio can be expressed in terms of the way in which sufficient statistics of securities 'add' to form sufficient statistics of their linear combinations. This means that it is at times convenient to think of consumption portfolios not simply as vectors in a state space, but as random variables. What is the relationship between such portfolios, random variables, and the associated probability densities?

5.C.1. States of nature, probabilities, and random variables

Let $h=[h_1\, h_2 \ldots h_S]$ be the S-vector of probabilities corresponding to state occurrences at $t=1$. With a given security program $\underline{Z}$ consider some specific set of portfolio fractions δ and therewith a portfolio $\underline{w}=\delta\underline{Z}$. Corresponding to the vector $\underline{w}$ define a discrete random variable, which we also indicate by the symbol $\underline{w}$ due to the directness of the relationship. The vector, and random variable, $\underline{w}$ represents the realization of return $\underline{w}_1$ with probability h_1, $\underline{w}_2$ with probability h_2, etc. Next, for some specific level of return $\underline{w}_*$ (a scalar) define the set $S_*=\{s\,|\,\underline{w}_s\leq\underline{w}_*$ for all $a\leq\underline{w}_s\leq b\}$, where the parameters a and b, respectively, represent minimal and maximal elements of $\underline{w}$. Associated with the vector $\underline{w}$ there is then a discrete cumulative probability density

$$F(\underline{w}_*)=\sum_{s\in S_*} h_s$$

with $F(a^-)=0$ and $F(b)=1$, where $a^-<a$. The associated probability density $f(\underline{w}_*)$ equals zero if $\underline{w}_*\neq\underline{w}_s$ for any s, otherwise it equals the sum of the state probabilities for all states for which $\underline{w}_*=\underline{w}_s$.

E5.4. Let there be five states of nature and consider the following portfolio:

$$\underline{w}=[0.9 \quad 1.0 \quad 1.5 \quad 1.6 \quad 1.0].$$

With state probabilities

$$h=[0.1 \quad 0.2 \quad 0.4 \quad 0.1 \quad 0.2],$$

the cumulative density $F(\underline{w}_*)$ and probability density $f(\underline{w}_*)$ are given by the following table.

$\underline{w}_*$	$F(\underline{w}_*)$	$f(\underline{w}_*)$
<0.9	0	0
0.9	0.1	0.1
1.0	0.5	0.4
1.5	0.9	0.4
1.6	1.0	0.1

■

The usual definitions of operations common in mathematical statistics follow, both when we think of w as a vector of returns or as the associated (discrete) random variable. More specifically, $E\underline{w}=\langle h, \underline{w}\rangle$ is the expected return of $\underline{w}$; $E(\underline{w}|\underline{w}')=\langle \hat{h}, \underline{w}\rangle$ is the expected return of $\underline{w}$ conditional on specific values realized for $\underline{w}'$, with $\hat{h}$ representing the appropriate conditional probabilities; $\mathrm{var}(\underline{w})=E[(\underline{w}-E\underline{w})(\underline{w}-Ew)]$ is the variance of $\underline{w}$; $\mathrm{cov}(\underline{w}, \underline{w}')=E[(\underline{w}-E\underline{w})(\underline{w}'-E\underline{w}')]$ is the covariance of $\underline{w}$ and $\underline{w}'$; etc.

Similarly, each security z^j has an associated (discrete) random variable and, in turn, the security program for the economy can be thought of as a random vector $\underline{Z}=[\underline{z}^1\ \underline{z}^2 \ldots \underline{z}^J]$. Moreover, corresponding to the random vector $\underline{Z}$ there is the usual variance/covariance matrix, which we indicate by $\underline{\underline{Z}}=[\mathrm{cov}(\underline{z}^j, \underline{z}^k)]$.

5.C.2. Expected utility and moments of the portfolio return distribution

It has long been recognized that the moments of probability distributions corresponding to consumption portfolios have descriptive content. That is, we can generally express the expected utility of any portfolio in terms of the moments of its probability distribution. For example, consider some portfolio $\underline{w}$ with mean $E\underline{w}$ and assume that the elementary utility function V is analytic. Expand $V(\underline{w}_s)$ about $E\underline{w}$ by Taylor's series yielding

$$V(\underline{w}_s)=\sum_{k=0}^{\infty} V_k(E\underline{w})(\underline{w}_s-E\underline{w})^k/k! \quad \forall s, \tag{5.C.1}$$

where V_k denotes the kth derivative of V and $V_0 \equiv V$. In turn, expected utility can be written as

$$EV(\underline{w})=\sum_{k=0}^{\infty} [V_k(E\underline{w})/k!]E[(\underline{w}_s-E\underline{w})^k]$$

$$=V_1(E\underline{w})E\underline{w}+V_2(E\underline{w})E[(\underline{w}_s-E\underline{w})^2]/2+\ \ldots\ ,$$

with $E[(\underline{w}_s - E\underline{w})^k]$ the kth central moment of the probability distribution. The second, simplified form of the expression has been reached by choosing the origin of V such that $V(E\underline{w})=0$.

Equation (5.C.1b) informs us that expected utility can be expressed as a weighted sum of the moments of a portfolio's return distribution, with the weights being appropriate derivatives of the elementary utility. When there are only a few non-zero derivatives of the utility function or only a few non-zero moments of the portfolio probability distribution, (5.C.1b) provides a practical basis for choosing portfolios on the basis of these moments. For example, suppose we restrict individuals to quadratic utility without limiting the returns distribution beyond the requirement that all portfolios have finite means and variances. Or, alternatively, we might consider all possible I2 individuals and restrict security returns to be distributed joint normally. In both cases terms of order three and greater in (5.C.1) vanish to give

$$EV(\underline{w}) = aE\underline{w} - b[\mathrm{var}(\underline{w}) + (E\underline{w})^2] \stackrel{\Delta}{=} g(E\underline{w}, \mathrm{var}(\underline{w})), \tag{5.C.2}$$

where a, $b>0$ and $(a/2b) \geq E\underline{w}$ when utility is increasing in wealth and exhibits risk aversion. Note that the function $g(\cdot)$ defined in (5.C.2) has as arguments the mean and variance of the consumption portfolio. And, given the parameter restrictions, it can be quickly shown that $g(\cdot)$ has the properties[4]

$$\partial g/\partial E\underline{w} > 0, \qquad \partial g/\partial\, \mathrm{var}(\underline{w}) < 0, \qquad \partial^2 g/(\partial E\underline{w})^2 < 0.$$

It is usual to refer to $g(E\underline{w}, \mathrm{var}(\underline{w}))$ as the *mean-variance equivalent preference* (or utility) *function*. When preferences are mean-variance equivalent, the choice of portfolios as S-vectors of state contingent returns with $K = \mathrm{rank}(\underline{Z})$ degrees of freedom is reduced to the simpler choice of portfolios with only two relevant degrees of freedom, mean and variance. Moreover, given the marginal properties noted above, for every individual there is a simple optimality criterion, the so-called *mean-variance maxim*: at any mean return choose the portfolio of least variance, or at any variance choose the portfolio of greatest mean. It follows immediately that the characteristics of securities which determine their value are those which contribute to the mean and variance of portfolios, which of course are the appropriate means and covariances of the securities.

We might look for somewhat greater generality by giving consideration to cubic elementary utilities. Then, three terms in the (5.C.1) expansion

[4]See Tobin (1958) and Feldstein (1968) for details.

would be relevant. Mean, variance, and skewness of portfolio returns would be choice objects, and a three-parameter equivalent preference function would be appropriate. And, in the manner of the two moment case, the mean and co-moments through order three of the security returns would form a basis for the theory of security price.

E5.5. While variance is a measure of risk for quadratic utilities, ordering *portfolios* of equal mean, what is the risk measure for cubic utilities? Let $V(\underline{w}_s)=\underline{w}_s-a\underline{w}_s^3$, where the parameter $a>0$ and outcomes are limited to the range $0\leq \underline{w}_s \leq (3a)^{-1/2}$. From (5.C.1) we can write expected utility as

$$\mathrm{E}V(\underline{w})=\mathrm{E}\underline{w}-a[\mathrm{E}(\underline{w}-\mathrm{E}\underline{w})^3+(\mathrm{E}\underline{w})^3+3\mathrm{E}(\underline{w}-\mathrm{E}\underline{w})^2\mathrm{E}\underline{w}],$$

where $\sigma^2(\underline{w})=\mathrm{E}(\underline{w}-\mathrm{E}\underline{w})^2$ and $k^3(\underline{w})=\mathrm{E}(\underline{w}-\mathrm{E}\underline{w})^3$ are, respectively, second and third central moments of $\underline{w}$. On what basis do we now choose from two portfolios, $\underline{w}$ and $\underline{w}'$, of equal mean? Portfolio $\underline{w}$ is preferred to $\underline{w}'$ with the cubic utility if

$$a\{3\mathrm{E}\underline{w}[\sigma^2(\underline{w}')-\sigma^2(\underline{w})]+[k^3(\underline{w}')-k^3(\underline{w})]\}>0.$$

From this expression it is apparent that the term

$$k^3(\underline{w})+3\mathrm{E}\underline{w}[\sigma^2(\underline{w})],$$

which involves the first three central moments of $\underline{w}$, is the relevant measure of risk ordering portfolios of equal mean. ■

While at first glance the choice of portfolio return distribution moments appears to be an empirically robust basis for a theory of price, it is not generally so.[5] Consider, for example, the complications arising with two moment, mean-variance preferences. In this case, the covariance of any security which is relevant to the determination of the security value is the covariance between the security's return and the distribution of marginal utilities yielded by each individual's optimal portfolio. That leads to two considerations: the observability of both the marginal utility and the optimal portfolio. When utility is quadratic, then marginal utility is linear and the personal (preference) information required for valuation seems minimal. Moreover, in this case all optimal portfolios follow the mean-

[5]See, however, Levy and Markowitz (1979), who have shown that mean-variance analysis can be applied as an approximation for a wide range of utility functions (with negligible error) as long as the distribution of returns is not too widely spaced.

variance maxim and thus are observable as a set, but which specific one corresponds to the optimal portfolio of each utility function (if it is required to differentiate the optimal portfolios at all in this case)? It is not difficult to see that these considerations are much more problematic when utilities and returns with terms of order three or greater in (5.C.1) are considered. Does this then imply that we are left with only the mean-variance foundation for a theory of security price?

The answer to this question is a qualified no. It is no because we can practicably expand the set of utilities and distributions beyond those giving mean-variance equivalent preferences. The no is qualified because the added generality comes at the expense of restricting attention to a class of 'linear pricing' models. It is to such models to which we turn our attention, beginning first with some basic properties of the set of optimal portfolios.

5.C.3. Efficient portfolios

In speaking of portfolios which are optimal for the collection of all I2 individuals it is usual to use (again, but now in a different sense) the notion of efficiency. Since the concept is fundamental a formal definition is useful.

D5.5. Efficient portfolio and efficient set. A portfolio $\underline{w} \in \theta(\underline{Z})$ is said to be *efficient* (with respect to $\underline{Z}$) iff it is optimal for some I2 individual, i.e., it solves (5.B.3).[6] The set of portfolios optimal for all such admissible utilities is termed the *efficient set* and indicated by $\theta^\circ(\underline{Z})$:

$$\theta^\circ(\underline{Z}) = \{\underline{w} \in \theta(\underline{Z}) \mid \underline{w} \text{ is optimal for some I2 individual}\}.$$

The notation $\mathring{\underline{w}}$ is used to indicate a typical element of $\theta^\circ(\underline{Z})$. All feasible portfolios that are not efficient are said to be *inefficient*.

How to determine whether or not a candidate portfolio is efficient? While in the end all such determinations are based on the existence or not of an I2 individual for which the portfolio is optimal, there are two sets of conditions which are helpful in avoiding the requirement for extensive enumeration. The first condition recognizes certain regularities in the ordering of consumption across states in optimal portfolios; the second isolates stochastic relationships between any two portfolios if every I2 individual is to prefer the first to the second. Consider these in turn.

[6]Recall S5.1 and the difference between utilities U and V. Wealth is suppressed in V and we regard the same U at different wealth levels as different V in (5.B.3).

P5.2. Efficient portfolio return patterns. For some candidate portfolio $\underline{w}$ number states in ascending order of return so that

$$\underline{w}_s \leq \underline{w}_{s+1}, \qquad s=1,2,\ldots,S-1.$$

Then this portfolio and all other portfolios which order states in the same fashion are efficient iff there is a nonnegative v-solution to

$$\sum_s h_s v_s \underline{z}_s^j = 1 \quad \forall j, \quad \text{where} \tag{5.C.3a}$$

$$v_s \geq v_{s+1}, \qquad s=1,2,\ldots,S-1, \tag{5.C.3b}$$

$$v_s \geq 0. \tag{5.C.3c}$$

Proof. See Peleg and Yaari (1975a, b) and Dybvig and Ross (1982) for a rigorous development. A sketch of the proof goes as follows. Equation (5.C.3a) corresponds to the optimality condition (5.B.3), with $v_s = \partial V(\underline{w}_s)/\partial \underline{w}_s \geq 0$ being the state s marginal utility (the utility function is scaled such that $\lambda = 1$). For concave utilities, $\underline{w}_s \leq \underline{w}_{s+1}$ implies $v_s \geq v_{s+1}$ for each s, as $V(\cdot)$ is an admissible elementary utility function only when marginal utility is positive and decreasing. With probabilities and the security program given, the only effect of the candidate portfolio $\underline{w}$ on the (5.C.3) conditions is through the ordering of states. Thus, when $\underline{w}$ is optimal and solves those conditions then so must every portfolio with the same ordering of states. □

Our intuition here is helped by writing equation (5.C.3a) in vector matrix form as $\hat{\underline{Z}}v = 1$, where the elements of $\hat{\underline{Z}}$ are $\hat{\underline{z}}_s^j = h_s \underline{z}_s^j$. In the case of complete security markets $\underline{Z}$ has full rank, and so does $\hat{\underline{Z}}$. As a result there is a unique v-solution and the ordering of states by returns is unique: once one efficient portfolio is found, then every efficient portfolio must order returns in the same way. And, corresponding to every portfolio which orders returns in this fashion there is an I2 individual.

In the alternative, incomplete market case there are in general many v-solutions to (5.C.3). For the simplest case of $S=3$ and $J=2$ the valuation equations are

$$\hat{\underline{z}}_1^1 v_1 + \hat{\underline{z}}_2^1 v_2 + \hat{\underline{z}}_3^1 v_3 = 1,$$

$$\hat{\underline{z}}_1^2 v_1 + \hat{\underline{z}}_2^2 v_2 + \hat{\underline{z}}_3^2 v_3 = 1.$$

The v-solution to these equations can be written as

$$v_1=\alpha_0 v_3-\alpha_1,$$

$$v_2=\beta_0 v_3-\beta_1,$$

where the α's and β's depend upon the $\hat{z}_s^j$. If on choosing a positive value for v_3 the resulting v_1 and v_2 are positive, then the ordering of states by the v's represents an ordering of states by wealth in an efficient portfolio (given the state probabilities and security program). Of course, changes in the $\hat{z}_s^j$, and in turn the α's and β's, will generally alter the orderings of the v's which are possible.

The alternative to tests of portfolio efficiency using a comparison of states ordered by returns relies on properties of one portfolio's return distribution which make it more, or less, preferred to another by all I2 individuals. For example, if one portfolio's returns were simply a downward shift of a second in all states, then every individual with increasing utility would prefer the second to the first. Or, if the two portfolios were of the same mean return, but the first had returns 'spread' further from the mean, then risk averse individuals would prefer the second to the first. In both cases, we could eliminate the first from the efficient set. That is roughly the intuition behind the use of 'stochastic dominance' as a test for efficiency.

D5.6. Stochastic dominance.[7] For the security program $\underline{Z}$ consider two portfolios $\underline{w}=\delta\underline{Z}$ and $\underline{w}'=\delta'\underline{Z}$ – both δ and δ' are portfolio fractions. It is said that $\underline{w}$ stochastically dominates $\underline{w}'$, written $\underline{w}D\underline{w}'$, iff

$$EV(\underline{w})\geq EV(\underline{w}')$$

for every I2 individual.

When we hereafter speak of individuals without a specific qualification we shall mean the class of I2 individuals. And, when speaking of preferred portfolios we shall mean preferred by I2 individuals unless there is a specific qualification. (Note that preference here is weak, including indifference.)

[7]Because individuals are here restricted only to be risk averse (I2), this concept is at times referred to as 2nd-order stochastic dominance. General, kth-order stochastic dominance would require individuals be limited to elementary utility functions whose derivatives alternate in sign through the kth derivative. Whitmore (1970), for example, has argued that individuals should be restricted to decreasing absolute risk aversion, which would make 3rd-order stochastic dominance the relevant concept. Less restrictively, Hadar and Russell (1969) have developed rules for 1st-order dominance, requiring only that individuals have positive marginal utility.

Stochastic dominance is an ordering relationship for pairs of consumption portfolios. $\underline{w}\mathrm{D}\underline{w}'$ iff there is no individual who prefers $\underline{w}'$ to $\underline{w}$; therefore, any portfolio which is optimal for some individual cannot be stochastically dominated by any other. It is, however, generally impossible to order all portfolios by stochastic dominance. For example, two portfolios $\underline{w}$ and $\underline{\hat{w}}$ may be such that neither $\underline{w}\mathrm{D}\underline{\hat{w}}$ nor $\underline{\hat{w}}\mathrm{D}\underline{w}$, which is to say that some individual prefers $\underline{w}$ while another prefers $\underline{\hat{w}}$. This does not mean that the two are equivalent in risk and expected return: that would require $\mathrm{E}V(\underline{w})=\mathrm{E}V(\underline{\hat{w}})$ for all individuals. Rather, it simply means that the two portfolios cannot be ordered by stochastic dominance and so the ordering is incomplete.

E5.6. Let there be four states of the world occurring with the probabilities $\mathrm{h}=[0.01\ \ 0.8\ \ 0.1\ \ 0.09]$ and consider the two portfolios:

$$\underline{w}=[0.1\ \ 0.001\ \ 0.1\ \ 0.1], \quad \text{and}$$

$$\underline{w}'=[1.0\ \ 0.01\ \ 0.01\ \ 0.01],$$

with means and variances given by

$$\mathrm{E}\underline{w}=0.0208, \qquad \mathrm{var}(\underline{w})=0.0015, \quad \text{and}$$

$$\mathrm{E}\underline{w}'=0.0199, \qquad \mathrm{var}(\underline{w}')=0.0097.$$

Note that $\underline{w}$ has greater mean and smaller variance, a combination that by the mean-variance maxim makes $\underline{w}$ preferred to $\underline{w}'$ for individuals with quadratic utility and would seem to indicate $\underline{w}\mathrm{D}\underline{w}'$. That, however, is not the case. For example, consider the concave utility function $V(\underline{w}_s)=\log(\underline{w}_s)$ which gives $\mathrm{E}V(\underline{w})=0.133$ and $\mathrm{E}V(\underline{w}')=0.34$. Since this risk averse individual prefers $\underline{w}'$ to $\underline{w}$, then $\underline{w}$ cannot be stochastically dominant. The portfolios cannot be ordered by stochastic dominance, which is to say, neither is dominated. ■

An extremely useful property of the stochastic dominance relationship is its transitivity, that is, if $\underline{w}\mathrm{D}\underline{w}'$ and $\underline{w}'\mathrm{D}\underline{w}''$ then $\underline{w}\mathrm{D}\underline{w}''$. This result follows since $\mathrm{E}V(\underline{w})\geq \mathrm{E}V(\underline{w}')$ and $\mathrm{E}V(\underline{w}')\geq \mathrm{E}V(\underline{w}'')$ jointly imply $\mathrm{E}V(\underline{w})\geq \mathrm{E}V(w'')$ for all I2 individuals.

E5.7. Suppose there are (just) five feasible portfolios $\{\underline{w}_1, \underline{w}_2, \underline{w}_3, \underline{w}_4, \underline{w}_5\}$. Let the portfolios be ranked in preference by all individuals according to one of three patterns:

Preference pattern	
1	$\underline{w}_1$ (>) $\underline{w}_5$ (>) $\underline{w}_2$ (>) $\underline{w}_4$ (>) $\underline{w}_3$,
2	$\underline{w}_2$ (>) $\underline{w}_3$ (>) $\underline{w}_1$ (>) $\underline{w}_5$ (>) $\underline{w}_4$,
3	$\underline{w}_3$ (>) $\underline{w}_1$ (>) $\underline{w}_5$ (>) $\underline{w}_4$ (>) $\underline{w}_2$,

where $\underline{w}^j$ (>) $\underline{w}^k$ indicates portfolio j is strictly preferred to portfolio k. A quick inspection shows optimal portfolios $\underline{w}_1$, $\underline{w}_2$ and $\underline{w}_3$ are not stochastically dominated, and portfolios $\underline{w}_4$ and $\underline{w}_5$ (which are not optimal) are dominated ($\underline{w}_1 \mathrm{D} \underline{w}_5$ and $\underline{w}_5 \mathrm{D} \underline{w}_4$). Does 'not dominated' therefore mean optimal?

Not necessarily, as the following, alternative pattern of preferences indicates:

Preference pattern	
1	$\underline{w}_1$ (>) $\underline{w}_5$ (>) $\underline{w}_2$ (>) $\underline{w}_3$ (>) $\underline{w}_4$,
2	$\underline{w}_2$ (>) $\underline{w}_5$ (>) $\underline{w}_4$ (>) $\underline{w}_3$ (>) $\underline{w}_1$,
3	$\underline{w}_3$ (>) $\underline{w}_5$ (>) $\underline{w}_1$ (>) $\underline{w}_4$ (>) $\underline{w}_2$.

Now $\underline{w}_5 \mathrm{D} \underline{w}_4$ and that is the only dominance relationship. Note particularly that, while not optimal, $\underline{w}_5$ is 'not dominated'. Thus, not being dominated by any other feasible portfolio is a necessary condition for portfolio efficiency, but it is not a sufficient condition. ■

Finally, observe that the transitivity of the stochastic dominance ordering should not be understood to mean that each efficient portfolio stochastically dominates every inefficient portfolio. Because of the incompleteness of the ordering it might, for example, be that $\underline{w}_1 \mathrm{D} \underline{w}_2$, $\underline{w}_2 \mathrm{D} \underline{w}_3$, $\underline{w}_4 \mathrm{D} \underline{w}_5$, $\underline{w}_4 \mathrm{D} \underline{w}_3$. If these were the only feasible portfolios and only dominance relationships, then $\underline{w}_1$ and $\underline{w}_4$ are candidate efficient portfolios, even though $\underline{w}_1$ does not dominate inefficient portfolio $\underline{w}_5$ nor does $\underline{w}_4$ dominate the inefficient $\underline{w}_2$.

5.C.4. Dominance criteria

A set of conditions necessary and sufficient for one portfolio to stochastically dominate any other is termed a *dominance criterion*. Such a criterion can (in principle) be applied pairwise to all feasible portfolios to determine those not dominated by any other. And, as noted above, a necessary condition for portfolio efficiency is that the candidate portfolio not be dominated in any such comparison.

Two dominance criteria are known. The first is particularly useful in empirical work, while the second is relatively more important in theoretical analysis. Even though the form of these criteria differ substantially, do not be mislead: being both necessary and sufficient conditions for stochastic dominance, they are equivalent in all essential regards.

P5.3a. Dominance criterion I. Let $\underline{w}, \underline{w}' \in \theta(\underline{Z})$ be two portfolios with associated probability density functions f and f', respectively, and denote by $y_1, y_2, \ldots, y_N$ the increasing sequence of returns where f_n and/or f'_n have a non-zero probability. Then, a necessary and sufficient condition for $\underline{w}\mathrm{D}\underline{w}'$ is:

$$K = \sum_{n=1}^{N-1} (y_{n+1} - y_n) \sum_{m=1}^{n} (f'_m - f_m) \geq 0 \quad \forall k \geq 2. \tag{5.C.4}$$

With F the cumulative density function associated with f, and similarly for F' and f', the proposition states that $\underline{w}\mathrm{D}\underline{w}'$ iff the *accumulated area* under the *cumulative* density function F' is not less than the area under F for any possible return level $y_k (k \geq 2)$. The reader is referred to Hanoch and Levy (1969) or Hadar and Russell (1969) for proof.[8]

E5.8. Let individuals be I2, but not otherwise restricted. Suppose there to be six possible states occurring with probabilities $h = [0.65\ 0.03\ 0.11\ 0.10\ 0.10\ 0.01]$ and consider two portfolios

$$\underline{w} = [0\ 1\ 1\ 1\ 2\ 1], \quad \text{and}$$
$$\underline{w}' = [0\ 1\ 0\ 0\ 2\ 2].$$

The following table results.

$\underline{w}, \underline{w}'$	f	f'	F	F'	$F'-F'$	K
0	0.65	0.86	0.65	0.86	0.21	0
1	0.25	0.03	0.90	0.89	−0.01	0.21
2	0.10	0.11	1.00	1.00	0	0.20

[8] Let $K = \mathrm{E}V(\underline{w}) - \mathrm{E}V(\underline{w}')$, the difference in expected utilities for $\underline{w}$ and $\underline{w}'$. For the case where probability densities are continuous, then $K = \int_a^b V(t)\mathrm{d}F(t) - \int_a^b V(t)\mathrm{d}F'(t)$ with a and b, respectively, the lower and upper bound on portfolio returns. Integrating twice by parts and using the non-negative signs of the first and second derivatives of V provides the sufficiency result.

As the (5.C.4) test expression K is everywhere non-negative we have the result $\underline{w}D\underline{w}'$. Note, however, that $E\underline{w}=0.45>E\underline{w}'=0.25$ and $\text{var}(\underline{w})=0.4475>\text{var}(\underline{w}')=0.407$. Even though the mean *and* variance of $\underline{w}$ is greater than that of $\underline{w}'$ it is possible to find $\underline{w}D\underline{w}'$. The utility of incremental mean (and other moment differences) must more than offset the disutility of the incremental variance (and other moment differences) in this case. Portfolio w' cannot be efficient. ■

From the statement of the dominance criterion and the above example it is clear that if stochastic dominance and the efficient set are to provide a useful reduction of the opportunity set, then there must be some restriction on the assignment of state probabilities by individuals. That is, when individuals are allowed to differ in their (subjective) estimates of probabilities, we can generally cause any portfolio to dominate any other. As a result every feasible portfolio would be potentially optimal and the efficient set could be no different from the overall opportunity set. Because it is possible to get such 'non-results' by allowing full freedom in the specification of probability assessments, it is usual to require, as in the specification of I2 individuals, that probability assessments are homogeneous.[9]

Consider now two portfolios with rectangular distributions: $\underline{w}$ has a constant probability density in the range $\underline{w}_a \leq w_s \leq w_b$, and $\underline{w}'$ has a constant density in the range $\underline{w}'_a \leq w'_s \leq \underline{w}'_b$. When $\underline{w}_a > \underline{w}'_a$ and $\underline{w}_b > w'_b$, then $\underline{w}$ is strictly preferred to $\underline{w}'$ for all non-decreasing utility functions. Or, when $E\underline{w}=E\underline{w}'$ with $\underline{w}_a > \underline{w}'_a$ and $\underline{w}_b < w'_b$ then strictly risk averse individuals will again strictly prefer $\underline{w}$ to $\underline{w}'$. These cases are intuitive and this intuition is part of the second criterion for stochastic dominance.

P5.3b. Dominance criterion II. Let $\underline{w}, \underline{w}' \in \theta(\underline{Z})$ be two distinct portfolios. Then $\underline{w}D\underline{w}'$ iff there exist two S-vectors (alternatively, two random variables) η and ℓ such that

$$\underline{w}' \cong \underline{w} + \ell + \eta, \tag{5.C.5}$$

where $\cong$ indicates equality in distribution across states, $\ell \leq 0$ has only non-positive elements, and η has the noise property $E(\eta)=E(\eta \mid \underline{w}+\ell)=0$.[10]

[9]There is one further consideration: to make the theory testable without a complex model of individual learning, it is generally assumed that these probabilities are objective in the sense that they are consistent with the probability distribution which would obtain if the economy were subject to a large number of trials.

[10]When the variance of η is strictly positive and ℓ has at least one strictly negative element, then $\underline{w}$ is strictly preferred to $\underline{w}'$ by all I2 individuals and the stochastic dominance is said to be *strong*.

Proof. The sufficiency of (5.C.5) is obvious: shifting returns downward and adding noise surely make any portfolio less preferred for every increasing, concave utility. As the proof of necessity is lengthy and technically complex, the reader is referred to Strassen (1967), Brunelle and Vickson (1975), and Ross (1976). □

When specifically choosing $\ell = \mathrm{E}\underline{w}'1_S - \mathrm{E}\underline{w}1_S$, which is admissible only when $\mathrm{E}\underline{w} > \mathrm{E}\underline{w}'$, then (5.C.5) can be rewritten as

$$S\underline{w}' = S\underline{w} + \eta,$$

where $S\underline{w} = \underline{w} - \mathrm{E}\underline{w}1_S$ is usually termed the *spread* of $\underline{w}$ and similarly for $\underline{w}'$. That is, portfolio $\underline{w}'$ is dominated by portfolio $\underline{w}$ if $\mathrm{E}\underline{w} \geq \mathrm{E}\underline{w}'$ and the spread of $\underline{w}$ is equal to that of $\underline{w}'$ plus noise.

E5.9. Let there be three states of nature occurring with probabilities $h_1 = 0.4$, $h_2 = 0.2$, and $h_3 = 0.4$. Consider the three portfolios

$$\underline{w}^1 = [3 \quad 6 \quad 3],$$

$$\underline{w}^2 = [2 \quad 6 \quad 4],$$

$$\underline{w}^3 = [1 \quad 5 \quad 3].$$

The following dominance relationships can be verified:

(a) $\underline{w}^1 \mathrm{D} \underline{w}^2$ since $\underline{w}^2 = \underline{w}^1 + \eta$ where $\eta = [-1 \quad 0 \quad 1]$ and $\mathrm{E}(\eta) = \mathrm{E}(\eta \mid \underline{w}^1) = 0$, and

(b) $\underline{w}^1 \mathrm{D} \underline{w}^3$ since $\underline{w}^3 = \underline{w}^1 - 1_S + \eta$ where again $\eta = [-1 \quad 0 \quad 1]$ and $\mathrm{E}(\eta) = \mathrm{E}(\eta \mid \underline{w}^1 + 1_S) = 0$.

Thus neither $\underline{w}^2$ nor $\underline{w}^3$ can be efficient portfolios. ■

5.D. *Efficiency and the Riskless Portfolio*

Suppose, as is usual, that the riskless portfolio is feasible. Although not efficient, this is a portfolio of importance beyond most others. There are several reasons for this. The first has two parts: (a) the riskless rate of return establishes a lower bound to the expected return on efficient portfolios, and (b) every portfolio made up of the riskless portfolio and strictly positive amounts of an efficient portfolio is also efficient. In addition, the riskless portfolio is observable (at least more so than most theoretical constructs in the non-experimental social sciences) and therefore a preferred element in an empirical statement of a theory of security price. While it is difficult to make these arguments for importance convincing at this juncture, it will be clear as we proceed. That leaves us here only to prove the above (a) and (b) assertions.

P5.4. Lower bound on efficient portfolio expected return. Let $\rho \in \theta(\underline{Z})$ and $\underline{\mathring{w}} \in \theta^{\circ}(\underline{Z})$, then $\mathrm{E}\underline{\mathring{w}} > \mathrm{E}\rho$ given that $\underline{\mathring{w}}$ is risky.

Proof. When $\underline{\mathring{w}}$ is riskless then $\mathrm{E}\underline{\mathring{w}} = \mathrm{E}\rho$ (given arbitrage gains are absent). In the alternative case, where $\underline{\mathring{w}}$ has uncertain returns, we can write $S\underline{\mathring{w}} = S\rho + \eta = \eta$ where η is noise. This condition plus the expected return requirement $\mathrm{E}\rho \geq \mathrm{E}\underline{\mathring{w}}$ would imply $\ell \leq 0$ and, by (5.C.5), $\rho \mathrm{D} \mathring{w}$. But $\underline{\mathring{w}}$ is efficient and cannot be dominated, therefore $\mathrm{E}\underline{\mathring{w}} > \mathrm{E}\rho$. □

When an I2 individual takes a risky portfolio as optimal its expected rate of return must be greater than the riskless rate. This suggests there is a premium received for the 'risk' taken. How to characterize the risk and price of risk to specify the premium? That comes later.

P5.5. Inefficiency of the riskless portfolio. The riskless portfolio is efficient iff $\underline{Z}$ is such that $\mathrm{E}\underline{z}^j = \mathrm{E}\rho\ \forall j$.

Note that $\mathrm{E}\underline{z}^j = \mathrm{E}\rho\ \forall j$ implies $\mathrm{E}\underline{w} = \mathrm{E}\rho$ for all $\underline{w} \in \theta(\underline{Z})$. That is, if the mean yield of *each* security equals $\mathrm{E}\rho$, then all feasible portfolios must also have mean return equal to $\mathrm{E}\rho$.

Proof. From (5.B.3) the optimal portfolio $\underline{\mathring{w}}$ is seen to solve $\mathrm{E}[V'(\underline{\mathring{w}})(\underline{z}^j - \rho)] = 0\ \forall j$ when $\rho \in \theta(\underline{Z})$. To prove sufficiency let $\mathrm{E}\underline{z}^j = \mathrm{E}\rho\ \forall j$, so that all portfolios have mean return equal to $\mathrm{E}\rho$. In this case $\mathring{w} = \rho$ solves the stationarity conditions, and by the strict concavity of V this solution will be unique. To prove necessity, let $\mathring{w} = \rho$ be the optimal solution. In this case the stationarity condition becomes $V'(\mathrm{E}\rho)\mathrm{E}(\underline{z}^j - \rho) = 0$ for all j – as ρ is not random $\mathrm{E}V'(\rho) = V'(\mathrm{E}\rho)$. Therefore $\mathrm{E}\underline{z}^j = \mathrm{E}\rho$ is necessary for $\mathring{w} = \rho$ to be optimal. □

The riskless portfolio (when it exists) will be optimal for I2 individuals only when all securities, and thus all portfolios, have the same mean return equal to the riskless rate. Because this requires the security program to be quite specialized, it is dismissed as a perverse case. Thus, when speaking of an optimal portfolio, and when the symbol $\mathring{\underline{w}}$ is used, we shall mean portfolios having risky returns. That, however, does not mean the riskless portfolio can be ignored, for it is a useful 'building block' in the construction of optimal portfolios.

P5.6. The Riskless portfolio in portfolio. Every portfolio formed using the riskless portfolio and an efficient portfolio in the manner $\underline{w} = \delta\mathring{\underline{w}} + (1-\delta)\rho$ is efficient when $\delta > 0$.

Proof. We proceed by showing that every portfolio $\underline{w} = \delta\mathring{\underline{w}} + (1-\delta)\rho$ with $\delta > 0$ is optimal for some I2 individual. Because $\mathring{\underline{w}}$ is efficient, there exists an I2 individual such that $\mathrm{E}[V'(\mathring{\underline{w}})(\underline{z}^j - \rho)] = 0\ \forall j$, see (5.B.3). Next consider a second utility function defined by $\mathrm{E}\hat{V}(\underline{w}) = \mathrm{E}V[\mathring{\underline{w}}/\delta + \rho(\delta - 1)]/\delta$. When $\delta > 0$, $\mathrm{E}\hat{V}$ is, because of similar properties of $\mathrm{E}V$, monotone increasing and strictly concave. In addition, the marginal utilities are related in the fashion $\mathrm{E}V'(\mathring{\underline{w}}) = \delta \mathrm{E}\hat{V}'(\underline{w})$, which means that the stationarity conditions of $\mathring{\underline{w}}$ with $\mathrm{E}V$ imply $\mathrm{E}[\hat{V}'(\underline{w})(\underline{z}^j - \rho)] = 0\ \forall j$. That is, $\underline{w}$ is optimal for $\hat{V}$ and therefore efficient. □

It is important to remark that this proposition does not mean that the efficient set is convex. That stronger conclusion would require convex combinations of every pair of efficient portfolios be efficient, rather than the limited case which requires only that all convex combinations of any efficient portfolio with ρ be efficient. But, while on the subject, are there reasonable conditions leading to such convexity?

5.E. Efficient Set Convexity

That $\theta^\circ(\underline{Z})$ is not necessarily convex can be shown by use of a counter-example.[11] Consider an economy with 4 equiprobable states and 3 securities and a security program given by

$$\underline{Z} = \begin{bmatrix} 1.65 & 2.05 & 1.80 \\ 1.10 & 1.30 & 1.20 \\ 1.30 & 0.95 & 1.20 \\ 1.25 & 1.25 & 1.20 \end{bmatrix}.$$

[11] See Dybvig and Ross (1982).

Think now of two I2 individuals (a and b) and two monotone increasing, concave elementary utility functions having marginal utilities

$$V'^a(1.65)=0.1, \qquad V'^b(2.05)=2.1,$$
$$V'^a(1.30)=4.0, \qquad V'^b(1.30)=2.8,$$
$$V'^a(1.25)=5.9, \qquad V'^b(1.25)=3.9,$$
$$V'^a(1.10)=6.8, \qquad V'^b(0.95)=4.0.$$

These marginal utilities would occur if individual a held the portfolio fractions $\delta^a=[1 \ \ 0 \ \ 0]$ and b held $\delta^b=[0 \ \ 1 \ \ 0]$; that is, individual a held only security one and b held only security two. It is a straightforward task to prove that these are, respectively, optimal portfolios for the individuals. This is shown using the optimality conditions (5.B.3a), which we repeat here:

$$\mathrm{E}[V'(\underline{w}_s)\underline{z}_s^j]=\lambda \quad \forall j.$$

For individual a these equations become:

$$\tfrac{1}{4}[0.1(1.65)+6.8(1.10)+4.0(1.30)+5.9(1.25)]=5.055,$$

$$\tfrac{1}{4}[0.1(2.05)+6.8(1.30)+4.0(0.95)+5.9(1.25)]=5.055,$$

$$\tfrac{1}{4}[0.1(1.80)+6.8(1.20)+4.0(1.20)+5.9(1.20)]=5.055.$$

A similar check verifies that δ^b is optimal for individual b.

Since the portfolios $\underline{w}^a=\delta^a\underline{Z}$ and $\underline{w}^b=\delta^b\underline{Z}$ are optimal for these two individuals, they are also efficient portfolios. If the efficient set is convex then all convex combinations of $\underline{w}^a$ and $\underline{w}^b$ must also be efficient. For example, the portfolio $\underline{w}^c=\frac{1}{2}\underline{w}^a+\frac{1}{2}\underline{w}^b$, which has returns

$$\underline{w}^c=[1.85 \quad 1.20 \quad 1.125 \quad 1.25],$$

would be efficient if $\theta^\circ(\underline{Z})$ were a convex set. As a check on the efficiency of $\underline{w}^c$ consider the portfolio fractions $\delta^*=[-1 \ \ -0.4 \ \ 2.4]$ and associated portfolio $\underline{w}^*=\delta^*\underline{Z}=[1.85 \ 1.25 \ 1.20 \ 1.13]$. Since the states are equiprobable and utility is state independent, every individual is indifferent to the order of returns across states and we can permutate these returns to give

$$\mathrm{E}V(\underline{w}^*)=\mathrm{E}V([1.85 \quad 1.20 \quad 1.13 \quad 1.25]).$$

Note now that with increasing utility

$$EV(\underline{w}^*) > EV(\underline{w}^c),$$

which means that $\underline{w}^c$ cannot be efficient. As a convex combination of efficient portfolios has been shown inefficient, the efficient set is here not convex.

While the above example shows that the efficient set is in general not convex there are two empirically important cases in which such convexity does occur.[12] One instance is when security markets are complete, as is shown first.

5.E.1. Complete markets

Recall P5.2, where it is shown that in complete markets all efficient portfolios have returns across states ordered in the same fashion. This, of course, means that the optimal portfolios of all individuals are similarly ordered in return across states, and this is the basis for the following proposition.

P5.7. Efficient set convexity with complete markets. Let individuals be I2 and let the security market be complete. Then the efficient set $\theta^{\circ}(\underline{Z})$ is convex.

Proof. Let $\underline{w}^1$ and $\underline{w}^2$ indicate any two efficient portfolios and consider the portfolio $\underline{w}^* = \alpha \underline{w}^1 + (1-\alpha)\underline{w}^2$ with $0 < \alpha < 1$. As both $\underline{w}^1$ and $\underline{w}^2$ are efficient then

$$\underline{w}_s^1 \leq \underline{w}_{s+1}^1 \quad \text{and} \quad \underline{w}_s^2 \leq \underline{w}_{s+1}^2 \tag{5.E.1}$$

for all s. And, as $\underline{w}^*$ is a convex combination of $\underline{w}^1$ and $\underline{w}^2$, then

$$\alpha \underline{w}_s^1 + (1-\alpha)\underline{w}_s^2 \leq \alpha \underline{w}_{s+1}^1 + (1-\alpha)\underline{w}_s^2, \quad \text{or} \tag{5.E.2a}$$

$$\underline{w}_s^* \leq \underline{w}_{s+1}^*. \tag{5.E.2b}$$

This last inequality implies that returns are ordered in portfolio $\underline{w}^*$ the same as in the two efficient portfolios, which means that $\underline{w}^*$ too is efficient (see P5.2). □

[12] Dybvig and Ross (1982) have also shown the efficient set is convex when there are less than three linearly independent securities or less than four states, which is a case of pedagogic importance.

5.E.2. Mean-variance efficiency

A second interesting case where the efficient set is convex occurs when individuals choose their optimal portfolios only on the basis of mean and variance. We work our way to this result in a somewhat indirect, but instructive, fashion.

D5.7. Mean-variance efficient set. Define the set of portfolios

$$\theta^e(\underline{Z})=\{\overset{e}{\underline{w}}\in\theta(\underline{Z})|\overset{e}{\underline{w}}\text{ solves min var}(\underline{w})\text{ for all E}\underline{w}>\rho\}$$

as the mean-variance efficient set. Let $\overset{e}{\underline{w}}$ represent a typical element of $\theta^e(\underline{Z})$.

As an aside we note that mean-variance (M-V) efficient portfolios have well-defined rules for construction – rules which are applicable for all specifications of $\underline{Z}$ providing only that all means and variances are finite. More to the present concern is the fact is that the M-V efficient set is the collection of optimal portfolios for individuals with mean-variance equivalent preferences.

P5.8. Mean-variance equivalent preferences and the efficient set. The mean-variance efficient set is exactly the efficient set when all individuals are restricted to mean-variance equivalent preferences.

Proof. Suppose that elementary utility functions or security returns are such that expected utility can be expressed as

$$\mathrm{E}V(\underline{w})=g(\mathrm{E}\underline{w},\,\mathrm{var}(\underline{w})), \tag{5.E.3}$$

with $g_1\equiv\partial v/\partial\mathrm{E}\underline{w}>0$, $\partial^2 v/\partial\mathrm{E}\underline{w}\partial\mathrm{E}\underline{w}<0$, and $g_2\equiv\partial v/\partial\,\mathrm{var}(\underline{w})<0$. Ignoring redundant securities, let $\underline{w}=\delta\underline{Z}$ and denote $\mathrm{E}\underline{z}$ as the J vector of expected security returns and $\underline{\mathit{Z}}$ as the (negative definite) $J\times J$ variance–covariance matrix of those returns. Under these conditions the utility maximization problem with mean-variance equivalent preference is written as the choice of portfolio fractions:

$$\max_{\delta} g(\langle\delta,\mathrm{E}\underline{z}\rangle,\delta\underline{\mathit{Z}}\delta)\quad\text{s.t.}\quad\langle\delta,1_J\rangle=1.$$

Stationarity conditions are, in part,

$$g_1\mathrm{E}\underline{z}+g_2\underline{\mathit{Z}}\delta+\gamma 1_J=0,$$

which we write as

$$\lambda \mathrm{E}\underline{z} - \underline{Z}\delta + \zeta 1_J = 0, \tag{5.E.4}$$

where $\lambda = g_1/g_2$ is the rate of substitution of mean per unit variance and $\zeta = \gamma/g_2$ is the rate of substitution of investment wealth (foregone initial period consumption) per unit variance.

By the obvious calculations it can be shown that equation (5.E.4) corresponds exactly to the solution of the problem which, treating expected return parametrically, generates $\theta^e(\underline{Z})$:

$$\min \operatorname{var}(\underline{w}) \quad \text{s.t.} \quad \mathrm{E}\underline{w} = k, \ \underline{w} = \delta\underline{Z}, \quad \text{and} \quad \delta 1_J = 1, \tag{5.E.5}$$

where $k > \mathrm{E}\rho$ is a continuously variable parameter. By the choice of the utility function parameters a and b, see equation (5.E.3), the marginal rates of substitution λ and ζ at the solution of (5.E.4) can be made to take on values equal to the Lagrange multipliers at the solution of the minimum variance problem (5.E.5). Thus, to each $\mathring{\underline{w}}$ solution of (5.E.5) there corresponds an individual with mean-variance equivalent preferences for whom $\mathring{\underline{w}}$ solves (5.E.4) and conversely.[13] □

It is from an intermediate step in the above problem that the efficient set convexity result can be shown.

P5.9. Convexity of the M-V efficient set. The *M-V* efficient set is convex.

Proof. Solve (5.E.4) for the portfolio fractions δ to yield

$$\delta = \lambda(\underline{Z}^{-1}\mathrm{E}\underline{z}) + \zeta(\underline{Z}^{-1} 1_J), \tag{5.E.6}$$

where λ and ζ are rates of substitution as noted in the proof to P5.8. There it was also shown that corresponding to any pair (λ, ζ) there is an individual with mean-variance equivalent utility. And, from the optimality condition (5.E.6) it is seen that every set of optimal portfolio fractions is written as a weighted sum of two identical vectors $\underline{Z}^{-1}\mathrm{E}\underline{z}$ and $\underline{Z}^{-1}1_J$. Thus convex combinations of any two efficient portfolios must also be a weighted sum of the same two vectors, yielding rates of substitution λ and ζ which correspond to the optimal portfolio fractions of some quadratic utility func-

[13] If a riskless security exists let it be $\underline{z}^0$. In turn, write the returns of each security j in excess return form $\underline{z}^{j\cdot} = \underline{z}^j - \underline{z}^0$. Let $\delta^0 = 1 - \Sigma_j \delta^j$ and then normalize $\delta^1, \delta^2, \ldots, \delta^J$ to form a portfolio of risky securities. In this case then interpret $\underline{Z}$ to be the matrix of *excess* security returns in the above analysis.

tion. With a given security program each $\underline{w}$ is a linear transformation of δ and therefore the portfolio set $\theta^e(\underline{Z})$ corresponding to the convex portfolio fraction set must also be convex. □

5.E.3. The market portfolio

Of special importance when the efficient set is convex is the portfolio of all securities in which each security is weighted in proportion to its market value relative to the value of all securities.

D5.8. Market portfolio. Let $\overset{*}{\delta}=[\overset{*}{\delta}_1\,\overset{*}{\delta}_2\ldots\overset{*}{\delta}_J]$ be portfolio fractions such that $\overset{*}{\delta}_j=v_0^j/\Sigma_\ell v_0^\ell\ \forall j$ and $\ell=1,2,\ldots,J$. The associated portfolio $\overset{*}{\underline{w}}=\overset{*}{\delta}\underline{Z}$ is called the market portfolio.

A key aspect of the market portfolio is its value in empirical analysis: the list of security fractions can be simply calculated from observable market data, the security prices. In particular, the construction of $\overset{*}{\underline{w}}$ does *not* require specific knowledge of individual preferences, probability estimates of state occurrences, the allocation of wealth across individuals, or any detailed property (other than market prices) of the security program.

E5.10. Suppose the security program is given by the S × J matrix

$$\underline{Z}=\begin{bmatrix}1.1 & 1.2 & 1.15\\ 0.9 & 0.8 & 0.85\\ 1.3 & 1.6 & 1.45\end{bmatrix}$$

and security prices are $v_0^1=15$, $v_0^2=21$, and $v_0^3=18$. Then the market portfolio weights are calculated as

$$\delta_1^*=\tfrac{15}{54}=\tfrac{5}{18},$$
$$\delta_2^*=\tfrac{21}{54}=\tfrac{7}{18},$$
$$\delta_3^*=\tfrac{18}{54}=\tfrac{6}{18}.$$

In turn, the market portfolio return is $\overset{*}{\underline{w}}=\overset{*}{\delta}Z=[1.15\ 0.83\ 1.47]$. With state probabilities $h_1=0.2$, $h_2=0.4$, and $h_3=0.4$ then $\mathrm{E}\overset{*}{\underline{w}}=1.156$, which is a 15.6% expected return. ■

A second useful property of the market portfolio in empirical work is the lower bound that can be placed on its expected return.

P5.10. Expected return of the market portfolio. Let the security market be in equilibrium with price system v_0 and the security program $\underline{Z}$. Then, the market portfolio and riskless asset are such that $\mathrm{E}\overset{*}{\underline{w}} > \mathrm{E}\rho$.

Proof. Let the ith individual's optimal portfolio at equilibrium prices v_0 be given by $\overset{\circ}{\underline{w}}{}^i = \Sigma_j \overset{\circ}{\delta}{}^i_j \underline{z}^j$, where $\overset{\circ}{\delta} = [\overset{\circ}{\delta}{}^i_1\ \overset{\circ}{\delta}{}^i_2 \ldots \overset{\circ}{\delta}{}^i_J]$ are the optimal portfolio fractions. The scalar $\lambda^i = \bar{w}^i / \Sigma_i \bar{w}^i$ indicates the fraction of aggregate investment wealth possessed by i – note that $0 \leq \lambda^i \leq 1$ and $\Sigma_i \lambda^i = 1$. Next, multiply $\overset{\circ}{\underline{w}}{}^i$ by λ^i and sum over all individuals to obtain

$$\sum_i \lambda^i \overset{\circ}{\underline{w}}{}^i = \sum_i \lambda^i \sum_j \overset{\circ}{\delta}{}^i_j \underline{z}^j = \sum_j \underline{z}^j \sum_i \overset{\circ}{\delta}{}^i_j \left(\bar{w}^i \Big/ \sum_i \bar{w}^i \right). \tag{5.E.7}$$

In exchange equilibrium it is required that $\Sigma_i \overset{\circ}{\delta}{}^i_j \bar{w}^i = v_0^j$ and $\Sigma_i \bar{w}^i = \Sigma_j v_0^j$. This implies

$$\sum_i \lambda^i \overset{\circ}{\underline{w}}{}^i = \sum_j \underline{z}^j \left[v_0^j \Big/ \sum_k v_0^k \right] = \sum_j \overset{*}{\delta}_j \underline{z}^j = \overset{*}{\underline{w}}. \tag{5.E.8}$$

As each $\overset{\circ}{\underline{w}}{}^i$ is efficient, then $\mathrm{E}\overset{\circ}{\underline{w}}{}^i \geq \mathrm{E}\overset{*}{\underline{w}}$ for each i and therefore $\mathrm{E}\overset{*}{\underline{w}} = \Sigma_i \lambda^i \mathrm{E}\overset{\circ}{\underline{w}}{}^i > \mathrm{E}\rho$ (by the fact that the λ^i weights are convex). When individuals differ then $\overset{\circ}{\underline{w}}{}^i \neq \overset{\circ}{\underline{w}}{}^n$ and the strict inequality holds generally as $\mathrm{E}\overset{\circ}{\underline{w}}{}^i > \mathrm{E}\overset{*}{\underline{w}}$ for some i. □

While the market portfolio can be written as a convex combination of efficient portfolios, it must be emphasized that P5.10 does *not* imply that $\overset{*}{\underline{w}}$ is efficient. Nor does the fact that all efficient portfolios have an expected return greater than ρ (see P5.4) allow us to conclude that $\overset{*}{\underline{w}}$ is efficient. That result does follow, however, when the efficient set is convex.

P5.11. Efficiency of the market portfolio. Let the security market be in exchange equilibrium and the efficient set $\theta^\circ(\underline{Z})$ be convex. Then, the market portfolio is efficient.

Notice that the convexity of $\theta^\circ(\underline{Z})$ and the presence of an exchange equilibrium are sufficient conditions for $\overset{*}{\underline{w}}$ to be an efficient portfolio; importantly, the proposition does not state that these are necessary conditions.

Proof. Trivial, since an exchange equilibrium assures (5.E.8). □

E5.11. On occasion the market portfolio is defined somewhat differently, as a market portfolio of only *risky* securities. This second definition derives in a straightforward way from that of $\underset{\sim}{\overset{*}{w}}$. Consider some efficient portfolio written as a portfolio of $\underset{\sim}{\overset{*}{w}}$ and ρ as follows: $\underset{\sim}{\overset{\circ}{w}}=\delta\underset{\sim}{\overset{*}{w}}+(1-\delta)\rho$. As a convenience we assume the riskless portfolio is the output of firm 1 and write, for $0<\gamma\leq 1$,

$$\begin{aligned}\underset{\sim}{\overset{\circ}{w}}&=\gamma\underset{\sim}{\overset{*}{w}}+(1-\gamma)\underset{\sim}{z}^1\\&=\gamma\sum_{j=2}\overset{*}{\delta}_j\underset{\sim}{z}^j+[(1-\gamma)+\gamma\overset{*}{\delta}_1]\underset{\sim}{z}^1.\end{aligned}$$

Next, normalize the $\overset{*}{\delta}_j$ $\forall j\geq 2$ to be portfolio fractions of the $J-1$ risky securities, i.e., choose

$$\delta^{**}_j=\overset{*}{\delta}{}^j\Big/\sum_{k=2}\overset{*}{\delta}_k=\overset{*}{\delta}_j/(1-\overset{*}{\delta}_1)\quad\forall j>2$$

so that $\Sigma_{j=2}\delta^{**}_j=1$. (Since by definition $1\geq\overset{*}{\delta}_j\geq 0$ for all $j=1,2,\ldots,J$ then $1>\delta^{**}_j\geq 0$). Now write

$$\begin{aligned}\underset{\sim}{\overset{\circ}{w}}&=\gamma(1-\overset{*}{\delta}_1)\sum_{j=2}\delta^{**}_j\underset{\sim}{z}^j+[1-\gamma(1-\overset{*}{\delta}_1)]\underset{\sim}{z}^1\\&=\gamma(1-\overset{*}{\delta}_1)\underset{\sim}{\overset{**}{w}}+[1-\gamma(1-\overset{*}{\delta}_1)]\rho,\end{aligned}$$

where $\underset{\sim}{\overset{**}{w}}=\Sigma_{j=2}\delta^{**}_j\underset{\sim}{z}^j$ is the 'risky market portfolio.' Each efficient portfolio is in turn seen to be a convex combination of $\underset{\sim}{\overset{**}{w}}$ and ρ – note that as necessary $1\geq\gamma(1-\overset{*}{\delta}_1)>0$, for $1\geq\gamma>0$ and $1\geq\overset{*}{\delta}_1\geq 0$. (It is also easy to show from the above expression that $E\underset{\sim}{\overset{**}{w}}>E\rho$, see P5.10.) ■

5.F. *Trading-off Mean and Spread*

The properties of $\theta^\circ(Z)$ established in this Chapter are useful, but they are not very extensive. While it would be nice if a robust theory of security demand and price could be developed on this limited basis, such results are not available. The answer to this insufficiency is obvious. Restrictions of some kind must be placed on the formulation of the theory in a way that allows the mean and risk trade-off to be measured explicitly and without undue data requirements. At a minimum the restrictions should provide for a way to measure all demand relevant characteristics of portfolios in a way that determines the prices for the characteristics by the operation of the appropriate markets and, simultaneously, allows the prices and characteristics themselves to be observed.

With the organization of conventional security markets given, we have already noted that the restrictions necessary to produce a useful theory are of two basic kinds: those concerned with the admissible class of individual utility functions (a limitation to some subset of I2 individuals) and/or those concerned with special properties of the security program $\underline{Z}$. The particular restrictions on utility functions and security returns that have been found to be most successful are those which result in a 'spanning' property for the efficient set. That is, they provide that all efficient portfolios are capable of being formed from only a few intermediate portfolios. The following several chapters are concerned with the nature of this particular kind of restriction (and especially the implications it has for the comparative statics of optimal consumption), for the prices of securities in market equilibrium, and, more generally, for the demand and supply behavior of individuals.

Chapter 6

LINEAR PRICING

It is at times useful to think of the opportunity set $\theta(\underline{Z})$ geometrically, as a subspace in an S-dimensional state space. Viewed in this way, a question which comes immediately to mind is whether or not some set of vectors smaller in number than the J original security vectors can generate that subspace. That is an interesting question, for under such conditions it would then be possible to formulate the individual's choice problem in terms of this smaller set of generating vectors. As one suspects, the ideas to be applied in this case are those similar to vector space spanning in linear algebra. In this analysis we do not restrict the spanning vectors to the underlying securities themselves, but instead employ the concept of a mutual fund.

D6.1. Mutual fund. A mutual fund is a financial intermediary whose only assets are securities of firms engaged in production and whose only liabilities are securities issued against these holdings. Further, the mutual fund performs this intermediation in a costless way.

It is to be stressed that the market value of securities issued by any mutual fund exactly equals the market value of the security portfolio it holds: this equality occurs as there are no fees or other drains involved in such intermediation (consistent with the continuing assumption of perfect markets). Specifically, when δ_j is the fraction of firm j's shares held by some mutual fund k, then $m^k = \Sigma_j \delta_j \underline{z}^j$ is the fund's state contingent return vector.[1] In turn, $v_0^k = \Sigma_j \delta_j v_0^j$ is both the value of the shares the fund holds *and* issues. Obviously, mutual funds are simply security portfolios. Why then introduce the terminology? A combination of notational ease, convenience of reference, and common usage are involved in the answer. Mainly, however, it is to provide an institutional setting for some of the discussion and to avoid problems of knowing which portfolio is being referred to when speaking of portfolios of portfolios.

[1]The organization of exchange and notation throughout this chapter and the next are the same as in Chapter 5.

6.A. Mutual Fund Spanning

A collection of mutual funds $M^K = [m^1\, m^2 \ldots m^K]$ is said to *span the portfolio opportunity set*[2] $\theta(\underline{Z})$ iff (i) $m^k \in \theta(\underline{Z})$ for all $k = 1, 2, \ldots, K$ and (ii) every $\underline{w} \in \theta(\underline{Z})$ can be written as a portfolio of these funds.[3] Perhaps the most obvious collection of spanning mutual funds is the J original securities themselves, in which case the number of spanning funds is $K = J$. From this it is seen that there will be non-trivial spanning of $\theta(\underline{Z})$ only when redundant securities exist; i.e., when the security program yields linearly dependent securities. When, alternatively, $K = \text{rank}(\underline{Z}) < J$ so that K is the minimum number of (linearly independent) funds to span $\theta(\underline{Z})$, then an optimal consumption portfolio can be equivalently formed either by a portfolio chosen from the (original) securities or by a portfolio formed from the fewer spanning funds (a portfolio of portfolios). The individual's indifference is assured in this case by the definition of mutual spanning and the fact that mutual fund intermediation is without cost – so that the market value of any consumption plan is identical regardless of whether it is made up indirectly from a portfolio of the mutual funds or directly from the original shares. While each individual is indifferent to the choice of portfolios from among the mutual funds or among the original securities in this case, when there are costs of information or transactions and these exhibit scale economies each individual would surely prefer to construct an optimal portfolio using the minimum number of mutual funds spanning the opportunity set.

6.A.1. Spanning the efficient set

A collection of mutual funds M^κ spans the portfolio opportunity set $\theta(\underline{Z})$ if every element of that set can be formed as a portfolio of the mutual funds. In an analogous way we may say that a collection of mutual funds M^κ *span the efficient set* $\theta^\circ(\underline{Z})$ if every efficient portfolio can be written as a portfolio of the M^κ funds. To indicate in a short-hand way that κ mutual funds span the efficient set we write $\kappa FS\theta^\circ(\underline{Z})$ or, when it is understood which security program obtains, $\kappa FS\theta^\circ$. It is intuitive that the properties of the spanning collection depend on the restrictions which are in the first instance placed on the efficient set.

[2]It should be noted that 'spanning' is not exactly the concept employed in linear algebra. The difference is that $\theta(\underline{Z})$ is not a vector space, for it is defined only by *portfolios* of securities and thus not closed under some multiplication operations. While important to recognize, this difference leads to complications only of a bookkeeping nature as we shall see.

[3]By definition a mutual fund is a portfolio of the original securities. To say that m^k is a mutual fund therefore implies $m^k \in \theta(\underline{Z})$. Thus, stipulation (i) above is for emphasis.

For some mutual fund collection $M^{\kappa}=[m^1\, m^2 \ldots m^{\kappa}]$ to span $\theta^{\circ}(\underline{Z})$ means that every efficient portfolio can be generated by a portfolio of these funds, it does not imply the converse. For example, one collection of funds spanning $\theta^{\circ}(\underline{Z})$ is the J original securities themselves. To be sure, all efficient portfolios can be generated from these securities, but so can all inefficient ones. This is generally an uninteresting collection of spanning funds, which indicates the problem of finding interesting conditions under which κ is small and the funds of M^{κ} are observable.

The above case points in turn to a second 'non-property' of the mutual funds spanning $\theta^{\circ}(\underline{Z})$: it is not generally required that the spanning funds themselves be efficient. The converse of this, that it is always possible to choose each such mutual fund as efficient, is both true and a useful property.

P6.1. Efficiency of spanning funds. Let $M^{\kappa}=[m^1\, m^2 \ldots m^{\kappa}]$ be κ linearly independent mutual funds spanning $\theta^{\circ}(\underline{Z})$. Each fund in M^{κ} can be chosen as an efficient portfolio.

Proof. We begin with a collection $\underline{\mathring{w}}^1, \underline{\mathring{w}}^2, \ldots, \underline{\mathring{w}}^{\kappa}$ of linearly independent, efficient portfolios. As m^{κ} spans $\theta^{\circ}(\underline{Z})$ write $\underline{\mathring{w}}^n=\Sigma_k \delta^k_n m^k$ for each of the $n=1,2,\ldots,\kappa$ portfolios where $\Sigma_k \delta^k_n=1$ for every n and $k=1,2,\ldots,\kappa$ indexes the mutual funds. Given the mutual funds are linearly independent, the portfolio fractions are distinct and these equations can be used to replace each m^k in the spanning set by a different $\underline{\mathring{w}}^n$. Finally, label $\mathring{m}^k=\underline{\mathring{w}}^k\ \forall k$. □

E6.1. A geometric interpretation of spanning is helpful at times. First, we can deal with *portfolio fractions*. The set of feasible portfolio fractions is a (J-1) dimensional hyperplane including the unit simplex (which would be the extrema of the set if short sales were prohibited). Non-trivial efficient set spanning means that the optimal portfolio fractions are a (J-2), or smaller, dimensional hyperplane which is included in the feasible set of portfolio fractions. The case where $J=3$ is illustrated in Figure 6.1a below. There, this feasible set is the plane labelled Δ. The set of *optimal* portfolio fractions might, for example, be a line in the Δ plane, say $\delta^a\delta^b$, or a point such as δ^c. In the first case, if two mutual funds are formed with portfolio fractions of the securities given by any pair of (distinct) points on $\delta^a\delta^b$, then all individuals can achieve their optimal consumption by selecting some portfolio of the mutual funds $m^a=\delta^a\underline{Z}$ and $m^b=\delta^b\underline{Z}$. Similarly, in the second case individuals would all choose the mutual fund $m^c=\delta^c\underline{Z}$. ■

Spanning can be, and more commonly is, thought of in the space of

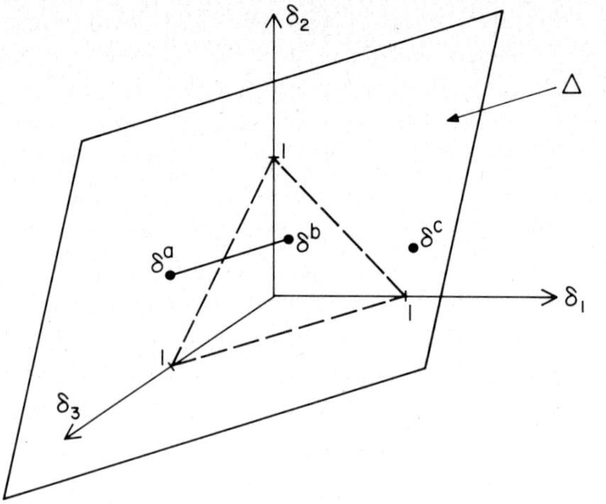

Fig. 6.1A. Portfolio fractions

portfolios. Once again let there be three linearly independent securities ($\underline{z}^1, \underline{z}^2$, and $\underline{z}^3$) and three states of nature. The securities are indicated in the returns 3-space given in Figure 6.1b along with the mutual funds m^1, m^2, and m^3 which yield the maximal returns in states 1, 2, and 3 (respectively) without non-negative returns in any other state. $\theta(Z)$ indicates the consumption portfolio set with these mutual funds as extrema. The efficient set might now, for example, be a line – more generally, a (J-2) or smaller

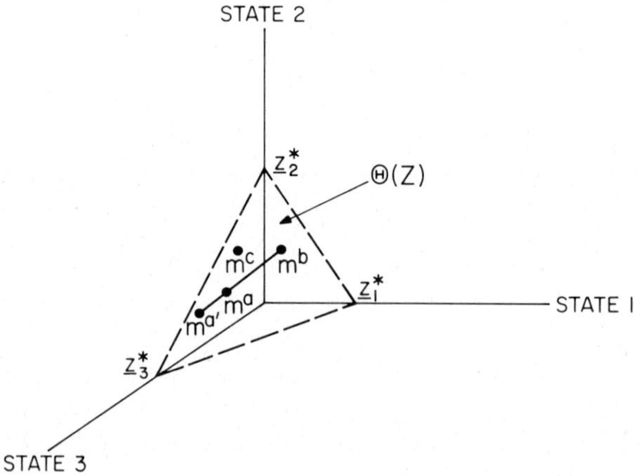

Fig. 6.1B. Consumption portfolios

hyperplane – in $\theta(\underline{Z})$, say that enclosed by the two portfolios m^a and m^b in the Figure. In this case m^a and m^b, or $m^{a'}$ and m^b, would be spanning mutual funds for $\theta^\circ(\underline{Z})$. As an alternative case, m^c might alone be the single efficient portfolio and there would be $1FS\theta^\circ(\underline{Z})$.

6.A.2. *Some properties of M^κ*

The efficient set is, of course, jointly determined by the properties of the security program and the characteristics of the I2 individuals. Given a detailed specification of the economy, we seek a nontrivial set of mutual funds which span the efficient set. There are two related aspects of this problem. First, what will be the smallest κ, the smallest number of spanning funds? And second, for any κ how can the spanning funds be specified to make them observable in practice? Using restrictions on the security program, Section 6.B provides an answer to the first of these questions. Without restricting $\underline{Z}$ or individuals, a partial answer to the second question is suggested by P6.1 above: it is always possible to choose efficient portfolios to form the spanning funds. And, there is one (generally) inefficient portfolio which too can be chosen.

P6.2. ρ in M^κ. Let $\rho \in \theta(\underline{Z})$. Then, it is possible to choose ρ as one mutual fund in M^κ.

Proof. If ρ were efficient then the proof would follow immediately from P6.1. But the riskless portfolio is not generally efficient (P5.5), and a second line of proof is necessary. In this case, first consider an arbitrary efficient portfolio $\underline{\mathring{w}} = \Sigma_k \delta m^k$ and then form a second portfolio from ρ and $\underline{\mathring{w}}$: $\underline{w}' = \zeta \underline{\mathring{w}} + (1-\zeta)\rho$. When $\zeta > 0$ then $\underline{w}'$ is efficient (again, see P5.5).

Next, form $\underline{w}'$ as a portfolio using the spanning mutual funds of M^κ: $\underline{w}' = \Sigma_k \gamma^k m^k$, which implies $\zeta \Sigma_k \delta^k m^k + (1-\zeta)\rho = \Sigma_k \gamma^k m^k$. Solving this yields $\rho = \Sigma_k \lambda^k m^k$ where $\lambda^k = (\gamma^k - \zeta\delta^k)/(1-\zeta)$. Thus $\Sigma_k \lambda^k = 1$ so that the λ^k are portfolio fractions. Since the numbering of mutual funds is arbitrary, choose mutual fund 1 such that $\lambda^1 \neq 0$, solve for m^1 in terms of $\rho, m^2 \ldots m^\kappa$, and use this expression to substitute ρ for m^1 in the spanning set. □

E6.2. Let $M^\kappa = [\rho\, m^2 \ldots m^\kappa]$ span $\theta^\circ(\underline{Z})$. Choose some efficient portfolio $\underline{\mathring{w}}$

$$\begin{aligned}\underline{\mathring{w}} &= \delta^1 \rho + \Sigma_{k=2}\, \delta^k m^k \\ &= \delta^1 \rho + (1-\delta^1) \sum_{k=2} \frac{\delta^k}{(1-\delta^1)} m^k = \delta^1 \rho + (1-\delta^1) m,\end{aligned}$$

where m, which we term the 'risky fund', has the obvious definition. The individual's optimization problem can then be written equivalently as

$$\max_{\delta^1,\ldots\delta^\kappa} \mathrm{E}V(\underline{w}) \quad \text{s.t.} \quad \sum_k \delta^k m^k = \underline{w}, \quad \text{or}$$

$$\max_{\delta^1, m} \mathrm{E}V(\underline{w}) \quad \text{s.t.} \quad \underline{w} = \delta^1 \rho + (1-\delta^1)m.$$

Now define $\mathrm{E}\hat{V}(\delta^1, m) = \mathrm{E}V(\delta^1\rho + (1-\delta^1)m)$, noting that with $(1-\delta^1)>0$ $\mathrm{E}\hat{V}$ is increasing and concave if $\mathrm{E}V$ is. We then have,

$$\max_{\delta^1, m} \mathrm{E}V(\delta^1\rho + (1-\delta^1)m) = \max_{\delta^1}\left\{\max_m \mathrm{E}\hat{V}(\delta^1, m)\right\}.$$

From the rightmost optimization we can define a two-stage problem for the individual. First the inner problem is solved by choosing the optimal 'risky fund', then the outer problem is solved to optimally form a portfolio of this fund with the riskless asset. While this separation of (a) the choice of the risky fund and (b) the choice of the portfolio of risky and riskless funds occurs for all individuals it should be remarked that the risky fund m will generally differ in the cross-section of I2 individuals. Under what specific circumstances will it not differ? That is our next subject. ■

6.B. $\kappa FS\theta°$: Restrictions on $\underline{Z}$

We state immediately the principal result, stressing in advance only that the proposition defines conditions on the security program, not individual preferences, for efficient set spanning.

P6.3. Security program and $\kappa FS\theta°$. Let individuals be I2, but otherwise arbitrary. For a collection of mutual funds $M^\kappa = [m^1\ m^2 \ldots m^\kappa]$ to span $\theta°(\underline{Z})$ it is necessary and sufficient that there exist a portfolio of the κ mutual funds $\sigma_j = [\sigma_j^1\ \sigma_j^2 \ldots \sigma_j^\kappa]$ such that for each security j

$$\underline{z}^j = \sum_k \sigma_j^k m^k + \eta^j, \quad \text{where} \tag{6.B.1}$$

$$\mathrm{E}(\eta^j) = \mathrm{E}\left(\eta^j \,\middle|\, \sum_k \sigma_j^k m^k\right) = 0.$$

Proof. To show sufficiency is straightforward. Let some portfolio $\underline{w}'$ result from portfolio fractions ζ: $\underline{w}'=\Sigma_j\zeta_j\underline{z}^j$. By hypothesis, $\underline{z}^j=\Sigma_k\sigma_j^k m^k+\eta^j$ which, in turn, implies

$$\underline{w}'=\sum_j\left[\zeta_j\left(\sum_k\sigma_j^k m^k\right)+\zeta_j\eta^j\right]=\sum_k\left(\sum_j\zeta_j\sigma_j^k\right)m^k+\eta,$$

where $\eta=\Sigma_j\zeta_j\eta^j$ is a portfolio of the η^j. Consider now some second portfolio $\underline{w}$ derived using weights $\gamma^k=\Sigma_j\zeta_j\sigma_j^k$ for each mutual fund k, that is, $\underline{w}=\Sigma_k\gamma^k m^k$. Notice that $\Sigma_k\gamma^k=\Sigma_j\zeta_j\Sigma_k\sigma_j^k=\Sigma_j\zeta_j 1=1$, so that $\underline{w}$ is a portfolio. We therefore have $\underline{w}'=\underline{w}+\eta$ where $\mathrm{E}\eta=\mathrm{E}(\eta|\underline{w})=0$, which implies $\underline{w}\mathrm{D}\underline{w}'$ when $\eta\neq 0$. For each $\underline{w}'\in\theta(\underline{Z})$ it is in this way possible to construct an associated portfolio $\underline{w}$ of the mutual funds, if it exists, such that $\underline{w}\mathrm{D}\underline{w}'$. By iteration of this process, all 'not dominated', and thus all efficient, portfolios can be generated from the collection M^κ. This provides the proof of sufficiency. Proof of necessity is considerably more complex and is not given here; instead, the reader is referred to Strassen (1966) and, especially, Ross (1976) for full details. □

For a collection of mutual funds to span the opportunity set $\theta(\underline{Z})$ requires exact replication of the security return of each firm. In contrast, for a collection of mutual funds to span $\theta^\circ(\underline{Z})$ it is only required that each firm's security can be written as a portfolio of these mutual funds plus idiosyncratic noise. What is the intuition for this requirement? Simply, it is that then all noise is eliminated in efficient portfolios. To see this, let $\mathring{\delta}$ be optimal portfolio fractions for some I2 individual and $\mathring{\underline{w}}=\delta\underline{Z}$. When the conditions of the proposition hold, the mutual fund collection M^κ is such that

$$\mathring{\underline{w}}=\sum_j\delta_j\left[\sum_k\sigma_j^k m^k+\eta^j\right]=\sum_k\gamma^k m^k+\sum_j\delta_j\eta^j, \tag{6.B.2}$$

where $\gamma^k=\Sigma_j\mathring{\delta}_j\sigma_j^k$ and therefore $\gamma=[\gamma^1\ldots\gamma^\kappa]$ are portfolio fractions. Given M^κ spans $\theta^\circ(\underline{Z})$ we can alternatively write $\mathring{\underline{w}}=\Sigma_k\gamma^k m^k$ which, by comparison with the above expression for $\mathring{\underline{w}}$, requires $\Sigma_j\mathring{\delta}_j\eta^j=0$. A portfolio is efficient then if and only if its portfolio weights are such that they diversity away all noise relative to the spanning mutual funds. This, however, does not mean that efficient portfolios are riskless. Rather, it only means that they do not contain the idiosyncratic risk of their constituent securities.[4]

[4]Section 6.D, to follow, deals with risk diversification.

Finally, we note that when a riskless portfolio exists it is usually taken as one of the spanning funds and (6.B.1) is rewritten compactly as

$$\underline{z}^j = \rho + \sum_{\ell} \sigma_j^{\ell}(m^{\ell} - \rho) + \eta^j, \tag{6.B.1'}$$

where $\ell = 2, \ldots, \kappa$.

6.B.1. The market model and efficient set spanning

When individuals are I2, but otherwise arbitrary, P6.3 informs us of the necessary and sufficient conditions for $\kappa FS\theta^{\circ}$: in short, it must be possible to write the return of each security as some portfolio of the same κ mutual funds plus noise. While this does not provide a practical theory of price, it is a very good start. To do better it is necessary to identify the κ spanning mutual funds in detail. A first question in that regard concerns the possibility that actual security markets will have a reasonably small κ.

P6.4. The Market model (*factor generating process*). Suppose it to be an empirical fact that the return of each security is generated by *market factors* $F^1, F^2, \ldots, F^{\kappa}$ in a linear process of the form

$$\underline{z}^j = \sum_k \zeta_j^k F^k + \eta^j \quad \forall j, \tag{6.B.3}$$

where $\zeta_j = [\zeta_j^1 \; \zeta_j^2 \ldots \zeta_j^{\kappa}]$ are portfolio fractions and the disturbances have the usual noise properties, are uncorrelated, and their variances are bounded. Without loss of generality, we also suppose the factors $F^k \; \forall k$ are linearly independent. Then, as the number of securities becomes large, $F^1, F^2, \ldots, F^{\kappa}$ span $\theta^{\circ}(\underline{Z})$ in an approximate way (described below).

The market factors that one might typically expect to be of importance are those determining aggregate demand (in both real and price components) in the short-run and, in the longer-run, those affecting the productive opportunities and consumer characteristics within the economy. Whatever the specific foundation for these common market factors, they are presumed in (6.B.3) to identify the underlying way in which security returns are generated. It is important to recognize that no detailed economic theory is advanced here as to what the common factors are or to support a linear generating process; rather, the model of equations (6.B.3) is simply maintained as an empirical fact. Given that fact, the indicated spanning follows in an approximate way as the number of securities becomes large.

Proof. Ross (1976) provides the original and rigorous proof, which we sketch here. Equations (6.B.3) satisfy the P6.3 necessary and sufficient conditions for the common factors $F^1, F^2, \ldots F^\kappa$ to span $\theta^\circ(\underline{Z})$ when each factor can be represented as a mutual fund, i.e., written as a portfolio of the underlying securities. We thus consider the portfolio fractions $\delta = [\delta_1\ \delta_2 \ldots \delta_J]$ such that

$$m^1 = \sum_j \delta_j \underline{z}^j = \sum_k \gamma^k F^k + \sum_j \delta_j \eta^j, \tag{6.B.4}$$

where $\gamma^k \equiv \Sigma_j \zeta_j^k \delta_j$ and, as both ζ and δ represent portfolio fractions, then so does $\gamma = [\gamma^1\ \gamma^2 \ldots \gamma^\kappa]$. If it is possible to choose simultaneously the elements of δ such that $\Sigma_j \delta_j \eta^j$ is a zero vector and $\gamma = [1\ 0\ 0 \ldots 0]$, then $m^1 = F^1$ and the first factor is represented by a mutual fund. This requires the portfolio fractions δ satisfy the following conditions:

$$\sum_j \delta_j = 1, \tag{6.B.5a}$$

$$\sum_j \delta_j \eta^j = \theta_S \quad (S \text{ equations}), \tag{6.B.5b}$$

$$\sum_j \delta_j \zeta_j^1 = 1, \quad \text{and for } k > 1 \tag{6.B.5c}$$

$$\sum_j \delta_j \zeta_j^k = 0 \quad (\kappa \text{ equations}).$$

Equation (6.B.5a) is the usual portfolio requirement. The S equations (6.B.5b) act to eliminate the noise term – note that when $J = S$, and the noise terms are linearly independent, there will be an exact δ-solution to *these* S equations. Finally, the κ equations (6.B.5c) provide, given there is no noise, that the δ portfolio fractions are formed in a way to specify F^1 as equivalent to a mutual fund. In total, there are $1 + S + \kappa$ equations and there are the J portfolio fractions of δ to be determined. If $J = 1 + S + \kappa$ then, with the independence assumptions, there will exist a set of portfolio fractions δ for which $m^1 = F^1$ exactly.

When J is not so large Ross describes an approximation argument to satisfy (6.B.5). He considers the 'well-diversified' portfolio fractions $\delta_j = c_j/J$ such that $|c_j| \le C_j < \infty$ with C_j independent of J for all $j = 1, \ldots, J$. For this case we can write $\Sigma_j \delta_j \eta_j = (1/J)\Sigma_j c_j \eta^j$. Since $|c_j|$ is bounded (independently of J) and the η^j are uncorrelated, the law of large numbers implies

$(1/J)\Sigma_j c_j \eta^j \to 0$, and therefore $(m^1 - F^1) \to 0$ as $J \to \infty$. Repeating the above argument for the remaining $k=2,\ldots,\kappa$ factors completes the proof. □

It is of interest that the approximation in the above proof does not rely on specific distributional characteristics either of the securities or noise terms. (Only the bounded variance of the noise terms along with the linear generating process are required.) The proposition therefore becomes of importance when the generating model is found to possess only a few factors. As empirical studies have generally found four or five factors to be significant in such a model, and the number of securities is 'large' relative to that, the approximation appears to rest on a reasonable foundation.[5]

What are the implications of $\kappa FS\theta^\circ$ for security pricing? That is the next issue of concern.

6.C. Linear Pricing with $\kappa FS\theta^\circ(\underline{Z})$

Let individuals be risk averse expected utility maximizers and suppose that the security program $\underline{Z}$ is such that the κ mutual funds $M^\kappa = [m^1 m^2 \ldots m^\kappa]$ span the efficient set. In this case there exist portfolio fractions $\delta_j = [\delta_j^1 \delta_j^2 \ldots \delta_j^\kappa]$ such that each security j has returns generated by the process

$$\underline{z}^j = \sum_{k=1} \delta_j^k m^k + \eta^j, \tag{6.C.1}$$

where η^j has the usual mean zero noise properties and k indexes the κ spanning funds. Taking the expectation of this expression yields the *linear pricing model*

$$\mathrm{E}\underline{z}^j = \sum_{k=1} \delta_j^k \, \mathrm{E}m^k, \tag{6.C.2a}$$

again for all j. Some later simplifications result if the riskless portfolio is used as a standard (assuming it is feasible), so choose $m^1 = \rho$ and, in turn, make the substitution $\delta_j^1 = 1 - \Sigma_{k=2} \delta_j^k$ in the above equation. On rearranging this gives

$$\mathrm{E}\underline{z}^{j\cdot} = \sum_k \delta_j^k \mathrm{E}m^{k\cdot}, \tag{6.C.2b}$$

[5]It is to be emphasized that the factors need not explain a large amount of the variation in each security. Rather, what is required is that the factors explain the covariation in returns among the securities. See Roll and Ross (1980) and Chen (1981) for an empirical investigation of factors significant in linear generating models.

where $\underline{z}^{j} = \underline{z}^{j} - \rho$ and $m^{k} = m^{k} - \rho$ define *excess returns* with respect to ρ, and the index k is used (here and hereafter unless noted explicitly otherwise) to indicate mutual funds from 2 (not 1) through κ. When the riskless portfolio is not feasible, any other distinct spanning mutual fund can be used instead and the mean returns in (6.C.2b) are then specifically the excess above that fund's returns.

Equations (6.C.2) relate the expected return on every security to the 'δ-weighted' sum of expected returns on the specific funds chosen to span $\theta^{\circ}(\underline{Z})$. Two questions concerning this relationship occur. First, how does one specify a collection of spanning mutual funds which can be constructed not simply in principle, but as a practical matter? Second, what are the underlying determinants of the δ_{j}^{k} weights and, specifically, do they relate to market parameters? Consider this latter question first.

6.C.1. Portfolio fractions as variances and covariances

Since $\kappa FS\theta^{\circ}(\underline{Z})$ results in a *linear* relationship between the expected returns on each security and that of the κ mutual funds, it follows that the δ-weights are simply appropriate variances and covariances. This result is shown in the following proposition, which employs the notations:

$M^{\kappa\cdot} = [m^{2\cdot}\ m^{3\cdot} \ldots m^{\kappa\cdot}]$, the collection of κ-1 excess return mutual funds, derived from the spanning collection M^{κ}, and,

$\not{M}^{\kappa\cdot}$ the variance–covariance matrix of order κ-1 associated with the excess return mutual funds $M^{\kappa\cdot}$.

P6.5. Covariance fractions. Suppose $\underline{Z}$ is such that equations (6.C.1) hold and $M^{\kappa} = [\dot{m}\, m^{2} \ldots m^{\kappa}]$ spans $\theta^{\circ}(\underline{Z})$. In turn, let $\not{M}^{\kappa\cdot}$ be the variance–covariance matrix of excess returns associated with M^{κ}.[6] Then,

$$\delta_{j}^{n} = \sum_{k} \not{m}_{kn} \operatorname{cov}(\underline{z}^{j\cdot}, m^{k}), \qquad n = 2, \ldots, \kappa, \tag{6.C.3a}$$

with $\not{m}_{kn}$ representing the k-n^{th} element of the inverse matrix $(\not{M}^{\kappa\cdot})^{-1}$ and, for δ to be portfolio fractions,

$$\delta_{j}^{1} = 1 - \sum_{k} \delta_{j}^{k}. \tag{6.C.3b}$$

[6]When the riskless asset is feasible the full variance–covariance matrix of returns is singular. Using the excess return form of the model eliminates this singularity problem without having to treat the singularity everywhere as a special case.

Proof. With κ representing the minimum number of mutual funds spanning the efficient set, the funds $\rho, m^2, \ldots, m^\kappa$ are chosen to be linearly independent. When choosing each of these as efficient, the excess return funds $m^{2\cdot}, m^{3\cdot}, \ldots m^{\kappa\cdot}$ have non-zero variances and $M^{\kappa\cdot}$ has an inverse. With these things understood, substitute from the (6.C.1) returns generating process for $\underline{z}^j$ in the definition of covariance to get

$$\operatorname{cov}(\underline{z}^{j\cdot}, m^n) = \operatorname{cov}\left(\sum_k \delta_j^k m^{k\cdot} + \eta^j, m^n\right). \tag{6.C.4a}$$

This equation holds for all $n = 2, 3, \ldots, \kappa$ and we shall use n, as well as k, in the following to index this specific range. The noise property of η^j implies $\operatorname{cov}(\eta^j, m^k) = 0$ for each m^k and therefore

$$\operatorname{cov}(\underline{z}^{j\cdot}, m^n) = \sum_k \delta_j^k \operatorname{cov}(m^{k\cdot}, m^n). \tag{6.C.4b}$$

Since this relation holds for all n, the following vector-matrix equation results,

$$\begin{bmatrix} \operatorname{cov}(\underline{z}^{j\cdot}, m^2) \\ \operatorname{cov}(\underline{z}^{j\cdot}, m^3) \\ \vdots \\ \operatorname{cov}(\underline{z}^{j\cdot}, m^\kappa) \end{bmatrix} = M^\kappa \begin{bmatrix} \delta_j^2 \\ \delta_j^3 \\ \vdots \\ \delta_j^\kappa \end{bmatrix}. \tag{6.C.5}$$

Finally, as $M^{\kappa\cdot}$ has an inverse (6.C.4) can be solved directly for (6.C.3a). □

Note that P6.5 does not require the security market be in equilibrium, nor does it place any explicit restrictions on individuals other than those required for $\kappa FS\theta^\circ$. Given such spanning, the mutual fund portfolio fractions are determined fully by the appropriate variances and covariances of the $m^{k\cdot}$ and the covariances between $\underline{z}^{j\cdot}$ and these same funds. Even though security returns are not required to follow two parameter distributions, only the second-moments of the joint distributions are sufficient to provide the δ_j^k weights. Again, this result stems from the linearity of the returns generating process implied by $\kappa FS\theta^\circ(\underline{Z})$.

6.C.2. Security prices with $\kappa FS\theta^\circ$

Since payoffs and consumption plans have been expressed in return form, security prices and, in turn, prices for consumption claims have entered only indirectly into the analysis. As our interest lies with a theory of price it is useful to restate the above results in dollar terms and thus to have prices take an explicit place.

P6.6. Security prices with $\kappa FS0^{\circ}$. Let the conditions of P6.5 hold, then the market price of each security j satisfies the following equivalent relationships[7]

$$v_0^j = \frac{\mathrm{E}z^j}{[\mathrm{E}\dot{m} + \Sigma_k \mathrm{E}m^{k\cdot} \Sigma_n \not{m}_{kn} \operatorname{cov}(\underline{z}^{j\cdot}, m^n)]}, \tag{6.C.6a}$$

$$v_0^j = \frac{\mathrm{E}z^j - \Sigma_k \mathrm{E}m^{k\cdot} \Sigma_n \not{m}_{kn} \operatorname{cov}(\underline{z}^{j\cdot}, m^n)}{\mathrm{E}\dot{m} - \Sigma_k \mathrm{E}m^{k\cdot} \Sigma_n \not{m}_{kn} \operatorname{cov}(\dot{m}, m^n)}. \tag{6.C.6b}$$

Proof. By definition $\underline{z}^j = z^j / v_0^j$, thus $\mathrm{E}\underline{z}^j = \mathrm{E}z^j / v_0^j$ and by (6.C.2) $\mathrm{E}\underline{z}^j = \Sigma_j \delta_j^k \mathrm{E}m^k$. Solve for v_0^j in terms of the $\mathrm{E}m^k$ and $\mathrm{E}z^j$, substituting for δ_j^k from P6.5. These steps give equation (6.C.6a). The second expression, (6.C.6b), then follows by substituting $\underline{z}^j = z^j / v_0^j$ in cov $(\underline{z}^j - \dot{m}, m^n)$ for each j and simplifying. □

The first of the two price equations, (6.C.6a), appears in a risk-adjusted discount rate form: the market value of each firm j is equal to its *expected* dollar value at the next period discounted to the $t=0$ market at a rate dependent on the riskiness of the dollar payoff. The equation precisely defines that discount rate in terms of the variances, covariances, and expected returns. An investigation of these components of the discount rate would therefore seem to provide a basis for a measure of each security's risk. Understanding exactly how the risk adjustment occurs is complicated by the unduly complex form of (6.C.6a), and so we delay any detailed discussion of the security risk measure until a simplified, but equivalent, expression for security price is developed.

The second price equation, (6.C.6b), is arranged in a certainty-equivalent form. There, the market value of firm j is equal to its next period expected dollar value less an amount appropriate to the risk it represents, that difference then discounted to period zero by the complex denominator rate. The equation defines the amount of the risk reduction and defines a

[7] Note carefully the distinction between return and dollar amounts, $\underline{z}^j$ and z^j, in these equations and recall that the indices k and n began at 2 unless specially noted otherwise.

common (riskless) discount rate.[8] Again, it is possible to gain insight into an appropriate measure of security risk from these definitions, but an equivalent form of (6.C.6b) developed below is a simpler basis from which to state such a measure.

6.C.3. *Some simplifications*

I2 individuals and the requirement that the security program $\underset{\sim}{Z}$ satisfy those conditions which lead to $\kappa FS\theta^{\circ}(\underset{\sim}{Z})$ are the crucial pre-conditions for the validity of the (6.C.6) price equations. While these equations do not reflect the imposition of equality in aggregate demand and supply required at a market equilibrium, they do represent necessary conditions for equilibrium prices based on each individual's conditions for a consumptive optimum and, consequently, they provide a useful basis for an empirical theory of price. Again, it is of note that the key feature of these valuation equations is that they do not involve parameters of individual utility functions (or preference): in the (6.C.6) expressions the expected return $\mathrm{E}z^{j}$, and therefore the price v_0^j, is stated solely in terms of potentially observable market parameters and properties of the security return distributions across states.

One must not, however, think these results to be more useful than they really are. In the general form given by equations (6.C.6), the price relationships are lacking in empirical content. For example, it is always possible to choose any set of non-redundant securities which span the opportunity set $\theta(\underset{\sim}{Z})$ also as a spanning set for the efficient set $\theta^{\circ}(\underset{\sim}{Z})$ and therefrom always specify the linear relationships of (6.C.6). In this polar case the equations become simple identities or, at least, only relate the fact that some security can be written as a linear combination of others and therefore (without arbitrage possibilities) must have a price which is that same linear combination of prices. The valuation equations become interesting only when something specific can be said about the efficient set and, in turn, the spanning mutual funds. That is yet to be done. But, first it is useful to reformulate the spanning mutual funds in a way that reduces the complexity of the (6.C.6) pricing expressions.

P6.7. $\kappa FS\theta^{\circ}$ with uncorrelated funds. Let the κ, linearly independent mutual funds $\hat{M}^{\kappa}=[\rho\ \hat{m}^2\ \hat{m}^3 \ldots \hat{m}^{\kappa}]$ span $\theta^{\circ}(\underset{\sim}{Z})$. Then, without loss of generality, there exists a second mutual fund collection $M^{\kappa}=[\rho\ m^2\ m^3\ \ldots\ m^{\kappa}]$

[8]Note that the choice of ρ as this 'common' mutual fund is arbitrary. Any fund in the M^{κ} spanning set can be chosen and, in fact, any mutual fund which is part of any spanning set can be chosen so long as all the proper adjustments are made.

which spans $\theta^{\circ}(\underline{Z})$ with the property that $\text{cov}(\rho, m^k)=\text{cov}(m^k, m^n)=0$ for all $k, n=2, \ldots, \kappa$ and $n \neq k$.

Proof. Given the original set of mutual funds $\hat{M}^{\kappa}$ are linearly independent, it is a routine task to construct an orthogonal set of κ mutual funds (vectors) to span the same subspace while retaining ρ in the new set. As the mutual funds are pairwise orthogonal, their returns have zero correlations and therefore zero covariances. □

When a pairwise uncorrelated set of mutual funds is selected to span $\theta^{\circ}(\underline{Z})$, the variance–covariance matrix $M^{\kappa\cdot}$ has (κ-1) strictly positive variance elements down the main diagonal and zeroes elsewhere. In this case $M^{\kappa\cdot}$ has an inverse and the δ-fraction of P6.5 simply omit off-diagonal elements, giving

$$\delta_j^k = \frac{\text{cov}(\underline{z}^{j\cdot}, m^k)}{\text{cov}(m^{k\cdot}, m^k)} = \frac{\text{cov}(\underline{z}^j, m^k) - \text{cov}(\rho, m^k)}{\text{cov}(m^k, m^k) - \text{cov}(\rho, m^k)} \quad \forall k \geq 2.$$

Since ρ is a constant this becomes

$$\delta_j^k = \text{cov}(\underline{z}^j, m^k)/\text{cov}(m^k, m^k) \quad \forall k \geq 2, \tag{6.C.7}$$

with, again $\delta_j^1 = 1 - \Sigma_k \delta_j^k$. In turn, the expected excess return of each security j, the linear pricing equation, is more simply written as

$$\text{E}\underline{z}^{j\cdot} = \sum_k b(\underline{z}^j, m^k)\text{E}m^{k\cdot}, \quad \text{where} \tag{6.C.8}$$

$$b(\cdot, m^k) \equiv \text{cov}(\cdot, m^k)/\text{cov}(m^k, m^k). \tag{6.C.9}$$

For each security j there are κ 'b's', each measuring the covariance of $\underline{z}^j$ with one of the m^k (then appropriately normalized by the variance of the m^k).

Equation (6.C.8) is the key relationship, the usual form of the *linear pricing model.* With some reworking, the (6.C.6) valuation equations too reflect the simplicity of using uncorrelated spanning funds, becoming

$$v_0^j = \frac{\text{E}z^j}{[\text{E}\rho + \Sigma_k b(\underline{z}^j, m^k)\text{E}m^{k\cdot}]}, \quad \text{and} \tag{6.C.10a}$$

$$v_0^j = \frac{[\text{E}z^j - \Sigma_k b(\underline{z}^j, m^k)\text{E}m^{k\cdot}]}{\text{E}\rho}. \tag{6.C.10b}$$

These correspond to risk-adjust discount rate and certainty-equivalent forms, respectively.

E6.3. A quick retrace of the developments to this point will verify for the reader that equations (6.C.1) through (6.C.10) apply not only to single securities but to all portfolios of securities. That is, for some portfolio $\underline{w} \in \theta(\underline{Z})$, efficient or not, the expected excess return can be determined as,

$$\mathrm{E}\underline{w}^{\cdot} = \mathrm{E}(\underline{w} - \rho) = \sum_k b(\underline{w}, m^k)\mathrm{E}m^{k\cdot}, \tag{6.C.11a}$$

with price v_0^w following therefrom as,

$$v_0^w = \frac{\mathrm{E}\underline{w}}{[\mathrm{E}\rho + \Sigma_k b(\underline{w}, m^k)\mathrm{E}m^{k\cdot}]}, \tag{6.C.11b}$$

or

$$v_0^w = \frac{\mathrm{E}\underline{w} - \Sigma_k b(\underline{w}, m^k)\mathrm{E}m^{k\cdot}}{\mathrm{E}\rho}. \tag{6.C.11c}$$

■

6.C.4. Constructing the spanning mutual funds

In equation (6.C.1) let $m^1 = \rho$ and choose the spanning mutual funds to have pairwise uncorrelated returns. This gives

$$\underline{z}^{j\cdot} = \alpha^j + \sum_k b(\underline{z}^j, m^k)(m^{k\cdot} - \mathrm{E}m^k 1_S) + e^j, \tag{6.C.12}$$

where e^j is mean zero noise and $\alpha^j \triangleq \Sigma_k b(\underline{z}^k, m^k)\mathrm{E}m^k 1_S = \mathrm{E}\underline{z}^j$. Ignoring some basic statistical difficulties, (6.C.12) can be treated as a simple linear regression, which explains why e^j is used instead of η^j to indicate noise – e^j would be required to have the usual Gauss–Markov properties if the resulting parameter estimates are to be efficient in a statistical sense. In any case, given a suitable specification of the mutual funds (and assuming their inter-relationship was stable over time) one could estimate the equation parameters.

As a practical matter, how is the regression to be set up? More exactly, how are we to select the set of mutual funds which both span $\theta^\circ(\underline{Z})$ and are orthogonal? There are several possible approaches to the problem. A strictly experimental approach would use the market model (see P6.4) and seek a set of generating factors, 'rotated' to be orthogonal, as the independent variables in the time-series regression for each security j. A candidate factor becomes relevant when every noise term, each e^j, is distributed independently of the factor. In addition, to assure the correct number of factors have been found, it would be required that the e^j be small in some sense, and tests could be developed to determine whether or not $\mathrm{E}\underline{z}^j = \alpha^j$ in the cross-section of securities.

A second, similar approach begins with two facts: first, that each of the κ mutual funds in the set spanning $\theta^\circ(\underline{Z})$ can be chosen as an efficient fund and, second, that mutual funds with minimum variance for given mean return are efficient. This approach proceeds by constructing a number of linearly independent, mean-variance efficient funds, these are then orthogonalized and tests made (as in the above experimental procedure with the 'factor model') to see if some limited number of the funds again minimizes the residual.

A final alternative to the above, largely empirical approaches, proceeds by placing additional restrictions on the underlying theory and, in turn, further limiting the structure of the efficient set in such a way that a well-defined set of spanning mutual funds is known and observable. This is the specific approach which is used in $2FS\theta^\circ(\underline{Z})$, the so-called capital asset pricing model. Regardless of how we arrive at a linear pricing model, meaningful statements can be made about the economics of the expression only when priced and unpriced sources of risk are clearly identified.

6.D. *Measures of Security Risk*

Recall the linear pricing model (6.C.8) which we rewrite as

$$\mathrm{E}\underline{z}^j = \mathrm{E}\rho + \sum_k b(\underline{z}^j, m^k)\mathrm{E}m^k. \tag{6.D.1}$$

The simple linear relationship between security (or portfolio) return and the 'b' coefficients of the security with the κ mutual funds accounts for the popularity of the model. The linearity too implies that the return variation of any asset is described by its normalized covariance with the several spanning funds – with the *risk premium* borne by the security, its expected return above the riskless rate, being proportional to these b's. A security positively correlated with each spanning fund earns a positive risk premium, one that is negatively correlated (valued as a hedge) sells at a discount, and the security with zero correlation to the funds (despite its possible uncertainty measured, for example, by variance) will bear no risk premium and earn the riskless rate of return.

While (6.D.1) has intuitive appeal, the relationship gains importance as a pricing model when the mutual funds can be identified in a fashion which assures that the *b*'s are measures of 'risk' which are consistent with the portfolio choice behavior of risk-averse individuals. Otherwise (6.D.1) is of limited economic content, being simply a mathematical relationship always holding among random variables. How are spanning mutual funds selected for the linear pricing model such that the *b*'s have the interpretation as risk measures. Or, is the choice of spanning funds inconsequential to the risk interpretation of the *b*'s?

An interesting first question is whether the *b*'s follow the stochastic dominance concept of increasing risk; that is, do the *b*'s of, say, securities *j* and *n* determine whether or not $\underline{z}^j$ dominates $\underline{z}^n$? The answer is no, but, as in all pedantic questions, understanding the reason for the answer is most important.

In this regard, first recall that the ordering of risks by stochastic dominance is generally incomplete. Thus, if the *b*'s indicated increasing risk by stochastic dominance then, depending on the distribution of return over states, it would generally be possible to find some pairs of securities which could not be ranked in risk relative to others and, consequently, for which no differentiating risk discount could be assigned. In contrast, equations (6.C.9) clearly assign risk discounts to every security which are either greater than, less than, or exactly equal to that for every other security. As (6.C.9) holds for all specification of $\underline{Z}$ consistent with $\kappa FS\theta^\circ$, the ranking is complete in all relevant cases and it appears that the *b*'s cannot, as a technical matter, measure risk simply by stochastic dominance.

A second, and really the essential, reason why the stochastic dominance ordering does not determine security risk is that it simply measures 'too much'. That is, the risk of any given security that must concern an individual, and thus the only risk to be considered in determining a security's value, is that portion which contributes to the overall riskiness of an *optimal* portfolio. To the extent that a security's total risk generally is made up of specific parts which can and can not be diversified away in the formation of optimal portfolios, then these risks need to be considered separately.

6.D.1. Diversifiable risk

Let individuals be I2 and suppose the κ mutual funds $M^\kappa = [m^1\ m^2\ \ldots$

m^κ] span $\theta^\circ(\underline{Z})$. Next write the optimal portfolio of each individual i in the form

$$\underline{\mathring{w}} = \sum_k \xi^k m^k = \sum_j \mathring{\delta}_i^j \underline{z}^j, \tag{6.D.2}$$

where $\mathring{\delta}_i$ indicates the optimal portfolio fractions and $\xi = [\xi^1 \ldots \xi^\kappa]$ defines an equivalent portfolio of the spanning mutual funds. Because M^κ spans $\theta^\circ(\underline{Z})$ it is also possible to write the return of each security as

$$\underline{z}^j = \sum_k \sigma_j^k m^k + \eta^j,$$

where, for each $j, \sigma_j^k\ \forall k$ represents portfolio fractions and η^j has the usual properties of noise. Substituting this into the rightmost side of (6.D.2) gives

$$\underline{\mathring{w}}^i = \sum_k \left(\sum_j \mathring{\delta}_i^j \sigma_j^k \right) m^k + \sum_j \mathring{\delta}_i^j \eta^j.$$

Finally, comparing this with the leftmost equation of (6.D.2) implies

$$\sum_j \mathring{\delta}_i^j \sigma_j^k = \xi^k \quad \text{for each } k, \tag{6.D.3a}$$

and

$$\sum_j \mathring{\delta}_i^j \eta^j = 0. \tag{6.D.3b}$$

While η^j is a part of what makes security j risky, each *efficient* portfolio is formed in a way to cancel this idiosyncratic component of its constituent securities. This leads to the following definition.

D6.2. Diversifiable (non-systematic, residual) security risk. Let the mutual funds $[m^1\ m^2 \ldots m^\kappa]$ span $\theta^\circ(\underline{Z})$ so that, for each security j, $\underline{z}^j = \Sigma_k \sigma_j^k m^k + \eta^j$ holds with $E\eta^j = E(\eta^j | \Sigma_k \sigma_j^k m^k) = 0$. In this case, define the noise term η^j as the diversifiable (non-systematic, residual) risk of security j.

The fact that the diversifiable risk of a security does not contribute to the riskiness of any efficient (optimal) portfolio means that in perfect markets the diversifiable risk (i) should not affect the demand for the security and, consequently, (ii) should not give rise to any risk adjustment in the determination of the security's market price. A measure of security risk which is to be relevant in a theory of security demand therefore must be related only to the security's randomness other than that created by this residual component.

6.D.2. Non-diversifiable risk

It should now be obvious that any measure of non-diversifiable risk must be relative to an individual's optimal portfolio, for we mean non-diversifiable in the sense that (even with perfect markets) the risk cannot be evaded. This suggests the necessary conditions for consumptive optimality must be the starting point of the definition. For individual i with expected utility function EV, these conditions are[9]

$$\mathrm{E}V'(\underline{\mathring{w}}^i)(\underline{z}^{j\cdot})=0 \quad \forall j. \tag{6.D.4}$$

where $\underline{\mathring{w}}^i$ is the optimal consumption portfolio. Note that these optimality equations hold whether there is nontrivial spanning of $\theta^\circ(\underline{Z})$ or not.

Let $\mathring{\delta}_j$ indicate the portfolio fraction of security j held in i's optimal portfolio, multiply (6.D.4) by this and sum over all j to derive

$$\sum_j \mathring{\delta}_j \mathrm{E}V'(\underline{\mathring{w}}^i)\underline{z}^{j\cdot}=\mathrm{E}V'(\underline{\mathring{w}}^i)(\underline{\mathring{w}}^{i\cdot})=0. \tag{6.D.5}$$

By the definition of covariance, the rightmost equation implies[10]

$$\mathrm{cov}(V'(\underline{\mathring{w}}^i),\underline{\mathring{w}}^{i\cdot})=-\mathrm{E}V'(\underline{\mathring{w}}^i)\mathrm{E}\underline{\mathring{w}}^{i\cdot}. \tag{6.D.6}$$

And, using a similar sequence of steps from (6.D.4), the covariance of $V'(\underline{\mathring{w}}^i)$ and any mutual fund (portfolio) can be derived as follows

$$\mathrm{cov}(V'(\underline{\mathring{w}}^i),m^{\cdot})=-\mathrm{E}V'(\mathring{w}^i)\mathrm{E}m^{\cdot}. \tag{6.D.7}$$

Solving these last two equations simultaneously for $\mathrm{E}V'(\underline{\mathring{w}}^i)$ and equating gives

$$\mathrm{E}m^{\cdot}=\beta^i(m^{\cdot},\underline{\mathring{w}}^i)\mathrm{E}\underline{\mathring{w}}^{i\cdot} \quad \forall J, \tag{6.D.8}$$

where $\beta^i(m^{\cdot},\underline{\mathring{w}}^i)\equiv\mathrm{cov}(V'(\underline{\mathring{w}}^i),m^{\cdot})/\mathrm{cov}(V'(\underline{\mathring{w}}^i),\underline{\mathring{w}}^{i\cdot})$. And, where there is no con-

[9]This is simply the optimality condition (5.B.3) with $\underline{\hat{w}}$ chosen as $\underline{\dot{w}}$. When a riskless fund exists, we let $\underline{\dot{w}}=\rho$.

[10]In equation (6.D.6), $V'(\underline{\mathring{w}}^i)=[V'(\underline{\mathring{w}}^i_1)\ V'(\underline{\mathring{w}}^i_2)\ldots V'(\underline{\mathring{w}}^i_S)]$ is notation for the S-vector of marginal utilities at this optimum. In turn, the covariance $\mathrm{cov}(V'(\underline{\mathring{w}}^i),\underline{\dot{w}}^{i\cdot})$ is defined in the usual way as $\Sigma_s h_s[V'(\underline{\mathring{w}}^i_s-\mathrm{E}V'(\underline{\mathring{w}}^i)][\underline{\mathring{w}}^{i\cdot}_s-\mathrm{E}\underline{\mathring{w}}^{i\cdot}]$.

fusion we shall use the simpler notation $\beta^i_m = \beta^i(m^\cdot, \underset{\sim}{\mathring{w}}^i)$. (As m is an arbitrary portfolio of securities, let $m = \underline{z}^j$ in which case the β^i_j refers to security j.)

It is important to call attention to several aspects of $\beta^i_{m^\cdot}$. (1) This proportionality measure follows simply from each individual's optimality conditions and does not presume any special spanning condition. (2) When a riskless asset exists then $\beta^i(m^\cdot, \underset{\sim}{\mathring{w}}^i) = \beta^i(m, \underset{\sim}{\mathring{w}}^i) + \beta^i(\rho, \underset{\sim}{\mathring{w}}^i) = \beta^i(m, \underset{\sim}{\mathring{w}}^i)$, as the covariance with respect to the riskless asset is zero. (3) From (6.D.8) it is seen that mutual funds with a larger β^i_m have a larger expected return ($\mathrm{E}\underset{\sim}{\mathring{w}}^{i\cdot} \geq 0$). (4) The β^i_m risk of any mutual fund (portfolio, security) is a covariability relative to the individual's optimal portfolio. As a result, that portion of the fund's dispersion which does not contribute to the optimal consumption (that is, it is diversified away in the optimal portfolio) is not reflected in β^i_m and therefore not measured as 'risk' by it.

Moreover, (5) β^i_m is invariant to equivalent specifications of the elementary utility function – let $\hat{V}(\cdot) = c_1 + c_2 V(\cdot)$, c_1 and $c_2 > 0$ constants, then β^i_m is identical for both $\hat{V}(\cdot)$ and its linear transform $V(\cdot)$; (6) β^i_m is such that any mutual fund contructed from a portfolio of securities, $m = \delta \underline{Z}$, has risk which is the same weighted average of the component security risk, $\beta^i(m, \underset{\sim}{\mathring{w}}^i) = \Sigma_j \delta_j \beta^i(\underline{z}^j, \underset{\sim}{\mathring{w}}^i)$; (7) β^i_m measures non-diversifiable risk as a simple proportionality with expected return – so that, if one mutual fund has twice the expected return as another, then it has twice the risk, see equation (6.D.8); and, (8) since the proportionality with expected return holds for all I2 individuals, the rank ordering of mutual funds in risk by $\beta^i(m, \underset{\sim}{\mathring{w}}^i)$ is the same as the rank ordering by $\beta^n(m, \underset{\sim}{\mathring{w}}^n)$ for all individuals i and n – that is, if individual i finds that two securities, or mutual funds, have betas in some specific ratio then so does every individual – again see (6.D.8).

We now have a choice. As a first alternative we may decide to use $\beta^i(m, \underset{\sim}{\mathring{w}}^i)$ to be individual i's measure of non-diversifiable risk of fund m, $\beta^n(m, \underset{\sim}{\mathring{w}}^n)$ to be individual n's measure, and so on for each individual in the economy. The problem with such a scheme is that there would be I separate measures of non-diversifiable risk. A second alternative is based on property (8) above. Rather than having individual-specific risk measures we might instead define each security's non-diversifiable risk in reference to a particular individual. While such a scheme would reduce the number of risk measures, the resulting risk ordering would then be unique only up to a constant ratio factor. In spite of this loss in specificity, such a definition is usually adopted.

D6.3. Non-diversifiable (systematic) risk. For any mutual fund $m \in \theta(\underline{Z})$ define $\beta(m, m^e) = \mathrm{cov}(m, m^e)$ as its measure of non-diversifiable (or systematic) risk, where m^e is the return on a mean-variance efficient portfolio.

Notice that there is no individual superscript to $\beta(m, m^e)$. We refer to this risk measure simply as the *beta* and, following convention, write it as β_m. That specific person for whom the mean-variance efficient fund m^e is optimal becomes the basis for defining the non-diversifiable risk measure.[11] Because the marginal utility function in this case is linear in its arguments and β^i_m is unaffected by equivalent linear transformations of utility functions, beta involves no individual-specific parameters. Lastly, note that the use of m^e means that the general mean-variance maxim rules for construction (which are independent of the specification of the security program $\underset{=}{Z}$) pertain and therefore the beta of any given fund or security is relatively easy to derive.

E6.4. It is to be emphasized that the definition of non-diversifiable risk as $\beta(\cdot, m^e)$ is relative to an optimal (efficient) portfolio. It is useful to show precisely why non-efficient portfolios when used as a reference fail to properly order securities in non-diversifiable risk. For concreteness, consider the orderings by $\beta(\cdot, m^e)$ and $b(\cdot, m'') = \text{cov}(\cdot, m'')/\text{cov}(m'', m'')$ where m'' is feasible but not efficient. Our intuition is that m'', since it is not efficient and includes diversifiable risk, will generally confuse the non-diversifiable risk ordering. This can, in fact, be shown.

Choose m^e particularly such that $\text{E}m^e = \text{E}m''$, which means that there exists a vector η such that $\text{E}(\eta) = \text{E}(\eta | m^e) = 0$ and $m'' = m^e + \eta$. In turn, beta can be written as

$$b(\cdot, m'') = b(\cdot, m^e + \eta) = \text{cov}(\cdot, m^e + \eta)/\text{cov}(m^e + \eta, m^e + \eta).$$

Since η is noise relative to m^e this yields

$$b(\cdot, m'') = [\beta(\cdot, m^e)\text{cov}(m^e, m^e) + \text{cov}(\cdot, \eta)]/[\text{cov}(m^e, m^e) + \text{cov}(\eta, \eta)],$$

where $\text{cov}(\cdot, \eta)$ can vary in sign and magnitude. Thus, for two securities, say j and k,

$$b(\underset{=}{z}^{j\cdot}, m'')/b(\underset{=}{z}^{k\cdot}, m'') = \frac{\beta(\underset{=}{z}^j, m^e)\,\text{cov}(m^e, m^e) + \text{cov}(\underset{=}{z}^j, \eta)}{\beta(\underset{=}{z}^k, m^e)\,\text{cov}(m^e, m^e) + \text{cov}(\underset{=}{z}^k, \eta)}.$$

From this last expression it is clear that the 'b' ordering of the two securities with respect to m'' depends on the sign and magnitudes of $\text{cov}(\underset{=}{z}^j, \eta)$ and $\text{cov}(\underset{=}{z}^k, \eta)$ and need not follow the beta ordering based on m^e. ■

[11]When not making specific assumptions about the security program, this means that the definition uses some individual with quadratic elementary utility as a reference.

6.D.3. The b's and β's of security risk

There are three measures of co-variation to be kept apart. First, there are the b's of the (6.D.1) linear pricing model:

$$b_m^k \equiv b(m, m^k) = \text{cov}(m, m^k)/\text{cov}(m^k, m^k),$$

where m^k is any mutual fund in a spanning collection. Second, there are the β_m^i occurring from each individual's optimality condition:

$$\beta_m^i \equiv \beta^i(m, \underline{\mathring{w}}^i) = \text{cov}(V'(\underline{\mathring{w}}^i), m)/\text{cov}(V'(\underline{\mathring{w}}^i), \underline{\mathring{w}}^i).$$

Third, there are the betas:

$$\beta_m \equiv \beta(m, m^e) = \text{cov}(m, m^e)/\text{cov}(m^e, m^e).$$

β_m^i and β_m *order* portfolios (securities) identically in risk, for β_m occurs with the choice of an individual having mean-variance preferences.

We now return to the linear pricing model of equation (6.D.1), asking if the b's of that relationship reflect the 'risk' of security j. The answer should be apparent: when the spanning mutual funds are selected to be efficient funds then the b's correspond exactly to betas and measure what is meant by non-diversifiable security risk. Specifically, in the linear pricing model

$$\text{E}\underline{z}^{j\cdot} = \sum_k b(\underline{z}^j, m^k)\text{E}m^{k\cdot},$$

if the κ funds are selected to be (uncorrelated and) efficient, then the b's and betas are identical as measures of the non-diversifiable risk of security j arising from its co-variation with these funds. And, to the contrary, when the spanning funds are inefficient, the ordering of the securities by b will not necessarily coincide with the non-diversifiable risk ordering.

Perhaps the most important reason for the popularity of the linear pricing model is its consistency with our intuition that asset returns have common sources of variability (the κ funds spanning θ°). The foundations for $\kappa FS\theta^\circ$ and linear pricing lie in the microeconomic theory of demand and that too has provided comfort to some. To others, however, this theoretical basis has been a source of unease, making too clear the long list of assumptions required for validity. As a reaction to this unease a simplified theory of asset price has arisen based primarily on the distinction between diversifiable and non-diversifiable risk.

This distinction takes the linear returns generating model as a primitive and adopts no assumptions about utilities other than their monotonicity and concavity. The absence of riskless arbitrage opportunities coupled with the linear generating model completes this simpler theory of linear pricing, as the next section shows.

6.E. *Arbitrage Pricing Theory*

Consider a security market economy with two *efficient* portfolios $\underline{\mathring{w}}$ and $\underline{\mathring{w}}'$ and a one factor generating model. In this case, then

$$\underline{\mathring{w}} = e + bF, \quad \text{and} \tag{6.E.1a}$$

$$\underline{\mathring{w}}' = e' + b'F, \tag{6.E.1b}$$

where the S-vector $e = \mathrm{E}\underline{\mathring{w}} 1_S$ (and similarly for e'), the b's are scalars, and the factor F has mean zero. Also, as the portfolios are efficient there is no additive noise. For arbitrage opportunities to be absent in the security market it is necessary that the two portfolios have the same value of b when they have the same expected return, see equations (5.B.2). But, how must the b's be related when the expected returns are not equal?

An answer to this last begins with a portfolio formed from $\underline{\mathring{w}}$ and $\underline{\mathring{w}}'$ as

$$\begin{aligned} \underline{w} &= \delta \underline{\mathring{w}} + (1-\delta)\underline{\mathring{w}}' \\ &= \delta(e-e') + e' + [\delta(b-b') + b']F. \end{aligned} \tag{6.E.2}$$

Now choose $\delta = b'/(b'-b)$, making the coefficient of F exactly zero. Thus, for this δ

$$\underline{w} = [b'(e-e')/(b'-b)] + e', \tag{6.E.3}$$

which is a riskless portfolio. When arbitrage opportunities are absent $\underline{w}$ must then equal the riskless portfolio ρ, and therefore

$$\frac{e-\rho}{b} = \frac{e'-\rho}{b'}, \quad \text{or}$$

$$e = \rho + b\left[\frac{e'-\rho}{b'}\right]. \tag{6.E.4}$$

Taking the expectation of this expression gives

$$\mathrm{E}e = \mathrm{E}\rho + b\lambda, \quad \text{with} \tag{6.E.5}$$

$$\lambda = \frac{\mathrm{E}e' - \mathrm{E}\rho}{b'}. \tag{6.E.6}$$

λ is commonly called a *factor risk premium* – it is the excess expected return on any portfolio with a factor coefficient equal to one.

Similar steps can be followed when arbitrage opportunities are absent and two or more factors generate security returns in a linear process. In this case the general result is

$$\mathrm{E}e = \mathrm{E}\rho + \sum_k b_k \lambda_k, \tag{6.E.7}$$

where k indexes the factors and the b_k, λ_k have interpretations analogous to the one factor case.

In closing this simple case, it is of interest that the portfolio expected return relationship allows the prices of efficient portfolios to be determined. That is, given $\mathrm{E}e = \mathrm{E}\mathring{w}/v_0$, with v_0 the market value of $\mathring{w}$, then

$$v_0 = \frac{\mathrm{E}\mathring{w}}{\mathrm{E}\rho + \Sigma_k b_k \lambda_k}. \tag{6.E.8}$$

6.E.1. Arbitrage prices generally

The above discussion suggests an alternative theory of security price built simply on two conditions: a factor generating model (6.E.1) and the absence of arbitrage opportunities. To make the theory interesting, however, it is necessary to extend the analysis to price all security portfolios, not just efficient ones as above. Given the extension is possible under not too restrictive conditions, then in what sense is the resulting theory of price of interest and an alternative to the linear pricing model with $\kappa FS\theta°$? Hold this question aside for the moment and consider first the preconditions for such a theory of price.

P6.8. Arbitrage Pricing Theory (APT). Consider an economy of I2 individuals with $S \times J$ security program $\underline{Z}$ for which each security's return is generated by a linear model with $k = 1, 2, \ldots, \kappa$ factors

$$\underline{z}^j = \mathrm{E}\underline{z}^j 1_S + \sum_k b_k^j F^k + \eta^j, \qquad j = 1, 2, \ldots, J, \tag{6.E.9}$$

where the expectations $E(F^k)=E(\eta^j)=E(\eta^j|\Sigma_k b^j_k F_k)=0$ and the η^j are uncorrelated with bounded variances. Then in the absence of arbitrage opportunities as defined below, 'most' securities are priced by the linear model

$$E\underline{z}^j=\lambda_0+\sum_k b^j_k\lambda_k, \tag{6.E.10}$$

with λ_0 and λ_k $\forall k$ being factor risk premia.[12]

Proof. The rigorous proof is given by Ross (1976) and Huberman (1982), which we sketch here. First, recall from linear algebra that the vector E (with jth component $E\underline{z}^j$) can be written as a linear combination of the J-vector of units 1_J, the J-vectors b_k (with jth component b^j_k) for each $k=1,2,\ldots,\kappa$, and a final J-vector ε which is orthogonal to 1_J and each b_k. That is,

$$E=\lambda_0 1_J+\sum_k \lambda_k b_k+\varepsilon, \tag{6.E.11}$$

with scalars λ_0 and λ_k, $k=1,2,\ldots,\kappa$ and the orthogonality conditions

$$1_J\varepsilon=\sum_j \varepsilon_j=0, \tag{6.E.12a}$$

$$b_k\varepsilon=\sum_j b^j_k\varepsilon_j=0 \quad \forall k. \tag{6.E.12b}$$

We think now of holding securities in fractions (of our wealth) proportional to the ε_j. From (6.E.12a) it is seen that the holdings use no wealth and therefore the fractions define an *arbitrage position.* From (6.E.12b) it is also seen that the position eliminates all the variation which is attributable to variations in $F^1, F^2 \ldots F^\kappa$ common factors, leaving only the variations associated with the η^j (as shown below). That is, the return on the position $\alpha\varepsilon$, α a scalar, is

$$\alpha\underline{Z}\varepsilon=\alpha\sum_j \varepsilon_j z^j=\left(\alpha\sum_j \sigma^2_j\right)1_S+\alpha\sum_j \sigma_j\eta^j, \tag{6.E.13}$$

using (6.E.11) and (6.E.12). Note that $E(\alpha\underline{Z}\varepsilon)=\alpha\Sigma_j\sigma^2_j$ and $\text{var}(\alpha\underline{Z}\varepsilon)=$

[12]Despite some similarities with the $\kappa FS\theta^\circ$ valuation equation, notice that the 'arbitrage pricing theory' does not rely on the concept of an efficient set and, in turn, spanning vectors of that set. Rather, being based simply on the absence of arbitrage its only presumption about individuals is that they have utilities increasing in wealth.

$\alpha^2 \Sigma_j \Sigma_\ell \varepsilon_j \varepsilon_\ell \operatorname{cov}(\eta^j, \eta^\ell)$, which has an upper bound of $\alpha^2 \Sigma_j \sigma_j^2$.

Now let the number of securities become large and suppose that each investor takes a sequence of arbitrage positions (if available) which yield expected returns increasing to infinity and variances decreasing to zero. Specifically, if $\Sigma_j \varepsilon_j^2$ goes to infinity with J, then arbitrage positions with such returns would occur when we choose (for example) the fractions $\alpha\varepsilon$ with the scalar $\alpha = 1/(\Sigma_j \varepsilon_j^2)^{3/4}$. In this case the return to the arbitrage position is such that

$$\mathrm{E}(\alpha \underline{Z}\varepsilon) = \left(\sum_j \varepsilon_j^2\right)^{1/4} \tag{6.E.14a}$$

$$\operatorname{var}(\alpha \underline{Z}\varepsilon) = 1 \Big/ \left(\sum_j \varepsilon_j^2\right)^{1/2}. \tag{6.E.14b}$$

With the η^j bounded above, we now see that the *absence* of arbitrage opportunities requires the sum $\Sigma_j \varepsilon_j^2$ not to increase unboundedly with the increase in J. That, in turn, requires 'most' of the ε_j be small and approximately zero.[13] Now look back to (6.E.11): for those (near) zero ε_j the no-arbitrage opportunity condition means that the idiosyncratic risk is eliminated and therefore

$$\mathrm{E}z^j = \lambda_0 + \sum_k \lambda_k b_k^j, \tag{6.E.15}$$

which proves the proposition.[14] □

Note that if there is a riskless security, say $j=0$, then $\mathrm{E}\underline{z}^0 = \lambda_0 = \mathrm{E}\rho$ and the pricing model may be written as

$$(\mathrm{E}\underline{z}^j - \mathrm{E}\rho) = \sum_k \lambda_k b_k^j, \qquad j = 1, 2, \ldots, J. \tag{6.E.10$'$}$$

[13]It is to be stressed that the proposition assures only that the linear pricing model (6.E.10) prices 'most' of the securities correctly, and all of them together with negligible error. More precisely, Huberman (1982) shows that if the securities are ordered by their absolute pricing errors so that $|\varepsilon_1| \geq |\varepsilon_2| \geq \ldots \geq |\hat{\varepsilon}|$, then for any $\hat{\varepsilon} > 0$ chosen arbitrarily small there exists an L where less than L of the securities are mispriced by an amount greater than $\hat{\varepsilon}$.

[14]In its most fundamental form the arbitrage pricing model (6.E.10), or (6.E.10′), holds for each individual separately. When taking this view, the model becomes an empirically useful market model only when making those homogeneity assumptions about individuals which permit aggregation. In this regard it is useful to assume the factor coefficients b_k^j and the expected returns $\mathrm{E}\underline{z}^j$ are agreed upon by all individuals. This agreement then implies that individual and market rate premia will be equal. See, for example, Roll and Ross (1980).

6.E.2. $\kappa FS\theta^\circ$ and APT

Notwithstanding the analytical similarity of the linear pricing model resulting from $\kappa FS\theta^\circ$ and APT, there is a profound difference in their underlying economics. We will later see that spannings sets of mutual funds for the efficient set will be identifiable in general only when conditions of security market equilibrium are satisfied. In contrast, few of the constructs of $\kappa FS\theta^\circ$ theory of price – particularly, the efficient set, spanning funds, and market equilibrium – are required for the APT. Of course, the lack of arbitrage opportunities characterizes a market equilibrium, but that is only a necessary condition for the equilibrium and ignores the usual supply and demand equality requirements. Moreover, the APT linear pricing model (6.E.10) obtains for subsets of security returns, providing they meet the conditions of P6.8. That is, with APT 'other' securities can be ignored so long as the included ones are 'sufficiently large' in number. Finally, with APT the specification of factors is a purely empirical exercise based simply on the distinction between the risk common to securities and that which is idiosyncratic (a distinction which is implicit in the linear generating process). Notice, however, that while risk premia are determined by the APT, the b's of the linear pricing model for this case are not given the interpretation of non-diversifiable risk.

Chapter 7

THE CAPITAL ASSET PRICING MODEL (CAPM)

While the detailed conditions leading to efficient set spanning are relatively recent, the sense – if not the precise analytics – of such spanning has been a recurring feature of capital theory. For example, it has long been common to assume that all relevant characteristics of security choice are those of mean return and a scalar risk measure. Given the price of the riskfree asset, it then followed that the problem of valuing risky securities in market equilibrium was that associated with determining the appropriate measure of risk and, with that, the appropriate price (premium) to be associated with that risk. Although this was a frequent conceptual framework, it was not until the 'mean-variance' analysis of Markowitz (1952) and Tobin (1958) that the determination of the trade-off between expected return and risk was made in a way consistent with utility maximizing behavior and the micro-economic theory of demand.[1]

In *mean-variance* (M-V) analysis each individual optimally considers only two parameters of the distribution of portfolio returns, the mean and variance. When risk averse, individuals trade-off variance (the 'bad') for greater expected return, variance being the single measure of portfolio risk. From that fact other results have followed: particularly, that two mutual funds fully reflect all recoverable information on security returns, that the efficient set is convex, that the so-called market mutual fund (see D5.7) is efficient when equilibrium conditions hold, and that security risk is measured by co-variability with the market fund. It is because of these results that the mean-variance theory is not only simple, but theoretically rich. And, it is because of this that the theory is frequently employed and developed here in detail.

7.A. Two Fund Spanning: The Efficient Set

What is the link between conditions for efficient set spanning and mean-variance analysis? In Section 5.E.2 it was shown that the optimal portfolio

[1] Recall Sections 5.C and 5.E, which develop the fundamentals of the mean-variance model.

of every individual with mean-variance equivalent preferences could be written as a portfolio of the same two mutual funds. Is the converse also true, that with two-fund spanning $\theta^\circ(\underline{Z})$ and the M-V efficient set $\theta^e(\underline{Z})$ are identical?

7.A.1. *Mean-variance efficiency*

P7.1. $2FS\theta^\circ$ (Z) and M-V efficiency. When two mutual funds span $\theta^\circ(\underline{Z})$ then every efficient portfolio is mean-variance efficient and therefore $\theta^e(\underline{Z})=\theta^\circ(\underline{Z})$.[2]

Proof. To begin, recall that $\theta^e(\underline{Z})$ is a subset of $\theta^\circ(\underline{Z})$, see D5.8. Choose a feasible portfolio $\underline{w}'=\Sigma_j\delta'_j\underline{z}^j$ with mean value $\mathrm{E}\underline{w}'=\Sigma_j\delta'_j\mathrm{E}z^j\geq\rho$. When conditions for $2FS\theta^\circ$ exist then a portfolio with the same mean $\mathrm{E}\underline{w}'$ can be constructed from two spanning funds m^1 and m^2 as follows

$$\mathrm{E}\underline{w}'=\lambda\mathrm{E}m^1+(1-\lambda)\mathrm{E}m^2, \tag{7.A.1}$$

where $m^1=\Sigma_j\delta_j^1\underline{z}_j$ and $m^2=\Sigma_j\delta_j^2\underline{z}_j$. Note that λ is unique given a choice of m^1 and m^2 for which $\mathrm{E}m^1\neq\mathrm{E}m^2$. Moreover, for each j the portfolio fraction δ'_j can be written as $\delta'_j=\lambda\delta_j^1+(1-\lambda)\delta_j^2+\alpha_j$, with α_j chosen to assure the equality. Now since

$$\sum_j\delta'_j=\sum_j[\lambda\delta_j^1+(1-\lambda)\delta_j^2]=1,$$

it follows that

$$\sum_j\alpha_j=0. \tag{7.A.2}$$

Hold this aside for the moment.

Next write

$$\begin{aligned}\underline{w}'&=\sum_j\delta'_j\underline{z}^j=\sum_j[\lambda\delta_j^1+(1-\lambda)\delta_j^2+\alpha_j]\underline{z}^j\\&=\lambda\sum_j\delta_j^1\underline{z}^j+(1-\lambda)\sum_j\delta_j^2\underline{z}^j+\sum_j\alpha_j\underline{z}^j\\&=\lambda m^1+(1-\lambda)m^2+\sum_j\alpha_j\underline{z}^j.\end{aligned} \tag{7.A.3}$$

[2]Note again that all security return means and variances are assumed to be finite.

This result and (7.A.1) imply

$$\sum_j \alpha_j \mathrm{E}\underline{z}^j = 0 \tag{7.A.4a}$$

and, in turn,

$$\mathrm{E}\left(\sum_j \alpha_j \mathrm{E}\underline{z}^j \,|\, \lambda m^1 + (1-\lambda)m^2\right) = 0. \tag{7.A.4b}$$

We can therefore write

$$\underline{w}' = [\lambda m^1 + (1-\lambda)m^2] + \eta, \tag{7.A.4c}$$

where η has noise properties. Thus, regardless of the choice of dispersion measure, the portfolio of the spanning mutual funds has minimum dispersion for the given expected return. And, when all variances are finite, then $[\lambda m^1 + (1-\lambda)m^2]$ must have minimum variance for the return level $\mathrm{E}\underline{w}'$. □

In the above proof it was assumed that the riskless asset was feasible, which meant that it provided the lower bound on the expected return to efficient portfolios. As the following proposition shows, when it is impossible to form a riskless portfolio then the minimum variance portfolio more generally gives the lower bound to the expected value of mean-variance efficient portfolios.

P7.2. Minimum variance portfolio. Let $\dot{m}$ be the portfolio with minimum variance, with $\dot{m} = \rho$ when the riskless portfolio is feasible. Then,

(i) $\dot{m}$ is mean-variance efficient when it is risky,
(ii) $\mathrm{E}\underline{\mathring{w}} \geq \mathrm{E}\dot{m}$ for all mean-variance efficient portfolios $\underline{\mathring{w}}$,
(iii) every portfolio of $\dot{m}$ and any mean-variance efficient portfolio $\underline{\mathring{w}}$ is also mean-variance efficient (with positive weight being given $\underline{\mathring{w}}$ when $\dot{m} = \rho$).

Proof. (i) Let $\dot{m}$ be risky and proceed by contradiction, i.e., assume $\dot{m}$ is not M-V efficient. In this case there then exists a M-V efficient portfolio $\underline{\mathring{w}} \neq \dot{m}$ with $\mathrm{E}\underline{\mathring{w}} = \mathrm{E}\dot{m}$ which stochastically dominates $\dot{m}$. We can then write $\dot{m} = \underline{\mathring{w}} + \eta$, with $\eta \neq 0$ being noise, so that $\mathrm{var}(\dot{m}) = \mathrm{var}(\mathring{w}) + \mathrm{var}(\eta) > \mathrm{var}(\mathring{w})$. But this must be false since $\dot{m}$ has minimum variance. Therefore $\dot{m}$ must be efficient. (ii) If $E\mathring{\underline{w}} < E\dot{m}$ then $\dot{m}$ has both smaller variance (less risk) and greater mean, a combination which implies that $\dot{\underline{w}}$ cannot be mean-variance efficient. Thus, by contradiction $E\mathring{\underline{w}} \geq E\dot{m}$. (iii) The case where $\dot{m}=\rho$ is covered by P5.6, so let $\dot{m}$ be risky. In this situation $\dot{m}$ is efficient and it can be chosen as one mutual funding spanning the efficient set by P6.1. Item (iii) follows from the convexity of the M-V efficient set, see P5.9. □

7.A.2. The mean-variance maxim

When conditions obtain for two fund spanning the efficient set is composed of only those portfolios with minimum variance at each possible level of mean greater than the riskless rate.[3] Details of the solution to this mathematical program provide some economic insights which are of interest. To begin, write the mean and variance of feasible portfolio $\underline{w}$, respectively, as

$$E\underline{w} = \delta E\underline{z}, \quad \text{and} \tag{7.A.5}$$

$$\mathrm{var}(\underline{w}) = \delta \underline{Z}\delta, \tag{7.A.6}$$

where δ is a vector of portfolio fractions, $\underline{w}=\delta\underline{Z}$, $E\underline{z}=[E\underline{z}^1\ E\underline{z}^2 \ldots E\underline{z}^J]$ is the vector of expected returns of the J securities, and $\underline{Z}=[\mathrm{cov}(\underline{z}^j, \underline{z}^k)]$ is again the $J \times J$ variance–covariance matrix. In turn, the efficient set can be constructively generated by minimizing $\mathrm{var}(\underline{w})$ subject to $E\underline{w}=k$ for all $k>\dot{m}$. For each value of k, the choice variable in this problem is δ and the associated Lagrangian is

$$L=\delta\underline{Z}\delta - 2\lambda(\delta E\underline{z} - k) - 2\xi(\delta 1_J - 1), \tag{7.A.7}$$

with λ and ξ multipliers. Stationarity conditions are

$$\underline{Z}\mathring{\delta} = \lambda E\underline{z} + \xi 1_J, \tag{7.A.8}$$

plus the two constraints. When the variance–covariance matrix has an

[3]To be somewhat more precise, we refer here to the *ex ante* (objectively perceived) distribution of returns. These in practices must be estimated from specific realizations (or by subjective methods), which requires that we distinguish the *ex post* efficient set, the set of minimum *sample* variance portfolios, from its *ex ante* counterpart. One can 'construct' population or sample efficient sets using either population means and variances or the corresponding sample statistics. The development and results of this section apply to either construction.

inverse, then all efficient portfolio fractions satisfy the condition

$$\mathring{\delta}=\lambda\underline{\mathcal{Z}}^{-1}\mathrm{E}\underline{z}+\xi\underline{\mathcal{Z}}^{-1}1_J. \tag{7.A.9}$$

This in turn implies that efficient portfolios are such that

$$\mathring{\underline{w}}=\underline{Z}\mathring{\delta}=\underline{Z}[\lambda\underline{\mathcal{Z}}^{-1}\mathrm{E}\underline{z}+\xi\underline{\mathcal{Z}}^{-1}1_J]. \tag{7.A.10}$$

Notice that all efficient portfolios can be written as a weighted sum of the *same* two vectors $\underline{Z}\underline{\mathcal{Z}}^{-1}\mathrm{E}\underline{z}$ and $\underline{Z}\underline{\mathcal{Z}}^{-1}1_J$, which is the usual method for verifying that two fund spanning obtains in this case.

Introduce now the $J\times 2$ matrix $[\mathrm{E}\underline{z}\ 1_J]$. If at least two securities have different means, this matrix has rank 2 and we can then rewrite (7.A.9) as

$$\mathring{\delta}=\underline{\mathcal{Z}}^{-1}[\mathrm{E}\underline{z}\ 1_J]A^{-1}\left[\begin{smallmatrix}\mathrm{E}\mathring{\underline{w}}\\ 1\end{smallmatrix}\right]. \tag{7.A.11}$$

Here, $\left[\begin{smallmatrix}\mathrm{E}\mathring{\underline{w}}\\ 1\end{smallmatrix}\right]$ is a 2×1 vector and the 2×2 symmetric matrix A^{-1} is defined by

$$A^{-1}\equiv\left[\begin{smallmatrix}\mathrm{E}\underline{z}\\ 1_J\end{smallmatrix}\right]\underline{\mathcal{Z}}^{-1}[\mathrm{E}\underline{z}\ 1_J].$$

The multipliers λ and ξ are eliminated from (7.A.9) by first premultiplying that equation by $[\mathrm{E}\underline{z}\ 1_J]$, then using the original constraints to solve for λ and ξ and finally substituting these back in (7.A.9). As the matrix A contains all means, variances, and covariances of the problem it is commonly referred to as the *parameter matrix* of the efficient portfolio set.

Equations (7.A.11) can be used to form the variance of $\mathring{\underline{w}}$ as

$$\operatorname{var}\mathring{\underline{w}}=\mathring{\delta}\underline{\mathcal{Z}}\mathring{\delta}=[\mathrm{E}\mathring{\underline{w}}\ 1]A^{-1}\left[\begin{smallmatrix}\mathrm{E}\mathring{\underline{w}}\\ 1\end{smallmatrix}\right]. \tag{7.A.12}$$

That is, the variance of any mean-variance efficient portfolio (and thus any efficient portfolio when two fund spanning obtains) is related to its mean return by the parabola[4]

$$\operatorname{var}(\mathring{\underline{w}})=(a_{11}-2a_{12}\,\mathrm{E}\mathring{\underline{w}}+a_{22}(\mathrm{E}\mathring{\underline{w}})^2)/(a_{11}a_{22}-a_{12}^2), \tag{7.A.13}$$

[4]It is to be stressed that this results in a parabolic relationship in the mean-variance plane; it has earlier been shown that all efficient portfolios lie along a (straight) *line segment* in the *S*-space of portfolios.

where the scalars $a_{11}=\mathrm{E}\underline{z}\underline{Z}^{-1}\mathrm{E}\underline{z}$, $a_{12}=a_{21}=\mathrm{E}\underline{z}\underline{Z}^{-1}1_J$, and $a_{22}=1_J\underline{Z}^{-1}1_J$ are the appropriate four elements of A^{-1}. In turn, the minimum variance unit plan $\dot{\underline{w}}$ is given by the solution of

$$\frac{\mathrm{d}\,\mathrm{var}(\mathring{\underline{w}})}{\mathrm{d}\mathrm{E}\mathring{\underline{w}}}=-a_{12}+a_{22}\mathrm{E}\dot{\underline{w}}=0, \tag{7.A.14}$$

and therefore

$$\mathrm{E}\dot{\underline{w}}=a_{12}/a_{22}. \tag{7.A.15}$$

Substituting this in (7.A.13) provides the minimum variance itself, also as one of the A^{-1} parameters

$$\mathrm{var}(\dot{\underline{w}})=1/a_{22}. \tag{7.A.16}$$

E7.1. In the above case a riskless, or zero variance, portfolio was specifically assumed to be infeasible (otherwise, $\underline{Z}$ would have been singular). It is straightforward, however, to extend the analysis and allow $\rho\in\theta(\underline{Z})$. To this end, keep the same J risky securities as before, but add a $(J+1)$th security with zero variance and mean return equal to $\mathrm{E}\rho$. Let $\delta^{J+1}=1-\delta 1_J$, where $\delta=[\delta^1\,\delta^2\ldots\delta^J]$ is, as above, the portfolio fractions of the J securities. Then, in a manner analogous to (7.A.7) the efficient set can be generated as the solution of the problem

$$L=\delta\underline{Z}\delta-2\lambda[\delta(\mathrm{E}\underline{z}-\mathrm{E}\rho 1_J)-(\mathrm{const}-\mathrm{E}\rho)], \tag{7.A.17}$$

with the constant (const) being treated parametrically. Notice that the constraint $\Sigma_{j=1}^{J+1}\delta^j=1$ does not now appear as part of the Lagrange function because δ^{J+1} is eliminated using this equality.

At a stationarity point of (7.A.17)

$$\underline{Z}\mathring{\delta}=\lambda(\mathrm{E}\underline{z}-\mathrm{E}\rho 1_J), \tag{7.A.18}$$

and the constraint $\mathrm{E}\rho=\mathrm{const}$ is satisfied. When $\underline{Z}$ is non-singular, the solution for $\mathring{\delta}$ is

$$\mathring{\delta}=\lambda[\underline{Z}^{-1}\mathrm{E}\underline{z}-\mathrm{E}\rho\underline{Z}^{-1}1_J]. \tag{7.A.19}$$

Finally, using the constraint equation to eliminate λ we obtain

$$\mathrm{E}\mathring{\underline{w}}=\mathrm{E}\rho+\mathrm{std}(\mathring{\underline{w}})[a_{22}(\mathrm{E}\rho)^2-2a_{12}\mathrm{E}\rho+a_{11}]^{1/2}, \tag{7.A.20}$$

where it is required that $\mathrm{E}\underset{\sim}{\mathring{w}} > \mathrm{E}\rho$ and $\mathrm{std}(\underset{\sim}{\mathring{w}})$ is notation for the standard deviation of $\underset{\sim}{\mathring{w}}$. Thus, the efficient set in mean-standard deviation space is a straight line segment. The (non-enclosed) vertical intercept of the efficient set line is the riskless return $\mathrm{E}\rho$ and the slope is given in terms of $\mathrm{E}\rho$ and the parameters of the A^{-1} matrix.

When it is additionally required that the security prices are at their equilibrium values, then the market mutual fund is efficient and can be used to determine the parameters in (7.A.20). In this case the valuation equation can be written in its common form

$$\mathrm{E}\underset{\sim}{\mathring{w}} = \mathrm{E}\rho + \lambda^{*}\mathrm{std}(\underset{\sim}{\mathring{w}}), \tag{7.A.21}$$

where $\lambda^{*} = (\mathrm{E}\overset{*}{m} - \mathrm{E}\rho)/\mathrm{std}(\overset{*}{m})$ and $\overset{*}{m}$ is the market fund. ■

7.B. *Two Fund Spanning Conditions*

The early security pricing literature justified $2FS\theta^{\circ}(\underset{\sim}{Z})$ and mean-variance analysis either on the basis of normal security return distributions or quadratic elementary utility functions. Both foundations have their drawbacks. With the non-zero probability of negative returns, normality is inconsistent with limited liability securities. And, in its increasing range, the region of interest, quadratic utility exhibits increasing absolute risk aversion and thus the uncomfortable implication that risky securities are inferior. As a reaction to these drawbacks, it is of interest to more generally catalogue the classes of utility functions which, for an arbitrary (but non-degenerate) specification of the security program $\underset{\sim}{Z}$, provide spanning, and particularly two fund spanning, of the efficient set.

7.B.1. *The utility functions*

The following proposition P7.3 characterizes an individual's 'expansion path' of state contingent claims with two fund spanning of the efficient set. P7.4 then identifies the class of utility functions yielding such an expansion path. We call attention to the fact that in the first of these propositions the security market can be complete or incomplete and contain a riskless portfolio or not.

P7.3. $2FS\theta^{\circ}(\underset{\sim}{Z})$ and optimal portfolios. Let the security program be arbitrary (except that it admit no arbitrage possibilities and be non-trivial), then a necessary and sufficient condition for two mutual funds to span the efficient portfolio set is that the elementary utility functions of all individuals yield a linear relation among optimal state contingent returns. That is, for each individual i the following relationship must obtain for all pairs of states s and e:

$$\mathring{\underline{w}}^i_s = a_s + b_{se}\mathring{\underline{w}}^i_e \, , \tag{7.B.1}$$

where the a_s and b_{se} parameters are common to all individuals and satisfy a further restriction noted below.

Proof. The case with three states $(s=1,2,3)$ is easily developed and generalizes directly. First, we show sufficiency. Let $\mathring{\underline{w}}^i_1 = a_1 + b_{12}\mathring{\underline{w}}^i_2$, $\mathring{\underline{w}}^i_2 = a_2 + b_{23}\mathring{\underline{w}}^i_3$ and by the appropriate substitutions and algebra solve for

$$\mathring{\underline{w}}^i_2 = \frac{\mathring{\underline{w}}^i_1 - a_1}{b_{12}} \quad \text{and} \quad \mathring{\underline{w}}^i_3 = \frac{\mathring{\underline{w}}^i_1 - (a_1 + b_{12}a_2)}{b_{12}b_{23}}.$$

In turn, the optimal consumption plan can be written as

$$\mathring{\underline{w}}^i = \begin{bmatrix} 1 & 0 \\ \mathring{\underline{w}}^i_1 \quad 1 & -a_1/b_{12} \\ 1/b_{12}b_{23} & (a_1 + a_2 b_{12})/b_{12}b_{23} \end{bmatrix},$$

$$= \mathring{\underline{w}}^i_1 m^1 + (1 - \mathring{\underline{w}}^i_1) m^2, \tag{7.B.2}$$

where the vectors m^1 and m^2 are defined in the obvious way from the a and b parameters. If the optimal portfolio of every individual has the linearity property given by equation (7.B.1), then every individual derives his optimal consumption from a portfolio of the *same* two vectors m^1 and m^2. The final step of the sufficiency proof, which results in a restriction on the a and b parameters, assures that both m^1 and m^2 can be written as mutual funds (i.e., as portfolios of the original securities). The reader is referred to Cass and Stiglitz (1970) for this step, see also P7.4 below. The proof of necessity proceeds in the obvious way and is omitted. □

P7.4. Utility functions and two-fund spanning. Let the security program admit no arbitrage opportunities but otherwise be arbitrary except as given below. Then the efficient set $\theta^\circ(\underline{Z})$ is spanned by two mutual funds iff I2 individuals are restricted to be such that one of the following three cases obtains.

Case (i). The security market is complete and all utility functions satisfy either

$$C^i[\mathrm{d}U^i(\underline{w}_s^i)/\mathrm{d}\underline{w}_s^i]^{D^i} + B[\mathrm{d}U^i(\underline{w}_s^i)/\mathrm{d}\underline{w}_s^i]^{B1} = \underline{w}_s^i, \tag{7.B.3a}$$

with individual-specific parameters C^i and D^i and common parameters B and $B1$, or

$$[\mathrm{d}U^i(\underline{w}_s)/\mathrm{d}\underline{w}_s^i]^{D^i}\ [C^i + b \log \mathrm{d}U^i(\underline{w}_s^i)/\mathrm{d}\underline{w}_s] = \underline{w}_s^i, \tag{7.B.3b}$$

with individual-specific parameters D^i and C^i and common parameter b.

Case (ii). The security market may be complete or not, but a riskless portfolio is feasible and all utility functions exhibit linear risk tolerance

$$T^i(\underline{w}_s^i) = a^i + b\underline{w}_s^i, \tag{7.B.4}$$

with individual-specific parameter a^i and common parameter b.

Case (iii). The security market may be complete or not, a riskless portfolio may be feasible or not, and all utility functions are either quadratic

$$\mathrm{d}U^i(\underline{w}_s^i)/\mathrm{d}\underline{w}_s^i = \hat{a}^i + \hat{b}\underline{w}_s^i, \tag{7.B.5a}$$

or exhibit constant relative aversion

$$\mathrm{d}U^i(\underline{w}_s)/\mathrm{d}\underline{w}_s^i = b'\underline{w}_s^{i'}, \tag{7.B.5b}$$

with $\hat{a}^i$ individual-specific and $\hat{b}$, b', and c' common parameters.

With a little algebra it is seen that the utility functions of case (iii) are a subclass of those in case (ii), and those in case (ii) are in turn a subclass of those in case (i): if $D^i = 0$ in (7.B.3a) and (7.B.3b), then (7.B.4) results; and, if in (7.B.4) it is further required that $b = -1$ then (7.B.5a) results, or when $a^i \equiv 0$ in (7.B.4) then (7.B.5b) results. The requirement that vectors m^1 and m^2 in fact be portfolios places such restrictions on the admissible parameters of the utility functions. As a complete security market provides the least restriction on admissible m^1 and m^2 it, in turn, places the least restrictive conditions on the utility function parameters. This logic continues through case (iii), which requires m^1 and m^2 be feasible in a fully general market (complete or incomplete and with or without ρ) and this places the maximum restrictions on the parameters of the riskless portfolio.

Proof. The essential logic of the proof is as follows. Given P7.3, it is only required (1) to show the above utility functions satisfy the (7.B.1) linearity relationship and (2) to further restrict the parameters of those utility functions to meet the requirement that m^1 and m^2 be mutual funds. In P1.9 it was shown that the linearity (proportionality) among any optimal state claims pair holds if and only if the demand for those state claims is linear (proportional) in initial wealth. That proof applies exactly to the complete markets case given above; all that is additionally required is to interpret the state claims as returns rather than dollar amounts. Cass and Stiglitz (1970), Pollack (1971), and Vickson (1975) give the final steps of the part (i) proof by showing that this linearity property of state claims demand is satisfied if and only if the utility function satisfies one of the two related functional equations (7.B.3).

The requirement that the same two mutual funds replicate every individual's optimal choice, and thus that the constants in (7.B.1) be common to all individuals, fixes the commonality of the parameters in case (i) of the proposition. The proofs for cases (ii) and (iii) then proceed simply from the case (i) results. The utility function parameters are restricted to assure m^1 and m^2 are mutual funds with the given specification of $\underline{Z}$. As the details of these final steps are both lengthy and algebraically tedious, the reader is again referred to Cass and Stiglitz or Vickson. □

When, in any of the three cases of P7.4, all individuals are constant relative risk averse with the same risk constant, then the parameters a_s $\forall s$ in (7.B.1) are identically zero and $\underline{\mathring{w}}^i_s = b_{se}\underline{\mathring{w}}^i_e$ $\forall s, e, i$. This implies $m^1 = m^2$, see (7.B.2), so that one mutual fund spans the efficient set and the same *portfolio* (not consumption plan in dollars) is optimal for all individuals.[5]

E7.2. Recall the individual's optimality condition of equation (4.B.1):

$$\partial U(w_s)/\partial w_s = \lambda(\pi_s/h_s) \quad \forall s,$$

where λ is the multiplier associated with the budget constraint. The security market may be complete or incomplete with this condition. Whichever case, suppose that there are two or more states for which the price-probability ratio is constant; that is,

$$\pi_\theta/h_\theta = c,$$

[5]This leads to $2FS\theta°(\underline{Z})$ since any two mutual funds which can be formed in a portfolio to equal the single spanning fund also spans the efficient set. That is, $1FS\theta°$ implies $\kappa FS\theta°, \kappa > 1$, albeit in a trivial way.

where c is constant for this subset of states (θ and e will indicate typical states in the subset). If U expresses strict risk aversion, then the marginal utility is an invertible function and

$$w_\theta = f(c\lambda),$$

where f is the inverse of the marginal utility. This equation informs us that in each of the θ states the individual's wealth w_θ is (optimally) identical. A consequence of this fact is that

$$w^i_\theta / w^i_e = 1 \tag{7.B.6a}$$

for *each* individual i. A similar constancy in wealth 'ratio' holds in rates of return. Multiply the preceding equation by $(c\bar{w}_0/c\bar{w}_0)$ to give

$$\underline{w}^i_\theta / \underline{w}^i_e = (w^i_\theta \pi_\theta / \bar{w}_0 h_\theta)/(w^i_e \pi_e / \bar{w}_0 h_e) = h_\theta / h_e. \tag{7.B.6b}$$

Equations (7.B.6) are the standard conditions for mutual fund spanning – individuals are indifferent between holding the pure state securities or holding a mutual fund which 'collects' those for which the price-probability ratio is the same constant. As every individual's period one utility depends on his wealth at that period and every individual holds the same wealth in the subset of states, there is no necessity to differentiate among the states of the subset. Rather, all that is required is to buy state claims in proportion to the state probabilities. ■

The specific case of two-fund spanning with a riskless asset and an incomplete security market is frequently considered. Given these conditions, but with the security program otherwise arbitrary [this is case (ii) of P7.4], two-fund spanning requires that utility functions exhibit linear risk tolerance. By specific choice of the a and b parameters in the expression of linear risk tolerance, the utility functions can be made to possess increasing, constant, or decreasing absolute and relative risk aversion. In this respect the limitation to linear risk tolerance and the finding of $2FS\theta^\circ(\underline{Z})$ – again, with $\rho \in \theta(\underline{Z})$, but $\underline{Z}$ otherwise arbitrary – does not appear restrictive. On the other hand, the requirement that the slope parameter b be common means that individuals in this case can differ only to the extent allowed by the parameter a^i and their investment wealth. Referring to P1.8, we see that the commonality of b requires that each and every utility function belong to a single subclass. For example, if one individual has logarithmic utility, then so must everyone, and this holds also for exponential utility. Further, if one individual has utility represented by a power function, then all individuals must have power functions of the same power. Finally, note too that the analysis has assumed homogeneity of probability estimates across individuals, so that on closer inspections individuals cannot differ by 'very much' at all if $2FS\theta^{\circ}(\underline{Z})$ is to occur by specification of individual characteristics.

While at first it appeared that placing restrictions on utility functions would be a reasonable foundation for a theory of security demand with $\kappa FS\theta^{\circ}(\underline{Z})$, we now see otherwise. That too is the conclusion of Cass and Stiglitz (1970, p. 144), who found that spanning '... turns out to be a property limited to a very, very few utility functions.' Because of these strong conclusions and because of the tractability and reasonableness of the alternatives, it is therefore not usual to consider limitations to utility functions alone as a method of achieving non-trivial mutual fund spanning of the efficient set. The polar alternative is to place no restrictions on individuals beyond the I2 specification, but limit the joint distribution of returns.

7.B.2. The security program

With I2 individuals P6.3 provides necessary and sufficient restrictions on the security program for $\kappa FS\theta^{\circ}(\underline{Z})$. From that proposition it is clear that two mutual funds, m^1 and m^2, span the efficient set if and only if

$$\underline{z}^j = \sigma_j m^1 + (1-\sigma_j)m^2 + \eta^j \quad \forall j, \tag{7.B.7a}$$

where η^j is the usual noise. Given the minimum variance portfolio $\dot{m}$ can be taken as one spanning fund, we write the above equation in its common form

$$\underline{z}^j = \dot{m} + \sigma_j(m - \dot{m}) + \eta^j \quad \forall j, \tag{7.B.7b}$$

(with the superscript to the second mutual fund being omitted for convenience). And, when a riskless portfolio ρ is available, then that final substitution for $\dot{m}$ is usual.

E7.3. What is the class of security return distributions which provide for equations (7.B.7) and therefore yield two-fund spanning? In Section 5.C.2 it was shown that the joint normality of security returns implied mean-variance equivalent preferences and this was shown in P5.9 (and P7.1) to imply $2FS\theta^{\circ}$. It is instructive to now consider an alternative proof of this fact. Let $\underline{Z} = [\underline{z}^1 \underline{z}^2 \ldots \underline{z}^J]$ be the vector of security returns with $\underline{\underline{Z}}$ the associated variance covariance matrix. Let $\underline{z}^1 = \rho$ and define the *excess returns* $\underline{z}^{j\cdot} = \underline{z}^j - \rho\ \forall j \geq 2$. Further, use $\underline{Z}^{\cdot} = [\underline{z}^{2\cdot}\, \underline{z}^{3\cdot} \ldots \underline{z}^{J\cdot}]$ and $\underline{Z}^{\cdot}$ as notation for the excess return matrix and associated variance–covariance matrix with the remaining $(J-1)$ securities. Using this notation (7.B.7) may be rewritten

$$\underline{z}^{j\cdot} = \sigma_j m^{\cdot} + \eta^j \quad \forall j \geq 2, \tag{7.B.8}$$

where $m^{\cdot} = m - \rho$ is the excess return (over the riskless rate) of m and η^j, again, has the usual noise properties:

$$\mathrm{E}(\eta^j) = \mathrm{E}(\eta^j | m^{\cdot}) = 0 \quad \forall j \geq 2. \tag{7.B.9}$$

Note, for later use, that these equations jointly imply the portfolio weights $\sigma_j = \mathrm{E}z^{j\cdot}/\mathrm{E}m^{\cdot}$.

Given there exist portfolio fractions and therefrom a mutual fund which satisfies (7.B.8) and (7.B.9), then $2FS\theta^{\circ}(\underline{Z})$ results. It is now to be shown that when securities are distributed multivariate normal such a portfolio exists.[6] We begin this proof by noting that it is sufficient for the conditional independence of normal variables that they be uncorrelated, i.e., a sufficient condition for (7.B.9) is that, for any fund $\hat{m}$,

$$\mathrm{cov}(\eta^j, \hat{m}) = \mathrm{cov}(\hat{\underline{z}}^j - \sigma_j \hat{m}, \hat{m}) = 0 \quad \forall j \geq 2, \tag{7.B.10}$$

where we substitute for η^j from (7.B.8). Multiplying both sides of this equation by ζ^j and summing over all $j \geq 2$ then gives

$$\mathrm{cov}\left(\sum_j \zeta^j (\hat{\underline{z}}^j - \sigma_j \hat{m}), \hat{m} \right) = 0. \tag{7.B.11}$$

If it is possible to show that there exists some portfolio of securities $\hat{m}$ solving this equation, then sufficient conditions exist for (7.B.10) and, in turn, for (7.B.8) and (7.B.9). This would prove that joint normality of the risky securities implies $2FS\theta^{\circ}(\underline{Z})$.

Proceeding along this line, let $\delta = [\delta_2\, \delta_3 \ldots \delta_J]$ be the portfolio fractions defining $m^{\cdot}$ and substitute this in (7.B.11) to give

$$\mathrm{cov}\left[\sum_j \zeta^J \left(\underline{z}^{j\cdot} - \sigma_j \sum_n \delta^n \underline{z}^{n\cdot} \right), \sum_n \delta^n \underline{z}^{n\cdot} \right] = 0.$$

[6]Here, the number of states must be infinite with each $\underline{z}^j$ an infinite dimensional vector (random variable) for the exact normality of the distributions.

Using the obvious notations rewrite this in vector-matrix form as

$$\zeta \underline{Z}^{\cdot}\delta - \delta \underline{Z}^{\cdot}\delta\langle\delta,\sigma\rangle = 0. \tag{7.B.12}$$

The δ-solution to this equation is $\delta = k(\underline{Z}^{\cdot})^{-1}\sigma$, with k a constant chosen to assure δ constitutes portfolio fractions. That this is a solution is shown by substitution:

$$k\zeta\underline{Z}(\underline{Z}^{\cdot})^{-1}\sigma - k\delta\underline{Z}(\underline{Z}^{\cdot})^{-1}\langle\zeta,\sigma\rangle = 0,$$

$$k\langle\zeta,\sigma\rangle - k\langle\zeta,\sigma\rangle\langle\delta,\sigma\rangle = 0.$$

As $\sigma_j = \mathrm{E}\underline{z}^j/\mathrm{E}m^{\cdot}$, we can write $\langle\delta,\sigma\rangle = \Sigma_j\delta_j\mathrm{E}\underline{z}^j/\mathrm{E}m^{\cdot}$. Finally, the definition of $m^{\cdot} = \Sigma_j\delta^j\underline{z}^{j\cdot}$ implies $\langle\delta,\sigma\rangle = 1$ and therefore $m^{\cdot}$ is a mutual fund. Given security returns are distributed multivariate normal over states, the mutual fund m and the riskless mutual fund ρ span $\theta^{\circ}(\underline{Z})$. ■

The nature of the above example would seem to suggest that any multivariate distribution with a two parameter description could also provide $2FS\theta^{\circ}(\underline{Z})$. This conjecture is false, however, as lognormally distributed security yields can be shown as a contradiction.[7] The problem with lognormal distributions in this regard is that they are not stable – a portfolio of lognormally distributed securities is not itself lognormally distributed in general. On this basis a second reasonable conjecture is that the class of Pareto–Levy stable distributions (of which the normal distribution is a limiting case) provides for $2FS\theta^{\circ}(\underline{Z})$. Using exactly the same procedure outlined above for the multivariate normal case, it is a straightforward task to show that such stable distributions do indeed provide for two fund spanning.[8] But, while stability in distribution is a sufficient condition for spanning of the efficient set, there are several counterexamples to its necessity.[9]

E7.4. Perhaps the most common of the counterexamples is the 'symmetric return' case where the multivariate distribution function of the securities is unchanged by their permutation.

More precisely, with $\underline{z}^1$ a riskless security, the multivariate distribution function of risky securities $f(\underline{z}^2, \underline{z}^3, \ldots, z^J)$ is symmetric if, for each set of outcomes, $f(\underline{z}^2, \underline{z}^3, \ldots \underline{z}^J)$ remains unchanged when any two arguments

[7] See Feldstein (1969).
[8] Fama (1965) develops this case in detail.
[9] See, for example, Agnew (1971).

of f are interchanged. That this sort of symmetry leads to $2FS\theta^{\circ}(\underline{Z})$ is immediately seen by reference to the conditions for an optimal portfolio. Obviously, if $f(z^2, z^3, \ldots, z^J) = f(z^j, z^3, \ldots, z^2, \ldots, z^J)$ then every risk averse individual chooses $\delta_2 = \delta_j \, \forall j$ as his optimal risky portfolio fractions; this is, each holds all *risky* securities in the same relative proportions. The result is that if $\hat{m}$ is the yield to a mutual fund with equal dollar amounts held in each risky security, then the pair $[\rho \, \hat{m}]$ spans $\theta^{\circ}(\underline{Z})$. It is important to observe, however, that the class of security distributions which lead to such symmetry is very specialized. For example, the most frequently considered instance of this case is where all (risky) securities have independently and identically distributed (i.i.d.) returns across states. ■

7.C. Valuation

One of the key aspects of the valuation equation with two-fund spanning is our ability to specifically identify the spanning funds. The following P7.7 provides the usual valuation equation in this case, the intervening P7.5 and P7.6 identify the spanning funds.

7.C.1. Spanning funds

P7.5. Two-fund spanning with uncorrelated funds. Suppose the security market is in equilibrium at some price system $\mathring{v}_0$. Let $\underline{Z}$ represent the security program of the economy at these prices, and further assume that conditions are such that two mutual funds span $\theta^{\circ}(\underline{Z})$. Then the pair $[\overset{*}{m} \, m^{\circ}]$ span $\theta^{\circ}(\underline{Z})$, where $\overset{*}{m}$ is the market mutual fund and m° is constructed such that $\operatorname{cov}(\overset{*}{m}, m^{\circ}) = 0$. Moreover, m° is an inefficient fund.

Proof. When the security market is in equilibrium and conditions for $2FS\theta^{\circ}(\underline{Z})$ are further satisfied, the market mutual fund $\overset{*}{m}$ is efficient (P5.10) and it can, therefore, be chosen as one spanning fund. It is also possible to choose $\dot{m}$, the minimum variance mutual fund, as the second fund (P7.2). Thus, $[\overset{*}{m} \, \dot{m}]$ spans $\theta^{\circ}(\underline{Z})$. We need now to show that there exists a fund m° such that (a) $m^{\circ} = \delta \dot{m} + (1-\delta)\overset{*}{m}$ and (b) $\operatorname{cov}(\overset{*}{m}, m^{\circ}) = 0$ hold simultaneously. Property (a) provides that m° can be substituted for $\dot{m}$ in the spanning pair, with property (b) further providing that m° and $\overset{*}{m}$ are uncorrelated. If it is additionally found that $\delta \geq 1$ when these two properties are satisfied, then $\mathrm{E}m^{\circ} \leq \mathrm{E}\dot{m}$ (with the strict equalities holding only when $\dot{m} = \rho$) which implies m° is inefficient.

For m° in (b) above, substitute from (a) and solve to yield $\delta = \text{cov}(\overset{*}{m}, \overset{*}{m}) / [\text{cov}(\overset{*}{m}, \overset{*}{m}) - \text{cov}(\overset{*}{m}, \dot{m})]$. In the case where $\dot{m} = \rho$, $\delta = 1$ and $m^\circ = \rho$, which makes m° inefficient. Consider next the case where $\dot{m} \neq \rho$ so that $\dot{m}$ is efficient. With $\overset{*}{m}$ and $\dot{m}$ distinct, then it must be that $\text{E}\overset{*}{m} > \text{E}\dot{m}$ which requires $\beta(\overset{*}{m}, \overset{*}{m}) > \beta(\dot{m}, \overset{*}{m})$. This implies $\text{cov}(\overset{*}{m}, \dot{m}) < \text{cov}(\overset{*}{m}, \overset{*}{m})$ and, in turn, $\delta > 1$. □

The fund m° is frequently termed the *zero-β mutual fund*, as its zero covariance with $\overset{*}{m}$ also means that it has zero systematic risk relative to $\overset{*}{m}$. Note finally that, because the solution for δ in the above proof is unique, m° is the only fund uncorrelated with $\overset{*}{m}$ that can be employed with $\overset{*}{m}$ as a spanning pair.[10]

P7.6. Covariance weights. Let the conditions of P7.5 be satisfied so that $[\overset{*}{m}\, m^\circ]$ span $\theta^\circ(\underline{Z})$. Then, $\forall j$

$$\underline{z}^j = \beta_j \overset{*}{m} + (1 - \beta_j) m^\circ + \eta^j, \tag{7.C.1}$$

where $\text{E}(\eta^j) = \text{E}(\eta^j | \overset{*}{m}, | m^\circ) = 0$. This, in turn, implies

$$\text{E}\underline{z}^j = \text{E}m^\circ + \beta_j \text{E}(\overset{*}{m} - m^\circ), \tag{7.C.2}$$

where the non-diversifiable risk of fund m is defined relative to $\overset{*}{m}$ as

$$\beta_j \equiv \beta(\underline{z}^j, \overset{*}{m}). \tag{7.C.3}$$

Proof. With $2FS\theta^\circ(\underline{Z})$ and equilibrium conditions, $\overset{*}{m}$ is mean-variance efficient. This proposition is thus simply a special case of P6.7 and equations (6.C.10). □

The notation $\beta_j \equiv \beta(\underline{z}^j, \overset{*}{m})$ follows the conventional usage for the non-diversifiable risk of each security j relative to the (mean-variance efficient in equilibrium) *market* fund. Moreover, equations (7.C.1), (7.C.2), and (7.C.3) follow not just for securities, but for every $m \in \theta(\underline{Z})$.

7.C.2. The CAPM

P7.7. Equilibrium values. Let the conditions of P7.6 be satisfied, then necessary conditions for an exchange equilibrium in a security market are

[10] This does not mean that there are not other funds uncorrelated with $\overset{*}{m}$. Generally there are other such funds which, as they have zero non-diversifiable risk, must also have the same mean return. See Black (1972) and Merton (1972).

that each security j be valued by the relationship

$$v_0^j = \mathrm{E}z^j/[\beta_j \mathrm{E}\overset{*}{m} + (1-\beta_j)\mathrm{E}m^\circ], \tag{7.C.4a}$$

or, equivalently,

$$v_0^j = [\mathrm{E}z^j - \hat{\beta}_j \mathrm{E}(\overset{*}{m} - m^\circ)]/\mathrm{E}m^\circ, \tag{7.C.4b}$$

where $\hat{\beta}_j \equiv \beta_j v_0^j$.

Proof. Substitute $\underline{z}^j = z^j/v_0^j$ into (7.C.2) and rearrange. □

From the above equations it follows that, for any feasible mutual fund $m = \delta\underline{Z}$, $v_0^m = \Sigma_j \delta_j v_0^j$. Finally, when $\rho \in \theta(\underline{Z})$ then $\dot{m} = m^\circ = \rho$ and the above equations are somewhat simplified:[11]

$$\underline{z}^j = \rho + \beta_j(\overset{*}{m} - \rho) + \eta^j, \tag{7.C.5a}$$

$$\mathrm{E}\underline{z}^j = \rho + \beta_j \mathrm{E}(\overset{*}{m} - \rho), \tag{7.C.5b}$$

$$v_0^j = \mathrm{E}z^j/[\rho + \beta_j \mathrm{E}(\overset{*}{m} - \rho)], \quad \text{and} \tag{7.C.5c}$$

$$v_0^j = [\mathrm{E}z^j - \hat{\beta}_j \mathrm{E}(\overset{*}{m} - \rho)]/\rho. \tag{7.C.5d}$$

Using the usual relationships between moments and comoments of joint distributions, (7.C.5b) can be rewritten as

$$\mathrm{E}\underline{z}^j = \rho + \lambda r(\underline{z}_j, \overset{*}{m})\,\mathrm{std}(\underline{z}_j), \tag{7.C.6}$$

where std(·) indicates standard deviation, $\lambda = \mathrm{E}(\overset{*}{m} - \rho)\,\mathrm{std}(\overset{*}{m})$, and $r(\underline{z}_j, \overset{*}{m})$ is the correlation coefficient between $\underline{z}_j$ and $\overset{*}{m}$. When held alone as a 'portfolio', the risk of security j can be measured simply by $\mathrm{std}(\underline{z}_j)$. When, alternatively, the security is held only as one security in an optimal portfolio the remaining risk *of the security* is measured by $r(\underline{z}_j, \overset{*}{m})\,\mathrm{std}(\underline{z}_j)$ and, in this case, the correlation coefficient has the interpretation of the percentage of total risk that is eliminated by the portfolio diversification.

A portfolio is efficient when all potentially diversifiable risk is in fact eliminated. In the present case this means

$$[1 - r(\underline{w}^e, \overset{*}{m})]\,\mathrm{std}(\underline{w}^e) = 0,$$

[11]These particular equations, with the riskless plan feasible, are often referred to as the SLM-CAPM, as Sharpe (1965), Lintner (1965) and Mossin (1966) provided the original derivation.

where $\underline{w}^e$ is an efficient portfolio. For this equation to hold it is required that $r(\underline{w}^e, \overset{*}{m})=1$, implying that *all efficient* portfolios are perfectly correlated with market portfolio.

E7.5. Consider some security j whose *dollar* payoff is jointly distributed with the market rate of return $\overset{*}{m}$ according to the following tableau:

	z^j		
$\overset{*}{m}$	5	10	15
1.0	0.2	0.1	0
1.1	0.1	0.2	0.1
1.2	0	0.1	0.2

From these data calculate the following statistics:

$$Ez^j=10,$$

$$E\overset{*}{m}=1.1,$$

$$\mathrm{cov}(z^j, \overset{*}{m})=0.2,$$

$$\mathrm{var}(\overset{*}{m})=0.006,$$

$$\hat{\beta}=0.2/0.006=33.3.$$

When $\rho=1.04$ then (7.C.5d) gives

$$v_0^j=[10\text{–}33.3(1.1\text{–}1.04)]/1.04=\$7.69.$$

Also,

$$\beta_j=\hat{\beta}_j/v_0^j=4.33,$$

which implies a strong covariation between security j and the market portfolio. Finally, from (7.C.5b) calculate

$$E\underline{z}^j=1.04+4.33(1.1-1.04)$$

$$=1.04+4.33(0.06)$$

$$=1.04+0.26,$$

where $E(\overset{*}{m}-\rho)=0.06$ is commonly called the market price of risk and 0.26 is security j's risk premium (in excess of the riskless rate of return). ■

7.D. *Equivalently Complete Markets*

When $2FS0^\circ(\underline{Z})$ all optimal portfolios lie on a plane spanned by $\dot{m}$ and $\overset{*}{m}$ in the S-dimensional space of portfolio returns. In general, changes in the specification of the security program $\underline{Z}$ will affect the definition of $\dot{m}$ and $\overset{*}{m}$ and, in turn, the plane defining the efficient set. That is, for two economies exhibiting $2FS0^\circ$, one with security program $\underline{Z}$ and the second with $\hat{\underline{Z}}$ but otherwise identical, the consumption opportunities of individuals will generally differ, different optimal portfolios will be chosen, the efficient sets (the planes) will differ, and finally the two mutual funds which span those efficient sets will differ. While all important consumption and market variables change with alterations of the security program, one important aspect of two fund spanning is that it is not required to 'fix' too much to keep optimal consumptions and prices unchanged. Specifically, if the market and minimum variance portfolios are identical in $\underline{Z}$ and $\hat{\underline{Z}}$, then despite all other differences in these two security programs the *efficient sets* are exactly the same, optimal consumption plans are the same, and the same sustaining state claim price systems will obtain in the corresponding market equilibria. We state this important fact formally.

P7.8. Two fund spanning and market economy equivalence. Consider two conventional security market economies identical in all respects except that one has security program Z and the second has program $\hat{Z}$ (where outputs are measured in dollar, not return, values). Let $v=[v^1\, v^2 \ldots v^J]$ be an equilibrium price system in the first market with $\pi=[\pi_1\, \pi_2 \ldots \pi_S]$ an associated sustaining state claim price system.

Assume conditions for $2FS0^\circ(\underline{Z})$ obtain in the first economy, where $\underline{Z}$ is the return form of Z at prices v. Further assume the following:

(i) with state claim prices π the prices of the $n=1, 2, \ldots, N$ securities in $\hat{Z}$ are given by $\hat{v}=[\hat{v}^1\, \hat{v}^2 \ldots \hat{v}^N]$, at these security prices $\hat{\underline{Z}}$ defines the security program, and with this program conditions for $2FS0^\circ(\hat{\underline{Z}})$ also obtains, and
(ii) the minimum variance plans are identical in Z and $\hat{Z}$, and
(iii) $\Sigma_j z^j = \Sigma_n \hat{z}^n$, which requires that the total of consumption claims in each state be identical in both economies.

Given these conditions $\theta^\circ(\underset{\sim}{Z}) \equiv \theta^\circ(\hat{\underset{\sim}{Z}})$, comparable individuals in the two economies choose the exact same consumption plans, and π is an equilibrium sustaining price system in both economies.

Proof. (For the special case where a riskless security exists and individual utilities are suitably homogeneous, then P4.7 applies. In the present, more general case a somewhat different proof is necessary.)

By definition π is an equilibrium sustaining state claim price system in the first economy. We want to show that it is also an equilibrium price system for the second economy and that this implies the efficient set in the second economy is exactly the same as in the first given the conditions of the proposition. To this end, assume prices π hold in economy two. With this assumption condition (i) assures $2FS\theta^\circ(\hat{\underset{\sim}{Z}})$ and, by hypothesis, $2FS\theta^\circ(\underset{\sim}{Z})$ obtains.[12] Given the minimum variance plan is the same in both economies, then the commonality of π implies $\dot{m}$ (ρ when that variance is zero) is the identical mutual fund in both. And, finally, the fact that the total of consumption claims is identical in both economies implies that, at common claims prices π, the market mutual fund is identical in both. This last result can be seen as follows:

$$\overset{*}{m} = \frac{\Sigma_j v_0^j \underset{\sim}{z}^j}{\Sigma_j v_0^j} = \frac{\Sigma_j z^j}{\langle \pi, \Sigma_j z^j \rangle} = \frac{\Sigma_j \hat{z}^j}{\langle \pi, \Sigma_j \hat{z}^j \rangle}.$$

The commonality of $\dot{m}$ and $\overset{*}{m}$ and the existence of conditions for two fund spanning at prices π means that, even though the opportunity sets may differ with $\underset{\sim}{Z}$ and $\hat{\underset{\sim}{Z}}$, the efficient sets are nonetheless identical. As a result each individual's consumption choice will be unaffected by a change from $\underset{\sim}{Z}$ to $\hat{\underset{\sim}{Z}}$. (Since the aggregate total of claims in each state is the same in the two economies, it too follows that π is an equilibrium state claims price system in both.) □

There are two important implications of P7.8 which, as we shall deal with them in detail in Chapter 8, are only mentioned briefly here. First, holding all production decisions constant, if some firm alters the packaging of its output into different securities without destroying the minimum variance portfolio and without changing the aggregate total of claims, then even

[12]When $2FS\theta^\circ(\underset{\sim}{Z})$ occurs because of restrictions placed on the preferences of individuals in the first economy, then two fund spanning will also occur for all (positive) sustaining state claim price systems in the second economy. However, when the two fund spanning results from properties of the security returns, then two fund spanning in the second economy at prices π is not assured.

though the unit opportunity set is altered, it is altered in an inconsequential way, for the efficient set remains the same, optimal portfolios remain the same, and individuals (including firm owners) are indifferent to the repackaging.[13] That is to say, repackaging, or the 'financing' decision of the firm, is irrelevant under these specific conditions.

The second key implication of P7.8 is evident if we choose one of the economies to have a complete security market. Under the conditions of the proposition, and even though the first economy may have an incomplete security market, equilibrium consumption plans and equilibrium prices are determined *as if* the market were complete. This means that, relative to the output plans of the firms, the allocation of consumption by every competitive security market exhibiting $2FS\theta^{\circ}(\underline{Z})$ must be fully (unconstrained) Pareto optimal. This brings us to the subject matter of Chapter 8.

[13]It is additionally required that the repackaging of state claims in the form of different securities does not change the total of state claims nor does it redistribute wealth. These possibilities are considered in greater detail in the following Chapter 8.

Chapter 8

THEORY OF THE FIRM: PRODUCTION AND CAPITAL STRUCTURE

In a riskfree world with prices given for all factors and products, each firm has a sure market value equal to the value of its output plan less the cost of inputs employed. In turn, stockholders unanimously support value maximizing decisions, for the increase in market value shifts each individual's budget constraint 'outward' to some new level, parallel to the original, unambiguously increasing his exchange opportunities. As was shown in Chapters 2 and 3, this result extends in a straightforward fashion to an economy with uncertainty when there is a complete set of forward markets and these markets are perfect and competitive. Again, production and capital structure decisions which maximize the market value of the firm receive unanimous stockholder support and result in a Pareto optimal resource allocation.

Beginning with the research of Modigliani and Miller (1958, 1963), Hirshleifer (1965, 1966) and Diamond (1967), there have been numerous attempts to extend these unanimity and value maximization results to incomplete and imperfect security markets. One frequently considered case concerns the firm's pure capital structure decision: the substitution of debt and equity as sources of capital while holding the production plan fixed. The irrelevancy of this decision, and thus the stockholder's unanimous indifference to capital structure, is then commonly shown using a 'homemade' leverage argument.[1] First, assuming that there is an optimal capital structure but it is not adopted by the firm, the focus is shifted to individual arbitrageurs. Every individual, it is said, can develop the optimal financing by buying an equal proportion of each of the securities issued by the firm and then issue whatever capital structure is optimal on personal account. If the market value of the firm is less than that achievable with the optimal capital structure, the individual increases his wealth by such arbitrage. In the absence of transaction and information costs all such

[1]Modigliani and Miller (1958, 1963) provide the original homemade leverage argument. See also Baron (1974, 1976).

arbitrage opportunities will be exploited and, as a consequence, the market value of the firm will be bid up so that its equilibrium value is independent of whatever capital structure it in fact selects.

There is also a second line of analysis, where homemade leverage is not used but instead each of the firm's securities always has a perfect market substitute. In this case the financing decision of the firm cannot create nor destroy consumption opportunities and, if the firm's output is 'small' relative to the market total, so that there are no significant price effects, such decisions are again irrelevant.[2] And, with each individual preferring more wealth to less there is then unanimous support for those corporate production decisions which maximize market value.

While the above discussion has been brief, and thereby somewhat incomplete, careful analyses of capital structure are quite complex. This in part owes to the variety of specializing assumptions and constructions which have appeared. Rather than adding generality to the analyses, these have left the essential source of financing irrelevance, or relevance, unclear. Is some sort of homemade leverage or the perfect substitutability of securities necessary to the proof? What are the effects of particular market imperfections, particular forms of monopoly power, or combinations of these? One objective of this chapter is to show that, in spite of the fragmented and highly specialized variety of model assumptions possible, there is a simple economic foundation to the relevancy and irrelevancy of the capital structure decision. Concomitant to the method of analysis is the recognition that the capital structure decision involves essentially the same issues as the firm's production, or investment, decision.

8.A. The Model Economy

Consider the usual two period, two good (current and future consumption denominated in dollars) state preference economy. As usual, the state of nature prevailing at $t=0$ is known while the particular state $s=1,2,\ldots,S$ to occur at the future period $t=1$ is uncertain. Individuals are endowed with amounts of the current consumption good and security holdings in the firms. Firms produce state-contingent amounts of future consumption using the current consumption good as the single input; the current investment is financed through the sale of conventional securities which provide claims against future output. Two firm decisions are considered: the choice of a production plan and, in turn, the choice of

[2]See Stiglitz (1969b, 1974) and Fama (1978).

conventional securities to issue as a source of funding for the required input.

The timing of the model economy along with the activity of all agents is usual. At the initial $t=0$ period firms make their production and financing (or capital structure) decisions. Knowing the production plans of firms and knowing how that output is allocated to its various classes of securities, individuals exchange claims to current consumption and the firm's various securities. At $t=1$ uncertainty is resolved, the true state of nature is revealed, and the payments stipulated by security contracts are made.

8.A.1. Firms and securities

The specification of firms, with extensions to include capital structure as well as production decisions, is similar to that of earlier chapters and can be briefly set out as follows. Each firm $j=1,2,\ldots J$ has production possibilities which are given by a *production set* Ξ^j made up of *production plans* $\xi^j=[z_0^j\, z^j]$ where $z_0^j \leq 0$ is the firm's (scalar) input and $z^j=[z_1^j\, z_2^j \ldots z_S^j]$ is its corresponding state contingent *output plan*. Each element of z^j occurs prior to any interest payment, taxes, security brokerage fee, or generally any drain or subsidy associated with the financial operations of the firm. Finally, to assure the existence of a unique production and exchange equilibrium for the economy, Ξ^j is assumed to be convex and closed, to contain the origin, and to be such that if a production plan for some j is feasible and $z_0^j=0$, then $z^j=0$. The choice of a specific plan ξ^j is referred to as the firm's *production*, or *investment, decision*.

Let $n=1,2,\ldots,N$ index the classes of securities (e.g., common and preferred stock, warrants, bonds, etc.) issued by each firm to finance its factor input. For each such class the payout across states is given by the S-vector $z^{jn}=[z_1^{jn}\, z_2^{jn} \ldots z_S^{jn}]$, with each z_s^{jn} indicating the dollars paid to (the holders of) firm j's class n security when state s obtains. Whatever the specific list of securities issued, the $S \times JN$ matrix $Z=[z^{11}\, z^{12} \ldots z^{JN}]$ designates the *security program* for the economy. And, in accordance with our earlier definitions, if rank $Z=S$, then the security market is said to be *complete* and when rank $Z=K<S$ it is said to be *incomplete*.

A change in the *capital structure* of some firm j is a revision in the collection of securities (payout vectors) offered by the firm leaving its overall output plan z^j unchanged. The general effect of such a change is an alteration in the consumption set spanned by the market securities. To summarize such changes it is useful to index the firm's choice of capital structure. We indicate each firm j's financial decision by δ^j and refer to changes in δ^j, holding j's output plan z^j fixed, as a *purely financial transaction*.

In summary, for each firm j the choice of z^j and δ^j means that the production plan and capital structure of the firm are determined, i.e., the S-vectors z^{jn} $\forall n$ are given. When these choices are made by all firms, a security program Z is specified for the economy.

8.A.2. *Individuals*

Let $i=1,2,\ldots,I$ index individuals. The (typical) ith individual's *consumption plan* is denoted by the $(S+1)$-vector $w^i=[w_0^i\, w^i]$ with w_0^i (a scalar) and $w^i=[w_1^i\, w_2^i \ldots w_S^i]$ indicating current and period 1 state-contingent consumption, respectively. Individuals are assumed to be I1 (see D1.15), each with utility given by $U^i(w_0^i, w^i)$.

Securities are issued by firms to finance planned production. Individuals obtain consumption at the future period by investing in these securities. To formalize these ideas, let α_{jn}^i be the fraction of firm j's security n demanded by individual i and, in turn, define the JN-vector $\alpha^i=[\alpha_{11}^i\, \alpha_{12}^i \ldots \alpha_{JN}^i]$ as i's post-exchange *security plan*. Prior to exchange it is assumed that only one class of security exists for each firm. This single class defines the *ex ante*, or original, firm *ownership*. Using the bar overscore as usual, let $\bar{\alpha}_j^i$ denote individual i's *endowed ownership share* in firm j; $0\leq\bar{\alpha}_j^i\leq 1$ and $\Sigma_i\bar{\alpha}_j^i=1$ are feasibility requirements. The JN-vector $\bar{\alpha}^i=[\bar{\alpha}_1^i\,\bar{\alpha}_2^i\ldots\bar{\alpha}_{JN}^i]$ represents i's *endowed ownership plan.*

With these notations the set of obtainable consumptions claims at period 1, the *claims set* for that future period, is

$$\Omega_C(z^j,\delta^j\ \forall j)=\left\{w^i\in R_+^S\,|\,w^i=\sum_j\sum_n \alpha_{jn}^i z^{jn}\ \forall\alpha^i\right\}.$$

As in earlier chapters, it is useful to think geometrically of $\Omega_C(z^j,\delta^j\ \forall j)$ as the space of period one consumptions generated by investment and capital structure choices. Constraining a plan w^i to be formed as a linear combination of the security vectors z^{jn} $\forall j,n$ is then equivalent to a requirement that the vector w^i lies in $\Omega_C(\cdot)$. The dimension of Ω_C, as usual, equals the rank of Z and this is the maximum number of linearly independent securities in the economy.

Hold fixed the capital structure and production decisions of all firms and, choosing current consumption as numeraire, define $v_0=[v_0^{11}\, v_0^{12}\ldots v_0^{JN}]$ as the *security price system*, where each v_0^{jn} represents the market value of firm j's security n. Using these prices individual i's budget constraint in the exchange of securities can then be written as

$$\sum_j \bar{\alpha}_j^i\left(\sum_n v_0^{jn} + z_0^j\right) + \bar{w}_0^i \equiv W^i = \sum_j \sum_n \alpha_{jn}^i v_0^{jn} + w_0^i. \tag{8.A.1}$$

The term $(\Sigma_n v_0^{jn} + z_0^j)$ is the *net* market value of firm j, which makes the first expression of the LHS the market value of i's security endowment (recall that $z_0^j \leq 0$). The LHS of (8.A.1) is the individual's *total endowed wealth*, being made up of the value of the security endowment (at prices v_0) and the $\bar{w}_0^i$ endowment of period zero consumption. This total endowment is labelled W^i. The right-most expression indicates the security ownership plans (and therefrom period one consumptions) and current consumption that are exchangeable with W^i. Finally, define individual i's *budget set* as

$$B^i(W^i, v_0) = \{\omega^i | w_0^i \text{ and } \alpha^i \text{ solve (8.A.1) above}\}. \tag{8.A.2}$$

Next, let $\pi = [\pi_1\, \pi_2 \ldots \pi_S]$ be a *sustaining state-claim price* system corresponding to the security price system v_0 and the security program Z, see P4.5. Specifically, we can write $v_0^{jn} = \langle z^{jn}, \pi\rangle\ \forall j, n$ and, in turn, restate i's budget constraint in terms of these state claims prices as[3]

$$\begin{aligned} w^i &= \sum_j \bar{\alpha}_j^i\left(\sum_n \langle z^{jn}, \pi\rangle + z_0^j\right) + \bar{w}_0^i \\ &= \sum_j \sum_n \alpha_{jn}^i \langle z^{jn}, \pi\rangle + w_0^i. \end{aligned} \tag{8.A.1$'$}$$

Holding aside the individual's endowment of period zero consumption, note from (8.A.1′) that wealth depends on the net market value $(\Sigma_n\langle z^{jn}, \pi\rangle + z_0^j)$ of each firm. A change in any firm j's decisions ξ^j and δ^j generally leads to a change in individual wealth and, if the market is incomplete, to a change in the period one claims set Ω_C. To be clear about these potential effects of corporate decisions on individual wealth, it will at times be useful to write the dependence explicitly as $W^i(\xi^j, \delta^j\ \forall j)$.

As a final bit of notation, denote individual i's *opportunity set* as those consumption plans which are jointly in the budget set and the set of period zero and period one feasible consumptions

$$O^i(\cdot) = \{\omega^i \geq 0 | w^i \in \Omega_C(\cdot) \text{ and } \omega^i \in B^i\}. \tag{8.A.3}$$

[3]Similarly the budget set can be reformulated in terms of the prices π as $B^i(W^i, \pi) = \{\omega^i | w_0^i$ and α^i solve (8.A.1′) with $W^i \leq \Sigma_j \Sigma_n \alpha_{jn}^i z^{jn}\}$.

8.A.3. Markets and competition

Holding fixed the output plans of all firms, the S-vector $m=\Sigma_j z^j>0$ will be used to denote the (economy-wide) aggregate supply of period one state claims; similarly the scalar $m_0=\Sigma_i \bar{w}_0^i+\Sigma_j z_0^j>0$ will denote the aggregate supply of the current consumption good. Using these notations the following specification provides a useful base case.

S8.1. Closed security market. A closed security market is such that there are no bankruptcy costs, taxes, or other costs which represent either a drain on or augmentation to aggregate supplies. In this case both firm and aggregate output totals, $\Sigma_n z^{jn}=z^j\,\forall j$ and $m=\Sigma_j\Sigma_n z^{jn}$ are independent of capital structure decisions, as is the aggregate period zero supply m_0.

In the following analysis it will be convenient to illustrate certain aspects of the firm's choice of a production plan and capital structure using a model where equity and debt are the only security classes and there are no taxes, transaction costs, or bankruptcy fees. That leads to the following definition.

D8.1. Simple debt and simple equity capital structure. Let specification S8.1 obtain and define the payout vector of simple (limited liability) equity $(n=e)$ and simple debt $(n=d)$ by, $\forall s$,

$$z_s^{je}=\max[z_s^j-b^j,0], \tag{8.A.4a}$$

$$z_s^{jd}=\min[b^j,z_s^j]=z_s^j-\max[z_s^j-b^j,0], \tag{8.A.4b}$$

where b^j is the promised payment to the total issue of debt.

Debt, being the senior claim, receives its promised payment if the firm's output in the state realized is not less than that payment; otherwise, the firm defaults, bankruptcy occurs, and the simple debt holders lay claim to the total output (without ownership transfer costs). If the firm does not default, then the holders of simple equity receive the excess over the promised (and actual) payment to debt. When bankruptcy occurs, however, equity receives nothing.

E8.1. Note that in varying b^j the firm alters the payouts to both debt and equity. For example, let $z^j=[5\ 3\ 4\ 6]$ and choose $b^j=2$. In this case $z^{jd}=[2\ 2\ 2\ 2]$, which is riskless, and $z^{je}=[3\ 1\ 2\ 4]$. Now choose $b^j=4$, giving the risky debt payoff $z^{jd}=[4\ 3\ 4\ 4]$ and a new, residual equity payment $z^{je}=[1\ 0\ 0\ 2]$. The effect of b^j on both payouts occurs even though the security market is closed and z^j is itself unaltered by the choice of b^j. Observe too, that when $b^j=0$ the security issued is labelled equity; alternatively, when $b^j=\max[z_1^j, z_2^j, \ldots, z_S^j]$ then the same security (in terms of payout) is issued, but it is in this case labelled debt. ■

The properties of markets and the extent of competition in both exchange and supply are critical in determining what constitutes an optimal plan of production and capital structure for the firm. For this reason it is appropriate to again set out these specifications in a systematic way. First, there are the usual conditions for market perfection.

S8.2. Perfect markets. All markets on which securities are traded are such that:

(i) (no price uncertainty) the basic elements of a security market are present, including full information expectations of prices on future spot markets, see D3.3–D3.5,
(ii) (frictionless exchange) there are no information or transaction costs,
(iii) (one price law) there are no arbitrage opportunities, meaning that all securities or combinations of securities which yield the same pattern of output across states carry the same market price, and,
(iv) (interior solution) all securities are infinitely divisible and short sales are permitted with neither margin nor escrow requirement.

The frictionless exchange condition (iii), it should be noted, assures that the security market is closed in the sense of S8.1.

Just as the perfection of markets is important so is the perfection in competition, or price-taking. While the role of price-taking in exchange is well recognized in this regard, the analytical role of price-taking in supply is less generally considered.

E8.2. Consider the case of a two-period, single commodity market economy under certainty. Taking current consumption as numeraire, let π_1 be the current price of a unit of (certain) period 1 consumption and denote by W^i individual i's endowed wealth, $W^i=\bar{w}_0^i+\pi_1\bar{w}_1^i$ where $\bar{w}_0^i$ and $\bar{w}_1^i$ are period 0 and 1 endowments, respectively. Thus W^i/π_1 is i's maximum of period 1 consumption. Finally, let d^j indicate some firm j's supply decision, either production or capital structure. Suppose now that π_1 is not independent of the specific choice of d^j. In this case, the period 0 consumption opportunities for each individual i are not generally maximized by the same d^j which maximizes period one consumption opportunities. In a cross-section of individuals with differing (time) preferences for current and future consumption, support for a specific choice of d^j generally will not be unanimous. Moreover, in the case of uncertainty this lack of unanimity will be further complicated by differing risk tolerances and preferences for consumption in future states. ■

As the above example suggests, the invariance of (state claim) prices to firm decisions is a key element in 'removing' individual differences to arrive at unanimous shareholder support for such decisions. We therefore provide the following pair of specifications.

S8.3. Competition (perceived price-taking) in exchange. Each individual perceives his choice to buy or sell appropriate amounts of any security not to affect the market price of that or any other security.

S8.4. Competition (perceived price-taking) in supply. Each individual owner of a firm when considering that firm's production and capital structure decisions perceives these decisions not to affect the market value of any feasible consumption plan.

Specification S8.3 indicates price-taking in exchange when each individual acts *as if* his demand for securities does not affect the price of securities. This specification is fine from the demand side, as it is clear exactly what the commodity (whose price is being held fixed) is when the individual's quantity demanded changes. A similar specification in supply is unsatisfactory, for as the firm changes its production and capital structure decisions, the commodities (that is, the securities) supplied generally change. We then do not know what it is that the firm is a price-taker of in supply. Is it the 'old' securities or the ones newly created by the variations in the supply decision? Specification S8.4 avoids the problem of 'commodity' definition by specifying competition in supply as perceived fixity of the prices of *all* feasible plans of consumption claims. To be sure, this is a fully satisfactory specification only if we then do not allow variations in the consumption claims set as firms choose alternative production and capital structure decisions. That is, S8.4 provides a well-defined notion of price-taking in supply if, and only if in general, $\Omega_C(\cdot)$ is fixed. The specifications S8.5 and S8.6 below are set forth out of this consideration.

S8.5. Financial completeness of the securities market. With fixed production decisions, the capital structure decisions of any firm does not affect the feasible set of consumption claims. That is, $\Omega_C(z^j, \delta^j\ \forall j)$ is independent of the choice of δ^k for each firm k, all other firm decisions constant.

Holding production decisions fixed and allowing changes only in capital structure for some firm, then (with the security market closed or not) new payout vectors can generally be created which alter Ω_C, the feasible set of consumption claims. The securities market exhibits *financial completeness* in the alternative case, when $\Omega_C(\cdot)$ is not altered by any firm using a purely financial transaction. But, what of production decisions and their effect on $\Omega_C(\cdot)$?

S8.6. Technical completeness of the securities market. With capital structure decisions fixed, the production decision of any firm does not affect the feasible set of consumption claims. That is, $\Omega_C(z^j, \delta^j \forall j)$ is independent of the choice of z^k for each firm k, all other firm decisions constant.

In contrast to financial completeness, technical completeness begins with changes in z^k. The complexity by which securities are usually defined, however, means that a purely technical change, leading as it does to changes in the output vector z^k, generally will *not* leave the associated security payouts, $z^{kn}\ \forall n$, unaltered.

E8.3. Suppose firm k issues only simple debt and equity. With b^k the promised payment to debt (and, again with states numbered such that $0 \leq z_1^k \leq z_2^k \leq \ldots \leq z_S^k$), write the payout to debt as

$$z^{kd} = [z_1^k\ z_2^k \ldots z_{\theta-1}^k\ r^k \ldots r^k],$$

where θ indicates the dividing state such that $z_{\theta-1}^k < b^k$ and $b^k \geq z_\theta^k$. When $\theta \geq 2$ and default is possible, the debt security is risky; otherwise it is riskless. The payout to simple equity in this case is the residual after the firm meets its debt obligation, i.e.,

$$z^{ke} = [0\ 0 \ldots 0\ (z_\theta^k - r^k)\ (z_{\theta+1}^k - r^k) \ldots (z_S^k - r^k)].$$

From the expression for z^{kd} and z^{ke} it is easily seen that the choice of a production plan generally changes both the debt and equity security payoffs.

It is also of interest that when debt is riskless and the firm increases its output (in every state) by a scale multiple, then with no change in the promised payment, the debt payoff would remain unaltered and the equity payoff would increase in every state. If, however, the debt was initially riskless and the firm *reduced* its output by a scale multiple, then there is the possibility that the debt may become risky (if the promised payment becomes greater than total output in some state) and the payoff vectors to debt and equity would change. ■

There will be occasions in the following analyses to require simultaneous financial and technical completeness of the securities markets, in which case *full completeness* is said to occur. While at first glance the various completeness specifications appear to impose very strong restrictions on markets, the reader should hold aside that judgment until some consideration (in Section 8.B.3) is given to ways in which markets can in fact achieve such properties.

As an end point for this section's basic definitions and conditions it is useful to provide a catalog of the conditions sufficient for what will soon be seen to be the critical price-taking in supply.

P8.1. Perceived price-taking in supply. Fix the production and capital structure decisions of all firms, except as noted below for firm j. Then the price of any consumption claims plan $w \in \Omega_C(\cdot)$ is perceived by j's owners to be independent of the choice of z^j and δ^j if those decisions are perceived not to affect one of the following price systems:

(8.1a) every system of sustaining state-claim prices, π,

(8.1b) each individual's implicit state-claim prices, π^i (the marginal rates of substitution of state-contingent consumption for current consumption at the individual's consumptive optimum), or

(8.1c) a price system for any set of securities spanning $\Omega_C(\cdot)$.

Proof. (8.1a) and (8.1b) follow immediately from the definition of a sustaining price system and the implicit state-claim prices. With respect to (8.1c), let $[z^1\, z^2 \dots z^K]$ be an arbitrary set of securities spanning $\Omega_C(\cdot)$, with market values as $[v_0^1\, v_0^2 \dots v_0^K]$. As the z's span $\Omega_C(\cdot)$, then for each $w \in \Omega_C(\cdot)$ it is possible to find numbers $[\alpha_1\, \alpha_2 \dots \alpha_K]$ such that $w = \Sigma_k \alpha_k z^k$. In turn, the market value of w can be written $v_0(w) = \Sigma_k \alpha_k v_0^k$. When the prices of the chosen vectors are fixed, then the price of the consumption plan w necessarily must be fixed. □

8.A.4. Exchange equilibrium

For convenience of reference we begin with the definition of an exchange equilibrium in a securities market.

D8.2. Security market exchange equilibrium. Let the production and capital structure decisions of all firms be given, thereby fixing the consumption set $\Omega_c(z^j, \delta^j \forall j)$ and aggregate supplies m and m_0. An exchange equilibrium is a collection of state-claim prices and an allocation of consumption $\{\mathring{\pi}, \mathring{\omega}^i \forall i\}$ such that:

(i) $\mathring{\omega}^i$ maximizes $U^i(\omega^i)$, subject to $\mathring{\omega}^i \in O^i(W^i, \mathring{\pi}) \forall i$, and,
(ii) $\Sigma_i \mathring{w}^i = m$ and $\Sigma_i \mathring{w}^i_0 = m_0$, which means that all markets clear.

With price-taking in exchange (S8.3), each individual's (interior) consumptive optimum is given by the usual equations:

$$\partial U_i / \partial w^i_0 = \lambda^i, \tag{8A.5a}$$

$$\sum_s \pi^i_s z^{jn}_s = v^{jn}_0 \quad \forall j, n, \quad \text{and} \tag{8A.5b}$$

$$W^i = \sum_j \sum_n \alpha^i_{jn} z^{jn} + w^i_0, \tag{8A.5c}$$

where λ^i is a Lagrange multiplier, $v^{jn}_0 = \Sigma_s \pi_s z^{jn}_s$, and individual i's implicit state-claims prices are $\pi^i_s \equiv (\partial U^i(\omega^i)/\partial w^i_s)/(\partial U^i(\omega^i)/\partial w^i_0) \forall s$. In an exchange equilibrium with complete security markets $\pi^i = \pi \forall i$ and both the price system and allocation of consumption $\omega^i \forall i$ are unique (assuming strict convexity of the opportunity set). Alternatively, when the security market is incomplete, π can be any (non-unique) sustaining price system, but the allocation $w^i \forall i$ remains unique.

Under conditions of perfect and complete markets and competition we have, in earlier chapters, shown that (1) the optimal production and capital structure decisions of a firm maximize net market value, independent of the details of individual tastes; (2) given production decisions, the firm's financing decisions are a matter of indifference to shareholders; and, (3) value maximizing decisions are Pareto optimal. With the specifications and the definitions set forth above, it is now possible to extend and qualify these results. The following Sections consider these issues in turn.

8.B. The Firm's Objective Criterion

Assume that (1) security markets are perfect, (2) there is perceived price-taking in both exchange and supply, and (3) financial and technical completeness obtain. Let $\overset{*}{z}{}^j$ and $\overset{*}{\delta}{}^j$ indicate the production and capital structure decisions of firm j which, when these market conditions hold, maximize the market value of firm j net of its factor cost with sustaining prices π. That is, $\overset{*}{z}^j$ and $\overset{*}{\delta}^j$ are such that the associated security payout vectors $\overset{*}{z}^{jn}\,\forall n$ and input level $\overset{*}{z}_0^j$ solve

$$\overset{*}{v}_0^j = \sum_n \langle \overset{*}{z}^{jn}, \pi \rangle + \overset{*}{z}_0^j \geq \sum_n \langle z^{jn}, \pi \rangle + z_0^j, \tag{8.B.1}$$

for all admissible production and capital structure decisions by firm *j*. Will the firm choose these net value maximizing decisions?

8.B.1. Unanimity and value maximization

Recall from (8.A.1′) that the individual's endowed wealth may be written as $W^i = \Sigma_j \bar{\alpha}_j^i [\Sigma_n \langle z^{jn}, \pi \rangle + z_0^j] + \bar{w}_0^i$. At the (fixed) sustaining state claim prices π, suppose that firm j chooses decisions $\overset{*}{z}^j$ and $\overset{*}{\delta}^j$ which yield $\overset{*}{v}_0^j$ and maximize i's wealth – let this maximum be given by $\overset{*}{W}^i$. Under these conditions the 'more wealth is better' proposition P1.1 holds and each individual orders his preference for corporate decisions simply by their effect on his wealth. That is, each individual with $\bar{\alpha}_j^i \geq 0$ prefers each firm j to adopt the decisions $\overset{*}{z}^j$ and $\overset{*}{\delta}^j$ which lead to $\overset{*}{W}^i$. This observation, in turn, leads to the following proposition.

P8.2. Unanimous support for net value maximization. Let the security market exhibit the degree of competition and completeness given by S8.3 through S8.6. Then *ex ante* shareholders of each firm j (i.e., those individuals i with $\bar{\alpha}_j^i \geq 0$) unanimously support production and capital structure decisions which maximize the net market value of the firm. Moreover, S8.3 through S8.6 are (in general) necessary for unanimous support of value maximization.

Proof. Sufficiency is demonstrated in the paragraphs leading to the proposition, leaving only necessity to be shown. As all key parts of the necessity arguments have been used before, only a sketch is given here.[4] First, we note that wealth effects accompanied by price changes need not be utility increasing for every concave utility, see P1.1, so that the price-taking conditions (S8.3 and S8.4) are necessary.

The completeness conditions (S8.5 and S8.6) are also required, for individuals contemplating a planned decision by some firm will not value the resulting payoff vector equally unless that state-contingent vector lies in Ω_C. Specifically, let Z indicate the security program before some firm j's planned

[4]See Radner (1974) for details.

change and Z^* after, with z^{j*} being the firm's planned output. For two individuals i and n with reservation demand prices π^i and π^n, then generally

$$\sum_s \pi_s^i z_s^{*j} \neq \sum_s \pi_s^n z_s^{*j},$$

when $z^{j*} \notin \Omega_C(Z)$. Moreover, the anticipated net value of firm j after the planned change might be more or less than the prechange value for one individual but not the other. Not only can unanimity fail in this case, value maximizing decisions are ill-defined, for whose claim prices should be used to assign a value? □

E8.4. Our intuition concerning the role of the completeness conditions is helped by a numerical example. Let the security program be given by the following tableau.

	State payoff			
	$s=1$	$s=2$	$s=3$	$s=4$
z^1	1	1	1	1
z^2	2	3	1	1
z^3	1	2	2	2
z^4	1.5	2.5	1.5	1.5

Note that $z^4 = (z^2 + z^3)/2$ so that the security market is incomplete: $\Omega_C(Z)$ is spanned by the three securities z^1, z^2, and z^3. Suppose that market values $v^1 = 0.9$, $v^2 = 1.6$, $v^3 = 1.5$, and $v^4 = 1.55$ obtain. Two sets of state-claim prices sustaining these values are $\pi^i = [0.3 \;\; 0.2 \;\; 0.2 \;\; 0.2]$ and $\pi^m = [0.3 \;\; 0.2 \;\; 0.3 \;\; 0.1]$, which we attribute to individuals i and m. Suppose now that firm 4 considers a change in its output to

$$z^{4*} = [1.5 \quad 2.5 \quad 1.4 \quad 1.7],$$

This new security is linearly independent of the other securities and therefore would complete the market: $z^{4*} \notin \Omega_C(Z)$.

Suppose now that individuals are price-takers in exchange and supply. Individual i values the planned output as

$$(v^{4*})^i = \sum_s \pi_s^i z^{4*} = 1.52,$$

and individual m as

$$(v^{4*})^m = \sum_s \pi_s^m z^{4*} = 1.54.$$

Notice that firm 4's value increases for i and decreases for m with the planned decision. As stockholders, they would disagree on the implementation of the decision. ■

While it is almost universally assumed that firms follow a value-maximization rule, the unanimity of such a rule among stockholders relies on (i) I1 individuals, (ii) price-taking, and (iii) full completeness as specifically set out in S8.3–S8.6. In addition to fixed prices, the relationship between an incomplete securities market and one which simply has financial and technical completeness is crucial to a clear understanding of the proposition. Once more, Ω_C need not have dimension S and the securities market need not be complete: rather, all that is required for unanimous support of the decisions which maximize the net market value of each firm k is that the claims set (whether of dimension S *or less*) not be altered by production or capital structure choices.

It should be stressed that the above model restricts attention to only one original class of security for each firm. Thus, when the firm considers a plan of production and a specific capital structure, the (net market) value consequences of those decisions are shared proportionately by every *ex ante* shareholder. If, alternatively, two or more original classes of securities existed, then there would be the possibility of non-proportional effects and potential problems for expropriation are created. To see how such difficulties might arise, assume for the moment that some firm has issued both debt and equity securities, bonds and stocks. Assume further that the firm is to be operated in the stockholders' (owners') interest. Our concern is with the case where, for example, the firm faces a stock market value maximizing production decision which makes the current bonds more risky (increasing the number of default states and/or reducing the amounts payable in default states) and thereby reduces their market value. By this decision stockholders would gain, but it would be 'at the expense' of bondholders. This would cause no difficulty for the class of stockholders, they would unanimously support this decision if they were not also bondholders. When those who hold the firm's bond and stocks are not distinctly separate groups, however, decisions which are less than stock market value maximizing would in general be preferred by the combined securityholders. More generally, maximizing stockholder wealth, bondholder wealth, and combined stockholder–bondholder wealth can imply three different firm decisions.

E8.5. Let the output of some firm j, z^j, be packaged as equity

$$z_s^{je} = \max[z_s^j - b^j, 0],$$

and debt

$$z_s^{jd} = z_s^j - z_s^{je} = \min[b^j, z_s^j],$$

for all s, where b^j is as usual the promised payment to debt (see D8.1). Consider now some current investment z_0^* having a payoff $z^* = [z_1^* \, z_2^* \ldots z_s^*]$ at period one. Let the investment be fully financed by a new bond issue, $b^* = z_0^*$. The post-investment total payoff of the firm is $z^{j*} = z^j + z^*$, made-up of equity $z^{j*e} = \max[z^j + z^* - b^j - b^*, 0]$ and debt $z^{j*d} = z^{j*} - z^{j*e}$ parts. Note that

$$\max[z^j + z^* - b^j - b^*, 0] \leq \max[z^j - b^j, 0] + \max[z^* - b^*, 0]$$

since the max function is convex (and the inequality is a property of convex functions). The post-investment payoff to equity (and thus its value) is generally less than firm j's pre-investment value plus the residual equity payoff of the stand-alone investment. Moreover, because $z^{j*} = z^j + z^*$ it must follow that

$$z^{j*d} \geq z^{jd} + z^{*d}.$$

In this way, bondholders might 'expropriate' the residual equity of the investment. ■

There are two usual 'solutions' to the difficulties presented by expropriation. First, each security contract may be written to include fully protective ('me-first') covenants which explicitly provide against such wealth transfers.[5] The second solution recognizes that if markets are suitably perfect, even such protective covenants would be unnecessary. When the firm's combined (debt and equity) market value is maximized, then in the absence of transaction and negotiation costs it would always be possible to find a compensation rule which makes every class of security (more exactly, every individual) better off. Quite simply, maximal combined value makes the 'pie' available for distribution to all claimants greatest, so that there must exist some way of allocating this maximum amount which is at least as preferred by all to any allocation of a smaller amount.[6] Both solutions, while frequently mentioned, generally involve contracting and transaction costs which may not be trivial.

[5]See Fama and Miller (1972, pp. 152–156).

[6]For this reason Fama (1978) has argued that combined value maximization yields the only *stable* market equilibrium. Acknowledging the costs of such compensation schema, Stiglitz (1972) alternatively argues that firms are likely to maximize stockholder wealth (even though it is less economically efficient than combined wealth maximization).

E8.6. Suppose firm j has value given by $v_0^j = v_0^{je} + v_0^{jd}$. A management decision is considered that will result in some new values $v_0^{j*} = v_0^{j*e} + v_0^{j*d}$, where $v_0^{j*} > v_0^j$ and $v_0^{j*d} > v_0^{jd}$ but $v_0^{j*e} < v_0^{je}$. In this case the firm might issue new stocks in amount v_0^{jd}, use the proceeds to retire the 'old' bonds and, *after* adopting the decision, then distribute a new sum of bonds worth v_0^{j*d}. This sequence of transactions results in a stockholder value

$$v_0^{j*e} - v_0^{je} = (v_0^{j*} - v_0^{jd}) - v_0^{je} = v_0^{j*} - v_0^j > 0.$$

When v_0^{j*} is greater than v_0^j, shareholder interests can always be made to coincide with (total) firm value maximization. (Note, however, that the above transactions are assumed to be costless and the old bonds are all tendered at the single price v_0^{jd}.)

8.B.2. Some special cases

Proposition P8.2 provides necessary (in general) and sufficient conditions for unanimous support of net value maximizing firm decisions. Why the (in general) qualification to necessity? Stylized cases can be constructed which yield such unanimity while not employing some (or all) of the S8.3 through S8.6 specifications. For example, in the extreme allow all individuals in the economy to be identical. Unanimity of course follows in this case and the perfection of markets and fixity of prices becomes unimportant as there simply will be no trading. Somewhat less pathological is the case where individuals generally differ in preferences and endowments, perceived prices change with production decisions, Ω_C either remains fixed or changes, and individuals are specifically 'constructed' such that each reaches a preferred consumption claims bundle at the firm's net value maximum.

These exceptions to S8.3 through S8.6 as necessary specifications for unanimity are, to be sure, highly stylized. There is, however, one quite reasonable, special case where the proposition does not provide necessity for unanimous support of purely financial decisions. Suppose that only the price-taking (S8.3 and S8.4) conditions hold, without completeness. In this case, P8.2 does not indicate unanimous support for net value maximization, as the firm is generally able to affect the consumption claims set through its capital structure decision. Now hold all production decisions constant, but permit each firm to change its choice of capital structure. While such choices alter the security program and thus generally affect the consumption claims set, if the set of consumption plans which are *optimal* for individuals remains unaffected, the 'new' exchange equilibrium will have all market values and optimal consumptions unchanged.

Consider specifically the case of the Capital Asset Pricing Model and refer to P7.8 (Two-Fund Spanning and Market Economy Equivalence). In this instance the 'market' and riskless funds span the set of consumption plans optimal for all individuals. With the aggregate supply of claims in each state the same (when the security market is closed, capital structure decisions have simple 'packaging' effects which do not disturb the given aggregate totals) and given that the riskless plan is not destroyed by the capital structure decision, the efficient set is unaltered by the change in capital structure even though the consumption claims set Ω_C in general changes. In this special case S8.3 and S8.4 (*without* financial completeness) provide necessary conditions for unanimous indifference for each firm's capital structure decision.

It is apparent that the above sets of circumstances are somewhat special, and that unanimity in the absence of the S8.3 through S8.6 conditions (specified in P8.2) is not to be expected. In this sense, the proposition provides conditions necessary *in general* for unanimous support of net value maximizing decisions by firms.

8.B.3. Financial and technical completeness

There are two, distinct ways by which *full* completeness of the securities market may arise. In the first case, we think of the firm as (1) inconsequential to the security market, meaning that in every state the firm's output is 'small' in the usual sense relative to the aggregate total of claims and either (2a) that, for all its possible choices of production and capital structure, the securities it offers are redundant relative to those of other firms, or (2b) that the firm simply has limited capability to change its securities. The (2b) case recognizes that the individual's consumption set depends not only on the trading opportunities provided originally by the *productive* firms' securities, it also depends on secondary market transactions that may repackage original securities. For example, if pooling and security creation strategies of financial intermediaries were to make a complete set of securities available, then the decisions of productive firms (who are small relative to the market) would have no effect on the trading opportunities of investors. Or, if individuals could borrow with limited liability, pledging as collateral only the securities purchased with the loan, then firm decisions could be replicated or undone, in a homemade way, on personal account. These conditions for market completeness are catalogued in the following proposition.

P8.3. Sufficient conditions for completeness. Let some firm k be small relative to the market in the sense that it cannot, by its own decisions, determine whether or not a positive or zero aggregate supply of state claims exists in any state. Then, the consumption set $\Omega_C(\cdot)$ is fixed independently of decisions z^k and δ^k (that is, S8.5 and S8.6 hold) if at least one of the following *perfect substitute* conditions holds:

(8.3a) (complete markets) $\dim(\Omega_C)=S$ for all possible choices of z^k and δ^k (which includes the case where $S=1$ so that there is no uncertainty at period 1), or

(8.3b) (spanning) some linear combination of the available securities are a perfect substitute for any security which can be created by firm k.

Alternatively, the period one claims set $\Omega_C(\cdot)$ is fixed for decisions by any or all firms if one or both of the following *equal access* conditions hold:

(8.3c) (costless intermediation) individuals and/or financial intermediaries can costlessly issue securities with any vector of payouts, the only requirement being that the aggregate claims in each state be unaltered, or

(8.3d) (homemade leverage) using a portfolio of firms' securities as collateral, individuals can costlessly issue personal securities to create any security that any firm is capable of creating.

Proof. Let $[z^{jn}]$ be the security program of the economy at some 'old' set of firm decisions. Now allow some specific firm k to alter its decisions thereby creating new securities and in turn alterning the security program. Represent the 'new' security program by $[\hat{z}^{jn}]$. The *perfect substitute* conditions (8.3a) and (8.3b) provide, in obvious ways, that the consumption claims set generated by $[z^{jn}]$ and $[\hat{z}^{jn}]$ are identical. In (8.3b), if it is possible that the firm issue primitive securities then (8.3b) and (8.3a) are the same. Even less restrictively, if the firm has a strictly positive level of output in each state *and* can issue debt with any face value (promised payment) then again spanning implies the market is complete (see E8.7 below). Thus, for (8.3b) to be different from (8.3a) it must be that some (exogeneous and unstated) restrictions exist on the range of securities the firm can create.

The *equal access* conditions (8.3c) and (8.3d) operate somewhat differently. Under these conditions no single firm nor any given group of firms can alter the consumption set as individuals and/or financial intermediaries usurp that 'capability'. Specifically, (8.3c) provides that individuals and/or financial intermediaries (neither of which has productive capabilities) can hold a portfolio of securities of productive firms and 'repackage' these by issuing new securities to fully complete the securities market. To be sure, the financial intermediary can complete the market by directly issuing a complete set of pure securities against its security portfolio, but such a restrictive type of intermediation is not necessary as the use of warrants and/or simple call options will suffice (again, see E8.7 below). In either case, given that the financial intermediaries and/or individuals can fully complete the market, firms in their choices of production plans and capital structure can not alter the fact that $\Omega_C(\cdot)=R^S_+$. Finally, (8.3d) also limits any firm's ability to affect the claims set since it allows individuals to create securities on personal account capable of spanning the set of consumption plans generated by all feasible production and capital structure decisions by firms. In this way individuals using 'homemade leverage' cause the claims set to be composed of those plans which are achievable by all combinations of decisions by the firms. □

E8.7. Consider some firm with a distinct, positive output in each state; i.e., the firm's output plan $z>0$ is such that $z_s \neq z_{s'}$ for any s and s'. Let $z^d(b)$ represent the simple debt security of this firm when the promised payment to debt is b:

$$z^d_s = \min[z_s, b] \quad \text{for each } s=1,2,\dots,S,$$

with

$$z^d(b)=[z^d_1\, z^d_2 \dots z^d_S].$$

Order the states such that $z_s > z_{s'}$ implies $s > s'$.

First, we show that the spanning condition (8.2b) implies a complete market. To begin, suppose the firm chooses $b=z_{S'}$ its debt looks just like its total output plan, $z^d(z_S)=z$, which can, by the spanning assumption (8.2b), be achieved using existing securities. When $b=z_{S-1}$, $z^d(z_{S-1})=[z_1\, z_2 \dots z_{S-1}\, z_{S-1}]$, which again can be achieved using existing securities. These two facts in turn imply $z^d(z_S)-z^d(z_{S-1})=[0\; 0\dots 0\; (z_S-z_{S-1})]$ can be achieved once more with only existing securities. In a like fashion we can form $z^d(z_{S-2})$ and $z^d(z_{S-1})-z^d(z_{S-2})=[0\; 0\dots 0\; (z_{S-1}-z_{S-2})\; (z_{S-1}-z_{S-2})]$. As both (z_S-z_{S-1}) and $(z_{S-1}-z_{S-2})$ are strictly positive then there exists a scalar $\lambda>0$ such that $\lambda(z_S-z_{S-1})=(z_{S-1}-z_{S-2})$. Thus the plan $[0\; 0\dots (z_{S-1}-z_{S-2})\; 0]$ too can be created from existing securities when (8.2b) holds.

By successively creating bonds with promised payments of z_{S-3}, $z_{S-4},\dots, z_1$ we are in this way able to generate a set of S securities each of which has a payout in one (different) state. Given that existing securities are capable of replicating all of these bonds, the security market is therefore complete. It is to be emphasized that $z>0$ and $z_s \neq z_{s'}$ for all s and s' are necessary conditions for this equivalence between (8.2b) spanning and market completeness to hold.

An equivalent, but institutionally different, method for completing the market goes as follows. Suppose that there exists a financial intermediary, designated by *, which holds a portfolio $[\alpha^*_{jn}]$ of the productive firms' securities $z^* = \Sigma_j \Sigma_n \alpha^*_{jn} z^{jn}$ such that $z^*_s \neq z^*_{s'}$ for all states s and s' and $z^*_s > 0\ \forall s$. As a convenience, number the states in a way that the payout increases with the index: $z^*_1 < z^*_2 \ldots < z^*_S$. Now, let the intermediary issue one security with payout z^*. A (European) call option is a security derived from z^* which promises a payment of $c^*(s, a) = \max\{z^*_s - a, 0\}$ in each state s; a is termed the exercise price of the call. When there are $S-1$ call options with exercise prices $z^*_1, z^*_2, z^*_3, \ldots, z^*_{S-1}$ written as indicated, the following table of S available 'securities' results.

	z^*	$c(., z^*_1)$	$c(., z^*_2)$	...	$c(., z^*_{S-1})$
State 1	z^*_1	0	0	...	0
State 2	z^*_2	$(z^*_2 - z^*_1)$	0	...	0
State 3	z^*_3	$(z^*_3 - z^*_1)$	$(z^*_3 - z^*_2)$...		0
	.	.	.	.	.
	.	.	.	.	.
State s	z^*_S	$(z^*_S - z^*_1)$	$(z^*_S - z^*_2)$	...	$(z^*_S - z^*_{S-1})$

The security of the intermediary (column 1) plus the call options (columns 2 through S) written on it span R^S, thus $\Omega_C(\cdot) = R^S$ and the market is complete. ■

P8.3 provides two different means by which market completeness may be accomplished. The first assures that no *one* firm in making its production and capital structure choice can offer new securities to the market which are not already available by some linear combination of the existing securities. The second market method is based on the assumption that individuals and/or financial intermediaries also deal in perfect and competitive securities markets. The crucial aspect of the intermediation is that it provides offsetting market actions which determine the claims set $\Omega_C(\cdot)$ independent of firm decisions. Finally, it is important to emphasize that the offsetting actions come from firms in the *perfect substitute* case and they come from individuals and/or financial intermediaries in the *equal access* case.

8.B.4. A special production technology

A frequently employed, quite special production technology, important to the issue of market completeness because of the manner in which it permits firm decisions to affect the consumption set, is that which 'decomposes' production decisions into additive and multiplicative effects.

D8.3. Decomposable production technology. The production technology of firm j is said to be decomposable if $z^j = f^j(z_0^j)1_S + g^j(z_0^j)\eta^j$ where f^j and g^j are scalar valued, suitably continuous functions such that: $f^j(0) = g^j(0) = 0$ and $f^j(z_0^j) \geq 0$, $g^j(z_0^j) \geq 0$ when $z_0^j \leq 0$; and, the S-vector $\eta^j = [\eta_1^j\, \eta_2^j \dots \eta_S^j]$ is the single source of uncertainty.

There are several specific subcases of decomposability which are commonly used:[7] *multiplicative uncertainty* when $f^j(z_0^j) \equiv 0$, *additive uncertainty* when $g^j(z_0^j) \equiv 1$, and *constant stochastic returns to scale* when $f^j(z_0^j) \equiv 0$ and $g^j(z_0^j) = \lambda z_0^j$ with $\lambda > 0$ as constant.[8] Two firms, j and k, are commonly said to be in the same *risk class* when there is multiplicative uncertainty and $\eta_s^j = \alpha\eta_s^k\, \forall s$ with $\alpha > 0$ a constant.[9] Finally, notice that when there is a continuum of states and η^j follows a standardized normal distribution, then the decomposable production technology replicates the frequently used case of normally distributed returns, with $f^j(z_0^j)$ being the distribution mean and $g^j(z_0^j)$ the associated standard deviation.

E8.8. Consider the *constant stochastic returns to scale* case:

$$z^j = \lambda z_0^j \eta^j,$$

with $\lambda > 0$ a constant and $\eta^j \geq 0$. Then two firms j and k with the same technology $(\eta^j = \eta^k)$ which have investment amounts differing by some constant $\alpha > 0$ $(z_0^k = \alpha z_0^j)$ differ in market values also by that same constant,

[7] Diamond (1967) provides one of the earliest analyses of the decomposable technology.

[8] Real technologies with intertemporally, identically distributed constant returns to scale are perhaps the most commonly assumed technology in multiperiod production economies. See, for example, Brock (1978), Prescott and Mehra (1978), Constantinides (1980), Breeden (1982), and Sundaresan (1984). Usually, power utility is also assumed for individuals in these cases. The popularity of such models arises from the fact that, given the homotheticity of power utility (see P1.8–P.10) and an intertemporally constant technology, a constant proportion of aggregate endowment is then reinvested in real technologies in equilibrium.

[9] Modigliani and Miller (1958) and Merton and Subrahmanyan (1978) use this case. Merton and Subrahmanyan argue that the equal risk class assumption defines 'free entry' to technologies.

i.e.,

$$v_0^k = \sum_s \pi_s z_s^k = \sum_s \pi_s \lambda z_0^k \eta_s^k$$

$$= \sum_s \pi_s \lambda (\alpha z_0^j) \eta_s^j$$

$$= \alpha \sum_s \pi z_s^j = \alpha v_0^j. \qquad \blacksquare$$

Much of the interest in decomposable production technologies is based on the fact that they, in quite simple ways, guarantee the (8.3b) spanning condition and therefore provide financial and technical completeness. The simple ways? Note that the investment decision z_0^j, while it in general changes the scale of the 1_S (riskless) and η^j (risky) patterns across states, does not change the patterns themselves, at least in several important cases.

P8.4. Sufficient conditions for spanning. Let the security market be closed and let some firm j have a decomposable production technology. When that firm's production is non-trivial ($z_0^j < 0$), then conditions for spanning exist and the claims set $\Omega_C(\cdot)$ is fixed independently of its production and capital structure decision if either (or both) of the following obtain:

(8.4a) a riskless security is available and the firm issues either equity alone or issues a combination of riskless simple debt and simple equity,

(8.4b) the firm always selects an all equity or all debt capital structure and either multiplicative uncertainty prevails and/or a riskless security is available.

Proof. That the two conditions are sufficient for financial and technical completeness simply requires showing the decisions z^j and δ^j of some firm j do not alter the consumption set. Condition (8.4a) is most frequently employed and can be used to sketch the proof. Let the firm choose a promised payment to debt of b^j: then $z^{jd} = b^j 1_S$, which is riskless for all choices of z^j. In turn, $z^{je} = z^j - b^j 1_S$, where $z^j = f^j(z_0^j) 1_S + g^j(z_0^j) \eta^j$. That is, all decisions z^j and δ^j (provided debt remains riskless) produce securities z^{je} and z^{jd} which are spanned by the vectors 1_S and η^j. $\Omega_C(\cdot)$ is therefore independent of the firm's specific decision. The (8.4b) cases are similarly shown and left to the reader. $\square$

8.B.5. Perceived and actual price-taking

We now call attention to the distinction between perceived and actual price-taking behavior in supply, noting then the implications of this difference for general and partial equilibrium analyses.

Recall the conditions provided in P8.1 for perceived price-taking in supply. As expected, a more restrictive case of price-taking occurs when prices are actually independent of firm decisions.

S8.4′. Actual price-taking (competition) in supply. The desicions of firms are such that they do not affect the market value of any feasible consumption plan $\omega^i=[w_0^i\ w^i]$ where $w^i \in \Omega_C$.

Of course, we would expect that actual price-taking leads to perceived price-taking, in which case S8.2, S8.3, S8.4′, S8.5 and S8.6 jointly provide conditions for unanimity by Proposition 8.2. But, what conditions lead to S8.4′?

P8.5. Actual price-taking in supply. Let S8.2, S8.3, S8.5, and S8.6 hold. Associated with some decisions z^j and $\delta^j\ \forall j$ and therewith aggregate supplies $m=\Sigma_j\Sigma_n z^{jn}$ and $m_0=\Sigma_j\bar{w}_0^i+\Sigma_j z_0^j$, designate an exchange equilibrium sustaining price system $\mathring{\pi}$. Then, there is actual price-taking in supply when all decisions by firms:

(8.5′a) leave unchanged the aggregate supplies m and $\mathring{m}$, and

(8.5′b) yield the same wealth $W^i\ \forall i$ at prices $\mathring{\pi}$.

Proof.[10] We proceed by showing that every set of production and capital structure decisions which satisfies the above conditions (8.5′a) and (8.5′b) implies an exchange equilibrium sustained by the same price system, $\mathring{\pi}$. First, assume as in the proposition that $\mathring{\pi}$ is such an equilibrium price system for some set of decisions $z^j, \delta^j\ \forall j$. In this case $\mathring{\pi}$ solves consumptive optimum equations (8.A.2) and markets clear. Consider now any other set of decisions $\overset{*}{z}^j$, $\overset{*}{\delta}^j\ \forall j$ such thai conditions (8.5′a) and (8.5′b) of the proposition hold. When S8.5 and S8.6 obtain then each individual i's opportunity set $\mathrm{O}^i(W^i, \mathring{\pi})$ is exactly as before (given $\mathring{\pi}$ is fixed), and therefore the same consumption plan is optimal for each i. By condition (8.5′a) all markets also clear at $\mathring{\pi}$ with the $\overset{*}{z}^j$, $\overset{*}{d}^j\ \forall j$ decisions. Thus $\mathring{\pi}$ is a sustaining exchange equilibrium price system at these 'new' as well as the 'old' decisions. □

[10]The logic of the following proof was first clearly stated by Stiglitz (1974) in his proof of the irrelevance of corporate financial policy in a general equilibrium model.

It is to be stressed that P8.5′ has both (8.5′a) *and* (8.5′b) as necessary conditions for *actual* price-taking in supply. While equilibrium consumption plans and thus state-claim prices are generally sensitive to the specification of wealth, there is one important case where this does not hold and condition (8.5′b) is not necessary for S8.5′ (but, condition (8.5′a) still is). When individuals are I3 (see D1.17), differences in wealth only affects the scale of an investor's risky portfolio and not its composition (see P1.6 and P1.7). Since all securities are held in equilibrium and every 13 individual holds risky assets in the same proportion regardless of wealth, then equilibrium prices are independent of the wealth distribution in this case.

Before ending this discussion two points should be addressed. First, note that when the conditions of P8.5′ are satisfied equilibrium consumption plans, and therefore state claim prices, are unaltered by corporate decisions. It follows in turn that the market values of the securities are the same, so that the perceived price-taking conditions of P8.3 are *actually* satisfied under the conditions of P8.5′. Second, when the conditions of S8.2, S8.3 and S8.5 hold, then changes in *capital structure* affect neither (i) aggregate supplies nor (ii) the allocation of wealth. As a result, equilibrium prices and the allocation of consumption is unaffected by capital structure decisions so that corporate financing is irrelevant. If, alternatively, the security market is not closed (S8.2 does not obtain) and/or variations are allowed in production plans, specific additional requirements must be made to assure (8.5′a) and (8.5′b) are met. Particularly, for a given change in the decisions of one firm, other firms must then make decisions which not only leave aggregate supplies unchanged, but also leave the allocation of wealth unaffected. One such special case occurs when S8.2 and S8.3 hold, there are two or more firms with *identical* production technologies exhibiting constant stochastic returns to scale, and there are exactly offsetting investment (and therefore output) decisions.

8.C. Theory of the Firm

8.C.1. Capital structure irrelevance

Suppose that the securities market is closed so that the equality $\Sigma_n z^{jn} = z^j$ is met independent of capital structure decisions. Assume also that specifications S8.2 through S8.6 hold: the market is perfect and there is both financial and production completeness. Finally, fix the sustaining price system, writing the net market value of each firm and the wealth of each individual as, respectively,

$$\langle z^j, \pi \rangle + z_0^j = \sum_n \langle z^{jn}, \pi \rangle + z_0^j \quad \forall j, \tag{8.C.1}$$

$$W^i = \bar{w}_0^i + \sum_j \bar{\alpha}_j^i \left(\sum_n \langle z^{jn}, \pi \rangle + z_0^j \right) \quad \forall i. \tag{8.C.2}$$

From these expressions it is apparent that (production decisions given) the market value of firms and the wealth of individuals are independent of the capital structure decision. That is, given that wealth orders preferences for individuals (P1.1), then equation (8.C.2) implies that all individuals are indifferent to the method by which any production plan is financed; (8.C.1), in turn, implies that the production plan which maximizes net wealth is independent of the financing. These facts are summarized in the following proposition.

P8.6. Capital structure irrelevancy in partial equilibrium. Let specifications S8.2 through S8.6 hold. Then, for any firm:

(8.6a) (value independence) given its production decision, the firm's net market value is independent of its capital structure decision,

(8.6b) (capital structure indifference) given the production decision, all individuals are indifferent to the choice of capital structure, and

(8.6c) (Fisher separation) there is unanimous shareholder support for the value maximizing production decision independent of the choice of capital structure.

There is also the problem of capital structure in general equilibrium, which the following proposition addresses.

P8.7. Capital structure irrelevancy in general equilibrium. Suppose S8.1, S8.2, S8.3, and S8.5 hold and fix the production decisions of all firms. Under these conditions, and for some specific set of capital structure decisions by all firms, assume a security market exchange equilibrium exists. Then corresponding to any other set of capital structure decisions there exists another exchange equilibrium such that:

(8.7a) (value independence) the net market value of each firm is the same as in the first equilibrium, and

(8.7b) (capital structure indifference) the allocation and prices in the two equilibria are identical so that there is unanimous indifference to the capital structure decisions of the firms.

Proof. Let $\mathring{\pi}$ be the original exchange equilibrium price system which yields a net market value for each firm j as $\langle z^j, \mathring{\pi}\rangle + z_0^j$. Given S8.1, capital structure decisions do not affect aggregate supplies and, by equation (8.C.2), every individual's wealth is independent of capital structure decisions when there is financial completeness. P8.5′ then provides that $\mathring{\pi}$ is a sustaining price system for the second (revised capital structure) exchange equilibrium, which means that the allocation is unchanged and thus there is unanimous indifference to any and all firms' capital structure under the given conditions. □

The basis of the propositions concerning unanimous shareholder support for net value maximization and for the irrelevancy of capital structure are those conditions which provide (1) that firm decisions affect individual consumption opportunities only by changes in personal wealth and, in turn, (2) that individuals order optimal consumption plans by wealth. While this fact has been used several times in the preceding sections, it is sufficiently critical to deserve a summary statement. To this end, recall first the indirect utility function

$$U^*(\pi, W) = \max U(w) \quad \text{s.t.} \quad w \in O(\pi, W). \tag{8.C.3}$$

When the sustaining state claims prices are fixed (see P8.4 or P8.4′), then U^* is increasing in W (P1.1) and the effect of firm decisions directly on W are of concern. Recall the expression for individual wealth

$$W = \sum_j \bar{\alpha}_j \left[\sum_n \langle \pi, z^{jn} \rangle + z_0^j \right] + \bar{w}_0. \tag{8.C.4}$$

With the prices π fixed one then sees that those decisions which maximize each firm's net market value, $\Sigma_c \langle \pi, z^{jc} \rangle + z_0^j$ for each firm j, will be optimal for every individual. The converse also holds: when the prices π are not fixed then increments to firm market value need not increase utility for all individuals (see P1.1).

This is the essential idea underlying P8.2: when conditions are such that wealth orders optimal consumption plans, there is shareholder unanimity with respect to net value maximizing decisions. It is an easy step from this result to the conditions for capital structure irrelevancy. With production decisions fixed (and the security market is closed, S8.1), then the value $\Sigma_n\langle \pi, z^{jn}\rangle$ is unaltered by the packaging of z^j into securities and individuals are obviously indifferent to the selected capital structure.

The proofs both of unanimous support for net value maximization and of capital structure irrelevancy are true in a partial equilibrium sense if the prices are perceived fixed, and they are true 'across equilibrium', or in a general equilibrium sense, if prices are actually fixed (and completeness is assured by equal access rather than perfect substitute means). Of course, the actual fixity of prices requires those restrictive conditions necessary to assure a constant supply of claims in all states.

8.C.2. Value additivity

In discussing the production decisions of firms it has been assumed that each firm had a fixed set of production plans. In this sense the technology of each firm was given. More generally, however, firms can also make decisions to adopt other firms' technologies. To analyze the market effects of this extended form of investment, suppose that firm $j=1$ chooses to purchase, or consolidate with, $(M-1)$ other firms. Further, suppose there to be no technical gains or losses to the consolidation of the firms (i.e., no 'synergies') so that the production set with the consolidated firm, $\cong^m$, simply equals the sum of the production sets of its constituents. That is, $\simeq^m = \{\xi^m \mid \xi^m = \Sigma_{j=1}^M \xi^j,\ \xi^j \in \simeq^j\ \forall j=1,\ldots,M\}$, where we let $j=1, 2, \ldots, M$ represent those of the consolidation and m indicates the consolidated firm.

P8.8. Value additivity. Let a production-exchange equilibrium exist with net value maximizing firms. Suppose further that there are no technical gains or losses to consolidations and that the securities markets are closed. Then if every security traded prior to a consolidation of firms can be represented as a linear combination of the securities traded after the consolidation (i.e., the claims set is unaltered by the changes), there exists a post-consolidation equilibrium with net value maximizing firms such that:

(8.8a) (unanimous indifference) the allocation, and prices, in the two equilibria are identical, so that there is unanimous indifference to the consolidation, and

(8.8b) (value independence) the net market value of the consolidated firm in the post-consolidation equilibrium equals the sum of the net market values of the constituent firms in the pre-consolidation equilibrium.

Proof. Let π denote a sustaining price system for the preconsolidation market, so that the net market value of each firm is $\Sigma_n\langle\pi, z^{jn}\rangle + z_0^j$, where $z^{jn}\,\forall j, n$ and $z_0^j\,\forall j$ are equilibrium values for net value maximizing firms. Now let firms $j=1, 2, \ldots, M$ merge under the conditions of the proposition and consider π as a candidate sustaining price system for the post-consolidation economy. By assumption the consolidation does not affect the consumption claims set (for example, appropriate *equal access* conditions may obtain) and there are no technical gains or losses created. By this second fact, the production plans available to the consolidated firm are exactly those which can be formed as all possible sums of the plans available to its constituents. Thus, at prices π the specific production plan which maximizes the net market value of the consolidated firm must be made up as the sum of the plans which were net value maximizing for the constituent firms in the pre-consolidation equilibrium. With the consumption claims set unaltered, with closed markets and thus aggregate supplies available to individuals in all time periods and states unaltered, and with individuals' wealth in turn unaltered, π must also be a sustaining price system for the post-consolidation markets. Optimal consumption plans must, of course, then be the same for the two equilibria leading to the (8.8a) indifference and, furthermore,

$$\sum_n \langle \pi, z^{mn}\rangle + z_0^m = \sum_n \left\langle \pi, \sum_j z^{jn}\right\rangle + \sum_j z_0^j$$

$$= \sum_j \left(\sum_n \left\langle \pi, z^{jn}\right\rangle + z_0^j \right),$$

so that the net market (equilibrium) value of the consolidated firm is exactly equal to the sum of the net market (equilibrium) values of its constituents. □

8.C.3. *Efficiency and value maximization*

The crucial feature of competitive markets in securities which provides for unanimous individual support for net market value maximizing firm decisions is that such decisions affect consumption possibilities only through changes in wealth. In Section 8.B it was argued that this factor was not only sufficient for such unanimity but, lacking very special conditions, it was also necessary.

Linked, in obvious ways, to the finding that net value maximizing decisions are unanimously supported is the conclusion that such decisions result in a Pareto optimal equilibrium allocation.

P8.9. Optimality of net value maximizing decisions. Suppose that the conditions of P8.2 hold and, therefore, that net value maximizing firm decisions are in the unanimous best interest of shareholders. Then, these decisions lead to a general equilibrium in which the allocation of resources is constrained Pareto optimal relative to the consumption claims set spanned by the securities available in the equilibrium.

Proof. Obvious from the definition of unanimity. When conditions for unanimity do not hold, then every decision by the firm generally makes one group of individuals better off at the expense of another. □

Chapter 9

MULTIPERIOD CONSUMPTION AND INVESTMENT

In the preceding chapters, as in much of the literature on asset valuation, it was assumed that individuals maximize the utility of current consumption and next-period wealth. In that 'static' two period model conditions occurring after the state is revealed at the future date are seemingly irrelevant, at least insofar as the individual's current decisions are concerned. The principal argument for imposing such myopia is analytical tractability; the cogent argument against the model is that individuals are certainly concerned with events beyond the very next period and, with markets opening periodically and with the accumulation of information, consumption and investment decisions will generally be revised over time.

These arguments need not be weighed against each other if the two period problem can be formed in the fashion of dynamic programming, as the first stage in a recursion sequence. In this case the second date of the two period problem would represent the entire future, with the 'derived utility' function of that second date providing the current value of the maximum utility that could be achieved throughout all future periods.[1] For the static two period model to be equivalent to the two period recursion then requires that the second period utilities be equivalent in these problems.

Being the maximum of future utility with respect to current decisions, the derived utility in the two period recursion reflects all future consumption–investment opportunities. That, in turn, means that these opportunities generally must be known with certainty in the present. Otherwise, the derived utility will be stochastic, and not the deterministic function that has heretofore been assumed in the static problem.[2] The dynamics of multiperiod investment–consumption choice and the conditions under which there is, in this fashion, a two period recursion equivalent to the static two period problem is the central issue addressed in this chapter.

[1] Fama (1970), Neave (1971), and Brush (1972) provide systematic analyses of the two period recursion equivalent to the multiperiod consumption–investment problem.

[2] The state-dependency of the 'next-period' utility function was earlier noted, in Section 3.D.1, and then assumed away in the (usual) definition of the two-period security market economy D3.5.

9.A. Two Period Equivalence

The simplest version of the multiperiod consumption–investment model considers an individual with current wealth which is to be consumed or used to purchase state claims to future consumption. Using only one good – a composite commodity of account – a consumption–investment decision of this sort is, moreover, made at the onset of every period in the individual's lifetime. This sequence of choices is based in part on the individual's *lifetime* expected utility

$$\mathrm{E}U(w_0, w_1, w_2, \dots, w_T), \tag{9.A.1}$$

where w_t indicates date $t=0, 1, 2, \dots, T$ *consumptions.* w_T is usually thought of as a bequest to heirs at T, the known *horizon* or *terminal date.* (Because individuals have a sequence of consumption–investment decisions, it is important to carefully distinguish between consumption of the composite good and wealth at each date; again, w_t is date t consumption). The dating convention, as usual, assumes $\mathrm{E}U(\cdot)$ to apply after the $t=0$ state has realized so that the current consumption choice w_0 is a scalar. Each element of the future consumption stream $(w_1, w_2, \dots, w_T)$ is, however, a vector of state-contingent quantities:

$$w_t = [w_{1t}, w_{2t}, \dots, w_{St}], \tag{9.A.2}$$

where St indicates the number of states at each date t. It will be convenient at times to think of each future w_t as a random variable.

9.A.1. The stochastic process

Unlike the situation in the static two period model, consumption choice with T risky periods introduces the problems of stochastic processes, including the need to consider compound events, jointness of probabilities, and strategies involving a revision of choice as events unfold over time. To deal with these things requires some additional definitions and notations. In this regard, first let $\underline{St}$ indicate the set of possible states at period t: $\underline{St} = \{1t, 2t, \dots, st, \dots, St\}$, where st is used both as an index and to indicate a particular realization of the state in period t. (At time 0 the state is known for sure and the set $\underline{S0}$ has a single element.) Next define the ordered t-tuple $nt = [s0, s1, \dots, st]$ to be a *specific evolution* of states up to date $t \leq T$, and denote the collection of *all possible evolutions* to date t by Nt, which is the cartesian product $Nt = \underline{S0} \times \underline{S1} \times \underline{S2} \times \dots \times \underline{St}$. For any two successive dates t and $(t+1)$ the number of elements in $N(t+1)$ is an $S(t+1)$-fold product of those in Nt. Finally, for $\tau<t$ define the first τ elements of a specific evolution $nt \in Nt$ as a *subevent* of nt.

E9.1. The above ideas can be illustrated in a three period economy. For this case let the $t=0$ state be known and, to keep things simple, assume two possible states $s=1$ and $s=2$ at $t=1$ and, similarly, two states $\theta=1$ and $\theta=2$ at $t=2$. There are thus four possible evolutions of the economy; these are labeled $n2_1$, $n2_2$, $n2_3$, and $n2_4$ corresponding to the (s, θ) pairs

$$[(s=1,\ \theta=1)\quad (s=1,\ \theta=2)\quad (s=2,\ \theta=1)\quad (s=2,\ \theta=2)]$$

and paths of the following *date-state tree*:

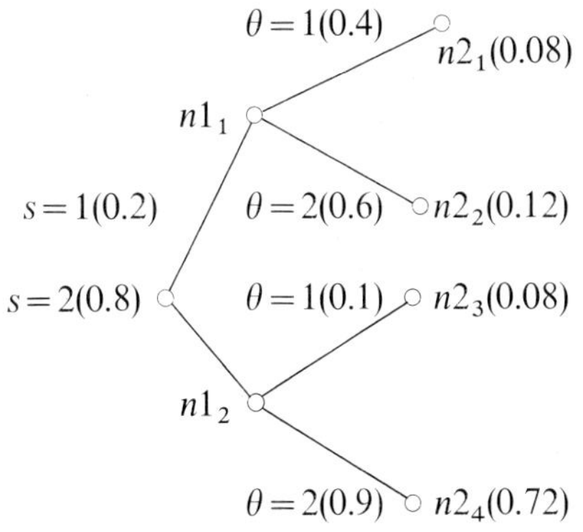

Note that $n1_1$ is a subevent of both $n2_1$ and $n2_2$; similarly, $n1_2$ a subevent of both $n2_3$ and $n2_4$. Nodes in the date-state tree correspond to subevents.

The probability that evolution $n2_1$ will occur is

$$\begin{aligned} h(n2_1) &= (\text{prob. } s=1)(\text{prob. } \theta=1 \mid s=1) \\ &= (0.2)(0.4) = 0.08, \end{aligned}$$

which is indicated in the figure. Probabilities of other evolutions are also marked along with subevent probabilities. ■

With these notations, the individual's lifetime utility can be written in expected utility form as

$$\sum_{nT \in NT} h_{nT} U(w_0, w_{n1}, w_{n2}, \ldots, w_{nT}), \tag{9.A.3}$$

where it is understood that $n1$ is a subevent of $n2$, $n2$ is a subevent of $n3, \ldots$ and $n(T-1)$ is a subevent of nT. Finally, by h_{nT} we mean the probability that the specific evolution nT will occur from among all those possible in NT. It is apparent that the individual's choice is over consumption *streams* associated with specific evolutions of the economy ('paths' through the tree of all possible date-state possibilities to T).

How do individuals trade claims to wealth when there are multiple periods with uncertain states? Our first inclination is to consider a set of forward markets occurring at $t=0$ in 'evolution claims', paying one unit of account at each date contingent on the particular subevent to occur (i.e., contingent on the node occurring in the date-state tree) and zero otherwise. This market arrangement is of course analogous to the two period contingent claims market economy of Chapter 2, only the claims across states at the 'second date' become instead claims to evolutions. And, just as there were prices for state claims in the two-period model, in this extended model there are prices for all possible subevents (evolutions). That is, the dimensionality of these problems differ, not their analytical structure. As Chapters 2 and 3 made clear, such an exchange arrangement has the merit of leading to a Pareto optimal allocation over time, providing all markets are perfect and competitive.[3]

Alternatively, P3.2 (and P3.3) provided conditions for the equivalence of allocations when such extensive forward markets are replaced by an appropriate sequence of markets. The general principle developed there was that individuals, with time additive and separable utilities, are indifferent between relatively rich forward markets with few future revision possibilities and relatively underdeveloped forward markets with extensive future markets opening to permit revisions. That is the usual basis for adopting a market organization in which trading occurs at each date to current consumption and state-contingent claims at the next market date.[4] When the markets in claims to the next date are complete, then the individual is fully capable of establishing a wealth position at the origin (node) of every possible (then-future) evolution of the economy.[5]

[3]See, especially, P2.9.

[4]See Samuelson (1969), Fama (1970), and Merton (1973b) for example.

[5]On the date 0 forward markets the current consumption good is traded as well as claims to the S1 states at date 1. At date 1 new markets open with trading in the then current consumption good and $S2$ claims to the states at date 2. Markets similarly open for each succeeding date. The markets at any date are complete, it should be noted, only in a particular sense. For example, at $t=0$ an 'unamibiguously' complete market for claims to dates 1 and 2 consumption would require claims (in addition to those available here) paying if *both*, and *neither*, $s1$ and $s2$ occurs for all combinations of states at both dates, i.e., all possible evolutions through the two dates. More generally, at $t=0$ the distinction is between the $S1$ state claims is used here and the complete set of $(S1 \times S2 \times \ldots \times ST)$ claims. When pure claims to *all*

An issue of special importance with the proposed sequence of markets concerns the current knowledge individuals have of future market prices. For example, with the sequential market arrangement, the prices of claims on markets, say, at period t (paying at $t+1$) are not known with certainty at period $t-1$. This is because those future market claim prices will generally depend on the state to occur – for example, because the wealth position of individual investors at the future date will be state dependent. With prices for claims on future markets uncertain in this fashion, so are the individual's future investment opportunities. And, the maximum utility that can be achieved over a sequence of future dates, which depend on the trading opportunities at those dates, too will be stochastic.

All this leads to a significant theoretical and practical difficulty: as current market choices (and resulting exchange equilibrium prices) are in general affected by uncertain future trading opportunities, current exchange is indeterminant without some clear specification of the manner in which individuals know those future opportunities. The major complications in the following analysis will arise from this state dependency.

9.A.2. Market organization

An overview of the market model to be generally used is as follows:

(i) individuals, with initial wealth $\bar{w}_0$ and without non-marketable income, maximize expected utility given by (9.A.3),

(ii) firms provide (exogeneously fixed) payoff streams (cash flows) over time,

(iii) conventional security markets in these risky payoffs open and close at each discrete date, current and future,

(iv) markets are complete in the sense that, at each date, individuals can separately purchase a then-current consumption amount and security claims paying in each state at the next date, and

(v) markets are perfect and competitive in the usual sense.

As individuals make their consumption-investment decisions in a market sequence, purchases of claims at one date provide (part of) the wealth

---

$S1 \times S2 \times \ldots \times ST$ future contingencies are available on current markets, then markets opening in the future are redundant – since no individual would revise his consumption plan at date 1 from that chosen at date 0. When these additional 'combination' claims do not exist, but markets open and close at each date (as here), it is possible for individuals to achieve the same allocation as if those additional claims did exist, providing that there is full information price expectations, see D3.3. In this case forward markets which are relatively 'rich' are equivalent to a mix of 'less rich' forward markets and a sequence of future markets.

constraint on future markets.[6] This 'accumulation' is clarified with the following notation:

$\bar{w}_{st}$ the individual's 'endowment' of claims when date and state st obtain,

w_{st} the individual's choice of consumption at date t given that state st obtains, and

$w'_{s(t+1)}$ the individual's choice of claims at date t which are payable at $(t+1)$ iff state $s(t+1)$ occurs.

The link between periods is made by requiring $\bar{w}'_{st} = w_{st}$, the number of claims chosen on markets at date $s(t-1)$ payable at st are the individual's 'endowment' given st occurs – w'_{st} is chosen at $(t-1)$. Non-marketable income is ignored in this link and it is assumed that, at each date, firms undertake (exogeneously specified levels of) production which provides the aggregate, state contingent, commodity supplies. Trading at each period $t = 0, 1, 2, \ldots, T-1$ is thus restricted to a budget balance where, for all st,

$$\bar{w}_{st} = w_{st} + \sum_{s(t+1)} \pi'_{s(t+1)} w'_{s(t+1)}, \tag{9.A.4a}$$

with each $\pi'_{s(t+1)}$ being the price on date t markets for a unit claim payable at date-state $s(t+1)$. That these are prices on future markets is emphasized by the prime. It is usual to refer to (9.A.4a) as the *accumulation*, or *transition*, equation. Finally, as there is no investment at the last period, only consumption, the period T budget restriction is simplified:

$$\bar{w}_{sT} = w_{sT}. \tag{9.A.4b}$$

In summary, markets in consumption claims open and close at each date. At each such trading period, which occurs after the state is known, the individual may choose to consume the payment from his previously purchased state claims or he may consume less, using the residual to purchase state claims payable at the next date. Of special note with the sequence of markets is the fact that at each date, say $(t-1)$, the individual only knows imperfectly his endowment position at any then-future date. As this uncertainty holds for every individual, all endowment positions on future markets are random from the present view and, in general, the state claim price system to obtain on future markets too will be random.

[6]The second 'part' of the wealth constraint is the prevailing price system for then-future claims – see (9.A.4a) below.

9.A.3. A basic assumption

Again, it is our purpose to set out the conditions under which risk averse expected utility maximizers, trading in a sequence of markets which are perfect and competitive, may replace their multiperiod decision problem at any date with an equivalent problem with only two periods. The pieces are nearly assembled for this analysis, with just one key assumption being additionally required. To understand its role, it is useful to consider the T-period problem as it stands now. At each period t with state st occurring, the individual chooses (then) current consumption w_{st} and the $S(t+1)$-vector $w'_{(t+1)}$ of claims to maximize (9.A.3). Part of the stationarity conditions for an interior solution are, for each $s(t+1)$,

$$\sum h_{nT}[\partial U(\cdot)/\partial w'_{s(t+1)}] = \lambda\pi'_{s(t+1)}, \tag{9.A.5}$$

where the sum is over all evolutions $nT \in NT$ and λ is a Lagrange multiplier. Since marginal utility has as its arguments consumption at all dates, its value depends on all past and future consumptions. Taking λ, the marginal utility of consumption in that (current) state which is the last occurring in specific evolution nt as numeraire, the price $\pi'_{s(t+1)}$ equals the expected marginal utility of the LHS in the above equation. This, in turn, means that equilibrium prices at each date and state too have the same dependencies on consumption at every other date and state.

Part of the original purpose in fashioning the T-period problem was to allow for complex interactions of events over time. With prices and consumption at every date and state dependent on prices and consumption at every other date and state, there is little hope of reducing the T-period problem to a 2-period equivalent. Some simplification is thus necessary to yield the equivalence. As the complex linkage between dates and states comes in part from marginal utilities, these must be dealt with first.

S9.1. Separable and Additive Utility. Each individual's utility of consumption at any period t is independent of consumption at any other period, giving the time additive and state separable utility function

$$U(w_0, w_1, w_2, \ldots, w_T) = \sum_t U(w_t, t) = \sum_t \sum_{st} h_{st}(w_{st}, t), \tag{9.A.6}$$

where the differences in the functions $U(\cdot)$ are understood.

9.A.4. Two period recursion

Using the separable and additive utility, the individual's choice problem can be represented as[7]

$$\max E_{nt} \sum U(w_t, t), \tag{9.A.7a}$$

choosing positive consumptions subject to:

$$\bar{w}_{st} - w_{st} = \sum_{s(t+1)} \pi'_{s(t+1)} w'_{s(t+1)} \tag{9.A.7b}$$

for each $t = 0, 1, \ldots, T-1$, and

$$\bar{w}_{sT} = w_{sT}. \tag{9.A.7c}$$

The expectation E_{nt} is with respect to all evolutions of the economy.

The solution to this problem proceeds conveniently with dynamic programming. It is easiest to begin with the last period, solving the problem at T first; the problem at $(T-1)$ is then solved assuming the optimal choice is made at T; in turn, the problem at $(T-2)$ is solved assuming all then-future decisions are optimal, etc. The solution procedure works backward in this fashion, employing the principle of optimality until the period 0 decision period is reached.[8]

[7]The rationale for the expected value of the sum of single period utility functions is based on the sequence of studies by Savage (1954), Koopmans (1960), and Debreu (1960). Savage shows that if an individual has preferences over the vector of future consumption amounts which obey complete ordering, transitivity, continuity, independence, complexity and unequal probability axioms, then there exists a scalar utility function of the consumption vector whose expected value individuals would maximize. This is the (9.A.1) criterion.

Debreu (1960) shows that the additive (undiscounted) utility function of the form (9.A.7a) follows when an additional independence axiom holds. Specifically, this axiom requires that preferences over consumption streams *after* any date are not affected by the consumption stream prior to that date. Finally, Koopmans (1960) shows that, assuming identical single period functions and that preferences over consumption streams are unaffected by delaying (all) the streams by one period (a property he calls stationarity), (9.A.7a) takes on the discounted form $E_{nt}\Sigma_t \gamma_t U(w_{st})$ where γ_t is the date t impatience factor and the $U(\cdot)$ are the same for all dates and states.

[8]The solution concept here is a simple one: in a multistage system it is unnecessary to consider, at any point, solutions which are nonoptimal. Stated conversely, this is Bellman's (1957) 'principle of optimality'

> An optimal policy has the property that whatever the initial (wealth) state and (consumption and investment) decisions are, the remaining decisions must constitute an optimal policy with regard to the state resulting from the first decision.

Proof of the principle is by contradiction. Simply, if the remaining decisions are not optimal then the entire policy could not be optimal.

Beginning at T is easy, for the optimal decision at that date has no real degrees of freedom. The individual 'dies' and a bequest is made, equal to the consumption claims available at the state to realize. (Alternatively, the individual dies after consumption and there is no bequest.) The decisions at the next-to-last period are more complicated and conventional, however, as consumption at $(T-1)$ is to be balanced with investment, the purchase of state claims to provide for the bequest.

When trading on the $(T-1)$ markets the individual knows the specific state then prevailing, say it is $s(T-1)$. Additionally, he knows the market value of his wealth $\bar{w}_{T-1}$ – this is just the state claims purchased at $(T-2)$ which have paid in state $s(T-1)$. He chooses the amount to then consume, w_{T-1}, allocating the remaining portion of his wealth to the purchase of date T, state-contingent claims. In choosing these amounts the individual maximizes an expected utility function based on the information available at $(T-1)$, including his revised probability estimates for the occurrence of date T states. That is, at $(T-1)$ the problem is to choose the 'current' consumption (scalar) w_{T-1} and the vector of consumption claims for the next period w'_T to solve

$$U^*(\bar{w}_{T-1}; \pi'_T, T) = \max\left[U(w_{T-1}, T-1) + \sum_{sT} h'_{sT}\, U(w'_{sT}, T) \right], \tag{9.A.8a}$$

subject to

$$(\bar{w}_{T-1} - w_{T-1}) = \sum_{sT} \pi'_{sT}\, w'_{sT}. \tag{9.A.8b}$$

Again: the expectation in (9.A.8a) is based on probabilities for state occurrences at date T *given* knowledge of the state occurring at $(T-1)$; the 'initial' wealth available to the individual is given by his previously chosen consumption claims,

$$\bar{w}_{T-1} = w'_{s(T-1)},$$

where $s(T-1)$ indicates the specific state that has occurred and is known at time $(T-1)$; and, the state claim prices π'_{sT} occurring on the $(T-1)$ markets too depend on the then prevailing state.[9]

[9]To complete the problem, non-negative consumption amounts are required. If the non-negativity constraints were explicitly imposed on the optimization problem, it would be necessary to modify the stationarity equations to include the usual Kuhn–Tucker conditions.

Since the market in date T claims is complete, the individual's investment opportunity set at $(T-1)$ depends only on his then-current 'initial wealth', $\bar{w}_{T-1}$, and the system of claims prices π'_T. In turn, the indirect utility function associated with the solution to (9.A.8) too is a function of these things. To draw particular attention to the intertemporal structure of the problem, it is usual to refer to $U^*(\cdot)$ in a more specific manner as the *derived utility* function. With competitive trading and state claim prices fixed with the individual's choice of claims, it is known from P1.1 that this derived (indirect) utility is strictly concave and increasing in $\bar{w}_{T-1}$ when the elementary utilities have that property in their consumption arguments.

It is important to emphasize that the intertemporal structure of the problem leaves the derived utility function state dependent even though the underlying elementary utilities are not, see (9.A.8a). To be explicit about how this occurs, first note that when state $s(T-1)$ specifically obtains at $(T-1)$, the individual's wealth is $\bar{w}_{s(T-1)}$, and similarly for other individuals. Generally, the distribution of wealth in the cross-section of individuals, and in turn the aggregate level of wealth, will be dependent on the state occurring. As the equilibrium price system on the $(T-1)$ markets for date T claims will in general depend on aggregate wealth and the wealth distribution to obtain at $(T-1)$, those claim prices too will be dependent on the state to occur at $(T-1)$.

We shall follow the usual custom, which is based on the above observation, and write the state dependency of the derived utility function in terms of the underlying wealth distribution, that is, we write $U^*(w'_{s(T-1)}; \tilde{w}_{T-1}, (T-1))$, where $\tilde{w}_{T-1}$ is the state dependent $(I-1)$-vector of individual wealth positions.[10] Note, finally, that the period $(T-1)$ choice of state claims appears in this expression, as we now view the derived utility from period $(T-2)$.

Using the derived utility an obvious analytical similarity develops between the individual's problem at $(T-1)$ and at the prior $(T-2)$ date. Specifically, at $(T-2)$ the 'current' consumption scalar w_{T-2} and the claims vector w'_{T-1} are chosen to

$$\max\left[U(w_{T-1}, (T-2)) + \sum_{s(T-1)} h'_{s(T-1)}\, U^*(w'_{s(T-1)};\ \tilde{w}_{T-1}, (T-1))\right], \tag{9.A.9a}$$

[10]Summarizing the state of information at any date by the distribution of wealth presumes, of course, that individual preferences and beliefs are known and that the aggregate supplies (from production) too are given (and exogeneous).

subject to

$$\bar{w}_{T-2} - w_{T-2} = \sum_{s(T-1)} \pi'_{s(T-1)} w'_{s(T-1)}. \tag{9.A.9b}$$

Once more, primes attached to the probabilities and state claim prices indicate that these are conditioned by the state 'then' occurring – here at date $(T-2)$. This problem is analytically the same as that at $(T-1)$ and yields a solution in the same fashion.

It is now apparent that in the general, date t problem the principle of optimality defines the derived utility

$$U^*(\bar{w}_t; \tilde{w}_t, t) = \max[U(w_t, t) + E_t U^*(w'_{t+1}; \tilde{w}_{t+1}, t+1)],$$

where the max is subject to the wealth transition equation (9.A.4a) and requires positive consumptions. In turn, the 'two period' problem at every date is analytically similarly to that of (9.A.8) and (9.A.9). Of particular interest in this period-to-period recursion sequence is the 'last' problem, at date $t=0$. This has the anticipated form

$$\max\left[U(w_0) + \sum_s h_s U^*(w'_s; \tilde{w}, 1)\right], \tag{9.A.10a}$$

subject to

$$(\bar{w}_0 - w_0) = \sum_s \pi_s w'_s, \tag{9.A.10b}$$

where s (for simplicity, without the date 1 indication) is now used to index states at period 1, $\tilde{w}$ is the period 1 wealth distribution, the π_s are the $t=0$ market prices for period 1 state claims, and $\bar{w}_0$ is (exogeneously given) initial wealth. The choice variables are initial consumption w_0 and the vector of state claims $w'_1 = [w'_{11}, w'_{21}, \ldots, w'_{S1}]$, which are also required to be non-negative. These results are stated formally:

P9.1. Two period recursion. Let (9.A.7) represent the lifetime utility maximization problem of some individual, with each elementary utility being monotone increasing strictly concave in consumption. In trading at each date, suppose the individual is a price-taker of claim prices. Then, the derived utility function $U^*(w_s; \tilde{w}, 1)$ in problem (9.A.10) is also monotone increasing, strictly concave in wealth. Moreover, w_0 and the $S1$-vector w'_1

which solve (9.A.10) are consistent with the solution of problem (9.A.7) for periods $t=0$ and $t=1$.

The (9.A.10) two period recursive model may be applied, as the name suggests, recursively: in this case $t=0$ always refers to the 'current' period and $t=1$ indicates the next period as the underlying chronology of the economy progresses.

9.A.5. *Some solution conditions*

The stationarity conditions for an interior solution to the date $(T-1)$ consumption–investment problem (9.A.8) are

$$\mu_{T-1}-\lambda=0, \tag{9.A.11a}$$

$$h'_{sT}\,\mu_{sT}-\lambda\pi'_{sT}=0 \quad \forall sT, \tag{9.A.11b}$$

where μ_{T-1} and μ_{sT} are the obvious marginal utilities and λ is the multiplier associated with the budget constraint. Eliminate λ and sum over at period T states to give

$$_{T-1}\rho_T\,E_{T-1}(\mu_T)=\mu_{T-1}. \tag{9.A.12}$$

$E_{T-1}(\mu_T)=\Sigma_{sT}\,h'_{sT}\,\mu_{sT}$, we think of μ_T as a random variable, and $_{T-1}\rho_T=(\Sigma_{sT}\,\pi'_{sT})^{-1}$ is the (one plus) riskless rate of return from $(T-1)$ to T which, for reasons noted above, is generally dependent on the state to occur at $(T-1)$. This, in turn, means that the riskless rate from $(T-1)$ to T is known only imperfectly at dates prior to $(T-1)$ and it is said that future riskless rates are *stochastic*. The above equation is consistent with our intuition: utility of 'current' consumption is equal to the expected marginal utility of 'future' wealth compounded at the riskless rate.

The (typical) period $(t-1)$ result is quite similar to that at $(T-1)$, only requiring that the future utility of wealth be measured by the derived utility function. That is, the individual solves

$$U^*(\bar{w}_{t-1};\tilde{w}_{t-1},t-1)$$

$$=\max\left[U(w_{t-1},t-1)+\sum_{st}h'_{st}\,U^*(w'_{st};\tilde{w}_t,t)\right], \tag{9.A.13a}$$

subject to

$$\sum_{st} \pi'_{st} w'_{st} = (\bar{w}_{t-1} - w_{t-1}), \tag{9.A.13b}$$

and non-negativity constraints. Stationarity conditions for an optimum are similar to those at $(T-1)$, and include

$$\mu_{t-1} - \lambda = 0, \tag{9.A.14a}$$

$$h'_{st}\mu^*_{st} - \lambda\pi'_{st} = 0 \quad \forall st. \tag{9.A.14b}$$

Again eliminating λ and summing over all st yields

$$_{t-1}\rho_t E_{t-1}\mu^*_t = \mu_{t-1}. \tag{9.A.14c}$$

Finally, for later use we note that the envelope theorem implies

$$\frac{\partial U^*(\bar{w}_{t-1}; \tilde{w}_{t-1}, t-1)}{\partial \bar{w}_{t-1}} = \mu_{t-1} = {}_{t-1}\rho_t E_{t-1}\mu^*_t, \tag{9.A.14d}$$

at the optimum,[11] where the right-most equation repeats from (9.A.14c).

9.A.6. Two period equivalence: state dependence and investment opportunities

P9.1, it should be emphasized, does not indicate that the static two period problem of preceding chapters is equivalent to the recursive two period problem (of the same date). At the center of the 'non-equivalence' is the difference between the next-period elementary utility U in the static case and the derived utility U^* in the recursive case, and particularly the fact that U^* is not simply a function of the individual's (next-period) wealth but also depends on the prevailing state claims prices and, more fundamentally, the distribution of wealth in the population (the $I-1$ dimensional variable $\tilde{w}_t$). That this difference is critical can be seen with a simple example. Let w^a_t and w^b_t be two plans of state claims purchased at $t-1$ and paying at t. Suppose further that the plans have equal means, $E_{t-1}w^a_t = E_{t-1}w^b_t$, but let b be risker than a in the sense that $w^a_t + \eta_t = w^b_t$ where η_t is noise with respect to

[11]See Mathematical Appendix. In the specific context of an intertemporal model Samuelson (1969) has shown that optimal consumption rules satisfy this envelope condition. When non-negativity constraints are explicitly imposed on consumption the envelope condition needs to be altered, see Benavie (1972, Chapter 5).

w_t^a, $E(\eta_t|w_t^a)=0$, so that

$$E_{t-1}U(w_t^a)>E_{t-1}U(w_t^b).$$

All risk-averse, expected utility maximizers (with the state-independent elementary utilities of the static problem) choose w_t^a relative to w_t^b.[12]

For the same plans and the derived utility function one cannot, however, generally show $E_{t-1}U^*(w_t^a;\tilde{w}_t,t)$ to be greater than $E_{t-1}U^*(w_t^b;\tilde{w}_t,t)$. Rather, when the function U^* is not separable in w_t and $\tilde{w}_t$, then the specification of the wealth distribution, and prices of state claims, will in general affect the relative magnitudes of the expected (indirect) utilities for the given plans a and b – recall E1.3–E1.5. As a result, the solution to the static problem will not generally agree with that of the two period recursion.

Not only does this simple example tell us how the difference occurs, when making no restrictive assumptions about elementary utilities (other than risk aversion) it tells us what is sufficient to make the static and recursive problems equivalent: η_t must be noise not only with respect to w_t^a but also with respect to the wealth distribution $\tilde{w}_t$, i.e., it must be that $E_{t-1}(\eta_t|w_t^a,\tilde{w}_t)=E_{t-1}(\eta_t)=0$. When this additional property obtains, then every risk-averse maximizer in the recursive system too will prefer w_t^a to w_t^b, just as in the static case.[13] This result is stated formally for the date 0 problem.

P9.2. Two-period equivalence. Let (9.A.7) represent the lifetime utility maximization problem of some individual, with elementary utilities being monotone increasing strictly concave in their arguments. Let (9.A.10) indicate the associated two-period recursion of this problem at date 0 and, alternatively, consider the 'static' problem made up of (only) the first two periods of (9.A.7), ignoring all then future periods. The solution to these two problems, the static and recursive, are identical when $E_0(w_1|\tilde{w})=E_0(w_1)$ for all consumption plans w_1 of the consumption set.

State dependence in the derived utility has several possible sources. It may, in the first instance, result from dependence in the underlying elementary utilities. Alternatively, it may arise from stochastic relationships among relative prices when several commodities are to be chosen. And lastly, it

[12]See P5.3.

[13]The proof follows closely that given for P5.2. First, note that $E_{t-1}U^*(w_t^b;\tilde{w}_t,t)=E_{t-1}[EU^*(w_t^b;\tilde{w}_t,t)|\tilde{w}_t,w_t^a]$. Also $E(U^*(w_t^b;\tilde{w}_t,t)|\tilde{w}_t,w_t^a)<U^*(E(w_t^b|\tilde{w}_t,w_t^a);\tilde{w}_t,t)$ by Jensen's inequality. The RHS of the inequality equals $U^*(w_t^a;\tilde{w}_t,t)$ by properties of the noise. Therefore, $E_{t-1}U^*(w_t^b;\tilde{w}_t,t)<E_{t-1}U^*(w_t^a;\tilde{w}_t,t)$.

may arise because the investment (trading) opportunities at future dates depend on the state then prevailing. The specification of individuals in S9.1 eliminates the first possibility by assumption. The second possibility is eliminated as we focus on a single commodity (or rely on a composite commodity theorem, see D3.4). That leaves the third source, the nature of future investment opportunities, to be dealt with.

The earliest, and most frequently used assumption for producing two period equivalence resolves the problem of state dependent (future) investment opportunities simply by assuming it away: the joint distribution on security returns, and thus all feasible consumption portfolios, is assumed to be independently and identically distributed over time.[14] In this case, the investment opportunity set is 'constant' over time and P9.2 clearly holds. The proposition too will hold when security returns are either completely random or when they vary over time in a non-stochastic manner. The final, well-known case in which P9.2 applies is when the individual utilities and security returns have special properties such that the consumption-investment decision is a function only of the date and unaffected by investment possibilities. We turn to two such special cases next.

9.B. Two Special Multiperiod Models

It was noted above that if the derived utility is separable as

$$U^*(w'_{st};\tilde{w}_t,t)=U_A^*(w'_{st};t)+U_B^*(\tilde{w}_{st};t),$$

then $\partial U^*/\partial w'_{st}=\partial U_A^*/\partial w'_{st}$ is a function only of the given individual's wealth and independent of the wealth distribution in the population (and thus independent of investment opportunities). It is apparent that, in this case, the static and recursive two period problems are equivalent in (interior) solution. While leading to obvious simplifications, this is of course not the general case; in fact, Hakansson (1970) has shown that the logarithmic elementary utility is the only risk-averse function to yield derived utilities separable in this fashion.[15] In the following section (9.B.1) we repeat his sufficiency proof and discuss some details of this 'base' case.

A second question concerning the two period equivalence is whether the derived utility function is of the same functional form at each date and, more specifically, of the same form as the underlying elementary utility. It

[14]See, for example, Fama (1970) and Merton (1971).
[15]See also Samuelson (1969) and Merton (1971).

should be clear from the development in Section 9.A. above that stochastically varying investment opportunities can in general act to destroy this conformity. When, however, some portion of the available investment opportunities are constant or vary deterministically over time an interesting class of elementary utilities does provide such conformity. The subsequent Section 9.B.2 develops that case.

9.B.1. Logarithmic utility

Consider an individual with 'logarithmic' elementary utility, $U(w_{st}, t) = \gamma^t \ln(w_{st})$, where γ is the impatience parameter. For this person the period $(T-1)$ stationarity conditions (9.A.11) become

$$\gamma^{T-1}/w_{T-1} = \lambda, \tag{9.B.1a}$$

$$h'_{s(T-1)}\gamma^T/w'_{sT} = \lambda\pi'_{sT} \quad \forall sT. \tag{9.B.1b}$$

Eliminating λ, summing over all states, and using the transition equation (9.A.8b) gives

$$h'_{sT}\,\gamma w_{T-1} = w'_{sT}\,\pi'_{sT},$$

$$\gamma w_{T-1} = (\bar{w}_{T-1} - w_{T-1}),$$

which can be solved for 'current' consumption as

$$w_{T-1} = \bar{w}_{T-1}/(1+\gamma). \tag{9.B.2}$$

With logarithmic utility the individual's optimal $(T-1)$ consumption level is simply proportional to his $(T-1)$ initial wealth and does not depend at all on the prevailing state claims prices. And, as expected, consumption is increasing in wealth and decreasing in the impatience factor γ.

What about the investment portfolio choice? Using (9.B.1) and (9.B.2), the optimal purchase of period T claims is

$$w'_{sT} = (h'_{sT}/\pi'_{sT})(\bar{w}_{T-1} - w_{T-1}) \quad \forall sT. \tag{9.B.3a}$$

And, for any two states sT and θT,

$$w'_{sT}/w'_{\theta T} = (h'_{sT}/\pi'_{sT})/(h'_{\theta T}/\pi'_{\theta T}). \tag{9.B.3b}$$

The optimal investment portfolio has state-claim holdings in direct ratio to the probability-price ratio of the states. Of course, this result is identical to that in the individual's optimal choice with the static two period model (recall E3.1).

Moving backwards one period, the derived utility function for the $(T-2)$ problem can be constructed using the envelope theorem (9.A.14) and the optimality condition (9.A.13):

$$\frac{\partial U^*}{\partial \bar{w}_{T-1}} = \gamma^{T-1}(1+\gamma)/\bar{w}_{T-1}.$$

Then integrating gives

$$U^*(\bar{w}_{T-1}; \tilde{w}_{T-1}, T-1) = \gamma^{T-1}(1+\gamma)\ln(\bar{w}_{T-1}) + \delta(\tilde{w}_{T-1}), \tag{9.B.4}$$

where $\delta(\tilde{w}_{T-1})$ is the constant of integration. The period $(T-1)$ derived utility is state dependent since, as we shall show below, $\delta(\cdot)$ is generally a function of the period T claim prices (and therefore the wealth distribution $\tilde{w}_{T-1}$).

First, however, it is of interest to prove that the derived utility at every date is logarithmic. We proceed by induction. Specifically, for some date t suppose that

$$U^*(\bar{w}_t; \tilde{w}_t, t) = \Gamma_t \ln(\bar{w}_t) + \Delta(t, \tilde{w}_t), \tag{9.B.5}$$

where Γ_t is a function of the individual's impatience factors only and $\Delta(\cdot)$ at each date t does not depend on any of the then-current choice variables – Γ_t and $\Delta(\cdot)$ are defined in detail below. Using the stationarity conditions (9.A.14) for the period $(t-1)$ problem, obtain

$$\gamma_t/w_{t-1} = \lambda, \tag{9.B.6a}$$

$$h'_{st}\Gamma_t/w'_{st} = \lambda\pi'_{st} \quad \forall st. \tag{9.B.6b}$$

Eliminating λ and summing over the states gives

$$w_{t-1}(\Gamma_t/\gamma^t) = \sum_{st} \pi'_{st} w'_{st} = \bar{w}_{t-1} - w_{t-1},$$

which, in turn, solves for the optimal $(t-1)$ consumption level

$$w_{t-1} = \bar{w}_{t-1}(\gamma^t/\Gamma_t). \tag{9.B.7}$$

Again, at each date consumption is strictly (positively) proportional to then-current wealth. And, the proportionality constants are known, non-stochastic functions of time (only).

Recall now the definition of the derived utility:

$$U^*(\bar{w}_{t-1}; \tilde{w}_{t-1}, t-1) = \max[U(w_{t-1}, t-1) + E_{t-1} U^*(w_t'; \tilde{w}_t, t)].$$

Substituting from (9.B.6) and (9.B.7) into this expression gives

$$\begin{aligned} U^*(\cdot) &= \gamma^t \ln(\bar{w}_{t-1}\gamma^t/\Gamma_t) \\ &\quad + E_{t-1}[\Gamma_t \ln(h_t'\bar{w}_{t-1}/\pi_t') + \Delta(t, \tilde{w}_t)] \\ &= (\gamma^t + \Gamma_t) \ln \bar{w}_{t-1} \\ &\quad + [\gamma^t \ln(\gamma^t/\Gamma_t) + E_{t-1}(\Gamma_t h_t'/\pi_t') + E_{t-1}\Delta(t, \tilde{w}_t)] \\ &= \Gamma_{t-1} \ln \bar{w}_{t-1} + \Delta(t-1, \tilde{w}_{t-1}), \end{aligned} \tag{9.B.8}$$

with the last two lines defining Γ_{t-1} and $\Delta(t-1, \tilde{w}_{t-1})$ in recursion. The derived utility is, for all stages, logarithmic in wealth. Moreover, from the definition of Γ_t it is apparent that this factor is always non-stochastic, being a function of γ and the date. Since Γ_t is non-stochastic, note for later use that (9.B.7) implies that aggregate consumption and aggregate wealth are perfectly correlated at each future date. Finally, as indicated above, the definition of $\Delta(t-1, \tilde{w}_{t-1})$ shows that it is a function of the claims prices and therefore state dependent.

Perhaps the most important feature of the logarithmic case is that the state dependence of the derived utility is 'additive' and therefore not problematic. That is, since the optimal choice of claims depends on the partial derivative of the derived utility with respect to the w_{st}, and Δ is not a function of these choice variables, the state dependence does *not* affect the individual's choice of consumption or investment plan.

9.B.2. Linear risk tolerance

Consider now an economy made up of a somewhat more general class of risk averse individuals, those with time additive elementary utilities exhibiting linear risk tolerance (LRT):

$$U(w_{st}) = \gamma^t (w_{st} - \alpha)^c / c, \tag{9.B.9}$$

with $\alpha \geq 0$, $\gamma > 0$, $c \neq 0$, and $c < 1$.[16]

At each date t the LRT individual solves the two period recursion problem (9.A.13), with solution equations being given by (9.A.14). Under these conditions assume a derived utility at date t of the form

$$U^*(\cdot) = \kappa_t[\bar{w}_t - \rho(t)\alpha]^c/c, \tag{9.B.10}$$

where κ_t is a (perhaps stochastic) function of the model parameters and $\rho(t) = 1 + \Sigma_{\tau=t+1}^{T}(1/{}_t\rho_\tau)$ with ${}_t\rho_\tau$ the riskless (one plus) rate from date t to τ. Note that U^* depends on future investment opportunities as reflected by the κ_t factor and the riskless rates in $\rho(t)$.

Using the envelope condition (9.A.14d) yields,

$$\kappa_{t-1}(\bar{w}_{t-1} - \rho(t-1)\alpha)^{c-1} = \gamma^t(w_{t-1} - \alpha)^{c-1},$$

and, solving for 'current' consumption,

$$w_{t-1} = (\gamma^t/\kappa_{t-1})^{1/c-1}(\bar{w}_{t-1} - \rho(t-1)\alpha) + \alpha. \tag{9.B.11}$$

With LRT utilities, demand for 'current' consumption is linear in wealth, just as in the static two period case. (And, when $\alpha = 0$, the power utility, demand is proportional.) To determine the individual's optimal investment plan (of state contingent claims paying at date t) use (9.A.14) to give

$$\gamma^t(w_{t-1} - \alpha)^{c-1} = \lambda, \tag{9.B.12a}$$

$$h'_{st}\kappa_t(w'_{st} - \rho(t)\alpha)^{c-1} = \lambda\pi'_{st}. \tag{9.B.12b}$$

With the elimination of λ and some algebra we then have, for all st,

$$\begin{aligned} w'_{st} &= \rho(t)\alpha + (w_{t-1} - \alpha)\xi_{st} \\ &= \rho(t)\alpha + \xi_{st}\alpha + \xi_{st}[(\kappa_{t-1}/\gamma^t)^{c-1}(\bar{w}_{t-1} - \rho(t-1)\alpha) - \alpha], \end{aligned} \tag{9.B.13a}$$

where

$$\xi_{st} \equiv (h'_{st}\kappa_t/\pi'_{st}\gamma^t)^{c-1} = (\kappa_t/\gamma^t)^{c-1}(\mu^*_{st}/\mu_{t-1})^{c-1}. \tag{9.B.13b}$$

[16]Equation (9.B.9) specializes to exponential utility when $c = -\infty$, $\alpha = 1$ and to logarithmic utility when $c = 0$. Also, when $c > 1$ then $U(w_{st}) = \gamma^t(\alpha - w_{st})^c/c$ and all of the following results hold. The α term can be time dependent without significantly altering any results. In the case where $\alpha \equiv 0$, then (9.B.9) is the usual power utility function.

The optimal choice of state claims is a linear function of the individual's consumption and, from (9.B.11), wealth. (Again, with power utility and $\alpha=0$ these relationships are ones of strict proportionality.)

From (9.B.13) it is seen that, at date t, $\rho(t)\alpha$ claims are held risklessly, equally in every state. The residual holdings, $w'_{st}-\rho(t)\alpha$, is therefore the *at risk* portion. This means that, for two states st and θt,

$$\frac{w'_{st}-\rho(t)\alpha}{w'_{\theta t}-\rho(t)\alpha}=\frac{\xi_{st}}{\xi_{\theta t}}. \tag{9.B.14}$$

The at risk portion of claims are proportionately held across states at each date. Moreover, when investment opportunities are constant over time, then state claim prices and probabilities will be constant over time, in turn the $(\xi_{\theta t}/\xi_{st})$ expressions in (9.B.14) will be constant, and the risky state claims *proportions* too will be constant. However, as $\rho(t)$ generally changes over time, the relative consumption–investment *amounts* change, see (9.B.11), and so will the investment amounts held both risklessly and at risk.

To verify the above results we need to show that the derived LRT utility assumed in (9.B.10) is in fact valid. Again, the proof is by induction. Using (9.B.10) and (9.B.12) in (9.A.13a) we have,

$$U^*(\bar{w}_{t-1};\tilde{w}_{t-1},t-1)=\gamma^t(w_{t-1}-\alpha)^c/c$$

$$+E_{t-1}\kappa_t[(\rho(t)\alpha+(w_{t-1}-\alpha)\xi_t-\rho(t)\alpha)]^c/c.$$

Substituting from (9.B.11) and rearranging then gives

$$U^*(w_{T-1};\tilde{w}_{t-1},t-1)=\gamma^t(\gamma^t/\kappa_{t-1})^{1/c-1}$$

$$\times[\bar{w}_{t-1}-\rho(t-1)\alpha]^c/c+\mathrm{E}_{t-1}\kappa_t[\xi_t(\gamma^t/\kappa_{t-1})^{1/c-1}$$

$$\times(\bar{w}_{t-1}-\rho(t-1)\alpha)]^c/c. \tag{9.B.15}$$

Assuming that the future riskless rates are non-stochastic, $[\bar{w}_{t-1}-\rho(t-1)\alpha]^c$ can be factored from the above expectation to give the LRT form

$$U^*(\bar{w}_{t-1};\tilde{w}_{t-1},t-1)=\kappa_{t-1}(\bar{w}_{t-1}-\rho(t-1)\alpha)^c/c, \tag{9.B.16}$$

where κ_{t-1} solves

$$\kappa_{t-1}=\gamma^t(\gamma^t/\kappa_{t-1})^{1/c-1}+E_{t-1}\kappa_t[\xi_t^c(\gamma^t/\kappa_{t-1})^{c/1-c}]. \tag{9.B.17a}$$

Using (9.B.13b) this can be written in a somewhat more instructive way as

$$\kappa_{t-1}=f(E_{t-1}\kappa_t(\mu_t^*/\mu_{t-1})^{c-1}) \tag{9.B.17b}$$

where $f(\cdot)$ is non-stochastic and depends in form on γ and the date. The argument of f, $E_{t-1}\kappa_t(\mu_t^*/\mu_{t-1})^{c-1}$, is, however, a random variable (when viewed from earlier dates) as this expectation generally depends on the date $(t-1)$ state. Thus, the derived utility, while LRT, is state dependent.

It should be emphasized that when the riskless rate is stochastic one cannot go from (9.B.15) to (9.B.16) and the derived utility is, in the first instance, not of the LRT form. That raises the question concerning conditions which lead to non-stochastic riskless rates.

E9.2. Between the two dates $(T-1)$ and T the one period (short) riskless rate of return is given by, see (9.A.12),

$$1/{}_{T-1}\rho_T=\sum_{sT}\pi'_{sT}=\gamma E_{T-1}[\mu(w_T)/\mu(w_{T-1})], \tag{9.B.18}$$

where the state claim prices $[\pi'_{sT}]$ are those occurring on the date $(T-1)$ markets and the probabilities underlying the expectation are those formed with the information available at date $(T-1)$. Again, we understand that ${}_{T-1}\rho_T$ depends on the state at date $(T-1)$ and, viewed from some prior date, is generally a random variable.

Consider now the special LRT case where individuals are identical and their elementary utility is CARA, i.e., of the (negative) exponential form:

$$U(w_{sT})=-\exp(-\alpha w_{sT}) \quad \text{for all } sT, \quad \text{and}$$

$$U(w_{T-1})=-\exp(-\alpha w_{T-1}),$$

with parameter $\alpha>0$. In this case ${}_{T-1}\rho_T$ will be independent of w_{T-1} (and thus non-stochastic) if $E_{T-1}\{\exp[-\alpha(w_T-w_{T-1})]\}$ is independent of w_{T-1}. How might this occur? Suppose that the individual's consumption follows an additive random walk: $w_T=w_{T-1}+\varepsilon_T$, where ε_T is noise with respect to w_{T-1}. Then,

$$1/{}_{T-1}\rho_T=\gamma E_{T-1}[\exp(-\alpha\varepsilon_T)], \tag{9.B.19}$$

which is independent of w_{T-1}. Given ${}_{T-1}\rho_T$ is non-stochastic viewed from $(T-2)$, then (9.B.16) follows from (9.B.15) at $(T-2)$. It is apparent that this analysis holds for arbitrary dates $(t-1)$ and t, and for riskless rates of all maturities. ■

E9.3. As a second, special LRT case let each individual's elementary utility by CRRA, i.e., of the power form

$$U^*(w_{st}) = \frac{1}{1-c}(w_{st})^{1-c} \quad \text{for all } st, \quad \text{and}$$

$$U(w_{t-1}) = \frac{1}{1-c}(w_{t-1})^{1-c},$$

with common risk measure c. Then, using (9.B.14c),

$$1/_{t-1}\rho_t = \gamma E_{t-1}[w_t/w_{t-1})^{-c}]. \tag{9.B.20}$$

Suppose now that the individual's consumption follows a geometric random walk: $w_t = (w_{t-1})\varepsilon_{t-1}$ where ε_{t-1} is noise with respect to w_{t-1}. Then, for all t,

$$1/_{t-1}\rho_t = \gamma E_{t-1}[\varepsilon_{t-1}^c], \tag{9.B.21}$$

which is independent of w_{t-1}, and again the riskless rate is non-stochastic. This result too easily extends to riskless rates of all maturities. ■

We conclude this section with a frequently used, special case.

P9.3. Two special cases. In an economy with identical individuals having time additive CRRA (CARA) elementary utility functions and aggregate consumption following a geometric (additive) random walk, then at each date:

(i) the derived utility function too is CRRA (CARA),
(ii) the derived utility function is non-stochastic, making the recursive two period problem equivalent to the static two period problem, and
(iii) aggregate consumption and aggregate wealth are perfectly correlated.

Proof. We shall treat the CRRA-geometric random walk case explicitly. The CARA-additive random walk case follows similar steps and is treated in detail in Section 10.C. Result (i) follows immediately from E9.3. To prove (ii) it is necessary to show that κ_t is non-stochastic at each date, see (9.B.16). First note from (9.B.11) that at the terminal date $(\kappa_T/\gamma) = \gamma^T$, making κ_T non-stochastic. Moving back one period, from (9.B.17b), it is then seen that κ_{T-1} will be non-stochastic when the argument of f, especially $E_{T-1}(w_T/w_{T-1})$, is non-stochastic. With identical individuals $w_T = W_T/I$ and $w_{T-1} = W_{T-1}/I$, where W_T and W_{T-1} are aggregate consumption levels (and the population I is assumed to be a known constant). In turn, proof of (ii) requires that $E_{T-1}(W_T/W_{T-1})^{c-1}$ be independent of the state to obtain at $(T-1)$. By assumption $W_T = W_{T-1}\varepsilon_{T-1}$ where ε_{T-1} is noise with respect to W_{T-1} – that is, aggregate consumption follows a geometric random walk – leaving $E_{T-1}(W_T/W_{T-1})^{c-1} = E_{T-1}(\varepsilon_{T-1})^{c-1}$, which is independent of W_{T-1} and therefore state independent. Since κ_{T-1} is non-stochastic, by a similar analysis so is $\kappa_{T-2}, \kappa_{T-3}, \ldots$ proving (ii). Result (iii) follows directly from the fact that κ_t is non-stochastic in (9.B.11). □

It bears re-emphasizing that in the very particular subcase where utilities are logarithmic there is always a simple non-stochastic relationship between aggregate wealth and consumption, see (9.B.7), without the requirement that aggregate consumption follow a random walk.

Developing a relationship between each individual's consumption and a general economic index, and then providing reasonable conditions under which this index follows an appropriate random walk will be considered in the next chapters. As a first step in this process we begin, in the next section, with an 'aggregation' theorem designed to produce an 'equivalent economy' of identical individuals from one where individuals are somewhat heterogeneous, therefore providing a link between individual and aggregate consumption at market equilibrium.

9.C. Demand Aggregation

In the multiperiod economy under uncertainty the wealth distribution across individuals at any date t is a state dependent (stochastic) vector. Unless all individuals are 'income neutral', asset prices, including the term structure of riskless rates, depend on this wealth distribution (and its derivative, the aggregate level of wealth). Thus, any multiperiod extension of, say, the two period capital asset pricing model would also have to include the asset's risk premium associated with its covariance with the $(I-1)$ wealth distribution variables in addition to the usual market (aggregate) wealth covariance. In an economy with a large number of diverse individuals such a valuation model would be intractable. This problem is avoided if individuals can be made homogeneous, for then the wealth is equal across individuals and the wealth distribution is (with a fixed population) given by a scalar. In turn, the stochastic processes of only aggregate variables are left to play a consequential role.[17]

[17]Constantinides (1982) has approached the heterogenity problem somewhat differently. He assumes markets are complete at every date, which means that the resulting competitive exchange equilibrium may be replicated by a central planner's allocation based on a weighted

9.C.1. An aggregation theorem

Demand aggregation is said to occur when it is possible to create a *composite* individual whose characteristics are an 'average' of those for the actual individuals of the economy and where the averaging is such that an exchange equilibrium price system reached in the economy made up only of composite individuals is identical to that occurring in the original economy with heterogenous individuals.[18] What characteristics are to be averaged? In this regard it is usual to allow that individuals differ in initial wealth, intertemporal patience parameter, probability beliefs, and risk aversion.

The interesting cases of aggregation generally assume the existence of a risk-free asset and limit attention to elementary utility functions which are linear in risk tolerance, that is of the form (see Section 1.C for details)

$$-U''(w_{st})/U'(w_{st})=a+bw_{st} \tag{9.C.1}$$

for each $t=0,\ldots,T$ and here primes indicate the obvious partial derivatives. The parameters a and b of the utility are the same for all st, but may differ with the date without adding substantively to the following results.

What differences among individuals permit aggregation? Resticting attention to the two-period case, the following proposition summarizes these conditions.

P9.4. Demand aggregation. Consider a two period economy with I3 individuals defined by equations (9.C.1) and intertemporal preference parameters as described above. Further, let a riskfree asset exist in the economy. Then the equilibrium prices for this economy are the same as in an economy of composite individuals if and only if the following *alternative* cases occur. For all individuals:

(i) initial wealth, probability beliefs, and risk preferences are common,
(ii) probability beliefs, rates of intertemporal preference, and risk preference $b\neq 0$ are common,
(iii) probability beliefs and risk preference $b=0$ are common,
(iv) initial wealth, probability beliefs, and risk preference $a=0$ and $b=1$ are common,

sum of the individual utilities being maximized. For the central planner he then substitutes a 'composite' individual. Equilibrium prices and the allocation of investment and consumption remain unchanged by this last substitution and the derived utilities of the composite individuals are state independent.

[18] It is occasionally said that the demand aggregation problem is 'solved' when equilibrium asset prices are independent of the distribution of wealth across individuals.

(v) $b=0$ and a complete market exists, and/or
(vi) initial wealth, rates of intertemporal preference and risk preference $a=0$ and $b=1$ are common and a complete market exists.

Proof of the proposition is algebraically complex and readily available in Rubinstein (1974) (sufficiency) and Brennan and Kraus (1978) (necessity).[19] We here note only the method of 'averaging' characteristics to define the composite individual:

(risk preference) $a=\Sigma_i a^i/I$ and
$b=b^i$ (which is always common),

(initial wealth) $\bar{w}_0=\Sigma_i \bar{w}_0^i/I$,

(probability beliefs) $h_s=\Pi_i(h_s^i)$ when $a\neq 0$ or
$h_s=\Sigma_s h_s^i/I$ when $a=0$, and,

(intertemporal preference) $\gamma=\Pi_i \gamma_i^{\alpha i}$ when $a\neq 0$
$=\Sigma_i(1+\gamma_i)^{-1}/I$ when $a=0$

where $\alpha^i\equiv a^i/a$. Of course, when individuals are identical in the first instance then aggregation obtains trivially.

Before closing this section an additional role for demand aggregation should be briefly mentioned. Purely financial contracts (insurance policies, put and call options, etc.) among individuals will be in zero net supply at an equilibrium in markets with composite individuals. Then as long as returns on real assets, in positive net supply, are independent of the state (non-stochastic investment opportunities) the derived utility will be state independent. If, for example, we were to make an assumption of joint normality in returns as part of a model to assure state independence of the derived utility, then the joint normality would only have to extend to the returns on real assets, not the financial derivatives, with demand aggregation. More on this in the following Chapters 10 and 11.

9.D. *Speculation*

Except in the special case with logarithmic elementary utilities, future investment possibilities generally affect the individual's current consump-

[19]The proofs noted here assume non-negative consumptions. To assure this, it is necessary that $b>0$ and $a<0$, so that marginal utility becomes infinite at $-a/b\geq 0$. These restrictions would, however, eliminate cases (iii) and (v) of the proposition. Finally, to assure a feasible consumption path in the multiperiod model we also require $\Sigma_{t=0}^{T}[a/b(\rho_t)]\leq\bar{w}_0$ where ρ_t is the 'long' (one plus) riskless rate from date 0 to t.

tion and investment decisions. While somewhat cumbersome, we could construct a Slutsky-like comparative static decomposition of this effect into intertemporal income and substitution parts. The results of that decomposition are obvious without actually doing the analysis: a perceived enhancement to future opportunities, in some state, make consumption in that future state cheaper relative to current consumption, and consumers 'substitute away' from current consumption. At the same time this enhancement in opportunities increases the wealth of the individuals and, with normal goods, that has a positive effect on current consumption. For logarithmic utility these intertemporal 'income' and 'substitution' affects are just offsetting. Otherwise, their magnitudes depend on the degree of risk aversion, wealth, intemporal impatience, etc.

There is a second reason for intertemporal substitution effects that has been ignored in the above developments, but deserves some attention. When individuals hold non-homogeneous probability assessments, then trading on markets for current consumption and future claims may be brought about by speculation based on the asymmetrical beliefs. In this section, we briefly look at what it means to say that prices reflect the diverse information possessed by individuals and then note the conditions for beliefs to be non-speculative. We also take this occasion to be somewhat clearer than heretofore about the operation of markets in sequence, and particularly about the attending process of probability and price revision.

9.D.1. A sequence of markets

For the moment suppose there to be only three dates for the economy: $t=0, 1, 2$. At the current date $t=0$ each individual chooses a certain consumption amount w_0 and tentative *plans* for consumption at $t=1$, w'_1, and $t=2$, w'_2 – we drop the i superscripts, understanding that the following analysis applies to each i.[20] Using the $t=0$ markets, each individual's plans for consumption are formed from date $t=1$ and $t=2$ pure securities: that is, w'_{1s} in plan w_1 is made up from pure securities which pay iff state s occurs at $t=1$, and similarly for all states at that date; in the same fashion, w'_{2s} in plan w'_2 is made from pure securities which pay iff state s occurs at $t=2$. Let π_1 and π_2 be the $S1$-vector and $S2$-vector, respectively, of prices for the date 1 and 2 pure securities on the $t=0$ forward markets.

Time evolves and at $t=1$ some state $s1$ occurs. Deliveries on $s1$ contingent claims are then made, and claims to all other states at $t=1$ expire

[20]To address the questions of probability, price, and portfolio revision explicitly, state claims to all future dates are now considered to be available on current markets.

without deliveries. In addition, the information provided by the occurrence of $s1$ will (in general) cause individuals to revise their probabilities assessment of states at $t=2$. We let $h_{s2|s1}>0$ denote the conditional probability that $s2$ will occur at $t=2$ given $s1$ has occurred; $h_{s2}=\Sigma_{s1} h_{s1} h_{s2|s1}$ follows by the laws of probability, where in general $h_{s2} \neq h_{s2|s1}$. With the occurrence of $s1$ and this revision in probability beliefs, equilibrium prices on date 1 markets for date 2 contingent claims will in general also be revised relative to their values on the earlier markets. It is convenient to adopt the similar notation $\pi_{s2|s1}$, for all $s2$ and $s1$, to indicate the date 1 market prices to date 2 contingent claims – generally, $\pi_{s2|s1} \neq \pi_{s2}$.

Each individual's wealth at date 1 depends on his prior choice of claims and the claims prices. For example, in specific state $s1$, the wealth is

$$w_{s1}=w'_{s1}+\sum_{s2} \pi_{s2|s1} w'_{s2}. \tag{9.D.1a}$$

and similarly for all date 1 states. Using this wealth, and in view of the revised prices and probabilities, it is to be expected that in state $s1$ the individual will choose to revise his tentative plan of date 2 claims and (then current) date 1 consumption. Let w_{s1} and $w_{s2|s1}$ (for all $s2$) indicate these revised choices on the date 1 markets. Again, generally $w_{s1} \neq w'_{s1}$ and $w_{s2|s1} \neq w'_{s2}$. And, the revised plan must satisfy the budget restriction

$$w_{s1}=w_{s1}+\sum_{s2} \pi_{s2|s1} w_{s2|s1'}, \tag{9.D.1b}$$

where w_{s1} is given by (9.D.1a) above. Finally, at the terminal date 2 markets do not open and each individual simply consumes the (previously) chosen amount $w_{s2|s1}$, given it is state $s2$ which occurs.

9.D.2. Optimal plans and intertemporal revision

In the market sequence the individual choices can be represented by the problem

$$\max\left[u_0(w_0)+\sum_{s1} h_{s1} u_1(w_{s1})+\sum_{s1} h_{s1}\left(\sum_{s2} h_{s2|s1} u_2(w_{s2|s1})\right)\right], \tag{9.D.2a}$$

subject to

$$(w_0-\bar{w}_0)+\sum_{s1} \pi_{s1} w'_{s1}+\sum_{s2} \pi_{s2} w'_{s2}=0, \tag{9.D.2b}$$

and for each state $s1$ at date 1,

$$(w_{s1}-w'_{s1})+\sum_{s2}\pi_{s2|s1}(w_{s2|s1}-w'_{s2})=0. \tag{9.D.2c}$$

The individual's decision variables are w_0, w'_1, and w'_2, at $t=0$ and w_1 and $w_{s2|s1}$ for all $s2$ and $s1$ at date 1. The budget constraint (9.D.2b) obtains for the date 0 market – $\bar{w}_0$ is (exogenously given) initial wealth – and (9.D.2c) obtains for each of the date 1 conditional markets. Using multipliers λ_0 and λ_{s1} for all states $s1$, (9.D.2c) can be rewritten in Lagrange form as

$$\begin{aligned}\max\Bigg\{ & u_0(w_0)+\sum_{s1}h_{s1}u_1(w_{s1}) \\ & +\sum_{s1}h_{s1}\left[\sum_{s2}h_{s2|s1}u_2(w_{s2|s1})\right] \\ & -\lambda_0\left[(w_0-\bar{w}_0)+\sum_{s1}\pi_{s1}w'_{s1}+\sum_{s2}\pi_{s2}w'_{s2}\right] \\ & -\sum_{s1}\lambda_{s1}\left[(w_{s1}-w'_{s1})+\sum_{s2}\pi_{s2|s1}(w_{s2|s1}-w'_{s2})\right]\Bigg\}. \end{aligned} \tag{9.D.3}$$

For an interior solution, stationarity conditions include

$$(h_{s1}/\pi_{s1})\mu_{s1}(w_{s1})=\mu_0(w_0) \quad \text{all } s_1, \tag{9.D.4a}$$

$$(h_{s2|s1}/\pi_{s2|s1})\mu_{s2}(w_{s2})=\mu_{s1}(w_{s1}) \quad \text{all } s_1 \text{ and } s2, \tag{9.D.4b}$$

$$\pi_{s2}=\sum_{s1}\pi_{s1}\pi_{s2|s1} \quad \text{all } s1, \tag{9.D.4c}$$

where μ_{s1} and μ_0 indicate the obvious marginal utility functions. In addition, there are the budget constraints (9.D.2b) and (9.D.2c).

Condition (9.D.4c), holding at each individual's optimum, is a no-arbitrage relationship among prices. Note the correspondence of this price relationship to that for probabilities, for $h_{s2}=\Sigma_s h_{s1}h_{s2|s1}$ by elementary probability rules. Conditions (9.A.4a) and (9.A.4b) are the usual two-period optimally relationships between the marginal utility of 'current' consumption, state claim prices, and the expected marginal utility of consumption at each state of the 'future' date. At an equilibrium in the date 0 and date 1 markets it would, of course, be required that the sum (across individuals) of consumption claims at each date and state exactly balance the endowments in those claims.

Following Rubinstein (1975), it is now usual to say that the prices at any date *fully reflect* new information received by an individual at that date when it is optimal for that individual not to revise his previously selected consumption plan. More specifically, given the set of claims prices on the date 1 market, an individual is said to have *non-speculative beliefs* if his revised probabilities to date 2 states leads him not to revise his consumption plan.

P9.5. Non-speculative beliefs. An individual will not revise his consumption plan at date 1 (relative to that chosen on markets at date 0) if

$$\frac{h_{s2}}{\pi_{s2}}=\frac{h_{s1}h_{s2|s1}}{\pi_{s1}\pi_{s2|s1}} \quad \text{for all } s1 \text{ and } s2. \tag{9.D.5}$$

Proof. Let $w^{\circ}_{s2|s1}$ and w°_{s1} (chosen at $t=1$ for all $s1$ and $s2$) solve (9.D.4) and be the individual's consumptive optimum. We first show necessary and sufficient conditions for $w^{\circ}_{s2|s1}$ to be independent of the state $s1$, leaving it to be shown in a second step that this plan is budget feasible on date 0 markets. To begin, eliminate μ_{s1} from (9.D.4a) and (9.D.4b) to get

$$\frac{\mu_0(w^{\circ}_0)}{\mu_{s2}(w^{\circ}_{s2|s1})}=\frac{h_{s1}h_{s2|s1}}{\pi_{s1}\pi_{s2|s1}}. \tag{9.D.6}$$

If $w^{\circ}_{s2|s1}$ is independent of the state $s1$ to occur then there must exist a scalar δ_{s2}, also independent of the $s1$ state, such that $\delta_{s2}=h_{s1}h_{s2|s1}/\pi_{s1}\pi_{s2|}{}^{s1}$. Summing this expression over all $s1$ and using (9.D.4c) then implies $\delta_{s2}\pi_{s2}=h_{s2}$. In turn, $h_{s2}/\pi_{s2}=h_{s1}h_{s2|s1}/\pi_{s1}\pi_{s2|s1}$ and therefore $\mu_0(w^{\circ}_0)/\mu_{s2}(w^{\circ}_{s2|s1})=h_{s2}/\pi_{s2}$ so that $w^{\circ}_{s2|s1}$ is independent of $s1$.

Proof that the optimal plan is budget feasible on the date 0 markets is routine and is left to the reader. See also Rubinstein (1975). □

The noteworthy aspect of P9.5 is that conditions for non-speculation depend only on the relationship of probability beliefs and market prices, but not on properties of the individuals' utilities or wealth.[21] While the date 0

[21] Hirshleifer and Rubinstein (1973) first noted this condition.

forward markets are not complete in the Debreu sense, this lack of dependence indicates that those markets nonetheless offer sufficient variety to satisfy permanently the wealth and taste differences across individuals.

E9.4. Rewrite the non-speculative beliefs condition (9.D.5) as

$$\frac{h_{s1}h_{s2|s1}}{h_{s2}}=\frac{\pi_{s1}\pi_{s2|s1}}{\pi_{s2}}$$

Suppose that the occurrence of state $s1$ at date 1 is publicly available information. All individuals trade in date 2 claims on the basis of the information. To stress that this information-trading sequence may occur at any date, let ϕ define the information set and let s (by itself) indicate the post information price and probability. The above equation becomes

$$\frac{h^i_\phi h^i_{s|\phi}}{h^i_s}=\frac{\pi_{s|\phi}\pi_\phi}{\pi_s}.$$

By the laws of conditional distributions the LHS of this is just the *likelihood function* $h^i_{\phi|s}$, so that the non-speculation condition becomes

$$h^i_{\phi|s}=\left(\frac{\pi_{s|\phi}}{\pi_s}\right)\pi_\phi.$$

Thus, if there is no trade at a post-information market equilibrium, then all individuals must have the same likelihood value, and the equilibrium prices fully reflect (reveal) this common value.[22] ■

Perhaps the most interesting case of non-speculative beliefs occurs when individuals have homogeneous probability assessments. Proof of this case proceeds simply, by contradiction. Note from (9.D.6) and $w^\circ_{s2|s1}>(<)w^\circ_{s2}$ iff $h_{s2}/\pi_{s2}<(>)h_{s1}h_{s2|s1}/\pi_{s1}\pi_{s2|s1}$. Suppose that one individual attempted to, say, increase his consumption in $s2$ on date 1 markets, so that $w^\circ_{s2|s1}>w^\circ_{s2}$, then in market equilibrium there would necessarily have to be some other individual(s) for which $w^\circ_{s2|s1}<w^\circ_{s2}$. But, from (9.D.5) that is seen to be a contradiction to the presence of homogeneous probability beliefs.

[22]See Bhattacharya (1975), Hakansson, Kunkel and Ohlson (1982), and Milgrom and Stokey (1982) for further details.

Chapter 10

MULTIPERIOD VALUATION

The first issue to be addressed in any theory of value is the underlying theory of demand. In valuing uncertain income streams, a theory of the individual's multiperiod consumption–investment decisions is prerequisite. Chapter 9 provided the first elements of that theory. While the developments there appeared promising at first glance, a complicating aspect of the resulting two period recursion of the multiperiod problem, one generally destroying its equivalence with the usual (static) two period model, was the state dependency of the derived utility of wealth function.

A variety of solutions of this state dependency are known in the literature. Restrictions on individual utilities have been imposed – as seen in Section 9.B.1, for example, logarithmic elementary utilities yield 'effective' state independence. The problem of state dependence is also trivially solved when future investment opportunities are constant, with all random variables independently and identically distributed (i.i.d.) across states at future dates.[1] And, as an alternative to these awkwardly polar cases, less restrictive, joint assumptions about utilities and the stochastic process of key economic aggregates over time too can provide state independence of the derived utility.[2] A final alternative is to simply set aside the two period recursion model and deal explicitly with the multiperiod problem in full detail.

In this chapter this last approach is taken. The analysis is not singular in focus, however, as it indirectly leads to insights concerning the range of assumptions about elementary utilities and stochastic processes which provide tractable forms of the two period recursion. In any regard, this concern for the individual's choice problem is by way of foundation, for the final interest of this chapter is with multiperiod exchange and the valuation of uncertain income streams.

[1]Rubinstein (1976) has argued for logarithmic utilities as the 'premier' model for analysis. The i.i.d. assumption has had a long history – see, for example, Samuelson (1969), Merton (1971) and Leland (1973).

[2]Recall P9.3.

10.A. Multiperiod Exchange

We consider a multiperiod, pure exchange security market economy. Production is exogeneously given and this, in turn, fixes the aggregate supply of claims at each date and state of nature. Trading in these claims occurs at a current period on forward markets and on a time sequence of forward markets. Let $t=0, 1, \ldots, T$ index the dates of the economy (T is, again, referred to as the terminal date, or horizon), and $st=1, 2, \ldots, St$ indexes states at each date t. Other aspects of the market organization are generally as in Section 9.A.1, with the following key features:

(i) individuals maximize expected utility, see (10.A.1) below,
(ii) firms provide (exogeneously fixed) payoff streams, or cash flows, over time,
(iii) conventional security markets in these risky payoff streams open and close at each discrete date, current and future,
(iv) markets are complete in the sense that, at each date, individuals can separately purchase claims to the then-current consumption and consumption at each then-future date-state pair, and
(v) markets are perfect and competitive in the usual sense.

We note that item (iv) is somewhat in contrast to the market organization in Chapter 9, except Section 9.D, as the following detailed specifications of the exchange organization make clear.

10.A.1. Firms and individuals

On the supply side there is the usual (composite) good, denominated in dollars, produced and paid out by $j=1, 2, \ldots, J$ firms. The (typical) jth firm's *payout*, or *cash flow, stream* is given by the vector $[z_0^j\, z_1^j \ldots z_T^j]$, where z_0^j is the (certain) date zero payout and $z_t^j=[z_{1t}^j\, z_{2t}^j \ldots z_{St}^j]$ is the St-vector of state-contingent payout at each date t. When the firm issues just one conventional security, the payout stream represents equity rights which can be thought of as a flow of dividends. Whatever its issue of securities, we take the payout stream of each firm to be fixed and focus on properties of the exchange equilibrium.

Firms represent the supply side of the economy and provide the consumption objects for individuals. At each date trading occurs in both the current consumption good and in the claims to future consumption issued by the firms. Using these markets each of the $i=1, 2, \ldots, I$ individuals chooses a plan of state and date contingent consumptions given by the vector $[w_0^i\, w_t^i \ldots w_T^i]$, where w_0^i is certain period zero (current) consumption and $w_t^i = [w_{1t}^i\, w_{2t}^i\, \ldots\, w_{St}^i]$ are state contingent claims for each future date t.

For each individual i the date 0 consumption–investment choice is in part based upon preferences represented by a time additive, state separable expected utility function of the form

$$\mathrm{E}U^i(w_0^i, w_1^i, \ldots, w_T^i) = U^i(w_0^i) + \sum_t \sum_{st} h_{st}\, U^i(w_{st}^i, t), \qquad (10.\mathrm{A}.1)$$

with every (state independent) elementary utility function $U^i(\cdot)$ exhibiting risk aversion, see S9.1. The homogeneous probabilities $[h_{st}]$ are assessments at time zero of the st date and state occurrence, and for each individual it is required that $\Sigma_{st} h_{st} = 1$ for each date t and $h_{st} \geq 0$ for every state and date pair.

10.A.2. Equilibrium conditions

On the $t=0$ markets, each individual's choice problem is written as

$$\max\left[U^i(w_0^i) + \sum_t \sum_{st} h_{st} U^i(w_{st}^i, t) \right], \qquad (10.\mathrm{A}.2\mathrm{a})$$

choosing $w_0^i \geq 0$ and each $w_{st}^i \geq 0$ subject to the budget constraint

$$\sum_t \sum_{st} \pi_{st}(w_{st}^i - \bar{w}_{st}^i) = (w_0^i - \bar{w}_0^i). \qquad (10.\mathrm{A}.2\mathrm{b})$$

Bar overscores, as usual, denote endowments in the particular date-state indicated and arise from decisions made at prior dates. The $[\pi_{st}]$ are state claims prices occurring with trade on the date 0 markets; current consumption is chosen as numeraire. Finally, throughout this chapter it is assumed that the markets on which individuals trade are perfect (see S4.2) and competitive (see S4.3) and that the solution to (10.A.2) occurs at a stationarity point with non-negative consumptions.

The date 0 exchange equilibrium in the model economy has the typical elements: a system of state claim prices and an allocation of consumption for each date and state, including the current period, such that utility is maximized for every individual and aggregate consumption equals the aggregate endowment (production) for each date and state. The equality of aggregate demand and supply requires

$$W_{st} \equiv \sum_i w^i_{st} = \sum_i \bar{w}^i_{st} \quad \forall st, \quad \text{and} \tag{10.A.3a}$$

$$W_0 \equiv \sum_i w^i_0 = \sum_i \bar{w}^i_0, \tag{10.A.3b}$$

where w^i_{st} represents individual i's equilibrium consumption at each st, W_{st} is *aggregate consumption* for date and state pair st (W_t will indicate the St-vector of W_{st} and associated random variable for date t) and, similarly, W_0 is aggregate consumption at $t=0$.

The following several propositions describe key properties of the individual consumptive optima and the associated multiperiod exchange equilibrium. Many of these have been developed indirectly in earlier chapters, but are now set out systematically for clarity and emphasis.

P10.1. Price-probability ratios. Let individuals satisfy (10.A.1) and suppose there are complete, perfect, and competitive markets in conventional securities. Then:

(i) across states at every date each individual's ordering of the ratio of price to probability is the same as his ordering of marginal utility of consumption and, therefore, the inverse of his ordering of optimal consumption amounts, and
(ii) at market equilibrium the ordering of price-probability ratios across states at every date is the inverse of the ordering of *aggregate* consumption levels.

Proof. The classical stationarity conditions for the problem (10.A.2) are, for all st dates and states,

$$\mu_{st} h_{st} = \mu_0 \pi_{st}, \tag{10.A.4a}$$

where $\mu_0 \equiv \partial U(w_0)/\partial w_0$ and $\mu_{st} \equiv \partial U(w_{st}, t)/\partial w_{st}$ are marginal utilities and the individual i superscript is omitted as a convenience. Rearranging gives

$$\mu_{st}/\mu_0 = \pi_{st}/h_{st}, \tag{10.A.4b}$$

again for all st dates and states. Part (i) follows immediately from this equation and the fact that risk aversion implies smaller marginal utility with greater consumption. In addition, it is required that $\Sigma_{st}\mu_{st}h_{st}=\mu_0/\rho_t$ at the optimum, where $\rho_t=(1/\Sigma_{st}\pi_{st})$ is the date 0 to date t (one plus) riskless rate.[3] Rearranging gives

$$\mu_0=\rho_t E(\mu_t), \tag{10.A.4c}$$

with E being with respect to the state probabilities h_{st} assigned at date 0 and we think of μ_t as a random variable.

For part (ii), let st and et represent any two states at date t. From (i) optimal consumption for individual i is ordered as $w^i_{st}>w^i_{et}$ if and only if $(\pi_{st}/h_{st})<(\pi_{et}/h_{et})$. With homogeneous probabilities and market prices, the same ordering holds for every individual at equilibrium; in turn, the ordering of aggregate consumption across states must be identical to the ordering of consumption by each individual. And, as price-probability ratios order every individual's consumption amounts across states they must also order aggregate consumption. □

The proposition identifies only a common ordering (across states at any date) of individual and aggregate consumption amounts. If it were known, say, that all individuals were identical, then $w^i_{st}=W_{st}/I$ would indicate each i's proportional relationship corresponding to the ordering. More generally, however, the proposition is not so informative as to tell us what the specific functional form is between individual and aggregate consumption amounts. Rather, that form depends on detailed properties of the individuals' utilities and the state contingent distribution of security payouts, among other things. Finally, it should be noted for completeness that the model underlying the above proposition is based on a finite number of dates and states and a nonstochastic population.[4]

[3]It is helpful to re-emphasize the notation being used, as it will be critical in later developments. We might more exactly write ${}_0\rho_t=(\Sigma_{st}\pi_{st})^{-1}$, where the $[\pi_{st}]$ are prices for date t claims on date 0 markets. This (one plus) riskless rate ${}_0\rho_t$ is a 'long' rate in the sense that, for $t>1$, it covers more than one trading (and consumption) period. Generally we write ρ_t for ${}_0\rho_t$, omitting the zero pre-script. The prices $[\pi_{st}]$, occurring on date 0 markets for each t, are known at that date and the ρ_t too are known (non-stochastic).

Alternatively, there are the 'short' (one plus) riskless rates ${}_{t-1}\rho_t=(\Sigma_{st}\pi'_{st})^{-1}$ arising on future date $(t-1)$ markets. In this case the prices $[\pi'_{st}]$, note the prime, are those to prevail on the date $(t-1)$ markets for claims paying at t. As these claims prices are generally dependent on the state to obtain at $(t-1)$, at dates prior to $(t-1)$ that price system is state dependent and, in turn, the ${}_{t-1}\rho_t$ riskless rate too will be state dependent (or stochastic).

[4]All of the results to be developed below (except, perhaps, for existence proofs) extent to a continuum of dates, states, and agents, with only the non-stochastic population being restrictive. See, for example, Brock (1978), and Dothan and Williams (1979).

E10.1. Consider an economy where all individuals have CRRA elementary utilities

$$U(w_{st}^i) = (w_{st}^i)^{1-k}/(1-k),$$

where k is the constant, common risk index. (We also assume the date t time preference parameter is common across individuals and choose it equal to one for convenience.) In this case stationarity conditions (10.A.4) take the form

$$w_{st}^i = (\pi_{st}/h_{st}^i)^{-1/k},$$

when the marginal utility of current consumption is set equal to one and, for the moment, probability beliefs are permitted to be heterogeneous. Summing over i gives

$$W_{st} = \sum_i (\pi_{st}/h_{st}^i)^{-1/k},$$

and, in turn,

$$\pi_{st} = (W_{st})^{-k}\left[\sum_i (h_{st}^i)^{1/k}\right]^k.$$

Substituting this back in the individual's demand yields a relationship between individual and aggregate consumption

$$w_{st}^i = k_{st}^i W_{st}$$

where the proportionality constant is a function of probabilities and the risk index,

$$k_{st}^i = (h_{st}^i)^{1/k} \Big/ \sum_i (h_{st}^i)^{1/k}.$$

Each individual's demand is determined by his weighted probability relative to the weighted probability of all others. In this case differences in probability beliefs cause the ordering of aggregate consumption across states at any date to differ (generally) from the ordering by individuals. With homogeneous probabilities, however, all individuals have the same state-to-state consumption ordering and it is identical to the aggregate consumption ordering. ■

10.A.3. Result-states and optimal allocations

A moment's reflection on P10.3 suggests the importance of states (at any date) having common aggregate consumption amounts. A concept useful in exploring the details of this importance is summarized in the following definition.

D10.1. Aggregate consumption result-state. Let the collection of all states at any given date which have the same level of aggregate consumption define an aggregate consumption result-state or, more simply, result-state.

E10.2. Consider an economy with 5 states at some date t, where aggregate consumption in each state is given by the following tableau:

state (st)	*aggregate consumption* (W_{st})
1	10.1
2	3.0
3	4.9
4	10.1
5	4.9

This economy is alternatively represented by three result-states, indexed by θ_t, at date t:

result-state (θt)	*aggregate consumption* ($W_{\theta t}$)
1	10.1
2	3.0
3	4.9

The definition of result-state implies a 'coarse' partitioning of underlying states on the basis of aggregate consumption. For the definition to be useful, states with the same level of aggregate consumption should have no consequential differences and need not be distinguished. In what circumstance might this occur?

P10.2. Individual and aggregate consumption. Let individuals be risk averse expected utility maximizers with time additive, state independent elementary utilities and homogeneous probability beliefs, see (10.A.1), and let security markets be complete, perfect, competitive and in equilibrium. Then each individual's optimal consumption plan is the same in all those states at each date having equal aggregate consumption amounts.

Proof. Under the stated conditions P10.1 shows that at market equilibrium the equality

$$\frac{\mu_{st}^{i} h_{st}}{\mu_{et}^{i} h_{et}} = \frac{\mu_{st}^{n} h_{st}}{\mu_{et}^{n} h_{et}}, \tag{10.A.5}$$

is satisfied for every two individuals (i and n) and state pairs (st and et) at any date t. Given individuals have homogenous probability beliefs, this simplifies to

$$\frac{\mu_{st}^{i}}{\mu_{et}^{i}} = \frac{\mu_{st}^{n}}{\mu_{et}^{n}}. \tag{10.A.6}$$

Since elementary utilities are state independent, marginal utilities which reflect risk aversion have the property

$$\mu_{st}^{i} > \mu_{et}^{i} \quad \text{implies} \quad w_{st}^{i} < w_{et}^{i}. \tag{10.A.7}$$

A comparison of this condition with (10.A.6) completes the proof, for when *aggregate* consumption in states st and et are equal these two conditions can hold simultaneously only if $w_{st}^{i} = w_{et}^{i}$. □

E10.3. It is possible to generalize P10.2 somewhat. Rather than assuming homogeneous probabilities, it might (less restrictively) be required only that individuals agree simply on state probabilities conditional upon the aggregate level of consumption at the date. In this case there would be individual specific probabilities h_{st}^{i} for each st such that,

$$h_{st}^{i} = h_{st|}W_{st} \cdot h_{W_{st}}^{i},$$

where $h_{W_{st}}^{i}$ is individual i's probability that aggregate consumption level W_{st} occurs at t and $h_{st|W_{st}}$ is the common conditional probability noted above. Equation (10.A.6) also obtains under these conditions. ■

The equilibrium relations between prices, probabilities and consumptions developed to this point are briefly summarized as follows. First, for any individual and any date and state pair (say *st*), the marginal utility of consumption is proportional to the ratio of the st claim price and probability. These first-order conditions imply that the ordering of price-probability ratios across states at any given date is the same as the ordering of each individual's marginal utility of consumption and, as a result, the inverse of the ordering of each individual's consumption amount (assuming risk aversion). To be consistent with market clearing conditions, at each date the ordering of price-probability ratios must be the inverse of the ordering of aggregate consumption. Finally, the conditions of market clearing also imply that if two states have the same level of aggregate consumption, then each individual must have the same consumption level in those two states (but that level generally differs across individuals).

The above summary suggests a translation in the 'kinds' of securities capable of providing all *ex ante* Pareto optimal allocations of a complete contingent claims market.

P10.3. Pareto optimality and result-states. Suppose individuals and markets satisfy the conditions of P10.2. A Pareto optimal allocation is then achieved at an equilibrium in the security markets when the securities span (only) result-states.

Proof. Under the assumptions of the proposition each individual's optimal consumption amount is the same in those states (at any date) with the same aggregate consumption. Thus the (unconstrained) allocation that is achieved in a complete claims market can also be achieved by an incomplete securities market providing only that these securities span the result-states. Finally, it has been shown earlier that the equilibrium allocation in an economy with perfect, competitive and complete markets in consumption claims is Pareto optimal,[5] so that the allocation by securities spanning result-states too will be Pareto optimal. □

In the absence of the homogeneous beliefs (or conditionally homogeneous beliefs, see E10.2 above) individuals might be willing to speculate on the occurrence of specific states as noted in Section 9.D. When that rationale is put aside, P10.2 demonstrates a lack of incentive for any individual to accept more risk than that achievable by trading only in claims to aggregate consumption at any date: aggregate (social) risk can therefore be measured by the state and date contingent properties of *aggregate consumption.* This means, for example, that when the level of aggregate consumption is the same in two (or more) states at some date, the diversity of outputs of the firms (and thus the distribution of payoffs of their securities) is immaterial to consumption choices. That is, in fact, precisely why trade in securities which span only result-states provide for an efficient allocation of risk-bearing.

Finally, as a convenience in summarizing the above results the following terminology is employed:

[5]See P2.8.

D10.2. Equivalently complete securities markets. Let the conditions of P10.2 and P10.3 obtain. Further, let the available securities span result-states at each date. In this case security markets are said to be *equivalently complete.*

10.B. Result-State Claim Prices and Security Valuation

P10.3 informs us that a collection of securities represents an equivalently complete market when trading in those securities span (only) the result-states $\theta t=1,2,\ldots,\theta t$ at each date t. There is, quite apparently, a set of 'pure' securities which span the result-states.

D10.3. Aggregate consumption result-state pure securities. Let $q_t=[q_{1t}\, q_{2t} \ldots q_{\theta T}]$ define the collection of date t, aggregate consumption result-state pure securities where each security $q_{\theta t}$ pays one unit of account if and only if the aggregate consumption level is $W_{\theta t}$ at date t, otherwise zero is paid.

With the (aggregate consumption) result-state pure securities the occurrence of every result-state is recorded as a different observable level of aggregate consumption. Can some form for the basic valuation equation be developed in a way which takes advantage of our ability to observe result-states by aggregate consumption amounts? The answer is of course yes, as the next section shows. One final construction is, however, useful before going on.

The key aspect of the aggregate consumption to result-state relationship is the one to one correspondence and not the specific levels of aggregate consumption. As an empirical touchstone, it is then common to speak not about aggregate consumption directly but of an *aggregate consumption security* (or portfolio) which pays a state contingent amount at each date equal to a scale multiple of aggregate consumption. We write that security's payoff as

$$z^*_{\theta t}=\xi_t W_{\theta t},$$

for all θt at each t, where the scalar ξ_t is a nonstochastic proportionality constant. As there is a one-to-one correspondence between $W_{\theta t}$ and $z^*_{\theta t}$ for each θt, it is also possible to identify result-states uniquely by z^*_t at each date.

10.B.1. Valuation relation 1

Consider a conventional security market where the securities issued by the firms constitute an equivalently complete securities market in the sense of D10.2. For each security the equilibrium market value net of current investment on the $t=0$ forward markets is given by the *fundamental valuation equation*

$$v_0 = v_0' - z_0 = \sum_t \sum_{st} \pi_{st} z_{st}, \tag{10.B.1}$$

where v_0' is the *gross value* of the stream associated with the security and v_0 is the *net value*, z_{st} is the *st* date and state payout, and π_{st} is a sustaining state claim price for *st* as established in trading at date 0 (with current consumption again numeraire). The date 0 payout, z_0, is a known constant and, for that reason, not treated explicitly. Rather, we shall be concerned with the net value of any income stream given by the RHS of (10.B.1). (Superscripts to indicate the specific security are omitted as a notational convenience.)

While the fundamental valuation equation is itself of little empirical use, its reformulation in terms of result-state pure securities provides a somewhat more practical valuation form. That translation is summarized in the following proposition.

P10.4. Valuation Relation 1 (VR1). Suppose that individuals satisfy the conditions of P10.2 and an equilibrium exists in equivalently complete, perfect, and competitive security markets with conventional securities. At this equilibrium the value of any payoff stream $[z_1\, z_2 \ldots z_T]$ can be written as

$$v_0 = \sum_t \left[\sum_{\theta t} \pi^*_{\theta t} E(z_t \mid z^*_{\theta t}) \right], \tag{10.B.2a}$$

where $\pi^*_{\theta t}$ is the (current) price of the θt result-state pure security and $E(z_t \mid z^*_{\theta t}) = \Sigma_{st} h_{st|\theta t} z_{st}$ is expected value of the date t payoff given θt occurs. Moreover, when intertemporal arbitrage opportunities are absent in the sense noted below, then

$$v_0 = \sum_{\theta 1} \pi^*_{\theta 1} E(r_1 \mid z^*_{\theta 1}), \tag{10.B.2b}$$

where $r_1 = z_1 + v_1$ is the security's period one *yield*, the payout (dividend) plus date one market value of shares (r_1, z_1, and v_1 being state contingent vectors).[6]

Equation (10.B.2a) is termed the *intertemporal* form of VR1. Its use requires estimates of the conditional expectation of the payout stream and the result-state prices at each date. No estimate of the stream's (expected) future market value is necessary, which makes this form useful in valuing non-traded assets – for example, capital budgeting projects. In contrast, the *recursive*, or *period-by-period*, form of VR1, (10.B.2b), uses an estimate of the asset's next-period market value (in addition to the payout) to create r_1. There is some compensation for this difficulty, however, as the formula uses result-state pure security prices only at date one. In this regard it is to be emphasized that the recursive form assumes an intertemporal no-arbitrage condition (as described below) in addition to those things necessary for the intertemporal form.

Proof. First consider (10.B.2a), the intertemporal form. Let $\overline{\theta t}$ indicate the set of states at date t having aggregate consumption level $z^*_{\theta t}$. Further, suppose st and et are two states in $\overline{\theta t}$. The ith individual's optimality conditions then include

$$\frac{h_{st}\mu_{st}}{h_{et}\mu_{et}}=\frac{\pi_{st}}{\pi_{et}}, \tag{10.B.3}$$

see (10.A.4). Moreover, as st and et are states in the same result-state, then the marginal utilities are equal, $\mu_{st}=\mu_{et}$, as are the individual's optimal consumption amounts, $w_{st}=w_{et}$, at market equilibrium (P10.2). Under these conditions (10.B.3) simplifies to

$$\frac{h_{st}}{h_{et}}=\frac{\pi_{st}}{\pi_{et}}. \tag{10.B.4}$$

Next recall the following properties of conditional probabilities:

$$h_{st}=h_{st|z^*_{st}}h_{z^*_{st}}, \tag{10.B.5a}$$

$$h_{et}=h_{et|z^*_{et}}h_{z^*_{et}}. \tag{10.B.5b}$$

where $h_{z^*_{st}}$ is the probability of z^*_{st} occurring and $h_{st|z^*_{st}}$ is the probability of state st given z^*_{st} has occurred. Similar notation is used for state et in

[6]Since $z^*_{\theta t}$ and θt are uniquely related, one-to-one, we can equivalently write $E(z_t|\theta t)$ or $E(z_t|z^*_{\theta t})$, but prefer the latter. For the same reason we may use summations with either θt or $z^*_{\theta t}$ as the index, but prefer the former.

(10.B.5b). As $z^*_{st}=z^*_{et}$, then $h_{z^*_{st}}=h_{z^*_{et}}$ and we have

$$\frac{h_{st|z^*_{st}}}{h_{et|z^*_{et}}}=\frac{\pi_{st}}{\pi_{et}}. \qquad (10.B.6)$$

Solve (10.B.6) for π_{st}, substitute that in (10.B.1), and sum over st $\in \theta t$ to give

$$v_0=\sum_t\left[\sum_{\theta t}\sum_{st\in\theta t}\left(\frac{\pi_{et}}{h_{et|z^*_{et}}}\right)h_{st|z^*_{st}}\right]z_{st}$$

$$=\sum_t\left[\sum_{\theta t}\left(\frac{\pi_{et}}{h_{et|z^*_{et}}}\right)\sum_{st\in\theta t}h_{st|z^*_{st}}\right]z_{st}$$

$$=\sum_t\sum_{\theta t}\left(\frac{\pi_{et}}{h_{et|z^*_{et}}}\right)E(z_t|z^*_{\theta t}). \qquad (10.B.7)$$

The 'adjusted' price $(\pi_{et}/h_{et|z^*_{et}})$ has the same value for each $et\in\theta t$, but generally differs as θt changes. As this is a valuation relationship, $(\pi_{et}/h_{et|z^*_{et}})$ therefore has the interpretation of the price of a security paying one dollar at period t if and only if θt occurs, that is, it is the (date 0 market) price of $q_{\theta t}$. This *result-state price* is labelled $\pi^*_{\theta t}$, which gives (10.B.2a):

$$v_0=\sum_t\left[\sum_{\theta t}\pi^*_{\theta t}E(z_t|z^*_{\theta t})\right].$$

To derive the recursive form (10.B.2b) begin again with the fundamental valuation equation (10.B.1),

$$v_0=\sum_t\sum_{st}\pi_{st}z_{st},$$

where the π_{st} are those date-state claims prices established in trading at the current $t=0$ date. When a particular state $s1$ occurs at period 1, a new value for the security occurs given by

$$v_{s1}=\sum_{t=2}\sum_{st}\pi_{st|s1}z_{st}, \qquad (10.B.8)$$

where $\pi_{st|s1}$ indicates the prices established on the markets at state-date $s1$. How are the date 0 and date 1 state claim prices related? Separate the period zero valuation relationship into two terms as

$$v_0 = \sum_{s1} \pi_{s1} z_{s1} + \sum_{t=2} \sum_{st} \pi_{st} z_{st}. \tag{10.B.9}$$

If there are to be no arbitrage opportunities in the sequence of markets, then it is necessary that

$$\pi_{st} = \sum_{s1} (\pi_{s1} \cdot \pi_{st|s1}) \quad \forall st, \tag{10.B.10}$$

see equation (9.D.4c). Using this condition, (10.B.9), and (10.B.8) give

$$\begin{aligned} v_0 &= \sum_{s1} \pi_{s1}(z_{s1} + v_{s1}) \\ &= \sum_{s1} \pi_{s1} r_{s1}. \end{aligned} \tag{10.B.11}$$

Again, the π_{s1}, all $s1$, are prices arrived at on the $t=0$ forward markets. Replacing r_1 for z_1 in (10.B.1) and following the development of (10.B.2a) from (10.B.1) provides (10.B.2b). In short, the value of any asset that is held for one period and then sold at its new value (including any dividend) is the same as its value if it were held to the terminal date T. □

It is to be emphased that the result-state prices $[\pi^*_{0t}]$ are based on the information individuals have in trading on the date 0 forward markets. At date 1, depending on the state to then obtain, new prices for date t result-state claims will generally arise, and we would properly indicate these changes, say by using $\pi^*_{0t|s1}$ given state $s1$ occurs at date 1 – recall equation (10.B.8) for example. A quick retrace of the recursion equation development shows, moreover, that dates 0 and 1 may more generally represent any dates $(t-1)$ and t in the model horizon, providing that all probabilities and result-state prices are then understood to be those obtaining on the date $(t-1)$ markets in the specific state to obtain at that date.

A short summary is helpful here. When individuals maximize time additive, state independent expected utilities and hold homogeneous probability beliefs (or agree on probabilities at each date conditional on aggregate consumption), and given markets are perfect and competitive, then each has an optimal consumption plan at every date derived from a collection of securities spanning only result-states. The multiperiod, equilibrium allocation achieved in this situation is Pareto optimal and VR1 results. It is of interest that that equation does not require the entire state and date contingent payout pattern to value an uncertain income stream; rather, at each date only the *expected* payouts (or the expected yield in the recursion form) conditional on aggregate consumption amounts are necessary data. These conditional expectations in turn are valued using the prices of aggregate consumption result-state securities.

In the (static) two period model with individuals having time additive, state independent expected utility and with homogeneous probabilities beliefs, Chapter 2 reached results similar to those of P10.4. In perfect and competitive markets it was there shown that every individual's optimal choice of next period claims could be written as a function only of the social total of claims, aggregate wealth. And, a (two period) valuation equation based on that social total, analogous to the (multiperiod) VR1, was set forth. It is important to stress that in the recursion form of the two period model, next period claims are not generally the same as next period consumption. It is, rather, necessary to distinguish between aggregate *wealth* which, depending on the state to occur, is allocated in various proportions (depending on the individual) to next period consumption and an investment in then-future period claims. In a multiperiod economy the allocation of consumption by securities spanning aggregate *wealth* is thus generally non-optimal. Instead, aggregate consumption at each date is the central factor.

On a moment's reflection it is seen that there are two cases in which the correspondence between the models is exact and the optimality of results extend to the static two period formulation. First, there is the simple situation where the recursive two period model arises because there are in fact only two periods remaining in the economy. In this instance aggregate wealth at the next period is aggregate consumption, for there is no distant future in which to invest. The second case is of somewhat more interest, occurring when there is perfect correlation between aggregate consumption and aggregate wealth at each date of the multiperiod horizon. Of course, when this occurs pure securities defined on aggregate wealth levels too will span (aggregate consumption) result-states and the prices and expectations conditional on aggregate wealth can therefore form a basis for valuation. As P9.3 noted, however, such perfect correlation occurs only under special conditions.

10.B.2. Derivative securities

Earlier chapters, in a variety of market economies, have developed forms of the fundamental valuation equation (10.B.1). In these instances the practical use of the pricing relationship has been generally hindered by the problem of state observability. VR1 solves that problem substantially:

under the conditions of P10.1 through P10.3 it is known that everything important about the state description can be summarized by the level of aggregate consumption. The measurement of that variable surely does not present the same degree of difficulty in observation as compared to a general state description. Moreover, as the distinguishable levels of aggregate consumption are likely less than the number of states, the entire pattern of date and state contingent payouts of an uncertain income stream need not be determined for its valuation: rather, only expected payoffs conditional on the realization of aggregate consumption at each date are required. Given these conditional expectations, VR1 allows us to value uncertain income streams in terms of the aggregate consumption result-state pure security prices. The rub in all of this is, of course, the need for ways to develop these prices from market observable variables. The following definition is a first step in that development.

D10.4. Derivative security. A derivative security (or asset) is one whose value at any date depends explicitly on the (exogenously determined) value of an *underlying* security (or asset).

Perhaps the most familiar examples of derivative securities are call and put options written on the yield of common equity. Specifically, if r represents the market yield of some asset, then

$$c(e,r)=\max[r-e,0],$$

defines the payoff of the call option, where e is a fixed and known exercise price.[7] Similarly, a put option has a payoff

$$p(e,r)=\max[e-r,0].$$

E10.4. Consider some firm with period t, state-contingent payout $z_t=[z_{1t}\, z_{2t}\, \dots\, z_{St}]$ and let b indicate the firm's promised payment to debt securities at each period. With limited liability, the payout to the firm's equity at each date and state is

$$z^e_{st}=\max[z_{st}-b,0], \qquad (10.B.12a)$$

which has the form of a call option on the payout z_t at exercise price b. In a like fashion the payout to debt can be written as

[7] A sometimes important difference occurs between European options, which can only be exercised at a given maturity date, and American options, with can be exercised at the holder's discretion at any moment up to the maturity date. As that distinction is not crucial in the following, only European options are here considered.

$$z_{st}^{d}=\min[z_{st},b]=z_{st}-\max[z_{st}-b,0], \tag{10.B.12b}$$

which is the same as holding a call option at exercise price b and the full amount z_t, termed a 'covered' call on z_t. (For more realistic details, see E11.4.) ■

With this as background, we now show that result-state securities can be formed from a portfolio of call options written on the aggregate consumption security. Result-state prices then arise as the (observable) market value of the associated call options, and VR1 given by (10.B.2) is a step closer to being empirically useful.

Proceeding along this line, first order result-states so that $\theta\tau>\theta t$ implies $z_{\theta\tau}^{*}>z_{\theta t}^{*}$ for all $\theta\tau$ and θt. Next, let the difference in the aggregate consumption security payoff between result-states θt and $(\theta+1)t$ be δ_θ, so that the security can then be written alternatively as $z_{1t}^{*}, z_{2t}^{*}=z_{1t}^{*}+\delta_1, z_{3t}^{*}=z_{2t}^{*}+\delta_2$, etc. Finally, let the θt-vector of payoffs of a call option on aggregate consumption at period t with exercise price of e be given by $c(e,z_t^{*})=[c(e,z_{1t}^{*})\ c(e,z_{2t}^{*})\ldots c(e,z_{\theta t}^{*})]$ and write its (current) market value as $v^{c}(e,z_t^{*})=\Sigma_t\Sigma_{\theta t}\pi_{\theta t}^{*}c(e,z_{\theta t}^{*})$.

The call with zero exercise price $c(0,z_t^{*})$ has $\max[z_{\theta t}^{*}-0,0]$ as elements, which is to say it has the same pattern of payoffs as aggregate consumption. The call option $c(z_{1t}^{*},z_t^{*})$ alternatively has $\max[z_{\theta t}^{*}-z_{1t}^{*},0]$ as payoff elements, or

$$c(z_{1t}^{*},z_t^{*})=[0\quad \delta_1\quad (\delta_1+\delta_2)\quad (\delta_1+\delta_2+\delta_3)\ \ldots]. \tag{10.C.13a}$$

Similarly,

$$c(z_{2t}^{*},z_t^{*})=[0\quad 0\quad \delta_2\quad (\delta_2+\delta_3)\quad (\delta_2+\delta_3+\delta_4)\ldots]. \tag{10.C.13b}$$

From the above two equations we see more generally that two 'successive' options, one held long and one held short in the manner $c(z_{\theta t}^{*},z_t^{*})-c(z_{(\theta+1)t}^{*},z_t^{*})=c(z_{\theta t}^{*},z_t^{*})-c(z_{\theta t}^{*}+\delta_\theta,z_t^{*})$ has a payoff vector with zeroes when $z_{\theta t}^{*}\le e$ and δ_θ for all $z_{\theta t}^{*}>e$. From this observation and a little addition it is further seen that the long and short combination of call options given by the RHS of

$$\begin{aligned}\delta_\theta q_{\theta t}^{*}&=[c(z_{\theta t}^{*}-\delta_\theta,z_t^{*})-c(z_{\theta t}^{*},z_t^{*})]\\ &\quad-[c(z_{\theta t}^{*},z_t^{*})-c(z_{\theta t}^{*}+\delta_\theta,z_t^{*})]\\ &=[c(z_{\theta t}^{*}+\delta_\theta,z_t^{*})-c(z_{\theta t}^{*},z_t^{*})]\\ &\quad-[c(z_{\theta t}^{*},z_t^{*})-c(z_{\theta t}^{*}-\delta_\theta,z_t^{*})],\end{aligned} \tag{10.B.14}$$

has a payoff of δ_θ in result-state θt and zero otherwise, which explains the LHS of the equation. Thus, when the indicated portfolio of calls is held in the amount $1/\delta_\theta$ we have exactly replicated a result-state primary security yielding one dollar if and only if $z^*_{\theta t}$ occurs at date and state θt. The formation of call options to give the entire collection, for all dates and states, of result-state primary securities proceeds routinely from the above case.[8]

Multiplying both sides of (10.B.14) by $\pi^*_{\theta t}$ and dividing by δ_θ, the value of any result-state primary security can be determined from the value of the portfolio of calls. That is, for each θt

$$\pi^*_{\theta t}=(1/\delta_\theta)\{[v^c(z^*_{\theta t}+\delta_\theta, z^*_t)-v^c(z^*_{\theta t}, z^*_t)] \\ -[v^c(z^*_{\theta t}, z^*_t)-v^c(z^*_{\theta t}-\delta_\theta, z^*_t)]\}. \tag{10.B.15a}$$

In the above equation the result-state prices are seen to be a function of the increment δ_θ. What happens when aggregate consumption is continuously distributed at date t? In this case the price of the portfolio of calls yielding one dollar if $z^*_{\theta t}$ occurs becomes the $\delta_\theta \to 0$ limit of the ratio $\pi^*_{\theta t}(\delta_\theta)/\delta_\theta$ evaluated at the exercise price $e=z^*_t$. That is,

$$\begin{aligned}\pi^*(z^*_t)&=\lim_{\delta_\theta\to 0}\pi^*_{\theta t}(\delta_\theta)/\delta_\theta \\ &=\lim_{\delta_\theta\to 0}\frac{[v^c(z^*_{\theta t}+\delta_\theta, z^*_t)-v^c(z^*_{\theta t}, z^*_t)]-[v^c(z^*_{\theta t}, z^*_t)-v^c(z^*_{\theta t}-\delta_\theta, z^*_t)]}{\delta_\theta^2} \\ &=\left[\frac{\partial^2 v^c(e, z^*_t)}{\partial e^2}\right]_{e=z^*_t}\end{aligned} \tag{10.B.15b}$$

We let π^*_t be shorthand for $\pi^*(z^*_t)$, understanding the aggregate consumption dependency. With aggregate consumption continuously distributed across result-states, the probability of any specific occurrence is, of course, zero. A probability density function for aggregate consumption nonetheless obtains and, associated with that, there is a price function for π^*_t given by the second partial derivative in the above equation (providing that the call valuation function $v^c(e, z^*_t)$ is twice differentiable in the exercise price).

[8]Breeden and Litzenberger (1978) provide full details.

E10.5. An alternative development of (10.B.15b) is as follows. When aggregate consumption is continuously distributed then the price of the aggregate consumption portfolio is

$$v_0^* = \int \pi_t^* z_t^* \mathrm{d}z_t^*,$$

where the variables are now understood to be continuous functions of the result-state at date t. When a call option is written on aggregate consumption at exercise price e its value is given by

$$v^c(e, z_t^*) = \int_e^\infty (z_t^* - e)\pi_t^* \mathrm{d}z_t^*.$$

Then, successive differentiation yields

$$\left[\frac{\partial^2 v^c(e, z_t^*)}{\partial e^2}\right]_{e=z_t^*} = \pi_t^*.$$

■

In summary, equation (10.B.15a) determines result-state security prices when aggregate consumption follows a discrete distribution over result-states. When that distribution is continuous, then (10.B.15b) is applicable. Substituting the appropriate form of this pricing function in VR1, either in the recursive or intertemporal form, however only shifts the search for an empirically useful valuation equation back one step, for we have neither a theoretical nor empirically useful expression for valuing call options on aggregate consumption (or any other non-trivial asset). Chapter 11 takes up that valuation problem, but some intermediate results are first helpful.

10.B.3. Valuation relation 2

Recall the fundamental valuation equation (10.B.1) written in its recursion form:

$$v_0 = \sum_{s1} \pi_{s1} r_{s1}, \tag{10.B.16}$$

where $r_{s1} = z_{s1} + v_{s1}$ is the period one yield. What are the implications of specific utility assumptions for claims prices? In answer to this question we write the claims prices in terms of 'utilities' as follows.

P10.5. Valuation Relation 2 (VR2). Consider some uncertain payout stream

$[z_1\, z_2 \ldots z_T]$. Suppose that individuals satisfy (10.A.1), that an equilibrium exists in an equivalently complete security market, and that the intertemporal no-arbitrage condition (10.B.10) obtains. Under these conditions the net value of the payout stream is given by the intertemporal valuation form

$$v_0 = \sum_t E[\psi_t(z_t) z_t)]/\rho_t, \tag{10.B.17a}$$

where $\psi_t(z_t) = E[\mu_t(w_t | z_t)]/E[\mu_t(w_t)]$ is the conditionally expected, relative marginal utility function. The accompanying recursive form is

$$v_0 = E(\psi_1(r_1) r_1)/\rho_1. \tag{10.B.17b}$$

with $r_1 = z_1 + v_1$ the one period yield.

Proof.[9] Optimality condition (10.B.4) along with (10.B.16) gives

$$v_0 = \mu_0 \sum_{s1} h_{s1} \mu_{s1} r_{s1} = E(\mu_1 r_1)/\rho_1 E(\mu_1), \tag{10.B.18}$$

with the expectation E here being with respect to the period 0 probabilities of period 1 states and $\mu_0 = \rho_1 E(\mu_1)$, see (10.A.4c). Properties of the expectations operator can be employed to write the alternative forms for (10.B.18):

$$\begin{aligned} v_0 &= E[E(\mu_1 r_1 | r_1)]/\rho_1 E(\mu_1) = E[r_1 E(\mu_1 | r_1)/E(\mu_1)]/\rho_1 \\ &= E[\psi_1(r_1) r_1]/\rho_1, \end{aligned} \tag{10.B.19}$$

which is the recursive valuation relationship (10.B.17b) with $\psi_1(r_1) \equiv E(\mu_1 | r_1)/E(\mu_1)$.

To derive (10.B.17a) consider some security t which has a non-zero payout only at date t. Using (10.B.1) and (10.B.18) that security's market value is

$$v_0^t = E(\mu_t z_t)/E(\mu_t)\rho_t = E[\psi_t(z_t) z_t]. \tag{10.B.20}$$

Similarly, a security which pays out only at two periods, t and t' has a current market value equal to $v_0^t + v_0^{t'}$, where both of these values are given by (10.B.20) using t and t' parameters. More generally, if some security has

[9]VR2 was originally stated by Beja (1971). Rubinstein (1976) and Brennan (1979) develop these formulae under specific utility and distributional assumptions.

the uncertain payout *stream* $[z_1\ z_s\ \ldots\ z_T]$ its date zero net value is the intertemporal sum

$$v_0 = \sum_t v_0^t$$

$$= \sum_t E(\mu_t z_t)/E(\mu_t)\rho_t = \sum_t E(\psi_t(z_t)z_t)/\rho_t,$$

which is equation (10.B.17a). □

We stress that VR1 and VR2 are equivalent, alternative valuation relationships. Both forms are based on the same underlying assumptions concerning individuals, markets and information.

Using (10.B.18) and the definition of covariance, it is sometimes useful to express VR2 in a slightly different format:

$$\begin{aligned} v_0 &= E(\mu_1 r_1) \\ &= E\mu_1 Er_1 + \text{cov}(\mu_1, r_1) \\ &= (Er_1/\rho_1) + \text{cov}(\mu_1, r_1), \end{aligned} \tag{10.B.21a}$$

where we use (10.A.4c) with the marginal utility of current consumption chosen to be one. Similarly, the period by-period form of VR2 also has a 'covariance' form:

$$\begin{aligned} v_0 &= \sum_t E(\mu_t z_t) \\ &= \sum_t [(Ez_t/\rho_t) + \text{cov}(\mu_t, z_t)]. \end{aligned} \tag{10.B.21b}$$

It is understood that random variables in the above equations (10.B.21) are defined with respect to date zero probabilities and prices are those occurring on markets too at date zero.

To complete our valuation catalog, use (10.B.21a) and a little algebra to derive the expected rate of return as

$$E\underline{r}_1 = E(r_1/v_0) = \rho_1 - \rho_1\, \text{cov}(\mu_1, \underline{r}_1).$$

(Note the difference between rates of return and yields: $\underline{r}_1 = r_1/v_0$.) As this relationship holds for any payout, then

$$E\underline{z}_1^* = \rho_1 - \rho_1 \operatorname{cov}(\mu_1, \underline{z}_1^*),$$

determines then expected return on an aggregate consumption security paying only at date 1 ($\underline{z}_1^* = z_1^*/v_0^*$). Dividing these last two equations gives

$$(E\underline{r}_1 - \rho_1) = (E\underline{z}_1^* - \rho_1)\frac{\operatorname{cov}(\mu_1, \underline{r}_1)}{\operatorname{cov}(\mu_1, \underline{z}_1^*)}. \tag{10.B.22}$$

And, as a final formula, we add the recursive valuation relationship between two general dates. Particularly, corresponding to (10.B.21a) there is

$$\begin{aligned} v_{t-1} &= E_{t-1}(\mu_t r_t) \\ &= [E_{t-1}(r_t)/_{t-1}\rho_t] + \operatorname{cov}_{t-1}(\mu_t, r_t). \end{aligned} \tag{10.B.23}$$

10.C. The Normal-CARA Case

While the valuation relationships in the various intertemporal and recursive forms given above seem quite detailed, without further restrictions they are not of any significant empirical use. The apparent problem is the presence of the individual-specific information in the marginal utilities. When conditions for demand aggregation occur that problem is partially solved, for it is then possible to deal with a composite individual. In turn, the valuation equations are simplified, at least to the extent that the relevant parameters of the marginal utility function would be common, or market-related, not individualistic. In this case there would be some hope in estimating those parameters from market data. But, even if it were appropriate to speak of a composite individual it is still necessary to make further assumptions about the marginal utility function to give simple, estimable valuation expressions. For example, if we were to assume all individuals are identical and risk neutral then $\mu_1(\cdot) = k$ for all i, and (10.B.17b) becomes $v_0 = kE(r_1)$. In this case value is determined by expectations alone and it would be necessary only to estimate k. Of course, with alternative specifications of utility it need not be such an easy task to identify and estimate the relevant variables and parameters.

In one frequently cited case it is possible to remove the utility-specific information from the valuation relationships without restricting individuals beyond the I2 specification. This generality comes at some expense, however, as it is required, alternatively, that underlying cash flows and aggregate consumption follow a bivariate normal distribution at each date. In this case the essential, enabling device is a *covariance property*:[10] subject to mild regularity conditions, if x and y are jointly normal in distribution and g is a differentiable function of x, then

$$\operatorname{cov}(g(x),y)=E(\partial g(x)/\partial x)\operatorname{cov}(x,y).$$

In the next several subsections we shall make the normality assumption and attempt to formulate a more practical theory of price, in an explicit T-date setting, on that basis. Two separate starting points are used corresponding to VR2 in the intertemporal and recursive forms given above.

10.C.1. Intertemporal analysis

Suppose that the cash flows z_t and z_t^* are jointly normal in distribution at each date and the covariance property holds. In turn, the intertemporal valuation equation (10.B.21b) can be significantly simplified:

$$v_0=\sum_t E(z_t)/[\rho_t+E(\partial\mu_t/\partial z_t^*)\operatorname{cov}(z_t,z_t^*)]$$

$$=\sum_t [E(z_t)-\lambda_t^i\operatorname{cov}(z_t,z_t^*)]/\rho_t, \qquad (10.C.1)$$

where $\lambda_t^i=-E(\partial\mu_t^i/\partial z_t^*)/E\mu_t^i>0$ (by monotonicity and risk aversion). In the usual way, each λ_t^i can be calculated using a security which has a payoff only at date t.[11] Specifically, let z_t^* be that payoff, then v_{0t}^* (the current price of z_t^*) is

$$\rho_t v_{0t}^*=E(z_t^*)-\lambda_t^i\operatorname{cov}(z_t^*,z_t^*).$$

Summing this over i and solving gives

$$\lambda_t=[E(z_t^*)-\rho_t]/\operatorname{var}(z_t^*),$$

where $\lambda_t=I/\Sigma_i(\lambda_t^i)>0$ has the interpretation of the date t 'price of risk'. Repeating this for each date t provides the final result, which we shall call

[10]See Rubinstein (1979) and Stein (1976) for proof.
[11]This specific payoff can be constructed since the security market is equivalently complete.

the *normal intertemporal valuation equation*:[12]

$$v_0 = \sum_t [E(z_t) - \lambda_t \text{cov}(z_t, z_t^*)]/\rho_t. \tag{10.C.2a}$$

Under the indicated normality assumptions, the value of any uncertain income stream is given as a period-by-period sum. Each term of the sum derives from mean and covariance parameters of z_t and z_t^* at each date t, being equal to the security's mean payoff reduced by a market-wide 'price of risk' (λ_t) times its 'risk' (covariance with z_t^*). This risk-adjusted mean is then discounted by the (one plus) riskless discount bond of the same date. The valuation equation bears a strong resemblance to the static, two-period CAPM (see Chapter 7) in that two factors are a basis for asset pricing. The intertemporal model, however, alters the factors somewhat: (1) the appropriate riskless rate is that associated with a riskless discount bond maturing at the date of the cash flow, not the current instantaneous rate; and, (2) the covariance with the market portfolio in the static CAPM is replaced by the covariance with the security which pays aggregate consumption at the date of the cash flow.[13] Moreover, in this intertemporal form it is (explicitly) the sum of future cash flows which add to current value.

It should be emphasized the VR2 generally, or (10.C.2) specifically, is not based on any assumption of exogeneously-given dynamics for aggregate consumption. Nor are the asset payoff distributions required to be linked over time in any fashion (other than by the fact that the cash flow is normal at each date). And, at the other pole, we have made no assumptions about individual elementary utilities beyond the I2 specification. While this generality is comforting, one feature of the resulting valuation model is not. Of particular interest to an empiricist is the properties of the price of risk: is λ_t stochastic and, if not, is it likely to be a stationary parameter over time? In this regard it is usual to make a final assumption, that there is demand aggregation and the composite utility is CARA; i.e., for each st, $U(w_{st}) = -\exp(\hat{\alpha} w_{st}) = -\exp(\alpha z_{st})$ where α scales for the (time constant) popula-

[12]Note that CARA utility implies a finite marginal utility at zero consumption and normally distributed variates means that there are non-zero probabilities of negative payoffs and 'consumption'. More exactly, then, the possibility of corner solutions, with Kuhn–Tucker inequalities at zero consumption, needs to be considered at this point. It is, however, usual to ignore this difficulty and proceed with normal-CARA analyses as an 'approximate' model. See, for example, Stapleton and Subrahmanyan (1978) and Brennan (1979).

[13]Recall from P9.3 that, with CARA composite utilities, the additional assumption of an additive random walk in aggregate consumption implies that aggregate wealth is perfectly correlated with aggregate consumption to each date, and properly scaled, we may then use the covariance of z_t with aggregate wealth as the risk measure in (10.C.2a).

tion. In this case, an even simpler valuation expression is reached, for $\lambda_t^i = E(\partial\mu_t^i/\partial z_t^*)/E\mu_t = \alpha$, in turn $\lambda_t = \alpha$, and the price of risk is a non-stochastic market constant for all dates, independent of probabilities and state claim prices. In turn,

$$v_0 = \sum_t [E(z_t) - \alpha \operatorname{cov}(z_t, z_t^*)]/\rho_t. \qquad (10.C.2b)$$

While CAPM-like, and now empirically tractable, the intertemporal model does not offer a clear rationale for the frequently used (static) two-period CAPM. That rationale, if it is to be forthcoming, will instead rest on conditions derived using the recursive form of VR2. It is to that derivation to which we next turn.

10.C.2. Recursive analysis

Assuming z_T and z_T^* are joint normal in distribution, then the $(T-1)$ market value of Z_T can be derived from (10.B.23) using the covariance property:

$$v_{T-1} = \{E_{T-1}z_T - [E_{T-1}(\partial\mu_T/\partial z_T^*)/E\mu_T] \times \operatorname{cov}_{T-1}(z_T, z_T^*)\}/_{T-1}\rho_T. \qquad (10.C.3)$$

(At this terminal date $r_T = z_T$, as there are no then future payoffs and $v_T \equiv 0$.) Assuming further that individuals have CARA composite utilities provides a non-stochastic price of risk α as above. Making that substitution gives the *normal-CARA recursive valuation equation* for date $(T-1)$:

$$v_{T-1} = [E_{T-1}(z_T) - \alpha \operatorname{cov}_{T-1}(z_T, z_T^*)]/_{T-1}\rho_T. \qquad (10.C.4)$$

We ask now whether there is a similar recursive equation for date $(T-2)$. While (10.B.23) by itself is applicable at that earlier date, for the marginal utility information to be 'removed' using the covariance property requires the yield $r_{T-1} = z_{T-1} + v_{T-1}$ and aggregate consumption to be joint normally distributed. That is problematic, for our fundamental assumption has been that cash flows, not yields, at every date are jointly normal with aggregate consumption. That is, z_{T-1} is normally distributed. If, in turn, r_{T-1} is to be normal, then the price v_{T-1} must be normal.[14] This returns our attention to

[14]It is crucial to distinguish between distribution assumptions on future prices and future cash flows. The difference can be illustrated for the simple case of risk neutral utilities. Consider some date t cash flow z_t. On date 0 markets z_t has a value of $E_0(z_t)$ discounted to periods at the

(10.C.4) and the following observations: (1) the conditioning variables for $E_{T-1}(z_T)$ are the sequence of aggregate consumption events $z_1^*, z_2^* \ldots z_{T-1}^*$, which are each normally distributed by assumption, making $E_{T-1}(z_T)$ normally distributed; (2) α is a deterministic constant from the CARA (and non-stochastic population) assumption; and, (3) the conditional covariance is non-stochastic due to the joint normal assumption.[15] Thus, a sufficient condition for v_{T-1} to be normally distributed is for the riskless rate ${}_{T-1}\rho_T$ to be nonstochastic. That leads to the following special case.

E10.6. Using (9.A.14c), the market value of a (riskless) security purchased at date $(t-1)$ and paying \$1 in each state at date t is

$$v_{t-1}^{\rho} = \gamma E_{t-1}\mu_t(w_t)/\mu_{t-1}(w_{t-1}).$$

Rearranging gives the one period riskless rate of return

$${}_{t-1}\rho_t = \mu_{t-1}(w_{t-1})/E_{t-1}\mu_t(w_t). \tag{10.C.5}$$

When conditions for demand aggregation exist, then $w_t = c_t z_t^*$, c_t a non-stochastic constant, for all t (with a constant population) and

$${}_{t-1}\rho_t = \hat{\mu}_{t-1}(W_{t-1})/E_{t-1}\hat{\mu}_t(W_t), \tag{10.C.6}$$

where the marginal utility $\hat{\mu}$ 'includes' c_t. Suppose further that the composite utility is CARA, i.e., of the (negative) exponential form:

$$U(w_{st,t}) = -\exp[-\alpha w_{st}]\gamma^t,$$

$$U(w_{t-1}, t) = -\exp[-\alpha w_{t-1}]\gamma^{t-1}.$$

Then (10.C.6) becomes

$${}_{t-1}\rho_t = \gamma E_{t-1}\{\exp[-\alpha(z_{t-1}^* - z_t^*)]\}. \tag{10.C.7}$$

In this case, ${}_{t-1}\rho_t$ will be independent of z_{t-1}^* (and thus non-stochastic as viewed from the earlier period) if the RHS of this last expression is

riskless rate, on date 1 markets it has value $E_1(z_t)$ discounted $(t-1)$ at the riskless rate, etc. If, by hypothesis, the changes in information are serially independent, then the indicated conditional expectation, and therefore the prices, will exhibit serial independence. That is, prices will 'fluctuate randomly' in the terminology of Samuelson (1965). In the text above we are asking a similar question about the link between the underlying cash flow stochastic process and that of prices, given CARA risk individuals and cash flows joint normally distributed with aggregate consumption at each date.

[15] See Feller (1966, p. 69), and Stapleton and Subrahmanyan (1978).

independent of z^*_{t-1}. Let $z^*_t = z^*_{t-1} + \varepsilon_{t-1}$ with ε_{t-1} noise with respect to z^*_{t-1}, then

$$_{t-1}\rho_t = \gamma E_{t-1} \exp[-\alpha \varepsilon_{1t-1}]. \tag{10.C.8}$$

That is, if the composite elementary utility is CARA and *aggregate consumption* follows an additive random walk, then riskless rates of return are non-stochastic. ■

Adding the assumption that aggregate consumption follows a (normal) additive random walk to the previous CARA and cash flow normality assumptions allows the covariance property to be used with (10.B.23) to produce

$$v_{T-2} = [E_{T-1}(r_{T-1}) - \alpha \operatorname{cov}_{T-2}(r_{T-1}, z^*_{T-1})]/_{T-1}\rho_T. \tag{10.C.9}$$

By similar arguments v_{T-2} is normal in distribution, and the date $(T-3)$ recursion too obtains. More generally, we have

$$v_{t-1} = [E_{t-1}(r_t) - \alpha \operatorname{cov}_{t-1}(r_t, z^*_t)]/_{t-1}\rho_t, \tag{10.C.10}$$

for every pair of dates $(t-1)$ and t. Recall from P9.3, and note 13 above, that with the additive random walk in aggregate consumption then aggregate wealth and consumption was perfectly correlated in this case. With some scaling of α and the substitution of aggregate consumption for the market mutual fund, this is precisely the form of the frequently used two-period (static) CAPM – see, for example, P7.5 and equation (7.D.5). Importantly, the equation is a price recursive relationship which can be 'folded back' in the fashion of dynamic programming to produce prices at every date of the horizon.

Equation (10.B.21b), the basic intertemporal form of VR2, and equation (10.B.23), the basic VR2 recursive form, are the foundations for the normal-CARA results. While based on rather general market and individual specifications (see P10.5), these valuation equations are of limited practical use since they involve individual-specific information in the form of marginal utilities. Assuming cash flows and aggregate consumption are joint normally distributed at each date, the individual-specific information is replaced by a market-wide price of risk parameter. When, further, demand aggregation occurs with composite CARA utilities, the price of risk is a non-stochastic constant. With these assumptions, the intertemporal model takes the empirically useful form given by equation (10.C.2b). Assuming, in addition, that aggregate consumption follows a (normal) additive random walk then, with CARA utilities, riskless rates of all maturities are non-stochastic, normally distributed (future) cash flows generated normally distributed (future) prices and a two period recursion equivalent to the static two period CAPM obtains. That result is stated in equation (10.C.10).

Chapter 11

MULTIPERIOD VALUATION AND OPTIONS

Recall generally the organization of exchange and notations of Chapter 10 and specifically valuation relation 2 (VR2), equation (10.B.17). Using that relationship, the market value of a derivative security with period one, state contingent payout $\phi(r_1)$ is

$$\begin{aligned} v_0^{\phi} &= E[\mu_1(w_1)\phi(r_1)]/E[\mu_1(w_t)]\rho_1 \\ &= E[\psi(r_1)\phi(r_1)]/\rho_1, \end{aligned} \tag{11.A.1}$$

where r_1 represents the yield on the underlying asset. Time indices 0 and 1 may more generally indicate any two dates, providing prices and probabilities are appropriately conditioned. The first purpose of this chapter is to develop an empirically useful form for v_0^{ϕ}. Then specializing that result to the case where the derivative security is a call option written on the aggregate consumption portfolio, the result-state prices necessary to practically implement valuation relation 1 (VR1), equation (10.B.2), are developed. As there are no 'free lunches', this final step requires some assumptions beyond those already made. One extremely simplifying assumption, for example, would be to require that the valuation relationship be risk neutral. While at first glance that seems unduly restrictive, it need not be. The next section makes that argument, and the theory of valuation then proceeds on that basis.

11.A. Risk Neutral Valuation

In a market equilibrium where securities are valued risk neutrally, prices are determined only by expected values and every security provides the same expected rate of return.

E11.1. With risk neutrality the value of a bond which promises b dollars against an uncertain period one cash flow of $z_1 = [z_{11}\ z_{21} \dots z_{s1}]$ is,

$$v^0 = E(\min[z_1, b])/\rho_1$$

$$= \left(\int_{-\infty}^{\infty} \min[z_1, b] f(z_1) dz_1\right) \Big/ \rho_1$$

$$= \left(\int_{-\infty}^{b} z_1 f(z_1) dz_1 + \int_{b}^{\infty} b f(z_1) dz_1\right) \Big/ \rho_1,$$

where ρ_1 is the riskfree rate of interest and $f(z_1)$ is the density function of z_1. When, for example, z_1 is normally distributed with mean 100 and standard deviation 25 and $\rho_1 = 1.1$, then a promised payment of $b = 86$ results in a current market value for the bond of $v^d = 74$. It is of particular note that this result is independent of individual preference-specific information. ■

As risk neutral valuation depends on (observable) market variables, it lays a (potentially) important empirical basis for a theory of valuation. The pivotal question concerns the kinds of economies which are capable of producing such valuation relationships. Is it specifically required that all individuals have linear elementary utilities? That answer is yes if the distribution on asset returns is to be taken as given in the analysis. Alternatively, is it possible to let individuals have quite general, and diverse, risk preferences and then impose restrictions on the joint distribution on returns used in the analysis to produce risk neutral valuation? Such 'preference free' results have been obtained, but are not pursued here as they, uncomfortably, require a riskless ('hedge') portfolio to be constructed from the available securities at each instant and thus require that actual trading in all assets occur and occur continuously.[1,2] Rather, the present

[1]Using only non-satiety as a preference requirement and the condition that prices not provide riskless arbitrage opportunities at any instant, Black and Scholes (1973) and Merton (1973a) have obtained risk neutral valuation formula for dividend protected European call option contracts. In that development, trading is assumed to take place continuously in continuously divisible assets and the price dynamics of the underlying security is assumed to follow an Itô process. The no arbitrage requirement produces a partial differential equation involving both the value of the call and the value of the underlying security. In turn, the solution of this differential equation, subject to appropriate boundary conditions, is also free of individual-specific preference information and thus is consistent with risk neutral preferences, see E11.3 below. Warrants, corporate debt, convertible bonds, put options, preferred stock, etc. are valued by essentially the same differential equation, with only the boundary conditions changing.

[2]Cox, Ross, and Rubinstein (1979) develop a preference free valuation formula for call

approach will be to develop risk neutral valuation relationships using a combination of restrictions on preferences and security payout (probability) distributions. As shall be clear in a moment, the key advantages of this approach are that it permits heterogeneous beliefs and a discrete time trading model. Moreover, there will be no requirement that assets be actually traded.

11.A.1. Risk neutral valuation relationships

Again, the notation and market organization are the same as in Chapter 10. For the moment, it is convenient to think of some underlying security (asset) j with a payoff, z_1, only at one date. (We might use either 1 or T as the date, but select the former.) In this case the period 1 yield $r_1 = z_1$ since there are no then-future payouts. Let the return on this security, z_1/v_0, have probability density $g(z_1/v_0)$. In turn, there is a conditional density function for the payoff z_1, given j's current market price, which we write as $f(z_1 | v_0)$, or more simply $f(z_1)$.[3]

Using this conditional density and VR2, the market value of the derivative security with date 1 payoff $\phi(z_1)$ is

$$v_0^\phi(v_0) = E[\psi_1(z_1)\phi(z_1)]/\rho_1$$

$$= \frac{1}{\rho_1}\int \psi_1(z_1)\phi(z_1)f(z_1)\mathrm{d}z_1. \qquad (11.A.2)$$

In the well-known case where the conditional marginal utility $\psi_1(z_1)$ is constant, (11.A.2) implies a risk neutral valuation relationship, with v_0^ϕ given simply as the expected value of $\phi(z_1)$. However, we mean more than this single case by risk neutral valuation as the following definition makes clear.

D11.1. Risk Neutral Valuation Relationship (RNVR). Let z_1 be the cash flow of some asset at a terminal period 1. The current value of z_1 is v_0, and there is the associated density $f(z_1)$. A risk neutral valuation relationship then exists if:

(1) there is a 'transformed' density function $f'(z_1)$, involving no parameters

---

options in a discrete time context. They too use a hedging argument, assuming the underlying asset has returns which follow a two state (binomial) jump process. See also Cox and Ross (1976).

[3] State contingent yields and returns at each date are generally interpreted as random variables in this chapter. See Section (5.C.1).

of individual preferences, such that

$$v_0^{\phi}(v_0)=\frac{1}{\rho_1}\int \phi(z_1)f'(z_1)\mathrm{d}z_1, \tag{11.A.3}$$

determines the value of the derivative security $\phi(z_1)$, and

(2) the conditional marginal utility function $\psi_1(z_1)$ is such that (11.A.2) and (11.A.3) provide the same value v_0^{ϕ}, i.e.,

$$\frac{1}{\rho_1}\int \psi_1(z_1)\phi(z_1)f(z_1)\mathrm{d}z_1=\frac{1}{\rho_1}\int \phi(z_1)f'(z_1)\mathrm{d}z_1. \tag{11.A.4}$$

It should be emphasized that $\psi_1(\cdot)$ on the LHS of (11.A.4) reflects individual specific information, but nothing on the RHS does. That is the basis for an RNVR: when $\psi_1(\cdot)$, $f(\cdot)$, and $f'(\cdot)$ are related in such a way that (11.A.4) holds, then the derivative security can be valued using the RHS of this equation, independent of individual preference parameters. It is apparent from (11.A.4) that an RNVR occurs when the conditional marginal utility ψ_1 bears the following, quite direct relationship to the probability densities:

$$\psi_1(z_1)=\frac{f'(z_1)}{f(z_1)}. \tag{11.A.5}$$

The usual RNVR case presumes no transformation of the underlying probability density, so that $f'(\cdot)=f(\cdot)$ and the utility function is required to be linear. It is possible, however, to have risk neutral valuation without individuals in the economy actually possessing risk neutral utilities. Taking the density $f(z_1)$ as given, this requires that the density $f'(z_1)$, to be used in the analysis, solve (11.A.5) for the specified utility function and associated $\psi_1(z_1)$. This transformed density, given $f(\cdot)$ and $\psi_1(\cdot)$, is not completely arbitrary, however. When $\phi(z_1)=z_1$ then (11.A.3) must solve for $v_0^{\phi}=v_0$, which requires that the mean of the distribution $f'(z_1)$ be $v_0\rho_1$. We shall use this restriction in the following analysis and, for simplicity, take all other parameters of $f(\cdot)$ and $f'(\cdot)$ to be identical.[4]

[4]The definition of a RNVR rule does not require that these other parameters be equal. Even more generally, the RNVR does not require that $f(\cdot)$ and $f'(\cdot)$ belong to the same class of distribution (e.g., lognormal). All that the RNVR does require is that $f'(\cdot)$ have the mean value given above and that it not involve individual-specific preference parameters.

11.A.2. Individuals

Whatever density function in fact occurs for asset payouts, there remains the task of choosing reasonable, *a priori* restrictions on individual preferences. Given $f(\cdot)$, then $f'(\cdot)$ can in general be unique and consistent with the market-observed prices only when $\psi(\cdot)$ too is unique. A RNVR thus seems impossible when there are a large number of different individuals in the economy, at least without some simplification. The obvious simplification in this regard is to adopt a composite or representative utility function applicable to all individuals. One basis for such a specification is the presumption that individuals are in fact identical. That strong restriction is fortunately not necessary; rather, all that is required is that diverse individuals possess the limited degree of homogeneity which permits 'demand aggregation.' Recall the conditions for such aggregation from P9.3, noting that the composite individual is formed in a way that, in an economy made up of identical individuals of this kind, prices would be determined exactly as in the original economy with the diverse individuals. Also, recall that when it is possible to create identical composite individuals in this fashion each possesses what is called a *composite utility function.*

11.A.3. Valuing derivative securities: Lognormal returns

That is the basic assumption about individuals. What about the second element of the analysis, the probability density $f(\cdot)$? As a first case, we suppose that the rate of return $z_1 \equiv z_1/v_0$ for security j is lognormal in distribution. In turn, the conditional density function[5]

$$f(z_1)=\frac{1}{z_1 K}\exp\{[-1/2\tilde{\sigma}_1^2][\tilde{z}_1-\tilde{m}_1)]^2\}, \qquad (11.A.6)$$

is also lognormal with expected value equal to

$$E(z_1)=\exp\{\tilde{m}_1+\tilde{\sigma}_1^2/2\}, \qquad (11.A.7)$$

where $\tilde{z}_1=\ln z_1$ is the corresponding normally distributed variate, $\tilde{m}_1=E(\tilde{z}_1)$, $\tilde{\sigma}_1^2=\text{var}(\tilde{z}_1)$, and $k=\tilde{\sigma}_1\ (2pi)^{1/2}$. The $\tilde{}$ overscore is used here and hereafter to indicate the natural logarithm of a variable and associated distribution parameters. As the transformed distribution $f'(z_1)$ must have

[5]Key properties of the lognormal distribution are developed in the Appendix to this chapter. See Aitchison and Brown (1963) for full details. Note too that, as the lognormal distribution is a continuous distribution, it is required that there be a continuum of states at each date.

mean equal to $v_0 \rho_1$, then

$$\exp\{\tilde{m}_1' + \tilde{\sigma}_1^2/2\} = v_0 \rho_1, \quad \text{and} \tag{11.A.8}$$

$$\tilde{m}_1' = \tilde{\rho}_1 - \tilde{\sigma}_1^2/2 + \ln(v_0) \tag{11.A.9}$$

define the underlying location parameter of $f'(\cdot)$. In turn,

$$f'(z_1) = \frac{1}{z_1 K} \exp\{(-1/2\tilde{\sigma}_1^2)[\tilde{z}_1 - \tilde{\rho}_1 + \tilde{\sigma}_1^2/2]^2\}, \tag{11.A.10}$$

where $\tilde{z}_1 = \ln(z_1/v_0)$ is the normally distributed rate of return. Notice that the transformed distribution of z_1 is written only in terms of the (observable) market parameters and contains no individual-specific preference information. This leads to the following proposition:

P11.1. Derivative security valuation: risk neutrality with lognormal returns. Let the conditions for VR2 be satisfied, see P10.5. Assume further (i) that, with one period remaining, the payoff on some underlying asset and the aggregate consumption outcome follow an arbitrary bivariate lognormal distribution, and (ii) that the conditions for aggregation of individual preferences occur. Then, the necessary and sufficient condition for risk neutral valuation of securities derived from the underlying asset is that the composite utility function exhibit constant relative risk aversion.

Proof.[6] First we show necessity. For an RNVR equation (11.A.4) must hold, with (11.A.6) and (11.A.10) giving the lognormal distributions for $f(z_1)$ and $f'(z_1)$, respectively. Substituting these in (11.A.5) and solving gives the conditional marginal utility supporting the RNVR:

$$\psi_1(z_1) \equiv E(\mu_1(w_1)|z_1)/E\mu_1(w_1) = c_1(\underline{z}_1)^{-c_2}, \tag{11.A.11}$$

where the RHS of the equation is the ratio of the distributions after simplification. The (non-stochastic) constants c_1 and c_2 arise from the underlying distribution parameters and the riskless rate of return:

$$c_1 = \exp\{c_2(2\tilde{m}_1 + 2\tilde{\rho}_1 - \tilde{\sigma}_1^2)/4\}, \tag{11.A.12a}$$

[6]Brennan (1979) provided the first systematic development of the lognormal-CRRA RNVR given here and the similar normal-CARA RNVR given in P11.2 below. See Merton (1973a), Rubinstein (1976), and Cox and Ross (1976) for earlier statements.

$$c_2=(2\tilde{m}_1-2\tilde{\rho}_1+\tilde{\sigma}_1^2)/2\tilde{\sigma}_1^2. \qquad (11.A.12b)$$

The problem is to solve (11.A.11) for the underlying utility function. As the immediate concern is with necessity, and the involved lognormal distributions are arbitrary, it is convenient to choose the correlation between w_1 and z_1 to be 1 exactly. This makes w_1 a non-stochastic function of z_1 and, for this special case, it is then true that the utility of the expectation is the expectation of the utility:

$$E(\mu_1(w_1)|z_1)/E\mu_1(w_1)=\mu_1(E(w_1|z_1))/\mu_1(Ew_1). \qquad (11.A.13)$$

As the RHS of equations (11.A.13) and (11.A.11) equal, that leaves us to derive the expression for the conditional expectation $E(w_1|z_1)$ and, on inverting this, solve for w_1 in terms of parameters.

With prices fixed, aggregate consumption W_1 and the security payoff z_1 are bivariate lognormally distributed by hypothesis. Moreover, with demand aggregation each identical individual's optimal plan is $w_1=W_1/I$, so $\ln w_1=\ln w_1-\ln I$. Given the number of individuals in the economy is fixed and nonstochastic, then $\ln w_1$ and $\ln z_1$ are bivariate normal and, in turn, the conditional distribution of $\ln w_1$ given $\ln z_1$ is degenerate normal (since w_1 and z_1 were assumed above to be perfectly correlated) with certain value equal to the mean

$$E(\tilde{w}_1|\tilde{z}_1)=\tilde{m}_1^w+\frac{\tilde{\sigma}_1^w}{\tilde{\sigma}_1}[\tilde{z}_1-\tilde{m}_1],$$

where $\tilde{m}_1^w=E(\ln\tilde{w}_1)$ and $\tilde{\sigma}_1^w=\text{std}(\ln\tilde{w}_1)$. Converting from the mean of lognormal variables to the corresponding normal variables and substituting in the marginal utility we have[7]

$$\mu_1(E(w_1|z_1))=\mu_1\left(\exp\left\{\tilde{m}_1^w+\frac{\tilde{\sigma}_1^w}{\tilde{\sigma}_1}[\tilde{z}_1-\tilde{m}_1]\right\}\right). \qquad (11.A.14)$$

From (11.A.11) this marginal utility must take the power function form, i.e.,

$$\mu_1\left(\exp\left\{\tilde{m}_1^w+\frac{\tilde{\sigma}_1^w}{\tilde{\sigma}_1}(\tilde{z}_1-\tilde{m}_1)\right\}\right)=[c_1(z_1)^{-c_2}]E\mu_1(w_1). \qquad (11.A.15)$$

[7]See the Appendix for the relationship between the mean and variance of corresponding lognormal and normal variables.

The remaining task is to express this marginal utility in terms of the consumption variable. As the argument of $\mu_1(\cdot)$ is w_1, solve for $\underline{z}_1$ from the LHS of the above expression, giving

$$w_1 = \exp\left[\tilde{m}_1^w + \frac{\tilde{\sigma}_1^w}{\tilde{\sigma}_1}(\tilde{z}_1 - \tilde{m}_1)\right], \quad \text{and}$$

$$\underline{z}_1 = c_3(w_1)^{c_4}, \tag{11.A.16}$$

with c_3 and c_4 constants determined by the distribution parameters. Substitute this expression for $\underline{z}_1$ in the RHS of (11.A.15) to give the sought-after form for the marginal utility function: $\mu_1(w_1) = (w_1)^{c_5}$, where the multiplicative scale is arbitrary and chosen as one and c_5 is, again, made up of distribution parameters and therefore non-stochastic. This proves necessity.

The proof of sufficiency is straightforward. Suppose $\mu_1(w_1) = (w_1)^k$, k a constant. As w_1 is lognormal then so is $\mu_1(w_1) = (w_1)^k$, which means the joint distribution of z_1 and $(w_1)^k$ is bivariate lognormal. The conditional expectation $E[(w_1)^k | z_1]$ is therefore lognormal and equal to

$$E((w_1)^k | z_1) - (z_1)^{b/\tilde{\sigma}_1} \exp - \{[b\tilde{m}_1/\tilde{\sigma}_1] + b^2/2\}, \tag{11.A.17}$$

where $b = k\tilde{\sigma}_1$. Substituting this expression in (10.A.3) for $E(\mu_1 | z_1)$ and then simplifying yields (11.A.6).[8] □

The RNVR definition generally, and proposition P11.1 specifically, apply to all derivative securities whose value depends on the payoff of an underlying asset. Put and call options, convertible bonds, stock warrants, and risky debt are typical specifications of $\phi(\cdot)$ that might be made. Consider, for example and later use, the specific case where the derivative security is a European call option written on the payoff z_1. The call provides the one period payoff $\phi(z_1) = \max[(r_1 - e), 0]$ where e is the option exercise price. Using (11.A.3) in this case, the lognormal-CARA RNVR is[9]

$$v_0^c(e, z_1) = \frac{1}{\rho_1} \int_0^{\infty} \max[(z_1 - e), 0] f'(z_1) \mathrm{d}z_1$$

[8] Rubinstein (1976) and Brennan (1979) provide full details of the sufficiency proof.

[9] It is understood that the call option price, like that of all derivative securities, is in part a function of the (current) market price of the underlying security. With this understood, the function dependence of v_0^c upon v_0 is generally suppressed in the notation.

$$=\frac{1}{\rho_1}\int_e^\infty (z_1-e)\frac{1}{z_1K}\exp\left\{\frac{-1}{2\tilde{\sigma}_1^2}[\tilde{z}_1-\tilde{\rho}_1+\tilde{\sigma}_1^2/2]^2\right\}\mathrm{d}z_1. \tag{11.A.18}$$

Making the change of variables $\hat{d}=[\tilde{z}_1-\tilde{\rho}_1+\tilde{\sigma}_1^2/2]/\tilde{\sigma}_1$ and performing the integration gives an empirically usable form for call option valuation, in terms of market-observable parameters only:

$$v_0^c(e,z_1)=v_0N(d_1+\tilde{\sigma}_1)-(e/\rho_1)N(d_1), \tag{11.A.19}$$

where $N(\cdot)$ is the standard normal cumulative density function and $d_1\equiv[\ln(v_0/e)+\tilde{\rho}_1-\tilde{\sigma}_1^2/2]/\tilde{\sigma}_1$.[10]

Inspection of equation (11.A.19) shows four parameters to be important in determining the price of a (European) call option with one period

[10]The function $f(w)$ is a normal density when

$$f(w)=(1/\sigma_w\sqrt{2pi})\exp[(-1/2\sigma_w^2)(w-m_w)^2],$$

with parameters m_w and σ_w being, respectively, the mean and standard deviation of w. $N(d)$ is the standard cumulative normal density, that is,

$$N(d)=\int_{-\infty}^{d}(1/\sqrt{2pi})\exp[-\xi^2/2]\mathrm{d}\xi.$$

A key property of normal densities used in deriving (11.A.19) is

$$\int_e^\infty f(w)\mathrm{d}w=N((-e+m_w)/\sigma_w).$$

The proof uses a change of variable $\xi=(w-m_w)/\sigma_w$ to convert $f(w)$ to a standard normal density:

$$\int_e^\infty f(w)\mathrm{d}w=\int_{(e-m_w)/\sigma_w}^\infty f(\xi)\mathrm{d}\xi.$$

As the normal density is symmetric about zero, the RHS of this expression then gives

$$\int_{-\infty}^{(-e+m_w)/\sigma_w} f(\xi)\mathrm{d}\xi\equiv N((-e+m_w)/\sigma_w).$$

A second fact used in deriving (11.C.19) is

$$\int_e^\infty \exp(w)f(w)\mathrm{d}w=\exp[m_w+\sigma_w^2/2]N((-e+m_w)/\sigma_w+\sigma_w).$$

Again, the proof involves a change to the standard normal deviate. To do this, first note that

$$-(1/2\sigma_w^2)(w-m_w)^2+w=m_w+\sigma_w^2/2-(1/2\sigma_w^2)(w-m_w-\sigma_w^2)^2,$$

and then choose $\xi=(w-m_w-\sigma_w^2)/\sigma_w$.

remaining to maturity: the price of the underlying security (v_0), the exercise price of the option (e), the variance of the logarithm of the asset payout ($\tilde{\sigma}_1^2$), and the logarithm of the riskfree rate of return for the period ($\tilde{\rho}_1$).

E11.2. Suppose the price of some non-dividend paying stock to be \$50 with one period variance $\tilde{\sigma}^2 = 0.20$. We consider a call option written on this stock with an exercise price of \$45. Let the riskfree rate of return be 10% over the period. Using these data in (11.A.19) gives

$$\begin{aligned} d_1 &= [\ln(50/45) + \ln(1.1) - 0.2/2]\sqrt{0.2} \\ &= [0.105 + 0.095 - 0.1]/(0.447) \\ &= 0.224 \end{aligned}$$

$$d_2 + \tilde{\sigma}_1 = 0.224 + 0.2 = 0.424$$

$$v_0^c = 50\, N(0.424) - (45/1.1)N(0.224),$$

$N(\cdot)$ is the standard cumulative normal deviate: $N(0.424)$ is the cumulative probability from minus infinity to $+0.424$ and $N(0.224)$ is similarly the cumulative probability to $+0.224$. From standard tables these values are

$$N(0.424) = 0.664,$$

$$N(0.224) = 0.588,$$

which gives

$$\begin{aligned} v_0^c &= 50(0.664) - 40.9(0.588) \\ &= \$9.15. \end{aligned}$$

From (11.A.19), note that the option price is (other things constant) an increasing function of the stock price. As a bit of terminology, when the stock price is below the option value, the option is said to be 'out of the money' and the call will have little value. As the stock price rises and $v_0 > e$, then the option is said to be 'in the money' and the option price increases towards its upper bound $[v_0 - e/\rho_1]$. ■

E11.3. Equation (11.A.19) is, with minor adjustments, equivalent to the Black and Scholes (1973) call option valuation formula with one period to maturity. Their original development was, however, based on the assumption that underlying security prices follow a continuous stochastic (Ito) process over time and that individuals costlessly and continuously revise their security holdings. In that case it is possible for the individuals to form a perfectly hedged (riskless) portfolio by selling a call option against a long position in the underlying security. At a competitive capital market equilibrium, the Black and Scholes call-security portfolio must then earn the riskless rate. Cox and Ross (1976) subsequently observed that, given the current security price, riskless rate, and homogeneous probability beliefs, the call's value must then be independent of the payoff characteristics of other securities *and* the preferences of individuals. That is, in a partial equilibrium analysis the call option value, being independent of investor preferences, may be derived under the assumption of risk neutrality without loss of generality.

In contrast to the Black and Scholes analysis, the present call option valuation equation (11.A.19) has been developed with discrete trading periods, so that it is not generally possible to create a call-security portfolio which is riskless at each instant. Instead of using the continuous time approach to create the instantaneously riskless portfolio and the RNVR, (11.A.19) is based on the combined lognormal-CARA assumptions to achieve the same result. In this sense, the same degree of approximation involved in developing the Black and Scholes valuation model is involved in the present lognormal-CRRA model. ■

P11.1 is restricted to the valuation of derivative securities whose payouts depend on a single random variate. There are, in contrast, many interesting situations where derivative securities payoff depending on the outcomes of two, or more, underlying state-contingent variables. For example, the equity of a firm may be viewed as call option on its debt (recall E10.4); in turn, a call option written on a stock index, a portfolio of equities, is an option on a portfolio of options. A second example is the case of a multiperiod bond. When the bond is risky (with some default states), the payoffs to the bondholders depend on the cash flow *stream* of the firm. The bond is then a derivative security depending on the joint probability distribution given by the period-by-period elements of that stream.

It is straightforward to generalize P11.1 and its proof to the case where a derivative security has its payoff depending on a vector of state contingent cash flows. After making the appropriate vector–matrix substitutions, that development closely follows the single variable case. Specifically, let $Z=[z^1 z^2, \dots z^N]$ be an N-vector of stochastic variables. In turn, $\tilde{\underline{Z}}=[\tilde{\underline{z}}^1\ \tilde{\underline{z}}^2 \dots \tilde{\underline{z}}^N]$ is the vector of logarithms of returns, with $\tilde{M}$ the associated vector of means and $\tilde{\Sigma}$ the variance–covariance matrix with elements $\mathrm{cov}(\tilde{z}^n, \tilde{z}^k)$ for all $n, k=1,2, \dots N$. When the returns of all the variables and aggregate consumption is joint lognormally distributed, then a necessary and sufficient condition for a RNVR is again that the composite individuals be CRRA. In this case, the RNVR is as anticipated

$$v_0^\phi = \frac{1}{\rho_1} \int\int \cdots \int \frac{\phi(Z)}{\sqrt{2pi}\,|\tilde{\Sigma}|(z^1 \cdot z^2 \ldots z^N)} \exp[\cdot] \mathrm{d}z^1 \mathrm{d}z^2 \ldots \mathrm{d}z^N, \qquad (11.A.20)$$

where $\exp[\cdot]$ is given by $\exp[-\frac{1}{2}(\tilde{\underline{Z}} - \tilde{\rho}_1 1_N + \frac{1}{2}\tilde{S})\tilde{\Sigma}^{-1}(\tilde{\underline{Z}} - \tilde{\rho}_1 1_N + \frac{1}{2}\tilde{S})]$, $|\cdot|$ indicates the determinant, 1_N is a N-vector of ones, and $\tilde{S}$ is the N-vector of own variances for the $\tilde{z}^j$.[11]

E11.4. Consider the valuation of multi-currency option bonds similar to those used in Euro-finance markets. In its pure discount form, the corporate issuer is contractually obligated to pay in either of two currencies as demanded by the bondholder. For example, at maturity the issuer might be bound to pay either \$1000 or 2000 DM. If the currency exchange rate is greater than 2 DM per dollar at that time, then bondholders will demand dollars; alternatively, DM will be chosen. The payoff is further complicated by the possibility that the bonds will enter default, in which case the underlying cash flow of the firm, in addition to the currency exchange rate, will be determinative of the bond's value.[12] Specifically, under the possibility of default the payoff structure will be

$$\phi(\delta_t, z_t; b, \bar{\delta}) = \min\{\max[b, b\delta_t/\bar{\delta}], z_t\},$$

where δ_t is the exchange rate between currencies at the maturity date, z_t is the firm's cash flow also at that date, b is the bonds promised payment in the base currency, and $\bar{\delta}$ is a contract-stipulated exchange rate. δ_t and z_t are random variables, b and $\bar{\delta}$ are parameters of the bond contract.

Assuming the firm's cash flow and the exchange rate at maturity are bivariate lognormal in distribution and that there is demand aggregate with composite CRRA utilities, then the (11.A.20) RNVR is applicable. Specifically,

$$v_0^\phi = \int_0^\infty \int_0^\infty \phi(\delta_t, z_t; b, \bar{\delta}) f'(\delta_t, z_t) \mathrm{d}\delta_t \mathrm{d}z_t,$$

[11] Stapleton and Subrahmanyan (1984) provide the full details of the (11.A.20) development and for the corresponding normal-CARA case in (11.A.25) below.

[12] When the bonds have new default probability, Feiger and Jacquillat (1979) show that such bonds are equivalent to a standard bond denominated only in the base currency and a call option contract on the currency exchange rate. Stulz (1982) and Stapleton and Subrahmanyan (1984) extent the analysis to the case of default, which requires the analysis of a single option on two risky variables.

with $f'(\delta_t, z_t)$ the transformed joint density as defined in (11.A.20). If all of the firm's cash flow is paid to the bondholders on default then the following intervals of integration provide a solution in terms of market parameters:

(1) $\delta_t \geq \bar{\delta}$ and $z_t \geq b\delta_t/\bar{\delta}$ $\quad\phi(\cdot) = b\delta_t/\bar{\delta}$

(2) $\delta_t \geq \bar{\delta}$ and $b \leq z_t \leq b\delta_t/\bar{\delta}$ $\quad\phi(\cdot) = z_t$

(3) $\delta_t \geq \bar{\delta}$ and $z_t \leq b$ $\quad\phi(\cdot) = z_t$

(4) $\delta_t < \bar{\delta}$ and $z_t > b$ $\quad\phi(\cdot) = b$

(5) $\delta_t < \bar{\delta}$ and $z_t < b$ $\quad\phi(\cdot) = z_t$.

To close this section, we re-emphasize that period zero and one in the above formulae may more generally represent any two periods. For example, consider a call option with exercise price e paying (only) on the basis of z_t^*, the period t aggregate consumption payoff (ignoring all $z_\tau^* \tau \neq t$). Assuming that z_t^* is lognormally distributed and individuals are CRRA, then (11.A.19) is applicable and specifically becomes

$$v_0^c(e, z_t^*) = v_0^* N(d_t^* + \tilde{\sigma}_t^*) - (e/\rho_t) N(d_t^*), \tag{11.A.21a}$$

where

$$d_t^* = [\ln(v_0^*/e) + \tilde{\rho}_t + (\tilde{\sigma}_t^*)^2/2]/\tilde{\sigma}_t^*. \tag{11.A.21b}$$

Here, v_0^* is the current price of the security paying z_t^* at t, $(\tilde{\sigma}_t^*)^2 = \text{var}[\tilde{z}_t^*]$, and $\tilde{\rho}_t$ is the logarithm of the return on the t-period pure discount (riskless) bond. We stress for later use that the call in this case is issued at date 0, with information and probabilities assessed at that time. ■

11.A.4. Valuing derivative securities: Normal returns

While the lognormal cash flow assumption provides tractable results, there are several arguments against adopting this as a single basis for a theory of asset price. First, the lognormal distribution is not a member of the class of stable distributions. As a result, portfolios of securities which are lognormally distributed are not themselves lognormally distributed – except in the special case where the variates are perfectly correlated. A theory developed using the lognormal security return assumption therefore cannot be readily applied to security portfolios and, for example, to the analysis of portfolio choice or to matters concerning the merger and partition of firms.[13] Second, when the underlying asset is not a limited liability security,

[13] It is, however, somewhat usual to acknowledge and then hold aside this problem, see Galai and Masulis (1977), and Stapleton and Subramanyan (1984).

but the right to payouts which may take on negative as well as positive values, the strictly positive lognormal distribution is an improper representation. Neither of these two limitations occur with the normal distribution, which in part explains its long history in models of capital asset valuation. But, when returns are normally distributed doesn't that also change the class of utility functions yielding RNVR?

P11.2. Derivative security valuation: risk neutrality with normal returns. Let the conditions for VR2 be satisfied. Assume further that (i) the payoff of some underlying asset and aggregate consumption follow an arbitrary bivariate normal distribution, and (ii) the conditions for aggregation of individual preferences exist. Then, the necessary and sufficient condition for risk neutral valuation of securities derived from the underlying asset is that the composite utility function exhibit constant absolute risk aversion.

A comparison of P11.1 and P11.2 shows that constant absolute risk aversion acts to produce an RNVR with normally distributed variables as constant relative risk aversion does with lognormal distribution.[14]

Proof. The distribution of z_1, given v_0, is

$$f(z_1)=\frac{1}{K}\exp\{(-1/2\sigma_1^2)(z_1-m_1)^2\}, \tag{11.A.22a}$$

which is normal, by hypothesis, with parameters $m_1 \equiv E(z_1)$, $\sigma_1^2 \equiv \mathrm{var}(z_1)$, and $K \equiv 1/\sigma_1\sqrt{2pi}$. The mean of the transformed (normal) distribution $f'(z_1)$ must again be $m'_1 \equiv E'(z_1) = v_0\rho_1$, giving

$$f'(z_1)=\frac{1}{K}\exp\{(-1/2\sigma_1^2)(z_1-\rho_1 v_0)^2\}. \tag{11.A.22b}$$

Substituting this in (11.A.5) and following solutions steps similar to those in the proof of P11.1 provides the result. □

Suppose that conditions for a RNVR occur under the normal-CARA assumption and consider again the case where the derivative security is a European call option having a payoff $\phi(z_1)=\max[(z_1-e),0]$ with e the

[14] By (11.A.5), the conditional marginal utility is the ratio of f' and f when an RNVR obtains. Some algebra and a moment's reflection on the ratio of f' to f bolsters the intuition relating lognormal returns to CRRA and normal returns to CARA.

option exercise price. In this case the call option value is

$$v_0^c(e, z_1) = \frac{1}{\rho_1} \int_{-\infty}^{\infty} \max[(z_1 - e), 0] f'(z_1) dz_1$$

$$= \frac{1}{\rho_1} \int_{e}^{\infty} (z_1 - e) \frac{1}{K} \exp\{(-1/2\sigma_1^2)(z_1 - \rho_1 v_0)^2\} dz_1. \quad (11.A.23a)$$

Using the change of variables $\hat{\xi}_1 = (z_1 - \rho_1 v_0)/\sigma_1$ gives

$$v_0^c(e, z_1) = \frac{\sigma_1}{\rho_1} \int_{\xi_1}^{\infty} (\hat{\xi}_1 / \sqrt{2pi}) \exp[\hat{\xi}_1^2/2] d\hat{\xi}_1$$

$$+ (v_0 - e/\rho_1) \int_{\xi_1}^{\infty} (1/\sqrt{2pi}) \exp[\hat{\xi}_1^2/2\} d\hat{\xi}_1, \quad (11.A.23b)$$

with the integration limit $\xi_1 = (e - \rho_1 v_0)/\sigma_1$. Integrating provides the final formula for the call option price,

$$v_0^c(e, z_1) = (v_0 - e/\rho_1) N(-\xi_1) + (\sigma_1/\rho_1) n(\xi_1). \quad (11.A.24)$$

Again, $N(\cdot)$ is the standard cumulative normal density function and we use $n(\cdot)$ to indicate the standard normal density function.[15]

As in the lognormal-CRRA case, the above results can be extended to provide a pricing formula for a derivative security whose payout is dependent on the joint cash flow of several underlying random variates. And, once more the extension mainly involves a substitution of vectors for scalars and requires attention be given to covariability. In a routine way, then, the 'multi-variate' normal-CARA formula becomes

$$v_0^\phi = \frac{1}{\rho_1} \int\int \cdots \int \frac{\phi(Z)}{\sqrt{2pi} |\Sigma| (z^1 \cdot z^2 \cdot \ldots z^N)} \exp[\cdot] dz^1 dz^2 \ldots dz^N, \quad (11.A.25)$$

with exp[·] given by

$$\exp[-\tfrac{1}{2}(\underline{Z} - \rho_1 1_N + \tfrac{1}{2}S) \overset{-1}{\Sigma} (\underline{Z} - \rho_1 1_N + \tfrac{1}{2}S)].$$

This valuation relationship corresponds to (11.A.20) in the lognormal-CRRA case.

[15] That is, $n(x) = \exp[-x^2/2]/\sqrt{2pi}$.

Again as in the lognormal case, it is straightforward to extend the normal-CARA RNVR to to evaluate call options issued at date 0 and paying (only) on an underlying security's (distant) period $t \geq 1$ outcome. Specifically, let z_t^* be the payoff of the state contingent period t aggregate consumption security, which we now assume is normally distributed. In this instance (11.A.24) becomes

$$v_0^c(e, z_t^*) = (v_0^* - e/\rho_t)N(-\xi_t^*) + (\sigma_t^*/\rho_t)n(\xi_t^*), \qquad (11.A.26)$$

where v_0^* is the current price of the security paying (only) z_t^* at date $t, \sigma_t^* =$ std(z_t^*), and $\xi_1^* = (e - \rho_t v_0^*)/\sigma_t^*$.

While normal-CARA results are analytically similar to those in the lognormal-CRRA case, they rest on a somewhat less convincing foundation. The presumptions that individual consumption, when establishing the RNVR, and z_t^*, in the above equation (11.A.26), follow normal distributions must be false, a compound error, because of the non-zero probability that is unrealistically assigned to negative consumptions. For this reason, it is not usual to pursue the normal-CARA call option on z_t^* as a basis for developing result-state prices.[16] For other purposes, however, where the RNVR call formula is not based on z_t^* as the underlying asset, the normal-CARA results have been used with less reservation as an approximation.

E11.5. Consider a corporate bond with promised payments b_1 and b_2 over two dates – the T-date analysis follows in a routine way. Following Geske (1977) suppose the corporation to be in default when, at any date, it is unable to issue new equity to cover the required payment to bondholders. Letting z_1 and z_2 be the normally distributed cash flows of the firm at dates 1 and 2, respectively, then b_2 is the first claim on z_2. In turn, b_1 represents a claim on z_1 plus the date 1 value of the date 2 equity claim, v_1^e. This equity value is

$$v_1^e = v_1^c(\max[z_2 - b_2, 0]), \qquad (11.A.27a)$$

where $v_1^c(\cdot)$ indicates the date 1 valuation function – given by (11.A.24), with appropriate substitutions, if the normal distribution and CARA utility restrictions obtain. In turn, the value of the firm's equity at date 0 can be

[16] As an exercise the reader may redo the following lognormal-CRRA development using the normal-CARA assumption and parameters. The results of that exercise can be checked, as they must give the valuation equations set out earlier in Section 10.B.4.

thought of as a call option against the sum $(z_1 + v_1^e)$:

$$v_0^e = v_0^c(\max[z_1 + v_1^e - b_1, 0]), \tag{11.A.27b}$$

where $v_0^c(\cdot)$, similarly, indicates a date 0 valuation function. The current value of the firm's bonds could be developed in a similar way.

Suppose now that, viewed from date 1, the date 2 cash flows and aggregate consumption are joint normally distributed and individuals have composite CARA elementary utilities. Then (11.A.24) obtains as a basis for the date 1 valuation function v_1^c, and v_1^e can be calculated. While v_1^e is generally a state dependent variable when viewed from date 0, it is not a normal random variate, as it is a call option written on z_2 and thus is the value of a variable with a truncated normal distribution. In short, $(z_1 + v_1^e)$ in equation (11.A.27b) is not normally distributed and there seems to be no basis for then using (11.A.24) as the function v_0^c, to determine the current equity value v_0^e.

Notice, however, that the date 1 value of the date 2 cash flow z_2, call it v_1, is normally distributed if z_2 is. In turn, v_1^e can be expressed as a function of v_1, and in (11.A.27b) we can then think of the underlying variate as v_1. If we additionally assume that elementary composite utilities are CARA and take the riskless rate of interest to be non-stochastic then the period 0 derived utility is CARA (see Section 9.B.2). A RNVR obtains at date 0 under these combined conditions and (11.A.27b) can be written as

$$v_0^e = \frac{1}{\rho_1} \int_{-\infty}^{\infty} \int_{v_1^b}^{\infty} (v_1^e + z_1 - b_1) f'(v_1, z_1) \mathrm{d}v_1 \mathrm{d}z_1, \tag{11.A.28}$$

where v_1^b is the date 1 critical value of the firm that is just sufficient to meet any current bankruptcy. The integration recognizes that v_1^e depends on z_1. $f'(\cdot)$, as usual, indicates the transformed density, now as given in (10.A.25).

Moving somewhat away from the technical details, we learn from this example that, as long as the underlying stochastic variables are joint normally (or lognormally) distributed, it is possible to use the RNVR to value derivative securities which themselves are not normally (or lognormally) distributed. ■

11.B. Multiperiod Valuation: The Lognormal-CRRA Case

The pieces are now at hand, more or less, to develop a multiperiod valuation rule. For this we have:

(1) VR1 in intertemporal (10.B.2a) and recursive (10.B.2b) forms, and
(2) call option price functions for use in (10.B.15) to calculate the aggregate consumption result-state prices appearing in VR1.

To be somewhat more specific, let $[z_1 z_2 \dots z_T]$ be the uncertain income stream of some asset j to be valued. When states at each date are continuously distributed VR1, equation (10.B.2), becomes

$$v_0 = \sum_t \int \pi_t^* E(z_t | z_t^*) \mathrm{d}z_t^*. \tag{11.B.1}$$

This valuation expression becomes empirically useful when result-state prices π_t^* can be stated in terms of market revealed data – the conditional expectation is naturally expressed in that form. Using the RNVR call option pricing formula as a basis for calculating π_t^* satisfies this purpose. Specifically, we use (10.B.15) to derive

$$\pi_t^* = \left[\frac{\partial^2 v_0^c(e, z_t^*)}{\partial e^2}\right]_{e=z_t^*},$$

where the call option price function $v_0^c(e, z_t^*)$ comes from (11.A.21) in the lognormal-CRRA case. That done, the conditional expectation $E(z_t|z_t^*)$ is calculated in a straightforward way from distribution parameters when these variables are assumed to be jointly lognormal in distribution.

11.B.1. Intertemporal analysis

Suppose that the cash flow of asset j and aggregate consumption are distributed bivariate lognormal and individuals possess (composite) elementary utilities which are constant relative risk averse. Risk neutral valuation of derivative securities based on the asset and/or aggregation consumption occurs under these conditions. In turn, equation (11.A.21) can be used with (10.B.15b) to determine π_t^*, the price of a call option which pays one dollar if and only if z_t^* occurs at t. That is,

$$\begin{aligned}\pi_t^* &= \left[\frac{\partial^2 v_0^c(e, z_t^*)}{\partial e^2}\right]_{e=z_t^*} \\ &= \left[\frac{\partial^2 [v_0^* N(d_t^* + \tilde{\sigma}_t^*) - (e/\rho_t) N(d_t^*)]}{\partial e^2}\right]_{e=z_t^*},\end{aligned} \tag{11.B.2}$$

where $d_t^* = [\ln(v_0^*/e) + \tilde{\rho}_t - (\tilde{\sigma}_t^*)^2/2]/\tilde{\sigma}_t^*)$, with other details of the notation being the same as associated with equation (11.A.21). Performing the indicated differentiation and evaluating the resulting expression at $e = z_t^*$ gives[17]

$$\pi_t^* = [1/\tilde{\rho}_t z_t^* \tilde{\sigma}_t^*] n(d_t^*), \tag{11.B.3a}$$

where

$$d_t^* = [\ln(v_0^*/z_t^*) + \tilde{\rho}_t - (\tilde{\sigma}_t^*)^2/2]/\tilde{\sigma}_t^*, \tag{11.B.3b}$$

and $n(\cdot)$ is, again, the standard normal density.

Next is $E(z_t | z_t^*)$. As z_t and z_t^* are jointly lognormal by hypothesis, then transforming from lognormal to normal variables yields[18]

$$E(z_t | z_t^*) = \exp\{\tilde{m}_t + \tilde{\sigma}_t^2/2 + \tilde{\beta}_t[\tilde{z}_t^* - \tilde{m}_t^* - \text{cov}(\tilde{z}_t, \tilde{z}_t^*)/2]\}.$$

$$= E(z_t) \exp\{\beta_t[\tilde{z}_t^* - \tilde{m}_t^* - \text{cov}(\tilde{z}_t, \tilde{z}_t^*)/2]\}. \tag{11.B.4}$$

As earlier, $\tilde{m}_t = E(\tilde{z}_t)$, $\tilde{m}_t^* = E(\tilde{z}_t^*)$, $(\tilde{\sigma}_t^*)^2 = \text{var}(\tilde{z}_t^*)$, and $\tilde{\beta}_t = \text{cov}(\tilde{z}_t, \tilde{z}_t^*)/(\tilde{\sigma}_t^*)^2$ are all parameters of the normally distributed payout distribution.

The two pieces to (11.B.1) are now in their final form. Substitute (11.B.4) and (11.B.3) in that valuation relationship, giving:

$$v_0 = \sum_t \int [(1/\rho_t z_t^* \tilde{\sigma}_t^*) n(d_t^*) \exp\{\cdot\}] dz_t^*, \tag{11.B.5}$$

with d_t^* from (11.B.3b) and the argument of $\exp\{\cdot\}$ from (11.B.4). Collecting terms, simplifying, and then integrating provides the (lognormal-CRRA) *intertemporal valuation equation,*[19]

$$v_0 = \sum_t E(z_t)/\exp[\tilde{\rho}_t + \tilde{\beta}_t(\ln(Ez_t^*) - \tilde{\rho}_t)]. \tag{11.B.6}$$

Equation (11.B.6) informs us that at each date t the payout to a security (asset) should be discounted at a rate appropriate to its particular systematic risk with date t aggregate consumption ($\tilde{\beta}_t$). Moreover, the appropriate riskless rate of interest for use in determining the discount rate is the

[17] Note that $\partial N(x)/\partial x = n(x)$ and $n(d_t^* + \sigma_t^*) = (e/v_0 \rho_t) n(d_t^*)$.

[18] Compare this with the developments leading to equation (A11.8) of the Appendix.

[19] Multiply the exponential terms and use the change of variables $\xi = \{\tilde{z}_t^* = [\tilde{\rho}_t + (\tilde{\sigma}_t^*)^2(\tilde{\beta}_t - \frac{1}{2})]\}/\tilde{\sigma}_t^*$.

rate of return on a riskless discount bond of the same maturity. These results are summarized in the following proposition.

P11.3. VR1: Risk neutrality with lognormal returns. Suppose that the conditions of P10.4 (VR1) and P11.1 (Derivative Security Valuation: Risk Neutrality with Lognormal Returns) obtain. Then the uncertain income stream $[z_1 \, z_2 \, \ldots \, z_T]$ has an (equivalent) market value given by (11.B.6).

An additional simplification to the intertemporal valuation equation occurs because of demand aggregation with composite CRRA utilities. In this case, let the marginal utility be written as $\mu_t(w_t) = (z_t^*)^{-k}$, where k is the CRRA measure and we hold aside the time preference discount factor. Using equation (11.A.1) the aggregate consumption payout at date t (only) has a current value of

$$v_0^* = E[(z_t^*)^{1-k}]/E[z_t^*)^k]\rho_t. \qquad (11.B.7)$$

If z_t^* is lognormal in distribution then so is $(z_t^*)^{\text{const.}}$, and therefore

$$\rho_t v_0^* = \frac{\exp\{(1-k)E(\tilde{z}_t^*) + (1-k)^2 \operatorname{var}(\tilde{z}_t^*)/2\}}{\exp\{kE(\tilde{z}_t^*) + k^2 \operatorname{var}(\tilde{z}_t^*)/\}}.$$

Reducing the RHS and taking logarithms gives

$$\tilde{\rho}_t = \ln(Ez_t^*) - \ln v_0^* - k \operatorname{var}(\tilde{z}_t^*).$$

which can be solved for the CARA measure as

$$k = \frac{\ln(E\underline{z}_t^*) - \tilde{\rho}_t}{\operatorname{var}(\tilde{z}_t^*)}. \qquad (11.B.8)$$

Finally, using this expression we rewrite the (lognormal-CRRA) intertemporal valuation equation as

$$v_0 = \sum_t E(z_t)/\exp[\tilde{\rho}_t + k \operatorname{cov}(\tilde{z}_t, \tilde{z}_t^*)]. \qquad (10.B.9)$$

In this form k has the interpretation of a 'price of risk'. Being an exogenous parameter given by the characteristics of the population and generally assumed to be known and fixed, the 'price of risk' is therefore a non-stochastic, intertemporal constant.

E11.6. While a relatively simple intertemporal valuation equation, (11.B.9) is still hindered in empirical usefulness by the measurement difficulties associated with the cov(·, ·) and $E(z_t)$ terms. One solution to this problem is to assume constant, non-stochastic growth rates for key parameters. Specifically, let $\bar{m}$ be the average instantaneous expected rate of return on the asset j payoff stream, $\ln(E\underline{z}_t)=\bar{m}t$; let $\bar{\sigma}_{j*}$ be the covariance rate, $\text{cov}(\tilde{z}_t, \tilde{z}_t^*)=\bar{\sigma}_{j*}t$; and, let $\tilde{\rho}_t=\bar{\rho}t$ with $\bar{\rho}$ the constant instantaneous riskless rate (implying a 'flat' term structure).[20] In this case the (10.B.9) model parameters can be estimated using the 'CAPM-like' equation

$$\bar{m}=\bar{\rho}+k\bar{\sigma}_{j*}. \tag{11.B.10}$$

■

E11.7. Rather than assuming the riskless rate to be non-stochastic, it is usual to produce that result by restricting the intertemporal dynamics of consumption (and, in turn, the state claim prices). Again, let there be demand aggregation giving CRRA composite elementary utilities. At date $(t-1)$, with z_{t-1}^* the prevailing level of aggregate consumption, then

$$U(z_{st}^*)=\frac{1}{1-k}(z_{st}^*)^{1-k}, \qquad U(z_{t-1}^*)=\frac{1}{1-k}(z_{t-1}^*)^{1-k}.$$

Using (9.A.14c) the riskless (one plus) rate from date $(t-1)$ to t is the ratio of expected marginal utilities, or

$$1/_{t-1}\rho_t=\gamma E_{t-1}[(z_t^*/z_{t-1}^*)^{-k}]. \tag{11.B.11a}$$

γ is the impatience factor. Observe that the riskless rate is in general a function of the prevailing level of aggregate consumption (state).

Suppose now that aggregate consumption follows a geometric random walk, i.e., $z_t^*=(z_{t-1}^*)\varepsilon_{t-1}$ with ε_{t-1} being noise with respect to z_{t-1}^*. Then, for all t,

$$1/_{t-1}\rho_t=\gamma E_{t-1}[(\varepsilon_{t-1})^k], \tag{11.B.11b}$$

which is independent of aggregate consumption at $(t-1)$ and therefore

[20] These assumptions are, for example, used by Black and Scholes (1973).

independent of the result-state to occur. It is, moreover, easy to extend this proof to show that default-free bonds of any maturity are non-stochastic.[21]

■

With the assumption of the geometric random walk in aggregate consumption P9.3 has shown that aggregate consumption and wealth are perfectly correlated at each date. With some scaling adjustments then, risk and the market price of risk can be written with respect to aggregate wealth in (11.B.9). Moreover, when the composite utility is logarithmic, this substitution of aggregate wealth in the pricing equations can be made without the random walk assumption, see Section 9.B.1.

11.B.2. Recursive analysis

We begin again with VR1, but now in the (10.B.2b) recursive form. On the date $(T-1)$ markets, the value of the payoff z_T (and nothing thereafter) is

$$v_{T-1} = \int \pi_T^* E_{T-1}(z_T \mid z_T^*) \mathrm{d}z_T^*. \tag{11.B.12}$$

Assuming individuals are CARA and z_T and z_T^* are bivariate lognormal produces, as expected,

$$v_{T-1} = E_{T-1}(z_T)/\exp[{}_{T-1}\tilde{\rho}_T + \tilde{\beta}_T(\ln(E_{T-1}z_T^*) - {}_{T-1}\rho_T)], \tag{11.B.13}$$

where $\tilde{\beta}_T = \mathrm{cov}_{T-1}(\tilde{z}_T, \tilde{z}_1^*)/\mathrm{var}_{T-1}(\tilde{z}_T^*)$ and ${}_{T-1}\tilde{\rho}_T$ is the one-period (one plus) riskless rate. With CARA composite utilities then (11.B.8) again holds, and

$$v_{T-1} = E_{T-1}(z_T)/\exp[{}_{T-1}\tilde{\rho}_T + k\,\mathrm{cov}_{T-1}(\tilde{z}_T, \tilde{z}_T^*)], \tag{11.B.14}$$

where k is the constant, market-wide price of risk. Further assuming that aggregate consumption follows a geometric walk, the (one-period) riskless rate ${}_{T-1}\rho_t$ is non-stochastic. In turn, v_{T-1} has the same lognormal distribution as the expectation $E_{T-1}(z_T)$.[22]

[21] Also using the CRRA assumption, Rubinstein (1977) has shown that geometric random walks arise in aggregate consumption with endogeneous production if real technologies have identically distributed (over time) constant returns to scale payoffs. The homotheticity of CRRA and the constancy of the technology provide that a constant proportion of aggregate output is reinvested at each date. See also Prescott and Mehra (1978) for an extension of this result to the infinite horizon, continuous time case.

[22] Again, the conditional covariance is non-stochastic since $\tilde{z}_T$ *and* $\tilde{z}_T^*$ are normal bivariates – see Feller (1966, p. 69).

Moving back one trading period, we would then expect to use the price recursion

$$v_{T-2} \overset{?}{=} E(r_{T-1})/\exp[{}_{T-2}\tilde{\rho}_{T-1} + k\,\mathrm{cov}(\tilde{r}_{T-1}, \tilde{z}^*_{T-1})], \tag{11.B.15}$$

where $r_{T-1} = z_{T-1} + v_{T-1}$ and $\tilde{r}_{T-1} = \ln(z_{T-1} + v_{T-1})$. From our earlier developments it is known that one of the prerequisites for the equality to hold in (11.B.15) is that r_{T-1} and z^*_{T-1} be bivariate lognormal. In contrast, the fundamental assumption that has been used to this point is that payouts z^*_{T-1} and z_{T-1} are lognormal. While it has also been shown that v_{T-1} is lognormal (with k and the riskless rate non-stochastic) that unfortunately is not enough. The problem is that the lognormal distribution is not stable, making even this list of assumptions insufficient to validate (11.B.15) and provide a recursive sequence for prices. This difficulty, of course, occurs for all dates $(t-1)$ and t (expect $t = T$).

There are two solutions to the lognormal-CRRA price recursion 'problem.' First, (11.B.15) may be viewed as an approximate result at any date.[23] Alternatively, we may amend our fundamental assumption and instead assume that the yield r_t and z^*_t (or the one period returns $\underline{r}_t$ and $\underline{z}^*_t$) are bivariate lognormal. This second fact clearly works and (11.B.15) holds as an equality; in turn the price recursion obtains for all dates $(t-1)$ and t. This recursion result, however, comes at the expense of some sacrifice in our original intent to derive price dynamics from the (exogenously given) underlying payouts.

[23]See, however, Aitchison and Brown (1963) for estimates of the approximation errors, which may be relatively large with just two variates.

Chapter 11 – Appendix

LOGNORMAL AND NORMAL DISTRIBUTIONS

If $\ln a$ and $\ln b$ are bivariate normal variates, then $a = \exp[\ln a]$ and $b = \exp[\ln b]$ are bivariate lognormal in distribution. Since $\ln a$ and $\ln b$ are normally distributed and since $d(\ln a) = da/a$ and $d/(\ln b) = db/b$, then the bivariate normal density function of a and b is $f(a, b) = f(\ln a, \ln b)/ab$, where $f(\ln a, \ln b)$ is the bivariate normal density function. In turn, the marginal lognormal density function, simply termed the lognormal density, is $F(a) = f(\ln a)/a$, where by definition

$$f(w) = \frac{1}{K}\exp\left\{\frac{-1}{2\,\mathrm{var}(w)}[w - E(w)]^2\right\},$$

with $K = \sigma(w)\sqrt{2pi}$. $E(\cdot)$ and $\mathrm{var}(\cdot)$, respectively, indicate the usual mean and variance parameters.

Now consider two rate of return variables $\underline{a} = a/v_a$ and $\underline{b} = b/v_b$. Suppose that these are distributed bivariate lognormally and that estimates of that distribution's parameters and the associated (marignal) lognormal densities of $\underline{a}$ and v_0 have been established. Letting $F(\underline{a})$ be the density function for $\underline{a}$ we have

$$F(\underline{a}) = \frac{1}{\underline{a}K}\exp\left\{\frac{-1}{2\,\mathrm{var}(\ln \underline{a})}[\ln \underline{a} - E(\ln a)]^2\right\}. \tag{A11.1}$$

The lognormal distribution of $\underline{b}$ is written similarly with parameters $E(\ln \underline{b})$ and $\mathrm{var}(\ln \underline{b})$. When prices are observed with certainty, it is relatively easy to shift attention to the (conditional) distribution of a and b directly, which can be written as

$$F(a|v_a) = \frac{1}{aK}\exp\left\{\frac{-1}{2\,\mathrm{var}(\ln \underline{a})}[\ln \underline{a} - E(\ln a)]^2\right\}, \tag{A11.2}$$

which is also lognormal. There is a similar expression for $F(b|v_b)$.

With v_0 a known constant the relationship between means and variances of lognormal variables are related to the means and variances of corresponding normal variables by

$$E(\underline{a}) = \exp\{E(\ln \underline{a}) + \mathrm{var}(\ln \underline{a})/2\}, \tag{A11.3a}$$

$$\mathrm{var}(\underline{a}) = E(\underline{a})^2 [\exp\{\mathrm{var}(\ln \underline{a})\} - 1]. \tag{A11.3b}$$

Some rearrangement of these gives the following useful expressions

$$E(\ln a) = \ln E(a) - \mathrm{var}(\ln a)/2, \tag{A11.4a}$$

$$\mathrm{var}(\ln \underline{a}) = \ln\left[\frac{\mathrm{var}(\underline{a}) + E(\underline{a})^2}{E(\underline{a})^2}\right]. \tag{A11.4b}$$

In addition, when the market prices v_a and v_b are certain the following relationships between $a, \underline{a}, b$, and $\underline{b}$ are easily shown:

$$E(a) = v_a E(\underline{a}), \tag{A11.5a}$$

$$\mathrm{var}(a) = v_a^2\, \mathrm{var}(\underline{a}), \tag{A11.5b}$$

$$\mathrm{cov}(a, b) = v_a v_b\, \mathrm{cov}(\underline{a}, b). \tag{A11.5c}$$

$$E(\ln a) = E(\ln \underline{a}) + \ln v_a, \tag{A11.5d}$$

$$\mathrm{var}(\ln a) = \mathrm{var}(\ln \underline{a}), \tag{A11.5d}$$

$$\mathrm{cov}(\ln a,\ \ln b) = \mathrm{cov}(\ln \underline{a}, \ln \underline{b}). \tag{A11.5e}$$

From the properties of conditional expectation for jointly normal variables we have

$$E(\ln a|\ln b) = E(\ln a) + \frac{\mathrm{cov}(\ln a, \ln b)}{\mathrm{var}(\ln b)} [\ln b - E(\ln b)], \tag{A11.6a}$$

and

$$\mathrm{var}(\ln a|\ln b) = \mathrm{var}(\ln a) - \frac{\mathrm{cov}(\ln a, \ln b)}{\mathrm{var}(\ln b)} \mathrm{cov}(\ln a,\ \ln b). \tag{A11.6b}$$

In turn, the conditional expectation of the lognormal variables can be written, following (A11.3a), as

$$E(\mathrm{a}|b)=\exp\{E(\ln a|\ln b)+\mathrm{var}(\ln a|\ln b)/2\}. \tag{A11.7}$$

Substituting in the RHS from (A11.6), this becomes

$$E(a|b)=\exp\left\{\mathrm{E}(\ln a)+\mathrm{var}(\ln a)/2+\beta\left[\ln \mathrm{b}-\mathrm{E}(\ln b)-\frac{\mathrm{cov}(\ln a,\ \ln b)}{2}\right]\right\}, \tag{A11.8}$$

where $\beta=\mathrm{cov}(\ln a,\ \ln b)/\mathrm{var}(\ln b)$.

Mathematical Appendix

MATHEMATICAL PRELIMINARIES

Many ideas in mathematics are of considerable use in economic analysis. The topics of special concern here are those relating to sets, functions, convex sets and functions, vector spaces, linear algebra, and optimization. The material presented below under each of these topics is synoptic and not intended to be either unduly formal or complete. Rather, the intent is (1) to inform the reader of those concepts and analytic procedures which should be mastered, and (2) to provide a uniform notation and terminology. Because of these limited objectives, most results are presented without proof and the task of constructing proofs, or finding them in some standard mathematical economics text, is left to the reader.

Throughout this discussion the following symbols are used:

iff reads 'if and only if',

$\forall i$ reads 'for all $i = 1, 2, \ldots$',

$\equiv]x$ reads 'there exists an x such that',

w.r.t. reads 'with respect to', and,

s.t. reads 'subject to'.

A.1. Sets

DA.1. A *set* is a collection of elements upon which certain operations, to be described below, can be performed.

Remark. To indicate that element x belongs to the set X we write $x \varepsilon X$ and say 'x is in X.' Conversely, if x is not contained in x, it is written that $x \notin X$. A set may be described either by listing its elements

$$X = \{1, 2, 3, \ldots\},$$

or according to its properties

$$X = \{\text{all } x \text{ such that } x \text{ has property } P\}, \quad \text{or}$$

$$X = \{x | x \text{ has property } P\}.$$

DA.2. Given any set X whose elements also are contained in another, possibly identical, set Y, it is said that X is a *subset* of Y written $X \leqslant Y$. If $X \leqslant Y$ but $X \neq Y$, then X is a *proper subset* of Y and this is written more concisely as $X < Y$.

DA.3. The *union* of two sets X and Y is defined as the set of elements that are in either X and/or Y and written $X \vee Y$. The *intersection* of two sets X and Y is defined as the set of elements that are in both X and Y and written $X \wedge Y$. If $X \wedge V$ is empty then X and Y are said to be *disjoint* sets.

Example. Let $X = \{1, 3\}$ and $Y = \{1, 2, 3, 5\}$. Then $X \leqslant Y$ and, more precisely, $X < Y$. It is easy to see that

$$X \vee Y = \{1, 2, 3, 5\},$$

$$X \wedge Y = \{1, 3\}.$$

Since $X \wedge Y$ is not empty, the two sets are not disjoint.

DA.4. Let $X = \{x_1, x_2, \ldots, x_N\}$ and $Y = \{y_1, y_2, \ldots, y_N]$ be two sets with equal numbers or elements. The *sum* of these sets, $X + Y$, is defined to be the set with respective elements summed: $X + Y = \{x_1 + y_1, x_2 + y_2, \ldots, x_N + y_N\}$.

DA.5. Let X and Y be two sets as given in DA.4. The *cartesian product* of X and Y, written $X \circ Y$ is the set of all ordered *pairs* $(x_n, y_m)m, n = 1, 2, \ldots, N$.

Remark. It is important to regard each element of $X \circ Y$ not as two objects, but as a single pair. The elements of the pair are ordered in the sense that the first is from the first set and the second from the second set.

Example. Let $X = \{3, 7\}$ be a set of period one outputs and $Y = \{5, 10\}$ be a set of period two outputs for an economy. Then the *cartesian product*

$$X \circ Y = \{(3, 5)(3, 10)(7, 5)(7, 10)\},$$

is a representation of all possible output sequences over the two periods.

DA.6. The extended set of real numbers is called the *real line* and denoted R^1.

DA.7. Fix a positive integer N and let R^N denote the cartesian product of the extended set of numbers with itself $(N-1)$ times. This is the extended N-space. Frequently used subsets of R^N are the non-positive orthant

$$R^N = \{x \in R^N \,|\, x \leq 0\},$$

the non-negative orthant,

$$R^N_+ = \{x \in R^N \,|\, x \geq 0\},$$

and the strictly positive orthant $R^N_{++} = \{x \in R^N \,|\, x > 0\}$.

DA.8. A space R^N is said to have a *metric* if for every two points $x, y \in R^N$ there exists a non-negative real number $m(x, y)$ such that

(1) $m(x, y) = 0$ if and only if $x = y$,

(2) $m(x, y) = m(y, x)$,

and if for every three points $x, y, z \in R^N$ the triangle inequality holds,

(3) $m(x, y) + m(y, z) \geq m(x, z)$.

The space with a metric defined is called a *metric space*. Use the symbol E to denote a metric space.

Example. (1) Let $E = R^1$. For any two points $x, y \in R^1$, define $m(x, y) = |x - y|$. First note that $m(x, y)$ satisfies conditions (1) and (2). The third condition follows from the computation

$$\begin{aligned} m(x, z) &= |x - z| = |(x - y) + (y - z)| \\ &\leq | - y| + |y - z| = m(x, y) + m(y, z), \end{aligned}$$

for any x, y, $z \in R^1$. Thus, m is a metric and we call the number $m(x, y)$ the *distance* between x and y.

(2) Let $E = R^N$. Define, for any two points $x = (x_1, \ldots, x_N)$ and $y = (y_1, \ldots, y_N)$ in R^N,

$$m(x, y) = [(x_1 - y_1)^2 + (x_2 - y_2)^2 + \ldots + (x_N - y_N)^2]^{1/2}.$$

It can be simply shown that m is a metric. The number $m(x, y)$ for $x, y \in R^N$ is called the *Euclidean distance* between x and y.

DA.9. Given a metric, a *neighborhood* of a point $x \in E$ is the set of all points y such that $m(x, y) < \delta$ where δ is a 'small', real, positive number.

DA.10. A set $X \lessdot E$ is said to be *open* if every $x \in X$ has some neighborhood (with δ sufficiently small) which lies in set X.

Example. The set $X = \{x \mid 0 < x < 1\}$ is an open set. For any point $x_0 \in X$ with $x_0 \leq 0.5$, a neighborhood can be defined for $\delta = x_0/2$ as the set of all points x such that $m(x, x_0) = |x - x_0| < x_0/2$, which is contained in X. Similarly for any point $x_0 \in X$ and $x_0 > 0.5$, the neighborhood defined for $\delta = (1 - x_0)/2$ lies in X. Therefore, every $x_0 \in X$ has a neighborhood contained in X, which proves X is an open set. The obvious association exists between strict inequalities and open sets.

Remark. The union of any number of open subsets of E is open. This clearly follows from the definitions of a union and open sets. Also, the intersection of a finite number of open sets $X_i \lessdot E$, $i = 1, 2, \ldots, N$, is open: Let $x \in X_1 \wedge \ldots \wedge X_N$. Since each X_i is open, x has a neighborhood lying about each X_i. The smallest of these neighborhoods lies in every X_i and therefore in the intersection.

Example. Since the two sets $X_1 = \{x \mid 0 < x < 2\}$ and $X_2 = \{x \mid 1 < x < 3\}$ are both open, $X_1 \vee X_2$ must be open

$$X_1 \vee X_2 = \{x \mid 0 < x < 3\}.$$

Likewise, the intersection, $X_1 \wedge X_2$, is open;

$$X_1 \wedge X_2 = \{x \mid 1 < x < 2\}.$$

DA.11. A point $x \in X$ is a *limit point* of the set $X \lessdot E$ if every neighborhood of x contains some points of X other than x. In the set $X = \{x \mid 0 < x < 1\}$ every point is a limit point, and the excluded points 0 and 1 are also limit points of X.

DA.12. If a set includes all its limit points it is said to be *closed*.

Example. The set $X = \{x \mid 0 \leq x \leq 1\}$ is closed. Also, given a point $x_0 \in R^N$, a real number r, and the metric m defined as the Euclidean distance, the set $X = \{x \in R^N \mid m(x, x_0) \leq r\}$ is closed. Notice the association between weak inequalities and closed sets.

Remark. The intersection of any number of closed subsets of E and the union of a finite number of such sets are closed.

DA.13. A set defined in a metric space is said to be *bounded* if the value taken on by the metric between any pair of points in the set is not greater than some finite number.

DA.14. A set is *compact* if it is both closed and bounded.

Example. Let $x=[x_1\, x_2 \ldots x_N]$ denote an individual's choice of a commodity bundle for consumption. The set of all physically feasible x, denoted by X, is called the consumption set. The set X is always assumed closed for anlaytical convenience. Since there is a lower survival limit to each x_i, X is bounded from below. If the assumption of upper boundedness is added, then the set X is compact.

$$X=\{x\in R^N \mid a_n \leq x_n \leq b_n;\ a_n, b_n \text{ finite};\ n=1,\ldots,N\}.$$

DA.15. A *correspondence* is a rule which assigns to each element of a set X, a nonempty subset of a set Y. A correspondence is said to be single-valued, or a *function* (denoted $f\colon X\to Y$)if each assigned subset of Y had exactly one element. If each element of Y assigned by f is real, then f is further said to be a real-valued function. The *domain* of f is X and we say f is defined on X; the *range* of f is the union of all points of $f(x)$ for all $x\in X$.

Example. $h\colon R^1\to R^1$ given by $h(x)=\{y \mid x^2\leq y\leq x^2+1\}$ for all $x\in R^1$ is a correspondence. $f\colon R^1\to R^1$ with $f(x)=x^2$ for all $x\in R^1$ a function.

A.2. Matrices, vectors and vector spaces

DA.16. An element of R^N is an ordered number collection termed a *vector* and denoted $x=[x_1\, x_2 \ldots x_N]$.

Remark. It is often convenient to think of an N-component vector as a point in N-dimensional space, that is, the geometrical interpretation of a vector is a point. The terms point and vector are thus used interchangeably.

DA.17. If $x, y\in R^N$, then the *line* through x and y is the set of points

$$\{z \mid z=\lambda x+(1-\lambda)y,\ \lambda \text{ real}\}.$$

Additionally, the *closed line segment* joining x and y requires $0 \leq \lambda \leq 1$, and the *open line segment* joining x and y requires $0 < \lambda < 1$ for the line segment to be open at both 'ends'.

DA.18. If $x = [x_1\ x_2 \ldots x_N]$ and $y = [y_1\ y_2 \ldots y_N]$ are two vectors in R^N, the *scalar or inner* product of x and y, denoted by $\langle x, y \rangle$ is defined as

$$\langle x, y \rangle = \sum_n x_n y_n.$$

Example. Let $x = [0.1\ 0.2\ 0.3\ 0.4]$ be a set of probabilities and $y = [2\ 3\ 5\ 7]$ the associated outcomes. Then the inner product

$$\langle x, y \rangle = (0.1)2 + (0.2)3 + (0.3)5 + (0.4)7 = 5.1,$$

is the expected value of the outcome.

DA.19. The set of N, N-component vectors given by

$$e^1 = [1\ 0 \ldots 0],\ e^2 = [0\ 1\ 0 \ldots 0], \ldots,\ e^N = [0\ 0 \ldots 1],$$

is termed a *coordinate system* for R^N and each vector is called a *unit vector.*

DA.20. Two vectors $x, y \in R^N$ are said to be *orthogonal* if $\langle x, y \rangle = 0$.

Remark. If for $x, y \in R^N$ it is the case that $x, y \neq 0$ and $\langle x, y \rangle = 0$, then the *angle between* x and y is 90°.

Example. Since $\langle e^n, e^m \rangle = 0$ for all $n, m = 1, \ldots, N$, $n \neq m$, the N unit vectors form an orthogonal coordinate system with an angle of 90° between any pair of the vectors.

DA.21. If y is any fixed non-zero vector in R^N and b is a constant, then the set of vectors x

$$\{x \mid \langle y, x \rangle = b\},$$

is called an $(N-1)$-*dimensional hyperplane* in R^N.

DA.22. Let the notation in the above definition hold. Then a (closed) *half space* in R^n is defined as $\{x \mid \langle y, x \rangle \leq b\}$.

DA.23. Consider J-vectors $\{x^1, x^2, \ldots, x^J] \in R^N$. These vectors are said to be *linearly dependent* if and only if there exist real numbers

$$a_1, a_2, \ldots, a_J, \text{ not all zero, such that}$$

$$a_1 x^1 + a_2 x^2 + \ldots + a_J x^J = 0.$$

Remark. If in the above definition the scalars a_j, not all zero, do not exist, then the vectors $\{x^1, x^2, \ldots, x^J\}$ are said to be *linearly independent*. If a finite set of two or more vectors is linearly dependent, then at least one of them can be written as a linear combination of the others.

Example. (1) Let $x^1 = [1\ 1\ 1]$, $x^2 = [0\ 1\ 0]$, and $x^3 = [1\ 0\ 1]$. Then the set of vectors $\{x^1, x^2, x^3\}$ are linearly dependent since

$$a_1 x^1 + a_2 x^2 + a_3 x^3 = 0,$$

when $a_1 = -a_2 = -a_3$. That is, $x^1 - x^2 + x^3$.

(2) Let $x^1 = [1\ 1\ 1]$, $x^2 = [1\ 1\ 0]$, and $x^3 = [2\ 0\ 1]$. If

$$a_1 x^1 + a_2 x^2 + a_3 x^3 = 0,$$

then $a^1 = a^2 = a^3 = 0$ necessarily. Hence, the three vectors are linearly independent.

Remark. If a set of J vectors is linearly independent then any subset of them is also linearly independent. For example, any number of nonequal unit vectors are linearly independent.

DA.24. A set of J vectors $\{x^1, x^2, \ldots, x^J\} \in R^N (J \geq N)$ is said to *span* R^N if every vector in R^N can be written as a linear combination of

$$\{x^1, x^2, \ldots, x^J\}.$$

DA.25. A *basis* for R^N is a linearly independent subset of vectors from R^N which spans the space.

Remark. Every basis for R^N contains precisely N vectors so that any set of N linearly independent vectors from R^N is a basis for R^N. Any $N+1$ or more vectors from R^N are linearly dependent.

Remark. The N unit vectors are a basis for R^N. Any set of basis vectors defines a coordinate system, not necessarily orthogonal, for R^N. The representation of any vector in terms of a set of basis vectors is therefore unique.

Remark. An important operation is that of changing a basis by replacing a single vector in the basis to yield a new basis. Given a set of basis vectors $\{x^1, x^2, \ldots, x^N\}$ for R^N and any other vector $y \neq 0$, consider $y = \Sigma_1^N a_n x^n$. If any vector x_n for which $a_n \neq 0$ is removed from the set of basis vectors and is replaced with y, the new collection of N vectors is also a basis for R^N.

Example. Take the unit vectors $e^1 = [1\ 0\ 0]$, $e^2 = [0\ 1\ 0]$, and $e^3 = [0\ 0\ 1]$ which forms a basis for R^3. Then the vector

$$y = 1(e^1) + 2(e^2) + 0(e^3) = [1\ 2\ 0],$$

can replace either e^1 or e^2 to form a new basis: the sets of vectors $\{y, e^2, e^3\}$ and $\{e^1, y, e^3\}$ each form a basis for R^3.

DA.26. The *dimension* of a vector space, written $\dim(R^N)$, is the maximum number of linearly independent vectors in the space.

DA.27. A *matrix* is a rectangular array of numbers arranged in rows and columns, for example, as

$$X = \begin{bmatrix} x_{11} & x_{12} & \cdots & x_{1N} \\ x_{21} & x_{22} & \cdots & x_{2N} \\ \vdots & & & \\ x_{M1} & x_{M2} & \cdots & x_{MN} \end{bmatrix}.$$

Remark. The above array is called an $M \times N$ matrix, and said to be of order $M \times N$ since it has M rows and N columns. Any matrix with the same number of rows as columns is called a square matrix. In turn, a square matrix with N rows and N columns is said to be of Nth-order.

Remark. A matrix of order $1 \times N$, containing only a single row of elements, is called a row vector. A matrix of order $M \times 1$ is called a column vector.

Remark. Two matrices X and Y are equal iff $x_{mn} = y_{mn}\ \forall m, n$; that is, the matrices are equal element by element.

DA.28. If X and Y are matrices of the same order then the *matrix sum*

$X+Y$ is defined to be a new matrix W such that, for all m and n,

$$w_{mn}=x_{mn}+y_{mn},$$

that is, corresponding elements are added to obtain $W=X+Y$.

DA.29. If λ is a scalar, then define *scalar multiplication* of a matrix such that

$$\lambda X=[\lambda x_{mn}],$$

that is, each element of X is multiplied by λ.

DA.30. If X is of order $M\times N$ and Y is of order $N\times K$, then the *product* XY is defined to be a matrix W of order $M\times K$ whose mkth element is

$$w_{mk}=\sum_n x_{mn}\,y_{nk}.$$

The mkth element in the product matrix is found by multiplying the elements of the mth row of the first matrix by the corresponding elements of the nth column of the second matrix and summing over all terms.

Remark. For matrix multiplication to be possible, the number of elements in a row of the first matrix must equal the number of elements in a column of the second matrix. The matrices are then said to be conformable with respect to multiplication.

Remark. It is important to note the order of the matrices in multiplication. In the product XY it is said that X is postmultiplied by Y, or that Y is premultiplied by X. XY is usually not equal to YX and may not even be conformable. Both products are conformable (i.e., exist) only if the matrices are of order $M\times N$ and $N\times M$. In this case XY is of order M and YX is of order N.

DA.31. The *rank* of a matrix X, written $\text{rank}(X)$, is the number of linearly independent columns in X.

Example. Let

$$X=\begin{bmatrix}2&1&1\\1&1&0\\3&1&2\end{bmatrix}.$$

Since the first column can be obtained by the sum of the last two columns, the three columns are linearly dependent. However, any pair of the columns are linearly independent. Thus, the rank of X is 2.

Remark. Let X be a $M \times N$ matrix. Since the columns of X can be viewed as vectors in R^M, the number of linearly independent columns in X, i.e., the rank of X, cannot exceed the dimension of R^M.

DA.32. A matrix X is said to have an *inverse* if there exists a matrix A such that $XA = AX = I$ where I is the identity matrix. It follows from this requirement that only square matrices have inverses.

Example. Consider the two matrices

$$X = \begin{bmatrix} 2 & -3 \\ 5 & -2 \end{bmatrix}, \qquad A = \begin{bmatrix} -2/11 & -3/11 \\ 5/11 & 2/11 \end{bmatrix}.$$

Since

$$XA = \begin{bmatrix} 2 & 3 & -2/11 & -3/11 \\ -5 & -2 & 5/11 & 2/11 \end{bmatrix}$$

$$= \begin{bmatrix} (-4/11 + 15/11) & (-6/11 + 6/11) \\ (10/11 - 10/11) & (15/11 - 4/11) \end{bmatrix}$$

$$= \begin{bmatrix} 1 & 0 \\ 0 & 1 \end{bmatrix} = I,$$

or

$$AX = \begin{bmatrix} -2/11 & -3/11 & -2 & -3 \\ 5/11 & 2/11 & -5 & -2 \end{bmatrix}$$

$$= \begin{bmatrix} (-4/11 + 15/11 & (-6/11 + 6/11) \\ (10/11 - 10/11) & (15/11 - 4/11) \end{bmatrix}$$

$$= \begin{bmatrix} 1 & 0 \\ 0 & 1 \end{bmatrix} = I,$$

each matrix is the inverse of the other.

Remark. An Nth order matrix X will have an inverse if and only if $\text{rank}(X) = N$. If rank $(X) = N$, X is called *non-singular;* otherwise when $\text{rank}(X) < N$, X is called *singular.*

A.3. Convex sets and functions

DA.33. A non-empty set $X < R^N$ is said to be *convex* if for any two points $x_1, x_2 \in X$ the line segment joining x_1 and x_2 is contained in X, i.e., if

$$[\lambda x_1 + (1-\lambda)x_2] \in X \quad \text{for all } \lambda \quad \text{when} \quad 0 \leq \lambda \leq 1.$$

Remark. If X and Y are convex sets then the set $Z = A \wedge Y$ is convex – the intersection of convex sets is convex.

Remark. If X and Y are convex sets, then their linear combination, $Z = \alpha X + \beta Y$ (α, β real numbers), is also a convex set.

DA.34. *A convex combination* of points $x^1, x^2, \ldots, x^K \in R^N$ is a point $x \in R^N$ satisfying

$$x = \sum_k^K a_k x^k,$$

where the $a_k \geq 0$ for $k = 1, 2, \ldots, K$ are real numbers and

$$\sum_k^K a_k = 1.$$

DA.35. An *extreme point* of a convex set is an element of the set which cannot be expressed as a convex combination of two other points in the set.

Example. The extreme points of a triangle (a convex set in R^2) are its vertices.

Remark. A set is *strictly convex* iff it is convex and all of its boundary points are extreme points. An example is the closed sphere in R^3. A convex set need not, however, have any extreme points; for example, consider any open convex set.

DA.36. A function $f: X \to R^1$ with X a convex subset of R^N is said to be a *convex function* if for any two points $x_1, x_2 \in X$ and any real number λ, $0 \leq \lambda \leq 1$,

$$f(\lambda x_1 + (1-\lambda)x_2) \leq \lambda f(x_1) + (1-\lambda) f(x_2).$$

If the strict inequality hold for all $x_1 \neq x_2$ and for all $0 < \lambda < 1$, then f is said to be *strictly convex.*

Remark. If $f(x)$ is convex then the line segment drawn between any two points on the graph of the function never lies 'below' the graph.

DA.37. A function $f: X \to R^1$, with X a convex set in R^N, is said to be *concave* (*strictly concave*) if $-f$ is convex (strictly convex).

Remark. If $f(x)$ is concave then the line segment drawn between any two points on the graph of the function never lies 'above' the graph.

Remark. Note that a linear function is both concave and convex, but neither strictly concave nor strictly convex.

Example. Let $X = \{x | 0 \leq x \leq 1\}$ and define a function $f: X \to R^1$ as $f(x) = x^2$. We want to show that f is convex in X. This is equivalent to showing that the inequality $f(\lambda x_1 + (1-\lambda)x_2) \leq \lambda f(x_1) + (1-\lambda) f(x_2)$ holds for all $0 \leq \lambda \leq 1$ and $x_1\, x_2 \in X$. In particular, it is necessary to show that $[\lambda x_1 + (1-\lambda)x_2]^2 \leq \lambda x_1^2 + (1-\lambda)x_2^2$ for all $0 < \lambda < 1$, since the equality obviously holds for $\lambda = 0, 1$. Square the left side and transpose terms

$$\lambda 2 x_1^2 - \lambda x_1^2 + (1-\lambda)^2 x_2^2 - (1-\lambda)x_2^2 + 2\lambda(1-\lambda)x_1 x_2 \leq 0,$$

which may be rewritten as

$$-\lambda(1-\lambda)x_1^2 - \lambda(1-\lambda)x_2^2 + 2\lambda(1-\lambda)x_1 x_2 \leq 0.$$

Multiply by $-1/[\lambda(1-\lambda)] < 0$ to get $x_1 + x_2^2 - 2x_1 x_2 \geq 0$ or $(x_1 - x_2)^2 \geq 0$. Consequently, f is convex and, since the last inequality is strict when $x_1 \neq x_2$, f is strictly convex.

Remark. The preceding example illustrates that it may be a matter of considerable difficulty to determine from the definition of convexity or concavity whether or not a particular function is or is not convex or concave. The following theorems provide help in that identification problem.

Remark. Let X be a convex set in R^N. If $f: X \to R^1$ then f is a continuous function on X.

Remark. Let a function f be defined and possess at least two derivatives on the closed interval $X=[x_1, x_2]$. If $d^2 f(x)/dx^2 \geq 0 \; \forall x \in X$, then the function f is convex on X. If $d^2 f(x)/dx^2 > 0 \; \forall x \in X$, then the function f is strictly convex on X.

Remark. Let $f: X \to R^1$ and $g: X \to R^1$ be convex functions defined on X then $f(x)+g(x)$, $\max[f(x), g(x)]$, and $\lambda f(x)$, for $\lambda \geq 0$, are all convex. It follows that the non-negative weighted sum of convex functions is convex.

DA.38. A function $f: X \to R^1$ with X a convex set of R^N, is said to be (strictly) *quasi-concave* if for every real number b the 'greater than or equal to' set

$$\{x \mid f(x) \geq b\}$$

is (strictly) convex.

Remark. An equivalent definition of quasi-concavity is commonly used. The function $f: X \to R^1$ is quasi-concave if given $x_1, x_2 \in R^N$, for any $0 \leq \lambda \leq 1$

$$f(\lambda x_1 + (1-\lambda) x_2] \geq \min[f(x_1), f(x_2)],$$

with the strict inequality holding for strict quasi-concavity.

Remark. If the function f is (strictly) concave, then it is also (strictly) quasi-concave. The converse, however, need not be true.

Remark. The above results imply that if the function g is (strictly) convex, then the 'lesser than or equal to' set

$$\{x \mid g(x) \leq b\},$$

is (strictly) convex.

A.4. Optimization

Remark. Let $f(x)$ be a real-valued function defined on $X < R^N$. If $f(x)$ is differentiable and concave then

$$f(x) \leq f(x^0) + \sum_n (x_n - x_n^0) \partial f(x^0)/\partial x_n,$$

for all $x, x_0 \in X$ where $\partial f(x^0)/\partial x_n$ are the first derivatives of f by x_n evaluated at the point x_0. The proof?

Use the definition of concavity to write

$$\lambda f(x) + (1-\lambda) f(x_0) \leq f(\lambda x + (1-\lambda) x_0),$$

where x is an arbitrary positive number. Since $\lambda > 0$ this inequality implies $f(x) \leq f(x_0) + [f(x_0 + (x - x_0)\lambda) - f(x_0)]/\lambda$ which must hold for all λ and therefore also in the limit as $\lambda > 0$ goes to zero.

DA.39. The vector $\mathring{x}$ is said to be a *maximum* of $f(x)$ in X, or $\mathring{x}$ is said to be the *constrained maximum* of $f(x)$ subject to the condition that

$$x \in X, \text{ if } \mathring{x} \in X \text{ and } f(\mathring{x}) \geq f(x) \quad \forall x \in X.$$

DA.40. Let $f(x)$ be a differentiable function on R^N. Necessary conditions for $f(x)$ to have a maximum at $\mathring{x}$ is that $\partial f(\mathring{x})/\partial x_n = 0$. These *stationarity* conditions are sufficient if $f(x)$ is concave.

Remark. Let X be the set of vectors x satisfying the constraints $g_m(x) = 0$ for $m = 1, 2, \ldots, M$. If $\mathring{x}$ is a maximum of $f(x)$ in X and if the Jacobian matrix $\mathring{J} = [\partial g_m(\mathring{x})/\partial x_n]$ has rank M, then there exists an M-vector of numbers $\lambda = [\mathring{\lambda}_1 \mathring{\lambda}_2 \ldots \mathring{\lambda}_M]$ such that

$$\partial f(\mathring{x})/\partial x_n + \sum_m \mathring{\lambda}_m \partial_{gm}(\mathring{x})/\partial x_n = 0 \quad \forall n.$$

The numbers $\lambda_m \, \forall m$ are termed *Lagrange multipliers.*

Remark. To determine the constrained maximum of a function f(x) we may write the necessary conditions of the above theorem and also

$$g_m(\mathring{x}) = 0 \quad \forall m.$$

These equations are equal in number to the elements of $\mathring{x}$ and $\mathring{\lambda}$. The solutions for $\mathring{x}$ and $\mathring{y}$ may include maxima, minima, or mixed maxima and minima ('saddle points'). More restrictive conditions are required for the exact determination of maxima or minima.

DA.41. The following two statements are equivalent:

(i) $\mathring{x}$ maximizes $f(x)$ over the set X defined by $g_m(x) = 0 \, \forall m$,

and

(ii) $\mathring{x}$ maximizes the Lagrange function

$$L(x, \mathring{\lambda}) = f(x) + \sum_m \mathring{\lambda}_m g_m(x).$$

Note that for every $x \in X$

$$f(x) = f(x) + \sum_m \mathring{\lambda}_m g_m(x).$$

Remark. If $f(x)$ and $g(x)$ are differentiable functions and if $\mathring{\lambda}$ exists such that at some $\mathring{x} \in X$, $X = \{x \mid g_m(x) = 0 \; \forall m\}$,

$$\partial f(\mathring{x})/\partial x_n + \sum_m \mathring{\lambda}_m \partial_{fm}(\mathring{x})/\partial x_n = 0 \quad \forall n,$$

and such that the associated Lagrange function

$$L(x, \mathring{\lambda}) = f(x) + \sum_m \mathring{\lambda}_m g_m(x)$$

is concave, then $\mathring{x}$ is the maximum of $f(x)$ in X.

Remark. If $f(x)$ is (strictly) concave and if the $g_m(x)$ are linear $\forall m$, the Lagrange function is concave and the 'first-order' conditions are sufficient to assure $\mathring{x}$ is a (unique) maximum.

DA.42. Consider the constrained optimization

$$\max f(x, s) \quad \text{s.t.} \quad g(x, a) = 0,$$

where a is a parameter and, for convenience, x is a scalar. For each value of a let $\mathring{x}(a)$ be the maximum of x in the above problem, and let $F(a) = f(\mathring{x}(a), a)$. Then the *envelope theorem* states that:

$$\partial F(a) \vdash \partial a = \frac{\partial f(\mathring{x}(a), a)}{\partial a} - \mathring{\lambda} \frac{\partial g(\mathring{x}(a), a)}{\partial a}.$$

The change in the constrained objective function adjusting x optimally is equal to the change when x is not adjusted. The proof is by direct calculation. Differentiating gives

$$\frac{\partial F(a)}{\partial a} = \frac{\partial f(\mathring{x}(a), a)}{\partial x} - \frac{\partial x}{\partial a} + \frac{\partial f(\mathring{x}(a), a)}{\partial a}.$$

Since $x(a)$ is optimal then

$$\frac{\partial f(\mathring{x}(a), a)}{\partial x} = \mathring{\lambda} \frac{\partial g(\mathring{x}(a), a)}{\partial x}.$$

Moreover, $\mathring{x}(a)$ must solve $g(\mathring{x}(a), a) = 0$ and so

$$\frac{\partial g(\mathring{x}(a), a)}{\partial x} \frac{\partial \mathring{x}}{\partial a} + \frac{\partial g(x(a), a)}{\partial a}.$$

Substituting the last two equations in the former completes the proof.

Remark. The envelope theorem provides a useful interpretation for the Lagrange multiplier in problems of the form

$$\max f(x) \quad \text{s.t.} \quad g(x) = a.$$

In this case $\partial[g(\mathring{x}) - a]/\partial a = -1$ and $\partial f(\mathring{x})/\partial a = 0$. Then by the envelope theorem $\mathring{\lambda} = \partial F(a)/\partial a$; that is, $\mathring{\lambda}$ provides the incremental change to f when relaxing the value of a by a small amount.

REFERENCES

Agnew, R.A., 1971, Counter-examples to an assertion concerning the normal distribution and a new stochastic price fluctuation model, *Review of Economics and Statistics*, 381–383.

Alchian, A.A., 1953, The meaning of utility measurement, *American Economic Review*, March, 26–50.

Aitcheson, J. and J. Brown, 1957, *The lognormal distribution* (Cambridge University Press, Cambridge).

Arrow, K.J., 1964, The role of securities in the optimal allocation of risk bearing, *Review of Economic Studies*, 91–96.

Arrow, K.J. and G. Debreu, 1954, Existence of an equilibrium in a competitive economy, *Econometrica*.

Arrow, K.J. and R.C. Lind, 1970 Uncertainty and the evaluation of public investments, *American Economic Review*, June, 364–378.

Arrow, K.J. and F.H. Hahn, 1971, *General competitive analysis* (Holden-Day, San Francisco, CA).

Baltensperger, E., 1976, The borrower-lender relationship, competitive equilibrium and the theory of hedonic prices, *American Economic Review*, June, 401–405.

Banz, R.W. and M.H. Miller, 1978, Some estimates of implicit prices for state-contingent claims, *Journal of Business*, Oct., 653–672.

Baron, D.P., 1974, Default risk, homemade leverage and the Modigliani-Miller theorem, *American Economic Review*, March, 176–182.

Baron, D.P., 1976, Default risk and the Modigliani-Miller theorem: A synthesis, *American Economic Review*, March, 176–182.

Baron, D.P., 1976b, Flexible exchange rates, forward markets, and the level of trade, *American Economic Review*, June, 253–266.

Barten, A. and V. Boehm, 1982, Consumer theory, in: K. Arrow and M. Intriligator, eds., *Mathematical approaches to micro-economic theory* (North-Holland, Amsterdam).

Bawa, V.S., 1975, Optimal rules for ordering uncertain prospects, *Journal of Financial Economics*, 444–455.

Beja, A., 1971, The structure of the cost of capital under uncertainty, *Review of Economic Studies*, Oct., 359–369.

Benavie, A., 1972, Mathematical techniques for economic analysis (Prentice-Hall, Englewood Cliffs, NJ).

Ben–Zion, U. and M. Balch, 1973, Corporate financial theory under uncertainty: A comment, *Quarterly Journal of Economics*, May, 209–295.

Bertsekas, D.P., 1974, Necessary and sufficient conditions for existence of an optimal portfolio, *Journal of Economic Theory*, June, 135–147.

Bhattacharya, S., 1981, Notes on multiperiod valuation and the pricing of options, *Journal of Finance*, March, 163–180.

Black, F., 1972, Capital market equilibrium with restricted borrowing, *Journal of Business:* 444–455.

Black, F., 1972, Equilibrium in the creation of investment goods under uncertainty, in: M.C. Jensen, ed., *Studies in the Theory of Capital Markets* (Praeger, New York).

Black, F. and M. Scholes, 1973, The pricing of options and corporate liabilities, *Journal of Political Economy*, May–June, 637–659.
Borch, K., 1962, Equilibrium in a reinsurance market, *Econometrica*, July, 424–444.
Borch, K., 1968, 'General equilibrium in the economics of uncertainty, in: K. Borch and J. Mossin, eds., *Risk and uncertainty* (MacMillan, London).
Borch, K., 1967, Economics and game theory, *Swedish Journal of Economics*, March, 215–228.
Borch, K., 1968, Indifference curves and uncertainty, *Swedish Journal of Economics*, March, 19–24.
Borch, K., 1969, A note on uncertainty and indifference curves, *Review of Economic Studies*, Jan., 1–4.
Breeden, D.T., 1979, An intertemporal asset pricing model with stochastic consumption and investment opportunities, *Journal of Financial Economics*, Sept., 273–296.
Breeden, D.T., 1982, Consumption, production, and interest rates: A synthesis, Working paper (Graduate School of Business, Stanford University, Stanford, CA).
Breeden, D.T. and R.H. Litzenberger, 1978, Prices of state-contingent claims implicit in options prices, *Journal of Business*, Oct., 621–651.
Brennan, M., 1971, A note on dividend irrelevance and the gordon valuation model, *Journal of Finance*, Dec.
Brennan, M., 1979, The pricing of contingent claims in discrete time models, *Journal of Finance* March, 53–68.
Brennan, M. and A. Kraus, 1976, The geometry of separation and myopia, *Journal of Financial and Quantitative Analysis*, June, 171–193.
Brennan, M. and M. Subrahmanyan, 1977, Intra-equilibrium and inter-equilibrium analysis in capital market theory: A clarification, *Journal of Finance*, Sept.
Brock, W.A., 1972, On models of expectations that arise from maximizing behavior of economic agents over time, *Journal of Economic Theory*, 348–376.
Brock, W.A., 1978, An integration of stochastic growth theory and the theory of finance, Mimeo., Department of Economics, University of Chicago, Chicago, IL.
Brunelle, S. and R. Vickson, 1975. A unified approach to stochastic dominance, in: W. Ziemba and R. Vickson, eds., *Stochastic optimization methods in finance* (Academic Press, New York).
Brush, S., 1979, Multiperiod stochastic consumption-investment decisions, Ph.D. dissertation, University of California, Los Angeles, CA.
Cass, D. and J. Stiglitz, 1970, The structure of investor preferences and asset returns, and separability in portfolio allocation, *Journal of Economic Theory*, June, 122–160.
Cass, D. and J. Stiglitz, 1972, Risk aversion and wealth effects on portfolios with many assets, *Review of Economic Studies*, July, 331–354.
Chamberlain, G., 1980, A complete characterization of Distributions allowing mean-variance portfolio analysis, Mimeo. (University of Wisconsin, Madison, WI).
Constantinides, G.M., 1980, Admissible uncertainty in the intertemporal asset pricing model, *Journal of Financial Economics*, March, 71–86.
Constantinides, G.M., 1979, Multiperiod consumption and investment behavior with convex transactions costs, *Management Science*, Nov., 1127–1137.
Constantinides, G.M., 1982. Intertemporal asset pricing with heterogeneous consumers and without demand aggregation, *Journal of Business*, 253–267.
Copeland, T.E. and J.F. Weston, 1979, *Financial theory and corporate policy* (Addison-Wesley, Reading, MA).
Cox, J.C., 1973, Properties of functions which are solutions to maximization problems, *Journal of Economic Theory*, 396–398.
Cox, J.C. and J. Ingersoll and R. Ross, 1980, A theory of the term structure of interest rates, *Econometrica*.
Cox, J.C. and S. Ross, 1976, A survey of some new results in financial option pricing theory, *Journal of Finance*, May, 383–402.
Cragg, J. and B. Malkiel, 1982, *Expectations and the structure of share prices* (University of Chicago Press, Chicago, IL).

DeAngelo, H., 1979, Three essays in financial economics, Ph.D. dissertation, University of California, Los Angeles, CA.

Debreu, G., 1959, *The theory of value* (Yale University Press, New Haven, CT).

Debreu, G., 1960, Topological methods in cardinal utility theory, *Mathematical Methods in the Social Sciences* (Stanford University Press, Stanford, CA).

Debreu, G., 1962, New concepts and techniques for equilibrium analysis, *International Economic Review*, 257–273.

DeGroot, M., 1970, *Optimal statistical decisions* (McGraw-Hill, New York).

Demsetz, H., 1969, Information and efficiency: Another viewpoint, *Journal of Law and Economics*, April, 1–22.

Diamond, P.A., 1967, The role of a stock market in a general equilibrium model with technological uncertainty, *American Economic Review*, Sept., 759–776.

Diamond, P.A. and R. Verrecchia, 1981, Informational aggregation in a noisy rational expectations economy, *Journal of Financial Economics*, 221–235.

Diamond, P.A. and M. Yaari, 1972, Implications of the theory of rationing for consumer choices under uncertainty, *American Economic Review*, June, 333–343.

Dieffenbach, B.C., 1975, A quantitative theory of risk premiums on securities with an application to the term structure of interest rates, *Econometrica*, May, 431–454.

Dothan, L.U. 1978, On the term structure of interest rates, *Journal of Financial Economics*, March, 59–70.

Drèze, J., 1970–71. Market allocation under uncertainty, *European Economic Review*, Winter, 133–165.

Drèze, J., 1972. A tatonnement process for investment under uncertainty in private ownership evonomies, in: G. Szegö and K. Shell, eds., *Mathematical methods in investment and finance* (North-Holland, Amsterdam).

Drèze, J., 1974, eds., *Allocation under uncertainty: Equilibrium and optimality* (Wiley, New York).

Drèze, J. and F. Modigliani, 1972, Consumption decisions under uncertainty, *Journal of Economics Theory*, 308–335.

Dybvig, P. and J. Ingersoll, 1982, Mean-variance theory in complete markets, *Journal of Business*, 233–252.

Dybvig, P. and S. Ross, 1982, Portfolio efficient sets, *Econometrica*, 1525–1546.

Ehrlich, I. and G.S. Becker, 1972, Market insurance, self-insurance, and self-protection, *Journal of Political Economy*, July–Aug., 623–648.

Ekern, S., 1973, On the theory of the firm in incomplete markets, unpublished Ph.D. dissertation (Graduate School of Business, Stanford University, Stanford, CA).

Ekern, S. and R.B. Wilson, 1974, On the theory of the firm in an economy with incomplete *markets, Bell Journal of Economics and Management Science*, Spring, 171–180.

Fama, E.F., 1965, Portfolio analysis in a stable paretian market, *Management Science*, Jan., 404–419.

Fama, E.F., 1970, Multi-period consumption-investment decisions, *American Economic Review*, March, 163–174.

Fama, E.F., 1972, Ordinal and measurable utility in: M.C. Jensen, ed., *Studies in the theory of capital markets* (Praeger, New York).

Fama, E.F., 1972, Perfect competition and optimal production decisions under uncertainty. *Bell Journal of Economics and Management Science*, Fall, 509–530.

Fama, E.F. and M.H. Miller, 1972, *The theory of finance* (Holt, Rinehart & Winston, New York).

Fama, E.F. 1978, The effects of a firm's investment and financing decisions, *American Economic Review*, June, 272–284.

Fama, E.F. and R. Roll, 1968, Some properties of symmetric stable distributions, *Journal of American Statistical Association*, 63, Sept., 817–836.

Fama, E.F. and G. Schwert, 1977, Human capital and capital market equilibrium, *Journal of Financial Economics*, Jan., 95–125.

Feiger, G. and B. Jacquillat, 1979, Currency option bonds, puts and calls on spot exchange and

the hedging of contingent foreign earnings, *Journal of Finance*, Dec., 1129–1139.
Feldstein, M., 1968, Uncertainty and forward exchange speculation, *Review of Economics and Statistics*, 50, May, 182–192.
Feldstein, M., 1969, Mean-variance analysis in the theory of liquidity preference and portfolio selection, *Review of Economic Studies*, Jan.
Feller, W., 1966, *An introduction to probability theory and its applications*, Vol. II (Wiley, New York).
Fischer, S., 1969, Essays on assets and contingent commodities, unpublished Ph.D. dissertation, Aug. (Department of Economics, M.I.T., Cambridge, MA).
Fischer, S., 1972, Assets, contingency commodities, and the slutsky equations, *Econometrica*, 40 March, 371–385.
Fishburn, P., 1968, Utility theory, *Management Science*, 14, Jan., 335–378.
Fishburn, P., 1975, Separation theorems and expected utilities, *Journal of Economic Theory*, 11, 16–34.
Fisher, I., 1930, *The theory of interest* (MacMillan, New York).
Foley, D.K., 1970, Economic equilibrium with costly marketing, *Journal of Economic Theory*, 2, 276–291.
Friedman, M. and L.J. Savage, 1948, The utility analysis of choices involving risks, *Journal of Political Economy*, 56, Aug., 279–304.
Galai, D. and R. Masulis, 1976, The option pricing model and the risk factor of stock, *Journal of Financial Economics*, 53–82.
Garman, M., 1977, A general theory of asset pricing under diffusion state processes, Working paper no. 50, Jan. (University of California, Berkeley, CA).
Garman, M., 1978, The pricing of supershares, *Journal of Financial Economics*, 6, March, 3–10.
Garman, M. and J. Ohlson, 1980, Information and the sequential valuation of assets in arbitrage-free economies, *Journal of Accounting Research* (Autumn), 420–440.
Geske, R., 1977, The valuation of corporate liabilities as compound options, *Journal of Finance and Quantitative Analysis*, Nov., 541–552.
Grauer, F.L.A. and R.H. Litzenberger, 1979, The pricing of commodity futures contracts, nominal bonds and other risky assets under commodity price uncertainty, *Journal of Finance*, March.
Green, J., 1964, *Aggregation in economic analysis* (Princeton University Press, Princeton NJ).
Grossman, S.J., 1977, The existence of futures markets, noisy rational expectations and informational externalities, *Review of Economic Studies*, Oct., 431–449.
Grossman, S.J., 1978, Further results on the informational efficiency of competitive stock markets, *Journal of Economic theory*, 81–101.
Grossman, S.J. and R.J. Shiller, 1981, The determinants of the variability of stock market prices, *American Economic Review*, May.
Grossman, S.J. and J.E. Stiglitz, 1976, Information and competitive price systems, *American Economic Review*, May, 246–253.
Grossman, S.J. and J.E. Stiglitz, 1980, Stockbroker unanimity in making production and financial decisions, *Quarterly Journal of Economics*, May, 543–566.
Grossman, S.J. and J.E. Stiglitz, 1980, On the impossibility of informationally efficient markets, *American Economic Review*, 393–408.
Guesnerie, R. and Y.Y. Jaffray, 1974, Optimality of equilibrium of plans, price expectations, in: J. Drèze, ed., *Allocation under uncertainty: Equilibrium and optimality* (Wiley, New York).
Hadar, J. and W.R. Russel, Rules for ordering uncertain prospects, *American Economic Review*.
Hadley, G., 1964, *Nonlinear and dynamic programming* (Addison-Wesley, Reading, MA).
Hagen, K.P., 1976, Default risk, homemade leverage, and the Modigliani–Miller theorem: Note, *American Economic Review*, March, 199–203.
Hahn, F.H., 1971, Equilibrium with transaction costs, *Econometrica*, May, 417–440.

Hakansson, N.H., 1969, Risk disposition and the separation property in portfolio selection, *Journal of Financial and Quantitative Analysis*, Dec., 401–405.

Hakansson, N.H., 1970, Optimal investment and consumption strategies under risk for a class of utility functions, *Econometrica*, Sept., 587–607.

Kakansson, N.H., 1977, The superfund: Efficient paths toward a complete financial market, in: H. Levy and M. Sarnat, eds., *Financial decision-making under uncertainty* (Academic Press, New York).

Hakansson, N.H., 1978, Welfare aspects of options and supershares, *Journal of Finance*, June, 759–776.

Hakansson, N.H., J. Kunkel and J. Ohlson, 1982, Sufficient and necessary conditions for information to have social value in pure exchange, *Journal of finance*, 1169–1181.

Hamada, R., 1969, Portfolio analysis, market equilibrium, and corporation finance, March, 13–31.

Hanoch, G. and H. Levy, 1969, The efficiency analysis of choices involving risk, *Review of Economic Studies*, July, 335–346.

Harrison, J.M. and D.M. Kreps, 1979, Martingales and arbitrage in multi-period securities markets, *Journal of Economic Theory*, June, 381–408.

Hart, O., 1975, On the optimality of equilibrium when the market structure is incomplete, *Journal of Economic Theory*, Dec., 418–443.

Hayak, F., 1945, The use of knowledge in society, *American Economic Review*, May, 519–530.

Hellwig, M., 1980, On the aggregation of information in competitive markets, *Journal of Economic Theory*, 477–498.

Hicks, J., 1939, *Value and capital* (Clarendon Press, Oxford).

Hirshleifer, J., 1965, Investment decision under uncertainty: Choice theoretic approaches, *Quarterly Journal of Economics*, Nov., 509–536.

Hirshleifer, J., 1966, Investment decision under uncertainty: Applications of the state-preference approach, *Quarterly Journal of Economics*, May, 252–277.

Hirshleifer, J., 1970, *Investment, interest, and capital* (Prentice-Hall, Englewood Cliffs, NJ).

Hirshleifer, J., 1971, The private and social value of information and the reward to inventive activity, *American Economic Review*, Sept., 561–574.

Hirshleifer, J., 1973, Where are we in the theory of information? *American Economic Review, Papers and Proceedings*: 31–40.

Hirshleifer, J., 1975, Speculation and equilibrium: Information risk and markets, *Quarterly Journal of Economics*, Nov., 519–542.

Hirshleifer, J., 1977, The theory of speculation under alternative regimes of markets, *Journal of Finance*, Sept., 975–999.

Hirshleifer, J. and M. Rubinstein, 1973, Speculation and information in securities markets, *Proceedings of the Institute of Management Science*, 799–802.

Huberman, G., 1982, A simple approach to arbitrage pricing theory, *Journal of Economic Theory*, March, 183–191.

Jarrow, R., 1980, Heterogeneous expectations, restrictions on short sales, and equilibrium asset prices, *Journal of Finance*, 1105–1113.

Jensen, M.C. and H. Meckling, 1976, Theory of the firm: Managerial behavior, agency costs and ownership structure, *Journal of Financial Economics*, 305–360.

Johnson, L.L., 1960, The theory of Hedging and speculation in commodity futures, *Review of Economics Studies*, June, 139–151.

Katzner, D., 1965, A note on the differentiability of consumer demand functions, *Econometrica*, 781–796.

Katzner, D., 1970, *Static demand theory* (MacMillan, London).

Kennan, W., 1981, The existence of expected utility maximizing decisions when utility is unbounded, *Econometrica*, 215–218.

Kraus, A. and R.H. Litzenberger, 1973, A state-preference model of optimal financial leverage, *Journal of Finance*, Sept., 911–922.

Kraus, A. and R.H. Litzenberger, 1975, Market equilibrium in a multiperiod state preference model with logarithmic utility, *Journal of Finance*, Dec., 1213–1228.

Krouse, C.G., 1972, Optimal financing and capital structure programs, *Journal of Finance*, Dec., 1057–1071.

Krouse, C.G., 1973, On the theory of optimal investment, dividends, and growth in the firm, *American Economic Review*, June, 269–279.

Krouse, C.G., 1976, Measuring allocative efficiency, *Journal of Finance*, June, 685–700.

Krouse, C.G., 1979, The optimality of risk allocation in competitive production and exchange: A synthesis, *Southern Economic Journal*, April, 762–777.

Krouse, C.G., 1985, Competition and unanimity revisited, again, *American Economic Review*, Dec., 950–959.

Koopmans, T., 1957, *Three essays on the state of economic science* (McGraw-Hill, New York).

Koopmans, T., 1960, Stationary ordinal utility and impatience, *Econometrica*, 11–121.

Kurz, M., 1974, Equilibrium with transaction cost and money in a single market exchange economy, *Journal of Economic Theory*.

Kydland, F.E. and E.C. Prescott, 1982, Time to build and aggregate fluctuations, *Econometrica*, Nov., 1345–1370.

Leland, H.E., 1968, Savings and uncertainty: The precautionary demand for saving, *Quarterly Journal of Economics*, Sept., 465–473.

Leland, H.E., 1972, On the existence of optimal policies under uncertainty, *Journal of Economic Theory*, 35–44.

Leland, H.E., 1974, Production theory and the stock market, *Bell Journal of Economics and Management Science*, Spring, 125–144.

Leland, H.E. and D. Pyle, 1976, Information asymmetries, financial structure, and financial intermediation, Research program in finance working paper no. 41, Graduate school of business administration, University of California, Berkeley, CA.

LeRoy, S.F., 1982, Expectations models of asset prices: A survey of theory, *Journal of Finance*, March, 185–217.

Levy, H. and H. Markowitz, 1979, Approximating expected utility by a function of mean and variance, *American Economic Review*, June, 308–317.

Lintner, J., 1969, The aggregation of investors' diverse judgments and preferences in purely competitive security markets, *Journal of Financial and Quantitative Analysis*, Dec., 347–400.

Lintner, J., 1965, The valuation of risk assets and the selection of risky investments in stock portfolios and capital budgets, *Review of Economics and Statistics*, 13–37.

Litzenberger, R.H. and H.B. Sosin, 1975, The theory of recapitalizations under incomplete markets and the evidence of dual purpose funds, Working Paper, Stanford University, Stanford, CA, May.

Lucas, R.E., Jr., 1972, Expectations and the neutrality of money, *Journal of Economic Theory* April, 103–124.

Lucas, R.E., Jr., 1978, Asset prices in an exchange economy, *Econometrica*, Nov., 1426–1446.

Malinvaud, E., 1972, *Lectures on microeconomic theory* (North-Holland, Amsterdam).

Markowitz, H.M., 1952, The utility of wealth, *Journal of Political Economy*, April, 151–158.

Markowitz, H.M., 1959 *Portfolio selection: Efficient diversification of investments*, Monograph 16, Cowles Foundation for Research in Economics, Yale University (Wiley, New York).

McCall, J., 1971, Probabilistic microeconomics, *Bell Journal of Economics and Management Science*, Autumn, 403–430.

McFadden, D., 1968, A simple remark on the second best Pareto optimality of market equilibria, *Journal of Economic Theory*, 26–38.

McKenzie, L., 1981, The classical theorem on existence of comparative equilibrium, *Econometrica*, 819–842.

Marshall, J.M., 1974, Private incentives and public information, *American Economic Review*, June, 373–390.

Marshall, J.M., 1976, Moral hazard, *American Economic Review*, Dec., 880–890.
Mayers, D., 1971, Non-marketable assets and capital market equilibrium under uncertainty, Ph.D. dissertation, Graduate School of Management, University of Rochester, NY.
Mayshar, J., 1983, On divergence of opinion and imperfections in capital markets, *American Economic Review*, 114–128.
Merton, R.C., 1971, Optimum consumption and portfolio rules in a continuous-time model, *Journal of Economic Theory*, 373–413.
Merton, R.C., 1972, An analytical derivation of the efficient portfolio frontier, *Journal of Financial and Quantitative Analysis*, Sept., 1951–1872.
Merton, R.C., 1973a, An intertemporal capital asset pricing model, *Econometrica*, Sept., 867–887.
Merton, R.C., 1973b, Theory of rational option pricing, *Bell Journal of Economics and Management Science*, Spring, 141–183.
Merton, R.C. and M.G. Subrahmanyan, 1974, The optimality of a competitive stock market, *Bell Journal of Economics and Management Science*, Spring, 145–170.
Merton, R.C., 1975, Theory of finance from the perspective of continuous time, *Journal of Financial and Quantitative Analysis*, 659–674.
Merton, R.C., 1980, Investment theory, in: K.J. Arrow and M.D. Intriligator, eds, Handbook of mathematical economics (North-Holland, Amsterdam).
Milgrom, P. and N. Stokey, 1982, Information, trade and common knowledge, *Journal of Economic Theory*, 17–27.
Miller, M.H. and F. Modigliani, 1958, The cost of capital and corporation finance, and the theory of investment, *American Economic Review*, 261–297.
Miller, M.H. and F. Modigliani, 1977, Debt and taxes, *Journal of Finance*, May.
Milne, F., 1974, Corporate investment and finance theory in competitive equilibrium, *Economic record*, Dec., 511–533.
Milne, F., 1975, Choice over asset economics: Default risk and corporate leverage, *Journal of Financial Economics*, June, 165–185.
Milne, F., 1979, Consumer preferences, linear demand functions and aggregation in competitive asset markets, *Review of Economic Studies*, 407–418.
Milne, F., 1963, Corporate income taxes and the cost of capital: A correction, *American Economic Review*, June, 433–443.
Mirman, L., 1971, Uncertainty and optimal consumption decisions, *Econometrica*, 179–185.
Modigliani, F. and M.H. Miller, 1958, The cost of capital, corporation finance and the theory of investmetn, *American Economic Review*, 261–297.
Mossin, J., 1966, Equilibrium in a capital asset market, *Econometrica*, Oct., 768–783.
Mossin, J., 1973, *Theory of financial markets* (Prentice-Hall, Englewood Cliffs, NJ).
Muth, J.F., 1961, Rational expectations and the theory of price movements, *Econometrica*, July, 315–335.
Myers, S., 1968, A time-state-preference model of security valuation, *Journal of Financial and Quantitative Analysis*, March, 1–33.
Neave, E., 1971, Multiperiod consumption-investment decisions and risk preference, *Journal of Economic Theory*, March, 236–247.
Negishi, T., 1960, Welfare economics and existence of an equilibrium for a competitive economy, *Metroeconomica*, 92–97.
von Neumann, J. and O. Morgenstern, 1947, *Theory of games and economic behavior*, 2nd ed. (Princeton University Press, Princeton, NJ).
Nielsen, N.C., 1974, The firm as an intermediary between consumers and production functions under uncertainty, unpublished Ph.D. dissertation (Graduate School of Business, Stanford University, CA).
Peleg, B. and M.E. Yaari, 1975a, A price characterization of efficient random variables, *Econometrica*, 283–292.
Peleg, B. and M.E. Yaari, 1975b, Efficient random variables, *Journal of Mathematical Economics*, 243–261.

Pollack, R.A., 1971, Additive utility functions and linear engel curves, *Review of Economic Studies*, Oct., 401–414.

Pratt, J., 1964, Risk aversion in the small and in the large, *Econometrica*, Jan., 122–136.

Prescott, E.C. and R. Mehra, 1978, Recursive competitive equilibrium and capital asset pricing, Working Paper, Columbia University, New York, June.

Prescott, E.C. and R. Mehra, 1980, Recursive competitive equilibrium: The case of homogeneous households, *Econometrica*, Sept., 1365–1379.

Pye, G., 1967, Portfolio selection and security prices, *Review of Economics and Statistics*, Feb., 111–115.

Quirk, J. and R. Saposnik, Admissibility and additive utility functions, *Review of Economic Studies*, 140–146.

Radner, R., 1968, Competitive equilibrium under uncertainty, *Econometrica*, Jan., 31–58.

Radner, R., 1970, Problems in the theory of markets under uncertainty, *American Economic Review*, May, 454–460.

Radner, R., 1972, Existence of equilibrium of plans, prices and price expectations in a sequence of markets, *Econometrica*, March, 289–303.

Radner, R., 1973, Optimal stationary consumption with stochastic production and resources, *Journal of Economic Theory*, 68–90.

Radner, R., 1974, A note on unanimity of stockholders' preferences among alternative production plans: A reformulation of the Ekern–Wilson model, *Bell Journal of Economics and Management Science*, Spring, 181–184.

Richard, S.F., 1978, An arbitrage model of the term structure of interest rates, *Journal of Financial Economics*, March, 33–58.

Riley, J., 1975, Competitive signaling, *Journal of Economic Theory*, April.

Robicheck, A. and S. Myers, 1966, Problems in the theory of optimal capital structure, *Journal of Financial and Quantitative Analysis*, June, 1–35.

Roll, R., 1977, A critique of the asset pricing theory's tests. Part I: On past and potential testability of the theory, *Journal of Financial Economics*, Feb., 129–179.

Roll, R. and S.A. Ross, 1980, An empirical investigation of the arbitrage pricing theory, *Journal of Finance*, 1073–1103.

Ross, S.A., 1973, The economic theory of agency: The principal's problem, *American Economic Review*, May, 134–139.

Ross, S.A., 1976, Options and efficiency, *Quarterly Journal of Economics*, Feb., 75–89.

Ross, S.A., 1976, The arbitrage theory of capital asset pricing, *Journal of Economic Theory*, Dec., 341–360.

Ross, S.A., 1977, The determination of financial structure: the incentive-signaling approach, *Bell Journal of Economics*, Spring, 23–40.

Ross, S.A., 1977, Discussion, *Journal of Finance*, 412–414.

Ross, S.A., 1978, Mutual fund separation in financial theory – The separating distributions, *Journal of Economic Theory*, 254–286.

Ross, S.A., 1978, A simple approach to the valuation of risky streams, *Journal of Business*, July, 453–475.

Rothschild, M. and J. Stiglitz, 1970, Increasing risk I: A definition, *Journal of Economic Theory*, June, 225–243.

Rothschild, M. and J. Stiglitz, 1971, Increasing risk II: its Economic consequences, *Journal of Economic Theory*, March, 66–84.

Rubinstein, M.E., 1974, An aggregation theorem for securities markets, *Journal of Financial Economics*, Sept., 225–244.

Rubinstein, M.E., 1975, Securities market efficiency in an Arrow–Debreu economy, *American Economic Review*, Dec., 812–824.

Rubinstein, M.E., 1976, The valuation of uncertain income streams and the pricing of options, *Bell Journal of Economics*, Autumn, 407–425.

Rubinstein, M.E., 1976, The irrelevancy of dividend policy in an Arrow-Debreu economy, *Journal of Finance*, Sept.

Rubinstein, M.E., 1977, The strong case for the generalized logarithmic utility model as the premier model of financial markets, in: H. Levy and M. Sarnat, eds., *Financial decision-making under uncertainty* (Academic Press, New York). Also abridged version in *Journal of Finance*, May, 551–571.

Rubinstein, M.E., 1978, Competition and approximation, *Bell Journal of Economics*, Spring, 280–286.

Rubinstein, M.E. and R.C. Merton, 1975, Generalized mean-variance tradeoffs for best perturbation corrections to approximate portfolio decisions. *Journal of Finance*, March, 27–40.

Samuelson, P.A., 1961, Using full duality to show that simultaneously additive direct and indirect utilities implies unitary price elasticity of demand, *Econometrica*, 791–796.

Samuelson, P.A., 1965, Proof that property anticipated prices fluctuate randomly, *Industrial Management Review*, Spring, 41–49.

Samuelson, P.A., 1969, Lifetime portfolio selection by dynamic stochastic programming, *Review of Economic Studies*, 234–246.

Sandmo, A., 1969, Capital risk, consumption and portfolio choice, *Econometrica*, 586–599.

Sandmo, A., 1970, The effect of uncertainty on saving decisions, *Review of Economic Studies*, 353–360.

Sandmo, A., 1974, Two-period models of consumption decisions under uncertainty: A survey, in: J. Drèze, ed., *Allocation under uncertainty: Equilibrium and optimality* (Wiley, New York),

Savage, L., 1954, *Foundations of statistics* (Wiley, New York).

Schall, L.D., 1972, Asset valuation, firm investment, and firm diversification, *Journal of Business*, Jan., 11–28.

Sharpe, W.F., 1964, Capital asset prices: A theory of market equilibrium under conditions of risk, *Journal of Finance*, 425–442.

Stapleton, R.C. and M.G. Subrahmanyam, 1978, A multiperiod equilibrium asset pricing model, *Econometrica*, Sept., 1077–1096.

Stapleton, R.C. and M.G. Subrahmanyam, 1984, The valuation of multivariate contingent claims in discrete time models, *Journal of Finance*, March, 207–228.

Stulz, R.M., 1982, Options on the minimum or the maximum of two risky assets, *Journal of Financial* Economics, July, 161–185.

Svensson, L.E.O., 1977, The stock market, the objective function of the firm, and intertemporal Pareto efficiency – The certainty case, *Bell Journal of Economics*, Spring, 207–216.

Smith, C., 1978, Options pricing: A review, Working paper no. 7523 (Graduate School of Business, University of Rochester, NY).

Smith, V., 1970, Coporate financial theory under uncertainty, *Quarterly Journal of Economics*, Aug., 451–471.

Smith, V., 1972, Default risk, scale, and the homemade leverage theorem, *American Economic Review*, March, 66–76.

Starr, R.M., 1973, Optimal production and allocation under uncertainty, *Quarterly Journal of Economics*, Feb., 81–95.

Stiglitz, J., 1969a, Behavior towards risk with many commodities, *Econometrica*, Oct., 468–479.

Stiglitz, J., 1969b, A re-examination of the Modigliani–Miller theorem, *American Economic Review*, Dec., 784–793.

Stiglitz, J., 1970, A consumption-oriented theory of the demand for financial assets and the term-structure of interest rates, *Review of Economic Studies*, July, 321–351.

Stiglitz, J., 1972, On the optimality of the stock market allocation of investment, *Quarterly Journal of Economics*, Feb., 25–60.

Stiglitz, J., 1972, Some aspects of the pure theory of corporate finance: Bankruptcies and take-overs, *Bell Journal of Economics*, Autumn, 458–482.

Stiglitz, J., 1974, On the irrelevance of corporate financial policy, *American Economic Review*, Dec., 851–866.

Stigum, B., 1969, Competitive equilibria under uncertainty, *Quarterly Journal of Economics*, Nov., 533–561.

Strassen, V., The existence of probability measures with given marginals, *Annals of Mathematical Statistics*, 432–439.

Sundaresan, M., 1983, Constant absolute risk aversion preferences and constant equilibrium interest rates, *Journal of Finance*, March, 205–212.

Svegö, J. and K. Shell, eds., 1972, *Mathematical methods in investment and finance* (North-Holland, Amsterdam).

Tobin, J., 1958, Liquidity preference as behavior towards risk, *Review of Economic Studies*, 65–86.

Townsend, R.M., On the optimality of forward markets, *American Economic Review*, March, 65–86.

Vickson, R., 1975, Separation in portfolio analysis, in: W. Ziemba and R. Vickson, eds., Stochastic optimization models in finance (Academic Press. New York).

Whitmore, G.A., 1970, Third-degree stochastic dominance, *American Economic Review*, June, 457–459.

Wilson, R.B., The theory of syndicates, *Econometrica* 26, Jan., 119–132.

Woodward, S.E., 1979, Two essays in the theory of competitive markets for contingent claims, Ph.D. dissertation (University of California, Los Angeles, CA).

Yaari, M., 1969, Same remarks on measures of risk aversion and their uses, *Journal of Economic Theory*, Oct., 315–329.

INDEX